Spectrum Guide to
JORDAN

INTERLINK BOOKS
An imprint of Interlink Publishing Group, Inc.
New York

Spectrum Guide to Jordan

First American edition published
in 1999 by

INTERLINK BOOKS
An imprint of
Interlink Publishing Group, Inc.
99 Seventh Avenue
Brooklyn, New York 11215
and
46 Crosby Street
Northampton, Massachusetts 01060

This book was designed and produced by
Camerapix Publishers International
PO Box 45048
Nairobi, Kenya

To order or request a catalog, please call
Interlink Publishing at 1-800-238-LINK

Website:www.interlinkbooks.com

Library of Congress Cataloging-in-Publication Data

Spectrum guide to Jordan/compiled and edited by Camerapix. — First American ed.
    p.   cm. — (Spectrum guides)
    ISBN 1-56656-235-X (pbk).
    1. Jordan—Guidebooks. I. Camerapix
    Publishers International.
II. Series: Spectrum Guides (Interlink Books)
DS 153.2.S64 1999
915.69504'4—dc21   97-24457
                                        CIP

Colour separations: Universal Graphics
Pte Ltd, Singapore.
Printed: Hong Kong/China.

The **Spectrum Guides** series provides a
comprehensive and detailed description of
each country it covers, together with all the
essential data that tourists, business visitors,
or potential investors are likely to require.

Spectrum Guides in print:
African Wildlife Safaris
Eritrea
Ethiopia
India
Kenya
Madagascar
Maldives
Mauritius
Namibia
Nepal
Oman
Pakistan
Seychelles
South Africa
Sri Lanka
Tanzania
Uganda
United Arab Emirates
Zambia
Zimbabwe

Publisher and Chief Executive:
Mohamed Amin
Editorial Director: Tahir Shah
Projects Director: Rukhsana Haq
Picture Editor: Duncan Willetts
Editors: Roger Barnard and Brian Tetley
Associate Editors: Jan Hemsing and
Bob Smith
Editorial Assistant: Rachel Musyimi
Cartographer: Terry Brown
Photographic research: Abdul Rehman

Editorial Board

Above: Jordanian pipers lead march past celebrating King Hussein's fortieth anniversary as monarch.

5

TABLE OF CONTENTS

PART FIVE: FACTS AT YOUR FINGER-TIPS

IN BRIEF

LISTINGS

MAPS

Half-title: Corinthian colonnades at Jerash, one of the finest and most elaborate provincial Roman cities ever constructed. Title page: Lake Tiberias from Jordan's most north-west corner. Overleaf: The legendary Desert Patrol pushes into the vastness of Wadi Rum. Following pages: Deep beneath the surface, a diver glances up through a bird's nest of wreckage in the Gulf of Aqaba. Pages 12-13: Towers of St Mary's Church and the King Abdullah Mosque mark the capital's skyline. Pages 14-15 The Colonnaded Street at Jerash, perhaps the finest of its kind to be built by the Romans outside Rome itself. Grooves made by chariot wheels are still visible on the cobbled streets.

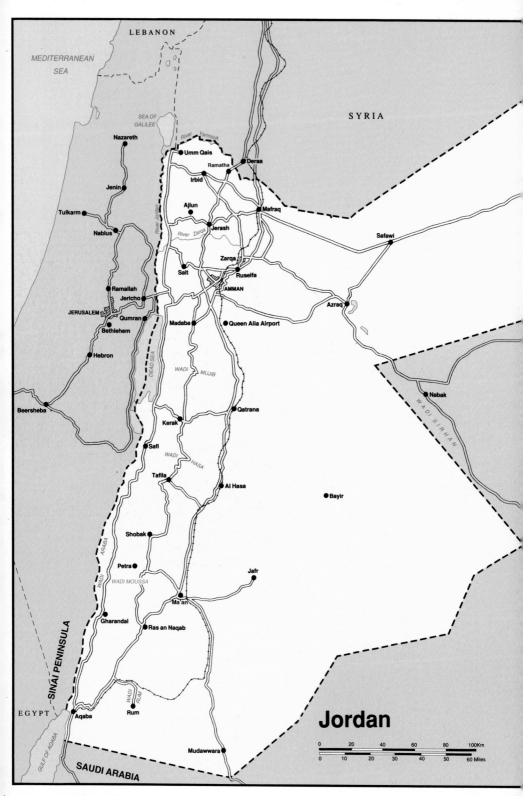

Jordan

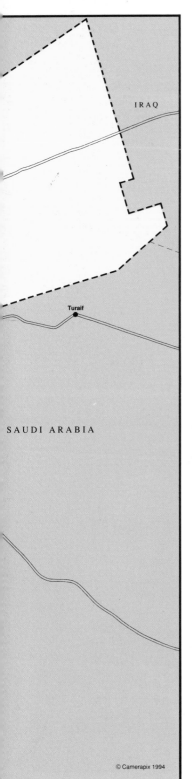

IRAQ

Turaif

SAUDI ARABIA

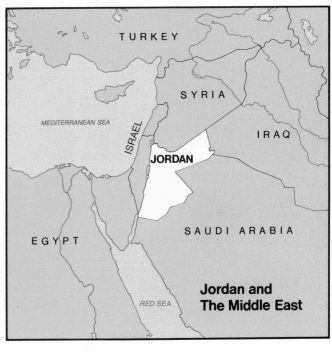

TURKEY

SYRIA

MEDITERRANEAN SEA

ISRAEL

IRAQ

JORDAN

EGYPT

SAUDI ARABIA

RED SEA

**Jordan and
The Middle East**

17

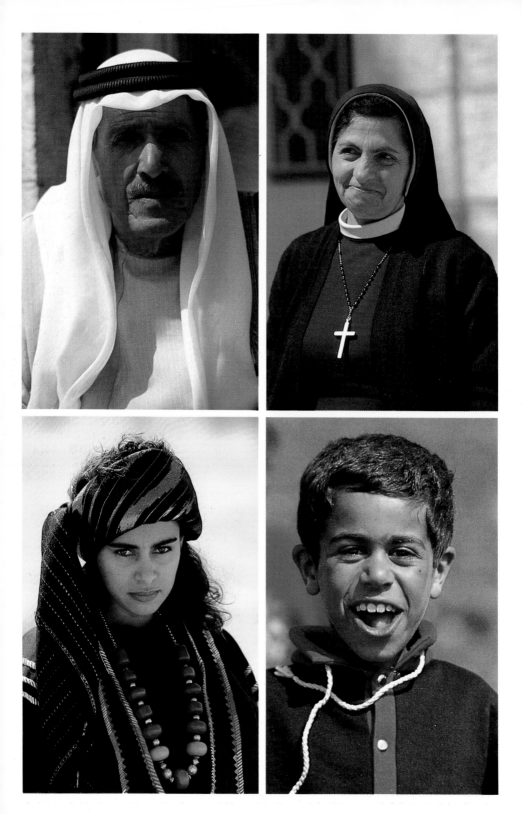

The Jordan Experience

An Arab stallion high steps its way through the narrow gorge at Petra, ancient capital of the Nabateans. This chasm, hewn by nature's hand, leads back to the dawn of civilisation like some enchanted tunnel.

The horse's hooves echo against sheer rock walls as the defile narrows further until, in the icy shadows of that slender passage, animal and rider arrive at a magnificent sight. Emblazoned in light, a monument is revealed, carved from the rock and soaring ever upwards. It is the fabulous Khazneh: the Treasury, a construction which has seldom been matched.

In a sense it is a perfect symbol of Jordan's colourful history which dates back to primeval times. At the crossroads of the Middle East, Neanderthal Man roamed these lands, hunting the creatures of pre-history. As far back as 10,000 years ago, the first settlements were fashioned at Beidha, near Petra. A succession of great leaders, whose names are still spoken and respected, strove to make the area their own. Commanders such as Solomon, Alexander the Great, Pompey, Constantine and Tamurlane swept into these lands, seeking to occupy them for their strategic importance.

They left behind their capitals and strongholds. Innumerable remnants cover the landscape of modern Jordan, reflecting the civilisations which took advantage of the region. Petra of the Nabateans, the Roman provincial city of Jerash, and the great Qasrs (castles and palaces) of the desert built by the Ummayeds, are but a few of the facets which make up the jewel that is Jordan today.

Wherever you visit — Amman (the ancient Roman city of Philadelphia), or Aqaba (the city whose waters flow to the Red Sea), you will discover a multitude of creations fashioned by both man and nature.

Visitors to Jordan find their own favourite, whether it is Madaba's 6th-century Map of the Holy Land; the frescoes at the Ummayed desert baths at Amra; the bustling back-streets of Salt or perhaps, most astonishing of all, Petra.

Complementing the diversity of the country's ancient wonders are its many peoples. The desert Bedouin are fabled for their chivalry and code of honour. But as well as Arabs, Jordan is home to minorities such as the Circassians, Druze and Armenians.

Each has its own cultural identity yet resides peacefully under the guidance of His Majesty King Hussein, who has navigated Jordan through troubled waters since his reign began. He has worked unceasingly for development, brotherhood, freedom and stability in the Middle East.

Amid Jordan's profusion of historical sites, peoples and modern development there is perhaps one place more suitable than any other to contemplate upon it all: Wadi Rum. Known as the Valley of the Moon, it stretches forth with an immensity that bewilders even those who live there.

It is at such desolate places that mankind began the foundations of his empires. Yet, Wadi Rum remains unconquered, its very size defying man's humble attempts to colonise. It is a fitting place to reflect upon the enchanted reaches of Jordan, and brings to mind the immortal words of the 12th-century Persian poet, Omar Khayyam:

The Worldly Hope men set their hearts upon
Turns Ashes — or it prospers; and anon,
Like snow upon the Desert's dusty Face
Lighting a little Hour or two — is gone.
Think, in this batter'd Caravanserai
Whose Doorways are alternate Night and Day,
How Sultan after Sultan with his Pomp
Abode his Hour or two, and went away.

Welcome to Jordan.

Top left: Jordanian man in an *aqal* and *keffiyeh*, the traditional headdress of the desert.
Top right: A nun at the Catholic school in Salt. Opposite left: Beautiful Jordanian girl adorned in traditional clothing. Opposite right: Smiling youngster at Jerash.

Travel Brief and Social Advisory

Some do's and don'ts to make your trip more enjoyable:

Getting around

The Middle East evokes images of mystery, romance, intrigue and excitement — a region of fascination for travellers and adventurers. No other area is so central to world history.

Anyone who has travelled extensively there knows the diverse landscapes, cultures, customs and traditions. Spend a few days in Jordan, the heart of the Middle East, and you will find yourself surrounded by peaceful people in a serene land where sensitivity to local beliefs and ways of life are reciprocated by exceptional hospitality.

There is no better place to explore biblical lands, the vestiges of ancient civilisations, deserts and rugged mountain landscapes.

The nation's ancestral code of honour ensures that you will be greeted with courtesy in all corners of Jordan: in the mountains or deep in the desert's wilderness.

The Ministry of Tourism is keen for visitors to take advantage of the services provided specifically for them. If you are unsure how to reach a particular place you will find travel agents, hotels, or the ministry willing to help.

With a wide range of accommodation and a fascinating choice of destinations, Jordan is an alluring country to visit. Nonetheless, unforeseen problems may arise, particularly in the desert.

Jordan is centrally located, and almost completely landlocked. Getting there is easy; there are flights to Amman's modern Queen Alia International Airport from all parts of the world. In addition, overland services carry passengers from Syria, Iraq, Saudi Arabia, the West Bank and Israel; with a regular ferry service connecting the kingdom to Egypt. A visa for certain nationalities can usually be obtained on arrival at the airport for a nominal fee. Jordan has embassies and consulates in numerous countries, where visas and information can be procured.

By road
Jordan has an excellent road network with many of the road signs in English. You might find that your local bookstore has only basic maps of Jordan and it is a good idea to buy them on arrival. In Jordan you can buy maps of the whole country and of specific areas. To find your way around Amman we recommend a 1:15,000 map, produced by the Jordan National Geographic Centre, which uses a numbering system to mark streets and points of interest. The Royal Jordanian Geographic Centre also produces first-class maps of Jerash (scale 1:5000); and a good tourist map of Aqaba (scale 1:10,000). One free national map is produced by Royal Jordanian Airlines. The best, and quite standard, map of Jordan (with a city map of Amman on the reverse) is the Ministry of Tourism's complimentary map offered to tourists.

Serviced by over 100 car-hire agencies in the kingdom, self-drive is no problem, but it is worth taking a few moments to go through the traffic signs. When hiring a car in Jordan it is not possible to waive all damage liability. This means that, in the event of a crash, the driver is liable to pay at least the first JD 100 of the claim. The car-hire agency usually requires a credit card slip to be signed by the driver and to be left at the agency until the car is returned. Make sure you know Arabic numbers. Do ensure that your vehicle is suited to your destination.

Opposite: Shadow and light display the wonders of El Khazneh, the Treasury, in the ancient rock-carved city of Petra.

Above: In a land where modern forms of transport mingle with ancient ways, a sign warns of one of the hazards on the road to Azraq in the east of Jordan.
Opposite: Mighty Desert Highway bisects Jordan from north to south.

Desert driving

It would be courting disaster to take an ordinary saloon car into the desert. If you do venture into the arid wastes take plenty of water, extra fuel, a compass and, if possible, a guide. If you can, set out with at least two vehicles. Leave early and avoid crossing sandy areas during the midday sun in summer as the sand gets very hot and softens. Follow existing tracks and trails, even if there seems to be a better route. If you are travelling in the desert during or soon after rain, remember that sand is harder to cross when waterlogged.

If you meet another vehicle that is unable to move do not drive alongside it: you may also get stuck. Stop some distance away before going to assist. When crossing dunes use low range gears or 4WD. Do not brake or accelerate hard as the tyres will dig into the sand.

Remember it is easy to get lost in the desert, so make a checklist before your journey. Ensure that you have an inflated spare tyre and tools to change it; that the vehicle is capable of such a trip; and that you leave details of your route, vehicle, and estimated time of arrival.

You should also carry at least one blanket per person (it gets extremely cold at night), as well as rope, boards, a spade, matches and medical equipment.

If you get stuck check the type of sand, and how deep the wheels are trapped. If the axles are embedded, gently straighten the front wheels. If they are not completely embedded, shovel sand from in front of the wheels. You may reach harder sand beneath. In any case, make a downhill ramp in front of each wheel for it is better to go forward than reverse.

Try to get something solid under the wheels. If, sensibly, you have taken along short planks these will do the job, for the desert seldom offers such a lifeline. Jack up the wheels or — if you have enough people — lift each corner of the vehicle. Start the engine and try driving away gently.

If you remain trapped, deflate the tyres to about half their usual pressure, unload

Above: Pride of the sky, a Royal Jordanian aircraft takes off.
Opposite: Once powerful steam engine spends its last years rusting away at Amman's railway station.

the vehicle as much as possible, and try again. When you do get clear remember to inflate your tyres. Most importantly: *If you are unable to get free, do not abandon your vehicle.* You will be placing yourself at greater risk. Stay near the vehicle, but investigate any tracks which look newly made. Consider your water and emergency supplies. Ration water to drink in the morning and evening. Take salt tablets.

You can collect small amounts of water in the desert by digging a series of holes, and covering them at night with plastic sheeting weighed down. Within a few hours you may well find that dew has formed on the underside.

There may be extra water in the vehicle's window-washer, but check there is no anti-freeze in it. Remember that drinking alcohol increases dehydration, as does drinking sugary carbonated drinks.

If you have told friends of your journey someone will be looking for you. Keep morale high by looking for ways to attract help. You can remove the rear view mirror

from the vehicle to use as a reflector. You can set fire to the seating material of the vehicle (having first removed it) to produce smoke — but be careful as the fumes will be toxic. More smoke can be made by removing a wheel, deflating a tyre, and setting fire to it with a little petrol.

By air

Jordan's three main airports are Queen Alia International, Aqaba International and Amman Civil. Royal Jordanian domestic flights connect Amman with the port of Aqaba.

By train

The great **Hijaz Railway Line** was constructed at the turn of the century, linking Damascus and Amman to Medina in Saudi Arabia.

It was one of the monumental engineering achievements of the 20th century, yet after only a few years of taking pilgrims to Medina, the line was destroyed during the Arab Revolt of 1917. Efforts to reconstruct derelict stretches, as well as modernise the rolling stock, have all ended in failure.

25

Above: Spectacular rock formations at Wadi Rum are an impressive backdrop to this section of the Damascus-Medina railway.

One service still runs weekly. It departs Amman every Monday and is supposed to reach Damascus about five hours later. But the service is erratic and can take much longer. If you are in a hurry, take the bus.

For railway lovers there is a unique annual event worth attending. Prince Ra'ad sponsors a journey by steam train on part of the old Hijaz line in honour of the Al-Hussein Society for the Education and Rehabilitation of the Physically Handicapped. The event, which usually takes place in mid-September, is open to all. The trip provides an experience of a bygone age, mixed with the modern delights of Jordan. A handful of the original Ottoman-built coaches, pulled by a magnificent old locomotive, ply their way slowly and majestically southwards out of the capital. After several hours the procession reaches the desert fortress of Daba'a which, cloaked in darkness, is the setting for a great banquet. You can find out more about this event by contacting the Marriott Hotel in Amman.

On foot

The best way to get to know Jordan is by walking. Many of its greatest places of antiquity, such as Petra, Jerash, and Umm Qais, give the pedestrian an advantage. Travelling on foot, you will hear the sounds unique to each place. At Petra, the wind swirls around the great Nabatean monuments, a counterpoint to the cries of birds of prey hovering above on thermals. Petra and Jerash have pathways leading around the ruins. Indeed, to really see Petra there is no other way than to hike the mountain paths to the city's hidden quarters. Or strike out for the desert; the perfect place is Wadi Rum. Its extraordinary valley, whose sheer rock faces soar up hundreds of feet, attracts hikers from all over the world.

Clothes

Western attire is frequently worn, and Jordanians like to dress well. For business it is suits and ties, even in the heat. Safari suits are also acceptable. While tolerant, the people are less well-disposed towards poorly dressed travellers.

Amman and other cities where business takes place have a much more conservative

Above: Azraq, in the east of Jordan, the last major centre before the Iraqi border, has been a stopping point for travellers for centuries.

code of dress than the resorts where casual dress is more common. Remember that, although at certain times of the year it gets extremely hot during the day, Jordan's desert regions become freezing at night. So if you plan an evening outing, it is advisable to take a sweater. Include a pair of shoes in which you can walk or hike comfortably.

If you plan to visit Petra and other sites, it is advisable to take a hat for shade. Women are not expected to veil, especially if from the West, but modest dress is appreciated. This means covering shoulders, upper arms and legs when in public. Loose cotton dresses are recommended.

Other essential items are sun-glasses and sun creams. Generally more expensive at tourist sites, all such things can be bought in Amman.

Many Jordanian men dress in long flowing robes known as *gumbaz*. They wear a checked red and white headdress held on by a circular band, known as a *keffiyeh*. This is not removed when entering a building. Jordanian women wear a traditional long robe, known as the *thob*. This is often ornately embroidered. You can tell a woman's origins from the embroidery design.

Tour options

Few countries offer such a variety of excellent tours as Jordan. Travel agents in Amman and outside Jordan will suggest various routes and options. If you are unsure which travel agent to use in Amman, ask at your hotel. Tours range in length from a morning to a week. Indeed, a week is ideal for sightseeing in Jordan. Some tours focus on specific historical periods, with visits to Roman or Nabatean historical sites. Others offer recreational activities such as diving at Aqaba.

Package tours are good value but be sure that they allow freedom to do your own thing. Two-centre holidays are becoming popular, allowing visitors to explore Jordan as well as one, two, or more Middle Eastern countries on the same trip. With the new-found climate of peace, tourists are able — not only to visit Jordan's popular neighbours Syria and Egypt — but they can now pass

relatively freely between Israel and the kingdom as well. Don't miss a visit to Petra, or a city tour of Amman. A suggested itinerary for a tour of Jordan's main sights might be:

    Day 1 Amman
    Day 2 Jerash, Ajlun, Umm Qais
    Day 3 Desert Castles: Kharana, Amra, Azraq
    Day 4 Mount Nebo, Madaba, Kerak
    Day 5 Petra
    Day 6 Aqaba, Wadi Rum
    Day 7 Back to Amman for shopping

Laundry

First-class hotels usually offer a good but expensive laundry service. Amman has a variety of shops with more competitive rates.

Alcohol

Although Jordan is an Islamic country, it is possible for non-Muslims to buy beer, wines and spirits except during the month of Ramadan. Most Muslims do not drink alcohol and most bars are located in hotels.

Health

Inoculations are generally only necessary if you are coming from an infected area. This especially applies to yellow fever. Preventive shots for hepatitis, polio, tetanus and typhoid are recommended. Amman and Jordan's other big cities have a selection of excellent hospitals, and blood is screened. Most doctors speak English. If in doubt about hospitals or doctors, ask your embassy.

Pharmacies have a wide selection of antibiotics and other remedies. Most medications in Jordan are expensive so if you need a particular drug it's wise to take supplies with you.

It is always safer to buy bottled water for drinking. When doing so, ensure the seal is unbroken. Soft drinks, especially soda water (which has no sugar and will not dehydrate you), are widely available. Water which has been boiled is also acceptable for drinking.

Make sure meat bought from street stalls is well-cooked. If you do get dysentery or diarrhoea seek medical advice. Remember to drink lots of liquid.

Photography

Amman has many photographic shops which sell films and offer processing services. Both colour and black and white film can be bought throughout Jordan. If you have a camera which uses the newly-developed Advanced Photographic film, you may have trouble buying extra film cartridges or having the existing ones developed in Jordan. Be wary of film sold at small souvenir kiosks; it may have been there for months and be out of date.

Before taking pictures of villagers, or even subjects in Amman, ask consent. The light in Jordan can be extremely bright, so low speed film is better than high. For places such as Petra and Jerash, you might find a wide-angled lens useful.

When to go

The best times to visit Jordan are spring and autumn, though it is rarely blisteringly hot or freezing cold. In the winter it snows, but to the romantic traveller this can add an extra dimension to the country's beauty.

Where to stay

The last five years have witnessed a great number of lavish new tourist and business hotels mushrooming up across the kingdom. These are generally located at key tourist sites (such as Petra) and at centres of international business (namely, downtown Amman). Most of Jordan's best hotels are in Amman, Aqaba, and at Petra, with the very best in the capital itself. In 1997, a number of ambitious new hotels were planned — largely to allow tourists to spend a night at some of the kingdom's more remote places of archaeological interest and staggering natural beauty. New hotels are being designed for the Dead Sea Valley, and for the northern reaches of the country. If you are on a tour you will probably be taken back to Amman each night when visiting parts of the north; and to Aqaba in the evening when visiting its environs and

Opposite: Rolling barren hills drift into the distance around the King's Highway.

Above: Rest house at Umm Qais enjoys fabulous panoramic views of both Lake Tiberias and the Golan Heights.

Wadi Rum.

The main sights are never a great distance from the cities, although towns such as Madaba and Kerak have little more than the barest overnight facilities for visitors. But even there an overnight stay is sure to give you a new insight into the country and its unending hospitality.

Most of Aqaba's big hotels are geared to beach holidays and facilities cater for all tastes, from water sports to just lounging by the pool. In the market area of Aqaba you will come across a wide range of more modestly priced hotels and pensions.

Camping

There are good and bad places to camp in Jordan. Camping at Petra is recommended. Officially you need a permit to camp within the ruins. This can only be obtained from the

Ministry of Antiquities in Amman but in practice a lot of people camp there without permission. In Petra and many other parts of the country there are caves in which you may spend the night. Wadi Rum is another excellent place to camp.

Take great care where you pitch a tent, and make sure you ask permission. Some people pitch tents near the rest house at Rum, but it is much more invigorating to wake in the morning further out in the valley. Jordanians are hospitable people and provided you do not leave rubbish, or cause fire, there should be no problems. Be considerate so that when you, or others, return you will be welcomed again.

National flag

Three horizontal stripes of black, white and a red triangle at the pole bearing a white 7-pointed star.

National flower

The Black Iris, *Iris nigricans*. It grows fairly extensively in Jordan, but it is not found in Europe.

Opposite: The beautiful Black Iris is the national flower of Jordan.
Overleaf: A flurry of hot air balloons above the rocks of Wadi Rum in celebration of King Hussein's fortieth anniversary as monarch.

PART ONE: HISTORY, GEOGRAPHY AND PEOPLE

Above: Jumble of ancient rocks at the edge of the Dead Sea.
Opposite: Bronze monument atop Mount Nebo represents the cross on which Christ was crucified and the serpent taken up in the desert by Moses.

An Ancient Pearl

Jordan's heritage stretches back to the dawn of mankind. It is a legacy that overwhelms not only tourists but archaeologists and historians. Each invading society has left its own mark. The Nabateans built their capitals there while others annexed the region and constructed provincial cities. From earliest times, when man roamed across what today is Jordan, the sweeping plains became a crossroads between Asia and Africa.

The chronology of Jordan is briefly as follows:

Above: Tall, weather-worn columns at Pella, ancient city of the *Decapolis*.

Palaeolithic Period: 500,000-17,000 BC
Neanderthal Man hunted around Azraq as well as in the south of modern Jordan.

Epipalaeolithic Period: 17,000-8000 BC
Evidence exists that settlements developed around Tabaga in south Jordan, as well as in the eastern desert regions, in the Jordan Valley, and at Pella.

Neolithic Period: 8000-4500 BC
Agriculture began to develop. Settlements at Beidha, near Petra, and at Jericho, point to the advanced nature of the society. The Ain Ghazal settlement, north of Amman, witnessed what is thought to have been man's first attempt to make statues.

Chalcolithic Period: 4500-3000 BC
Copper was smelted for the first time. The village of Teleilat Ghassul, unearthed in the Jordan Valley, dates to this period. Walls in the stone and mud-built houses are known to have had decorative frescoes. Substantial finds of pottery and tools from this era have been unearthed.

Early Bronze Age: 3000-2100 BC
Settlements expanded in their size, diversity and cultural output. These developments were perhaps due to the influence of the Canaanites who planned towns, developed architectural methods and tools. Invasions may be the reason why this thriving civilisation was brought to an end.

Middle Bronze Age: 2100-1500 BC

A resurgence in the development of civilisation and trading took place, making the era one of ancient Jordan's most prosperous. Excavations show an enormous wealth of artistic know-how. People moved from one land to another and some are believed to have gone from Jordan to Egypt, where they became rulers, known as *Hyksos* ('leaders from a foreign land'). Abraham is thought to have arrived in the Land of Canaan in about 1900 BC.

Late Bronze Age: 1500-1200 BC

Two great dynasties — those of the Egyptians and the Hittites of Anatolia — dominated the Late Bronze Age. Jordan and Palestine fell to the Egyptians. Trading between all parts of the Middle East and beyond seems to have been well developed.

Iron Age: 1200-330 BC

The bulk of Old Testament events took place during this era. Several kingdoms, including those of the Ammonites, the Edomites, and the Moabites, emerged in Jordan, dividing up the land. A well-developed agricultural community is known to have existed at Tawilan near Ain Mousa in southern Jordan. Numerous Iron Age settlements were dotted about Jordan, including those at Kerak, Mount Nebo, Madaba and Amman.

Hellenistic Period: 332-63 BC

Alexander the Great's conquest of West Asia brought the Hellenistic culture in its wake. To the Arabs, Alexander was known as *Dhu al-Qarnain*, meaning 'the one with two horns'. Much of the Middle East took up the Greek language and was influenced by Greek culture. Alexander's death in 323 BC resulted in the splitting up of his empire between two generals, Ptolemy and Seleucus.

Nabatean Period: 400 BC-AD 160

The Nabatean's magnificent civilisation, with its capital at Petra, developed through trading. Much of its achievements and settlements were annexed by the Roman Emperor, Pompey, in AD 106.

Top: Curious carving from Jordan's unique history thought to represent a Nabatean citizen or god.

Above: Ancient, many-wicked lamp, the handle of which is adorned with the pattern of a peacock's tail.

Roman Period: 63 BC-AD 330

A wealth of provincial Roman cities were constructed around what today is Jordan. Of most consequence is the federation of ten cities, known as the *Decapolis*, many of which lie within the territory of modern Jordan. Among these were Philadelphia (Amman), Gerasa (Jerash), Gadara (Umm Qais), Pella, and Dion (Irbid). *Pax Romana* led to a stable environment for trading and, with additional benefits such as excellent Roman roads, much important development took place.

Byzantine Period: AD 324-AD 632

Trading routes were extended into the Far East, alongside advances in agriculture. After the conversion of Roman Emperor Constantine, Christianity spread rapidly through the Middle East. The era is marked by dozens of churches which are home to some of the finest mosaic friezes.

Arab Empire: AD 634-AD 1099

By AD 635 most of the Middle East had fallen to Arab control. The advent of Islam, which swept across Jordan between AD 633 and AD 636, defeated the last remnants of the Byzantine Period. The legendary battle of Yarmouk marked the decisive victory for Islam in the region.

Crusader Period: AD 1099-AD 1268

Crusade invasions established Christian strongholds in the Middle East. Fortresses, like those at Kerak and Shobak, helped defeat the forces of Islam and acted as toll points for commercial travellers. Saladin (Salah el-Din) overcame the Crusaders, storming and besieging their strongholds, the jewel of which was Jerusalem (which he took in AD 1187).

Mamluk Period: AD 1263-AD 1516

Originating from Egypt, they replaced the dominant Ayyubids, taking control and re-modelling many of Jordan's great fortresses. In 1400 came the Mongol invasion of Tamurlane which was beaten back by the Mamluks. The empire gradually weakened and fractionalised before giving way to the Ottoman Empire.

Ottoman Period: AD 1516-AD 1918

Turkish supremacy, which lasted over 400 years, held much of the Arab World in its grip. Jordan's importance was largely due to its position as a route for pilgrims heading for Mecca and Medina. The empire was brought to an end during World War I, when the Arab Revolt occurred, laying the way for an independent Arab nation in Jordan.

Modern Jordan

A British Mandate over Palestine and Jordan was enforced in 1920. Transjordan became a self-governing region under the British Mandate. The Mandate came to an end in 1946 when, on 25 May, full independence was declared.

Early times

Historians and archaeologists have never disputed the importance of the regions that fall inside Jordan's contemporary boundaries. But in recent years, using new methods of dating and experimentation, the extraordinary diversity and age of its ancient settlements has become apparent.

Under every rock, it seems, there is a vestige of the past. From Palaeolithic times Jordan's deserts were home to hunters. Some flocked to a large expanse of water known to have existed near Azraq; others stalked the great plains with their primitive weapons in search of food. Flint tools, from earliest times, have been found at Bayir, south of Tuba, where even today only the most adventurous go.

Rock carvings, which have been located in different parts of the country, are thought to be the work of various civilisations which existed during the Palaeolithic, Neolithic and Chalcolithic eras.

Palaeolithic Man was predominantly a hunter-gatherer who tended to live near water. He followed the great herds of animals. Palaeolithic man has left us evidence of his existence through rock carvings, tools and other artefacts.

Implements such as flint and basalt hand-axes, knives and scraping tools for using on skins have all been found in Jordan.

Above: Recently excavated ruins of the Neolithic village of Beidha.

It was during the Epipalaeolithic era (the same as Mesolithic, or Middle Stone Age) that man began to settle. He developed specific ways of constructing buildings; he domesticated animals such as dogs and gazelles and began to cultivate the land to supplement meat acquired through hunting. During the Epipalaeolithic era settlements developed at Jericho and Beidha, near Petra.

As soon as man settled in one place, civilisation developed rapidly. As we move into the Neolithic era (New Stone Age) we find the remnants of surprisingly advanced communities. One is the settlement at Ain Ghazal, just north of Amman. There, a large number of buildings have been excavated, some of which had plaster floors. The dwellings were divided into three distinct districts. Ancestors of the group are known to have been venerated, especially at Beidha. Various skeletons, jawbones, and skulls have been found, some buried under the floors of houses. In some cases skulls had been removed from skeletons, covered in plaster, with bitumen filling in the eye sockets.

In other areas of what is now Jordan, developments were taking place. For example, in the eastern desert, pre-pottery Neolithic settlements were springing up. Commerce in stones, such as obsidian (from what is now Turkey) malachite, and others, began on routes that led deep into the desert.

Above: Qasr al-Abed, meaning The Castle or Palace of the Slave, was reconstructed by a lone French archaeologist. Its stone blocks are the largest ever used in any ancient construction of the Middle East.

Left: Lioness sheltering a cub at Qasr al-Abed. The Qasr was constructed by the Tobiad family, before being devastated by the great earthquake of AD 362.

Above: Weathered by centuries of wind and rain, the ruins at Petra remain perhaps the most magnificent of their kind on earth.

Experts conclude that migration from the eastern desert regions indicates that the area became hotter and drier over the centuries. The Neolithic Age's most significant accomplishment was the making of pottery vessels. Armed with this new and developing technique, Neolithic Man was ready to progress towards newer and greater things.

It was during the Chalcolithic (Copper-stone Period) that copper was smelted for the first time. The village of Teleilat Ghassul developed in the Jordan Valley. Settlements had become self-sufficient, no longer reliant on hunters. Livestock was then kept in pens. Cultivation of cereals, dates, olives and other produce escalated.

Houses at Teleilat Ghassul were planned around expansive courtyards. Foundations were of stone with mud bricks making up the walls. Wall paintings, some of the first of their kind, depicted processions of masked figures as well as geometric designs.

As copper hooks, knives, arrowheads, weapons and tools became more advanced, flint tools became less popular. The Bronze Age brought developments that would have been unthinkable to Neolithic Man, and planning became important. Settlements were given strategic positions on hilltops, and were defended with barricades and concentric walls. Life was no longer left to chance; water was channelled from one place to another, reservoirs were built and precautions were even taken against earthquakes and floods. In short, life was becoming civilised.

Jawa, a town in the eastern desert, is a good example of the sophistication of the Early Bronze Age. It was probably home to about 2,000 people. Defence walls encircled it and a mixture of animal breeding, agriculture and hunting ensured prosperity. Vast stone ramparts also encircled the ancient settlements at Beidha and Jericho.

Perhaps the most mysterious and strangest of all Bronze Age discoveries was that of 20,000 graves at Bab edh-Shra. The corpses were interred in shaft tombs with multiple chambers, which included jewellery, pots and other articles as well as skeletons. It is not known for certain what

Above: The Temple of Zeus and South Theatre are two of Jerash's most important ancient structures.

brought an end to the Early Bronze Age settlements.

The last decade or so has seen archaeologists altering their theories substantially concerning the Middle and Late Bronze Age periods of the Middle East. This revival and re-interpretation has come about through newly found fragments relating to Bronze Age Man. It seems that, during the middle and latter stages of the Bronze Age, large and distinct communities arose in areas of what is now north and central Jordan while a nomadic Bedouin-type people, called the *Shasu*, are thought to have roamed the southern lands.

During the mid-Bronze Age people started to move about the Middle East to a far greater extent. Trading between Egypt, Syria, Arabia, Israel and Jordan continued to develop, resulting in the development of civilisation and culture. Finer pots were produced and better metal work as new techniques and raw materials became available. It was then that the *Hyksos* (a Greek term, equivalent to the ancient Egyptian *hkaw haswt* translated roughly as 'leaders from other lands') arrived in Egypt. They seem to have originated from Jordan or Palestine, before embarking for Egypt and becoming rulers for a time.

The refining of bronze was an important step forward. This realisation, together with inventions such as the potter's wheel and hotter furnaces, saw the transition to a completely new era. Man was then capable of fashioning tools of great flexibility, and with them he set out to shape the society around him.

In the twilight of the Bronze Ages, various new kingdoms emerged. In the south there were the Edomites; in the centre the Moabites; and to the extreme north was the Aramaean kingdom's capital at Damascus. Commerce on an unprecedented scale led to the mushrooming of different trading civilisations. These kingdoms prospered as precious metals, spices and a range of extraordinary goods were produced, traded and transported. The accumulation of wealth made the rich prone to attack. Much of the warring, feuds, and rape of one civilisation by another, is recorded in the pages of the Old Testament.

Alexander and Beyond

Before Alexander's conquest a new society developed. Its populace nurtured the arts and, in their time, constructed some of the finest monuments of any ancient people. They were the Nabateans.

Fundamental details about them are still unknown, but they seem to have been a nomadic people — herders of flocks, who came from Arabia. Nabatean society was almost certainly based on trading at which few were more skilled. Their commercial expertise brought rare and exotic artefacts from Egypt, Greece, Rome, India, China and the farthest outposts of the East. Soon ivory, perfumes, medicines, gold and a complete spectrum of goods and wares became available. Alongside their talents as traders, the Nabateans were skilled at building and in water management. It was an era that prospered for over 500 years in which unrivalled excellence was created from little more than bare rock.

We know that the Nabateans spoke a dialect of Arabic and later on adopted Aramaic. Their capital stands at Petra, but the site was inhabited for a considerable time before they arrived. The nearby Neolithic settlement at Beidha supports this assertion, although when the Nabateans arrived they made changes on an unprecedented scale.

A wall was constructed to fortify the city and to supplement the natural seclusion of the narrow gorges. Various Roman writers — few of whom actually visited the city — record that Petra, which means 'rock', was a glorious sight. Strabo wrote about Petra when he told of the Nabateans and their society. He concluded that the Nabateans had no slaves but shared duties between everyone. He maintained that they were a democratic people, with no social classes, no family restrictions and few disputes; in short, Nabatean life was idyllic.

Petra and other settlements tell us a good deal about these people. Sacrificial shrines were given great importance and it is probable that human sacrifice occurred. There were tombs, baths, market-places and ordinary houses, as well as many venerated places where the pantheon of Nabatean deities could be extolled. Principal of these was *Dushara*, the sun god. Petra was referred to by David in Psalm 108 as 'The Strong City'. After the collapse of Roman civilisation (and after a short visit in Crusader times) Petra remained hidden for over a thousand years.

Above: Lone watchtower enabled a Byzantine community to survey the flat desert landscape for miles around.

It was not until Swiss explorer John L Burckhardt rediscovered the spot in 1812 that its whereabouts became known throughout the world again.

Alexander the Great's conquest of Jordan, along with much of the Middle East and Central Asia, brought the Hellenistic culture firmly into the heart of the region. Yet, soon after vanquishing the Middle East, Alexander was dead. Jordan was incorporated in the empires of the Ptolemies and the Seleucids (who hailed from Syria) until it became the property of Roman General Pompey, when he marched through Syria in 63 BC.

A few remnants of Greek civilisation still remain in Jordan, although many are only fragments of later societies built on Greek foundations. One of the most spectacular Hellenistic creations in Jordan is the exquisite and extraordinary Qasr al-Abed ('the Castle

Above: Mosaic frieze at Deir Ain Abata, the newly-discovered Sanctuary of Lot, depicts an almost unique leaf design.

or Palace of the Slave') at Iraq el-Amir, a short distance from modern day Amman. You can still make out some of the wonderful sculpted lions which, like the massive stone blocks, are cut from a gloriously-hued yellow stone.

The castle, or palace, belonged to the mighty Tobiad family. Its design was intriguing — although extremely large, archaeologists have noticed that there was only one small entrance leading inside. This was possibly to prevent an attacking army from marching into the palace, as only one man could enter at a time.

Pompey's conquest of Jordan and the surrounding areas in 63 BC brought about the fabled federation of the *Decapolis* cities.

This loosely-knit group of cities varying in number, spread across Jordan, Palestine and Syria, had common bonds of economic and cultural interest. Many of the cities still thrive, though most have changed their names. Of the original ten cities, five are thought to be in modern Jordan. These are: Philadelphia (Amman), Gerasa (Jerash), Gadara (Umm Qais), Pella and Dion (Irbid). Among these Jerash appears to have been the most splendid. No expense was spared in making it one of the greatest provincial cities anywhere in the Roman Empire. Hadrian himself visited Jerash in AD 130, the occasion being marked by the monumental arch at the south of the ruins.

In the year AD 106 the Romans annexed the southern regions of Jordan and absorbed them into their new Province of Arabia. Petra was included in the same year. Rather than fall into decline, it seems that Petra enjoyed a new lease of life. Many Roman buildings were constructed, among which were the amphitheatre, the colonnaded street and houses, monuments and shops of all kinds.

The Via Nova Traiana ('Trajan New Road') which linked the Red Sea with Damascus, and everything in between, was a great boon to traders such as the Nabateans. Then, strangely, almost as suddenly and silently as they arrived, the Nabateans left Petra. No one is quite sure why. The exodus was unhurried: it was well planned. With the departure of the Nabateans and the decline of the Roman Empire, which had grown too big and mismanaged to stay together, a new era began: the Byzantine Period.

With its capital at Constantinople (Istanbul), the newly divided Eastern Roman Empire became known as the Byzantine Empire. The Byzantine era began with Constantine's conversion to Christianity and dates from AD 324. Innumerable churches sprouted all over what is now Jordan, many clustered together on the foundations of ancient Roman settlements. All over Jordan, Roman buildings were plundered to build churches — an activity assisted by a number of substantial earthquakes. Emperor Justinian's rule (AD 527-565) witnessed an extraordinary growth in

Above: Exterior of Qasr Amra in Jordan's eastern desert — an ancient and elaborate bathing complex.

church construction. These new houses of worship boasted some of the finest mosaic floors. The mosaics around Madaba are perhaps the greatest of all, the jewel in their crown being the 6th-century map of the Holy Land in Madaba itself.

The latter years of the Byzantine era were marred by onslaughts of different kinds. There were outbreaks of plague that depopulated the region horrifically, especially that of AD 542, as well as campaigns by the Sassanians and others. But perhaps the greatest change came with the advent of Islam in the 7th century AD. From then on Jordan, and the Middle East, took a new path — the Islamic Way.

The Islamic Era

When the Prophet Mohammed heard the Word of God for the first time he tried to convert the pagan people of his native Mecca. But they threatened him and his followers. So in AD 622, he left for Medina, a city north of Mecca. This migration is known as the *Hijira*, and marks the advent of Islam. From this date the Islamic calendar begins (1 AH). In the year AD 630 Mohammed returned to Mecca and converted the city. From that point, the Word of Islam spread rapidly through the Middle East and North Africa.

A new and powerful dynasty was founded in Damascus in AD 661 — the dynasty of the Ummayeds. It lasted until the year AD 750 and gave yet another lease of life and prosperity to Jordan. Pilgrims flocked through the country from Damascus, Jerusalem and beyond, en route to the holy city of Mecca. Jordan is filled with evidence of the Ummayed love of hunting, sport and leisure. Caravanserais, bath complexes, meeting places and palaces were constructed in Jordan's desert lands. They are collectively known as the desert palaces or castles. The latter is something of a misnomer, as many of the buildings were certainly not defensive strongholds, although some, such as Qasr Kharana, were designed that way.

The *Qasrs*, meaning 'palaces', demonstrate not only the Ummayed love for the

Above: High above the surrounding valleys, the Crusader fortress at Shobak was once considered impenetrable.

desert, but show the dynasty's expertise in construction. Qasrs Tuba and Mushatta illustrate the refined nature of their brickwork, while Qasr Amra (a bathing complex) houses some of the most exquisite frescoes in the Middle East. Perhaps the greatest building of all constructed by the Ummayeds is the Dome of the Rock in Jerusalem.

The Ummayeds were succeeded by the Abbasid Dynasty. They transferred the seat of the Khalifate from Damascus to Baghdad, leaving the desert palaces empty or inhabited by wandering Bedouins.

In AD 969 Jordan fell yet again into the hands of another power. This time it was the Fatimids of Egypt who gained control and they maintained a hold over Jordan until 1071. Then the Crusaders from Europe marched through Palestine and into Jordan in 1099. Their aim was to retake all the former Christian regions that had fallen into the hands of Islam. In doing so they took Jerusalem and established a kingdom there. A line of Crusader fortresses was constructed down the backbone of Jordan, the most substantial of which were at Kerak and Shobak.

The legendary Muslim leader and warrior, Saladin, brought an end to the Crusader presence in AD 1187 at the battle of Hattin. From then on Jordan's history is dominated by Islamic peoples. The region prospered under the Mamluks, who restored not only the Ayyubid and other Islamic strongholds, but many of those constructed by the Crusaders as well.

The people who claimed Jordan had to be willing to fight for control of such a strategic crossroads. The year 1516 saw yet another defeat and victory. This time it was the Mamluks who were overthrown by the growing Ottoman Empire. The Turkish realm expanded through the Middle East from Constantinople.

Although the era saw little progress for Jordan, the Ottoman presence continued into the 20th century. A great railway was planned and built by the Ottomans to link Damascus to Medina. This, the fabled Hijaz Railway Line, was conceived to transport pilgrims to and from Mecca and Medina, although the extension to Mecca

46

was never realised. Despite building the Hijaz line, the Ottoman Empire's lack of advances left Jordan underdeveloped.

With time there arose a movement for independence, to cast off the mantle of colonisation. The Ottoman Turks allied with the Germans during World War I while a new Arab movement was growing under the leadership of the Hashemite, Sharif Hussein.

On 10 June 1916, after negotiations with the British, the Great Arab Revolt began. Britain affirmed that it would support the revolt as long as the Arabs strove to defeat the Ottomans. But, in secrecy, the British and French agreed to the Sykes-Picot Accord which effectively divided between them all the lands pledged to Sharif Hussein.

Meanwhile, the Turkish positions were overcome. The Hijaz Railway (although newly built) was made inoperable, as were other key Ottoman lines of defence and communication. The Ottoman Empire collapsed, and with the collapse came the end of the war.

Britain divided up what it called 'the Fertile Crescent'. France acquired Syria and Lebanon while Britain got Iraq, Palestine and Jordan. In 1917, the British Government announced the Balfour Declaration, which noted that Britain would support the Zionist dream of creating a Jewish state in Palestine. Attempts by Sharif Hussein to resist this reshaping of the map failed.

However, in 1921, Emir Abdullah, his second son, met Churchill in Jerusalem to secure recognition for the Emirate of Transjordan. This became fully established in 1923 with the Emir Abdullah as its first head of state. Transjordan was excluded from the clauses concerned with the establishment of a Jewish homeland in Palestine.

An agreement was signed with Britain in 1928 that led to Transjordan's virtual self-governing. Yet it was not until after World War II that Jordan became a completely sovereign state. With the British mandate's end, full independence came on 25 May 1946. Emir Abdullah became the first King of Transjordan. In 1950 Transjordan and Central Palestine merged to form the Hashemite Kingdom of Jordan.

Modern Jordan

Since its full independence, Jordan has been subjected to a series of gruelling and daunting problems. But these traumas have united the nation behind strong leadership. Even as the cries of joy over independence were dying, trouble flared up.

The United Nations General Assembly had recommended, in 1947, that Palestine be divided. A great number of Jewish refugees, fleeing Europe after World War II, set their eyes on Palestine as the Promised Land. Yet when it came to partition, the Jews were not only given the greater half, but the valuable coastal strip as well. This

Above: Minarets soar above the bustling streets of Amman.

Above: Part of the Hijaz railway line destroyed during the Arab Revolt in 1917, which saw the collapse of the Ottoman Empire and paved the way for the modern state of Jordan.

controversial decision by the UN initially led to an Arab boycott of the situation, and eventually to war. When, in 1948, hostilities broke out, the highly trained and well-equipped Israeli militia overcame the Jordanian army.

Following the massacre of many Arabs, Palestinian refugees gathered their belongings and headed for the West Bank. This exodus of almost a million Arabs fuelled Jewish territorial ambitions.

By the end of the war, the Israelis found themselves with not only Galilee, but the Negev desert (a substantial strip giving them access to the Red Sea), most of the Mediterranean coast and almost the whole of Jerusalem. The loss of territory, as well as the massive influx of refugees, affected Jordan badly. However, things were to get worse.

On 20 July 1951 King Abdullah was murdered as he entered the Al-Aqsa Mosque in Jerusalem for Friday prayers. At his side was his grandson, Hussein (later to become King) who flung himself at the assassin. The killer fired a shot at Hussein, and had it not ricocheted off a medal on his chest, the future king might also have perished. In his autobiography, *Uneasy Lies the Head*, King Hussein wrote of the assassination:

'On that terrible day . . . I learned the importance of death; that when you have to die, you die, for it is God's judgement. Only thus have I found (the) particular inner peace granted to those who do not fear death.'

Abdullah's second son, Naif, became regent while his eldest son, Talal, was in Switzerland receiving medical treatment. Talal, who was favoured by Jordanians, assumed power but was forced to abdicate later, due to illness. News of the abdication greeted Hussein at school at Harrow in England. When he turned eighteen, Hussein returned to his homeland, swore allegiance to his people and became king.

Above: King Talal bin Abdullah, the father of King Hussein.

Above: Portrait of Sharif Hussein bin Ali, leader of the Arab Revolt, at the Military Museum, Amman.

The Time Of King Hussein

In a reign of over forty years, King Hussein has been an outstanding and courageous leader. He has gripped the reins of authority ever since his accession, and has steered the Kingdom of Jordan on a positive course towards development, stability and a lasting peace.

The path, which has navigated many of the region's most trying ordeals, has put the king at considerable risk. Yet even in the most difficult circumstances his leadership has been firm and fair. Jordan's people look upon their monarch as a father figure: and as a man committed to equality and peace beyond all else.

Hussein's reign has witnessed enormous changes not only in Jordan, but also in the Middle East at large. The Suez Crisis of 1956 was followed by the infamous Az-Zarqa Affair, where the king had to overcome a serious threat to his monarchy.

The young Kingdom of Jordan felt the waves of conflict among its neighbours.

One was the *coup d'etat*, in Iraq, on 14 July 1958 which brought to an end the reign of King Feisal II (Hussein's own cousin) when he and his family were assassinated.

Following the coup Iraq pulled out of the newly signed Arab Federation, as well as the Baghdad Pact.

In August 1960 Jordan's Prime Minister, Hazza al-Majali, was assassinated. It happened just as the nation was making its first steady steps towards development. On 1 April 1965 the king proclaimed his younger brother Prince Hassan as crown prince. A new era had begun: one in which Jordan's progress was consistent and rapid, yet fraught with new dangers.

At a summit in Jerusalem in 1964, The Palestine Liberation Organisation (PLO) was formed. It was designed to act as a mouthpiece for the Palestinian people and to further the liberation of Palestine from Zionism. Jordan's alliance with the PLO led to massive retaliation by Israel on Jordan itself.

In May 1967 President Nasser of Egypt ordered the withdrawal of the United

Above: King Hussein and Crown Prince Hassan pose with their father, King Talal.

Opposite top: King Hussein as a young man with Crown Prince Hassan, Prince Mohammed and Princess Basma.

Opposite: Young King Hussein and a sports car.

Nations Emergency Force from its Sinai region (where it had been positioned since 1957). Then Nasser proclaimed that the Straits of Tiran, at the threshold of the Red Sea, would be a prohibited area for Israeli vessels.

At the end of May 1967 Jordan signed a military alliance with Egypt. Within a week Israel began to attack Egyptian positions in the Sinai.

The Israeli airforce destroyed the Egyptian airforce before it was even airborne. Then they turned their attentions to Egyptian troops in the Sinai, and Jordanian soldiers on the West Bank, as well as Arab forces protecting the Golan Heights.

Some 6,000 Jordanians were listed as

dead or missing, and more than 200,000 refugees flooded from the West Bank into Jordan. Later, the Israelis annexed the whole of Jerusalem and the West Bank.

These hostilities damaged Jordan's economy and injured its social framework. The influx of so many Palestinians, together with the loss of tourism and agricultural revenue (largely from the West Bank), put Jordan in an extremely difficult position. Added to this were the implications of the growing militant activities of the PLO. The situation was explosive.

It was in September 1970 that Palestinian guerrillas hijacked four commercial aircraft, three of which were flown to northern Jordan, with the crew and passengers kept as hostages.

King Hussein could not condone such actions and dispatched his army to put an end to the hijacking. A ten-day civil conflict ensued, which was ended by the signing of an agreement in Cairo between Hussein and Yasser Arafat, the leader of the PLO. Palestinians were given the choice of leaving Jordan or conforming to its laws.

The October War of 1973 did not directly concern Jordan, although the country sent a nominal force to help Syria. A spate of Arab summits in the years that followed seemed to smooth relations between the Arab nations. But, all the while, Israel manoeuvred for an even stronger power base. It was to this end that Israel launched an attack on Lebanon in the summer of 1982.

Peace in the Middle East seems short-lived. With the Iran-Iraq carnage at an end, the 1990s began with another Gulf War. This invasion by Saddam Hussein into Kuwait sent shock waves through the West, fearful of Kuwait's oil reserves falling into 'enemy' hands.

The largest massing of allied troops since 1945, and the eviction of Iraq's despot, left the Hashemite Kingdom in an unenviable position. Seen by the Arab and Western Worlds as too sympathetic to Iraq before the Gulf Crisis, King Hussein's position seemed, at many points, to be untenable. But, characteristically, the monarch managed to sweep back from the brink of calamity. In the months that followed the ending of the 1991 Gulf War, Hussein embarked on a

Above: Military display marks the fortieth anniversary of King Hussein's accession to the throne.

daunting series of informal talks aimed at thawing his isolated position with the international community.

As at so many times during his long and extraordinary reign, sceptics were too quick with their pessimistic predictions. Hussein is a survivor in the grand tradition of Arab leaders who, despite crippling odds, saved the day through indomitable charisma and shrewd strategy.

On 12 October 1991, as his kingdom struggled to bounce back after the earlier conflict of the year, Hussein announced Jordan's participation in a planned Middle East Peace Conference, scheduled for Madrid at the end of the month.

Those first steps on the road to peace were difficult, with slow progress. The Palestine question, as ever, formed one of the major stumbling blocks to any agreement. But, behind the scenes, intense talks continued.

Early in 1993 it emerged that secret negotiations, held in Norway, between the Israeli government and the PLO had led to an agreement. A 'Declaration of Principles' was drafted and, as the world's press recorded

history in the making, the Declaration was signed — and sealed with a handshake — on the White House lawn on 13 September 1993.

The sight of Yasser Arafat, King Hussein and Israeli Prime Minister Yitzak Rabin shaking hands was, perhaps, one lasting memory we shall keep from the decade. On 26 October 1994, in a tent straddling the Jordan-Israeli border at Arava, Jordan signed a comprehensive peace treaty with Israel.

With so many years of hostility between Israel and its Arab neighbours, forging a lasting Peace was never expected to be easy. As the ink was still drying on the official document of reconciliation, militant forces in Israel, the West Bank, and beyond, sought revenge.

The infamous Hebron Massacre, and the slaying of Yitzak Rabin — by a right wing Jewish extremist — were two sordid events with the power to derail any fragile rapprochement.

As Jordan moves towards the next century a lasting era of stability is on the cards.

Optimism has to prevail that the

Above: His Majesty King Hussein bin Talal of the Hashemite Kingdom of Jordan in 1997.

continuing reconciliations cease to be punctuated by outbursts of violence and that, either in this century or, at least, early in the next, Jordan can look forward to a lasting era of stability in which future generations can live peacefully side by side.

Overleaf: Sundown over Aqaba.

The Land of Yesterday and Tomorrow

'Jordan is itself a beautiful country. It is wild, with limitless deserts where the Bedouin roam, but the mountains of the north are clothed in green forests and, where the river flows, it is fertile in summer and winter. Jordan has a strange haunting beauty and a sense of timelessness. Dotted with the ruins of empires once great, it is the last resort of yesterday in the world of tomorrow. I love every inch of it. I love Amman, where I was born, and which I have seen grow from a township. I am still awed and excited each time I set eyes on Petra, approaching by a defile so narrow that a dozen Nabateans could hold an army at bay. Above all I feel at home in the tribal black tents in the desert.' (King Hussein, from his autobiography, *Uneasy Lies the Head*.)

Above: Spring flowers adorn a Jordanian hillside.

King Hussein's pride for his land is reflected by all Jordanians, for it is a place, fashioned by the forces of nature, with unending diversity and untamed splendour.

Including the Dead Sea, Jordan is a small country of about 96,188 square kilometres (37,138 square miles) yet within its borders is a plethora of physical features that are the envy of many larger nations.

There are vast deserts and rich forested valleys, as well as mountains rising to a thousand metres, and dry land at nearly 400 metres below sea level, giving Jordan the honourable distinction of being home to the lowest region on earth.

The Great Rift Valley, slicing down the western flank of Jordan, is the country's most prodigious natural feature. This immense crack in the surface of the world stretches from Lake Tiberias (the Sea of Galilee), cleaving a path through Jordan, the Red Sea, and on through eastern Africa. In its mighty fissure (created some 20 million years ago by the shifting of tectonic plates), the Jordan River has carved a watery path, 320 kilometres (200 miles) long. Kindled by the melted snows of Syria's Mount Hermon, the Jordan River courses silently into the Dead Sea: the lowest point on Earth.

The Jordan Valley is the nation's most fertile region. Along its sides a warm climate ensures excellent crops of vegetables and fruit, irrigated by the East Ghor canal. This sub-tropical climate nourishes most of Jordan's agricultural output. Temperatures in the Jordan Valley range from about 14.9°C in January to as high as 40°C in July.

The Dead Sea is a barren expanse of water whose mineral contents are about eight times denser than the world's oceans. The salt content, which is over 20 per cent, has been extracted in recent years to provide potash and other minerals to be sold on the international market.

At 394 metres (1,293 feet) below mean sea level, the Dead Sea's extraordinary mineral-laden water is capable of supporting a human body. The salts are extremely irritating to the eyes, although they are known to have

Above: Wadi Araba, the Valley of Arabs, testifies to Jordan's stark beauty.
Overleaf: The northern reaches of Jordan, around Ajlun, are well known across the Middle East for their fertile fields.

beneficial properties for the bather.

South of the Dead Sea the Jordan Valley runs on, forging its way through the Wadi (valley) Araba, until it reaches the Gulf of Aqaba. This valley is one of the most spectacular in the Middle East, with its barren sides, where the searing wind batters against its walls in search of an escape. The narrow Gulf of Aqaba, which leads into the Red Sea, gives Jordan access to the oceans. A coastline of 40 kilometres (25 miles), bordered with coral reefs as fine as any, houses not only a port but an aquatic playground. The serene waters of Aqaba, where diving is superb, teem with fish of all kinds.

But the Rift Valley, with its many features, is just one of Jordan's natural attributes. On the West Bank (presently occupied by Israel), the mountains of Judaea and Samaria — extolled in biblical times — rise up in desolation. Within the valleys nestle cities and settlements whose very foundations were forged in the days of the Old Testament. Their names, which include Jerusalem and Bethlehem, are central to Christianity.

In the north of Jordan, from Lake Tiberias and the Syrian border, another terrain sweeps down to Amman, Jordan's capital. This, the Land of Gilead, straddles the region between the Wadis of Zarqa and Yarmouk. Much of Jordan's populace dwells in the fertile northern valleys, with their rich soils and charming glades. Well-watered by the prevailing westerly winds, these highlands are an idyllic setting whether in the summer's heat or the winter's frosty breeze.

There could be no place more beautiful, more elegant and awe-inspiring than the deserts of the east. They extend over four-fifths of Jordan, providing a landscape that is chillingly barren. This wilderness, with its volcanic black basalt, yellow sand, and granite panoramas, commands a stark and enchanting splendour that can only be marvelled at by man. The pinnacle of this cryptic region is surely Wadi Rum: the Valley of the Moon.

The People: Ancient Cultures, Age-old Country

For more than nine millennia man has made Jordan his home. As one civilisation replaced another, monuments to their passage were left behind. Each year new treasures of these epochs are discovered while the climate ensures their preservation.

Jordan's population of 4.4 million (not including the West Bank) is made up of several cultural groups. The vast majority of inhabitants are of Arab origin, most of whom follow Islam and are of the Sunni branch.

About 7 per cent of the nation's people are Christian; another small percentage is made up of Circassians (Sunni Muslims brought by the Ottomans from the Caucasus to what is now Jordan). A small percentage of Armenians and other cultural minorities live in Amman, as well as in other parts of the country.

Jordan's population escalated during the 1948 and 1967 wars with Israel, when there was a massive influx of Palestinian refugees. Palestinians now make up a large proportion of the population while nomadic peoples, predominantly Bedouin, account for about 10 per cent. Another great population increase took place with Iraq's 1990 invasion of Kuwait. Tens of thousands of Jordanians living elsewhere in the Middle East, fled home as the prospect of war in the Gulf loomed ever closer.

Of all the people in the Middle East, none has a reputation as exalted as the Bedu, or Bedouin. Largely a nomadic people, they cling to ancient ways, living by fabled codes of hospitality and kinship. Totalling about seven per cent of the population, they wander in Jordan's deserts, and those of Saudi Arabia, Syria and Iraq.

The Bedouin

The word *Bedu* comes from the Arabic word, *badawi*, meaning 'a dweller of the desert'. The Bedouin endure the desert and have learnt to survive its unforgiving climate. They treat it with due reverence, knowing that the wilderness has no respect for fools.

Today, most of Jordan's Bedouin reside in the vast wasteland that extends eastwards from the great Desert Highway. When driving on the Highway, or some of the country's other eastern roads, you may well see a scattering of tents and goats denoting one of the nomadic communities. Alas, the 20th century has begun to catch up with the Bedouin. Many have resorted to a semi-nomadic lifestyle, or have taken to living in settled communities.

The traditional Bedouin way of life has come about by adopting measures that ensure survival. Philip K Hitti, in his encyclopaedic volume, *A History of the Arabs* (1937), observes:

'To its denizen the desert is more than a habitat: it is the custodian of his sacred tradition, the preserver of the purity of his speech and blood and his first and foremost line of defence against encroachment from the outside world. Its scarcity of water, scorching heat, trackless roads, lack of food-supply — all enemies in normal times — prove staunch allies in time of danger. Little wonder then that the Arabian has rarely bent his neck to a foreign yoke.'

There are few societies whose existence is as harmonious as that of the Bedouin. They walk a tight line between life and death, balancing with tenacity and skill. They understand their flocks of goats and camels, forging a symbiotic relationship with them so that each depends on the other for survival. The herds rely on their masters for protection, the masters depend on their herds for milk, meat and skins.

The constant wandering is no aimless venture; it is a carefully planned expedition for new pastures.

In desert conditions, where vegetation is slow to grow and scarce, even at the best of times, it may be many months before old pastures are revitalised. The vast herds of camels which, until the early years of this century, could be found moving through the desert, have all but disappeared. Some writers put the number of camels in these great herds at about 100,000. Today the

Above: A shepherd boy minds his family's flock.

Bedouin tend only a few camels and goats.

The clan is at the centre of Bedouin society. Each family has its own tent, a collection of which (known as *hayy*), constitutes a *qawn*, or 'clan'. A number of these clans make up a 'tribe' (a *qabilah*). People living in the same clan are considered to be of the same blood. There are no lengths to which a man of the clan will not go to safeguard another.

In traditional Bedouin society there are few items of material importance, little more, in fact, than the tents, animals, a few utensils and perhaps some jewellery. These are communally owned by the family. Yet in Bedouin eyes, the land is not owned by any one man. Leadership of the clan is the responsibility of the Sheikh, an elder to whom matters of strife or decision are brought for adjudication.

In Islam no man is more venerable than the next: any can lead the prayer. This spills over to Bedouin society at large where all men are seen as equal, with elders commanding extra respect gained through experience. In Arab lands the concept of a monarch is a relatively new one. *Malik*, which means 'king', was traditionally only used when referring to a ruler of Persian, or other, dynasties. In Bedouin and Arab societies each man commands great dignity and responsibility.

Genealogy is of supreme importance. It was probably people from the Middle East who first elevated genealogy to a science. In Islamic lands, tracing one's family back to the Prophet Mohammed is seen as extremely prestigious. Such people take the honorary title of *Sharif* (or *Sharifa* for a woman).

The Bedouin are seen as a fearless people who, although basically peace-loving, will engage in a blood feud if necessary. In cases where one man slays another in the same clan, no one will defend him. The murderer will usually be killed or forced to leave his tribe to become an outlaw (*tarid*).

There is no worse punishment than excommunication from the clan and tribe. In circumstances where one man has been murdered by another from outside his own clan, the situation calls for vendetta. Blood

Top: Friendly face of an Orthodox priest.
Above: Jordanian girl fetches water wearing the traditional costume of Jordan's Salt area.

demands blood. Such feuds can last for generations. They may lie dormant for decades before being revived once again.

Hostilities do not cease until total vengeance has been gained. The values of Bedouin society are vested in an ancient code of honour. This calls for total loyalty to the clan and tribe, and to one's position of work, in upholding the survival of the group. There is a sense of honour and pride in the Bedouin's hospitality. The word *Asabiyah* refers to the Bedouin clan's soul and spirit. With it comes an unwavering allegiance to the group through which that community can survive.

Since World War II the Bedouin lifestyle has changed in many ways and in some respects their existence has improved. With the advent of modern medicine in Jordan, Bedouin who attend clinics receive excellent treatment. But some fear that drugs will weaken their immunity to their harsh surroundings.

As Jordanian society changes, so the Bedouin are forced to change. Once, as the sole providers of meat to settled communities, they were assured of a good existence. Now villages and towns have other sources of meat, forcing the Bedouin to reduce their herds. As their children are drawn to study, they are also drawn to Western ways.

The government of Jordan, which in the past contemplated settling the nomadic Bedouin, seems to be coming to terms with their existence. For they have achieved something no other society has managed ... the ability to survive in Jordan's vast barren lands.

The Circassians

Circassians are a non-Arab Islamic people of the Sunni branch, who, originating from the Caucasus in Russia, fled during the 19th century following persecution to live in other Islamic lands. They are known as *Sharakisah* in Arabic. Their origin is traced to Indo-European Muslim tribes, in particular to Iassi and the Kossogs of the Caucasus.

The exodus and migration began in the year 1878, reaching its height between 1864 and 1878. This migration, in which thousands of Circassians sought new homes, continued until the turn of the century.

The migration occurred because of persecution by Christians in Russia. They searched for a place to safeguard their Islamic faith. The majority who fled the Black Sea region settled in Turkey, Syria and Jordan. For political reasons the Ottoman regime encouraged the migration and about 600,000 Circassians left Russia.

Many thousands of Circassians now live in Jordan. Their groups are spread through Amman, Jerash, Wadi el-Seer, Suweilih, Zarqa, Azraq, and other parts of the north.

When they arrived, Amman was little more than a tiny settlement. An abandoned mosque, dating back to the Ummayed era, and a tall tower were refurbished by the Circassians as a place of worship. They began to construct dwellings on the site of modern Amman. It was thanks to Circassian immigrants that Amman developed into a thriving city.

Most came with nothing. They worked hard, like the Palestinians, to rebuild their lives. Amman's natural sources of water were an important start for the new civilisation. Circassians brought with them traditions from the Caucasus: weaving, basket-making and carpentry.

The Ottomans managed the resettlement of the Circassians to some extent, using them almost as a security belt in various parts of their empire. Circassians were recruited into the police and also formed a special cavalry division which protected the building of the great Hijaz Railway Line.

Historically there has been some friction between the Bedouin and the Circassians. The former saw the Circassians as a threat to their lands, water supplies and life in general. Today Circassians have managed to carve a niche for themselves in Jordan. They are a well-educated and socially responsible people who have sought to develop and improve society.

Many of the older Circassians in Jordan worry about the preservation of traditional beliefs and customs that they brought from the Caucasus.

Top: Jordanian Lady working on a sculpture.
Above: Smiling young shepherd boy.

Above: Abu Fadel, a Bedouin chief, ensures that the ancient codes of the Bedouin are continued.

Crafts

Circassians have methods of craftsmanship, which are totally different from those of their Arab counterparts. These include special equipment for bee-keeping — a Circassian passion — and tools and methods for blacksmiths. Circassians were able to earn their living in new lands by offering services, in addition to the artefacts that they made. Their carpentry allowed them to build not only carts, windows and ploughs, but entire houses and specialised equipment for use in agriculture and other activities. They also brought a knowledge of crafting with gold, and created superb jewellery and ornamented weapons, belts and brooches.

Circassians are known for their acts of charity to the community. The famous black and white mosque in Amman (known as the Abu Darwwish Mosque) was constructed by a Circassian. Their society has always been divided into small clans and tribes, presided over by chieftains, known as the *Besh*. Below the *Besh* was another leader, known as a *Lava Lash*, beneath whom came the *Warq*.

A supreme council took care of general affairs of the community and ensured that the chieftain did not stray from the path of good leadership. An unwritten constitution, known as the *Adigha Khabza*, guided the society and was referred to for direction. The constitution is still used to give advice and guidance.

Although the Circassians have always put great store by their leader's judgements, they resort to democratic means to arrive at the most favourable decision.

Teaching through proverbs and stories sought to give new generations a grounding in behaviour. Sadly, these proverbs and tales are slowly being lost. There are many Circassian maxims. One declares: Think before you utter and do not sit down before you know your place.

Above: A liberal culture in all respects, Jordan's young generations are free to pursue their interests.

Right: Weaver at work on a traditional loom.

Above: Father and daughter represent Jordan's past and future generations.

Above: A fruit seller in Amman displays the pick of the crop.

The Druze

The Druze (who get their name from the Arabic *Duruz* and *Darazi*), are a sect descended from the Ismaili branch of Shia Muslims. Although most Middle East Druze reside in Lebanon, Syria and Israel, a small number live in Jordan, mainly near the Syrian border. Azraq has a Druze community.

The Druze have safeguarded their beliefs and traditions, many of which are at odds with those around them. This has been achieved by concealment of their heritage and adhering to strict rules on marriage. Conversion to other religions is not permitted. This practice of secrecy, known as *taqiyah*, allows the Druze to go to any lengths to prevent clandestine details of their faith from becoming known. This is so important to them that Druze are permitted — and even expected — to conform superficially to the religious observances of those in whose company they may be.

In Druze society only the elite, referred to as *'uqqal* ('knowers'), are entrusted with the cryptic details central to the faith. The exact history of the Druze is not entirely known.

According to *Encyclopedia Britannica*, they first proclaimed their faith in Cairo in AD 1017. A group of Druze had as their leader a man named Hamzah ibn 'Ali ibn Ahmad. But it was from a junior of the clan, named Darazi, that the Druze are thought to have acquired their name.

Their faith seems to comprise a mixture of many things. Included are a belief in a Messiah, incarnation, mystical knowledge and transmigration. These elements are combined with a doctrine which maintains the divinity of al-Hakim bin-Amri-llah (the sixth Fatimid khalifah of Egypt). It is thought that the Druze believe al-Hakim will be incarnated once again and subsequently inaugurate a new golden age.

Above: Coffee is prepared at a Bedouin encampment in the deserts near Wadi Rum.

Above: One of the many desert policemen who protect the remote areas of the country.

Other minorities

Other small scattered communities are dotted about Jordan. Among these are various Christian communities who make up about 7 per cent of Jordan's population. They live mostly in Amman and around Madaba, Kerak, Salt and Ajlun.

A large percentage of Jordan's Christians are members of the Greek Orthodox Church, having scriptures in both Greek and Arabic. Jordan has a substantial number of Roman Catholics, as well as others of the Catholic faith from Armenia and Syria. Various Protestant denominations are also found in Amman and in small numbers elsewhere.

The north Jordan Valley contains a small community of Turkomans and Bahais, who moved from Iran to Jordan in 1910. They settled on land in Jordan that was bought in 1879 by Abdul Baha Abbas, the leader of their Bahai faith.

There are also a few small communities of Samarians, people claiming to belong to an ancient Jewish sect, with a descent that stems from the House of Joseph. They accept the first five books of the Bible's teachings — the *Pentateuch* — refusing to regard any others as credible.

PART TWO: PLACES AND TRAVEL

Above: Statue outside the Jordanian parliament commemorates the great Arab Revolt.
Left: Abu Darwwish Mosque, Amman, with its distinctive chequered pattern.

Amman: Great Seven-Hill Metropolis

Amman is a city which geographically straddles seven hills and historically sits astride many centuries. The city's modern buildings blend with the remnants of ancient civilisations. The profusion of gleaming white houses, kebab stalls with roasting meat, and tiny cafés where rich Arabian coffee is sipped in the afternoon sunshine, conjure a mood straight from *A Thousand and One Nights*.

It is a city with a timeless ambience, where a slight detour off the beaten track reveals the wonders of a Bronze Age settlement or a Byzantine monastery. In its *souqs* (markets), you can bargain for fruit, perfume, gold or other exquisite luxuries of the Middle East.

For businessmen Amman offers the most up-to-date convention and communication facilities. Its strategic position and cosmopolitan atmosphere, make it one of the foremost centres of finance and trade in the Middle East today.

By the end of the 1991 Gulf War, Amman was bursting its seams with the influx of repatriated Jordanians. Tens of thousands had fled lives elsewhere in the Gulf, returning home with Saddam Hussein's invasion of Kuwait. The result: a dire housing crisis. But, so characteristically, Jordan's people turned misfortune into prosperity. The returning Jordanians began to build vast new housing expanses, new offices and companies. As Amman heads toward the new millennium, its role as a leading Middle Eastern hub of communication and industry seems set. When one wanders about the capital, charged as it is with awe-inspiring dynamism, it is hard to imagine how it was in less modern times.

Although Amman was selected for the capital of the Hashemite Kingdom by King Abdullah as late as the 1920s, its historical role has been both varied and significant. The city was the focal point of three distinct regions: these were woodland, desert, and semi-arid. Its fertile surroundings with traditionally high water reserves, have ensured Amman's prosperity throughout history.

As man travelled further in pursuit of trade, communities on the site of modern Amman, took advantage of the newly formed routes.

The Bible speaks of Rabbath-Ammon, an area thought to have been located where the Citadel, probably built around 1200 BC, now stands. Flint tools in the area have reinforced beliefs that this part of the city is the oldest. Rabbath-Ammon crops up quite frequently in the pages of *Deuteronomy* and other chapters of the Bible. The first is *Deuteronomy 3:11*: 'For only Og king of Bashan remained of the remnant of giants; behold, his bedstead was a bedstead of iron; is it not in Rabbath of the children of Ammon? Nine cubits was the length thereof, and four cubits the breadth of it, after the cubit of a man.'

The Ammonites, thought to be the ancestors of Lot, waged innumerable wars against Saul, David, and others. David campaigned against them with ferocity. The Bible states: 'And he brought out the people that were in it, and cut them with saws, and with harrows of iron, and with axes. Even so dealt David with all the cities of the children of Ammon. And David and all the people returned to Jerusalem.' (*1 Chronicles 20:3*)

Despite its intriguing and eventful biblical years, most of the ruins dotted about the city come from Amman's distinguished Roman and Byzantine eras. The city, which was rebuilt during the Roman and Hellenistic periods, was renamed Philadelphia by the Hellenistic ruler Ptolemy II. It was incorporated into the *Decapolis* following Emperor Pompey's conquest southwards through Jordan. The Romans reconstructed vast areas of the city, making it the envy of other societies for its sumptuous architecture and enlightened cultural centres.

Opposite: Bird's eye view of the city of Amman. The striking Abu Darwwish Mosque in the foreground is built on Jabal Ashrafieh.

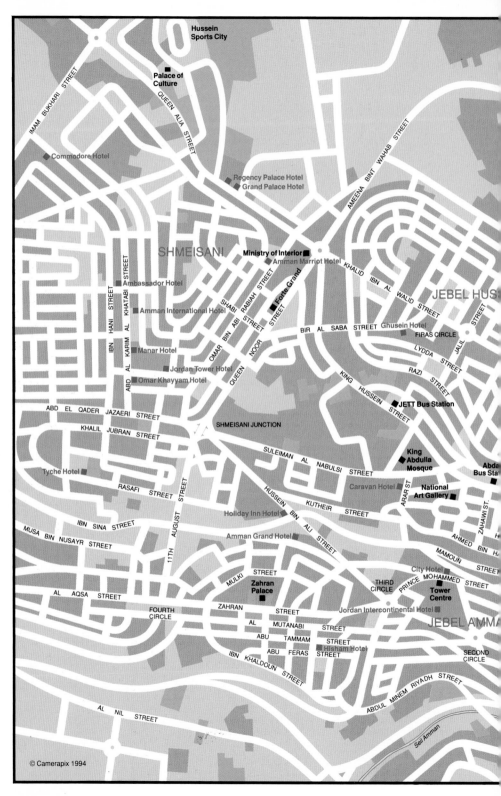

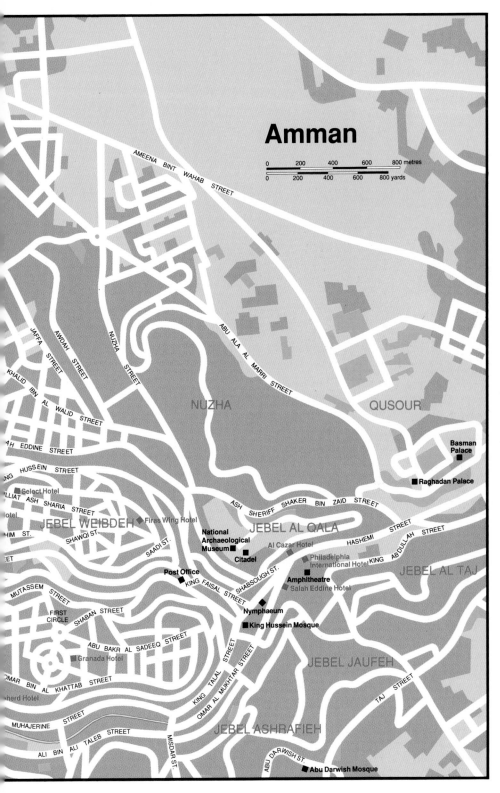

Amman

0 200 400 600 800 metres
0 200 400 600 800 yards

AMEENA BINT WAHAB STREET

JAFFA STREET
AWDAH STREET
NUZHA STREET
ABU ALA AL MARRI STREET

KHALID IBN AL WALID STREET

'H EDDINE STREET

NUZHA

QUSOUR

Basman
Palace ■

■ Raghadan Palace

NG HUSSEIN STREET

■ Select Hotel

'LLIAT ASH SHARIA STREET

otel

ASH SHERIFF SHAKER BIN ZAID STREET

JEBEL WEIBDEH ◆ Firas Wing Hotel

JEBEL AL QALA

HASHEMI STREET

IM ST.

SHAWQI ST.

National
Archaeological
Museum ■

Al Cazar Hotel

ABDULLAH STREET

ET

SAADI ST.

■ Citadel

Philadelphia
International Hotel KING

JEBEL AL TAJ

Post Office

SHABSOUGH ST.

■ Amphitheatre

■ ◆ KING FAISAL STREET

Salah Eddine Hotel

MUTASSEM STREET

Nymphaeum ■

FIRST
CIRCLE

SHABAN STREET

■ King Hussein Mosque

ABU BAKR AL SADEEQ STREET

JEBEL JAUFEH

OMAR BIN AL KHATTAB STREET

KING TALAL STREET
OMAR AL MUKHTAR STREET

TAJ STREET

■ Granada Hotel

herd Hotel

MUHAJERINE STREET

ALI BIN ALI TALEB STREET

MISDAR ST.

JEBEL ASHRAFIEH

ABU DARWISH ST.

■ Abu Darwish Mosque

Later, during the Byzantine period, Amman was home to a bishop and several splendid churches. Indeed, the great Temple of Hercules at the Citadel, was later transformed into a Byzantine church. Following the Persian onslaught in the early 7th century, Philadelphia reverted to being known by its Semitic name. Thus Ammon evolved to become Amman.

Again, during the Ummayed era, Amman held importance through its location on trade routes and for its strategic military position. But Amman's entry into modern times did not happen until the 19th century. The neighbouring city of Salt had stolen much of the limelight as an administrative and political centre. Yet in 1878 a group of Circassian emigrants, many of whose descendants still reside in the capital, were transported to Amman by the Ottoman Sultan Abdul Hamid. It was in 1921 that the Emir Abdullah bin Hussein moved his capital to Amman. The rest is history.

Getting there

At the heart of the Middle East, Amman

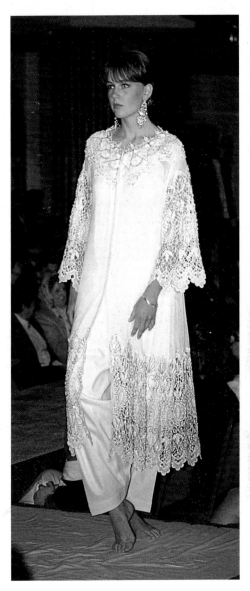

has excellent air links with major centres the world over. It is linked by road to Saudi Arabia, Iraq, Syria and Israel. The rail link between Damascus (Syria), Amman and Medina (Saudi Arabia) has fallen into disuse over much of its length but there is a weekly passenger train from Amman to Damascus which makes the return journey with freight only. Jordan is also linked to Egypt by daily ferry services across the Gulf of Aqaba.

Left: Modern Amman — a thriving city with a history that stretches back to ancient times.

Above: Jordanian model on the catwalk at a fashion show in Amman.

When to go

Amman has a comfortable year-round climate though winter is sometimes below freezing point. The best time of the year is spring (March to May) and early autumn.

Where to stay

Amman has a wide range of accommodation ranging from 5-star hotels and reasonably-priced guest houses. With the building boom of the early- and mid-1990s, a variety of new hotels have sprung up. These tend to cater for the businessman, but many are known for providing excellence at competitive rates. See Listings for "Hotels" and accommodation.

Entertainment

The city's nightclubs mostly feature discotheques with occasional live shows and offer friendly bars and excellent snacks. A number of clubs will only admit couples.

Sightseeing

For those seeking the atmosphere of the **Old City,** it is best to venture to the district **east** of **Jabal Amman.** There, in the bustle of daily life, you can explore the capital's greatest *souqs*, fine museums, ancient constructions, monuments and cultural sites.

The **Citadel** is a hill with an elongated summit. Inhabited for centuries, its importance as a military and religious strategic site derives from its position above the regions below. Its view to the **south,** over the **Roman theatre** is spectacular. Valleys lie on all sides but the north, where an escarpment was quarried to give security from the underlying areas.

The Citadel area, known in Arabic as *Jabal el Qala*, is about 850 metres (2,789 feet) above sea level. Even though it is high, be warned that the midday sun will easily burn the skin. Recent excavations by Jordanian and foreign archaeologists have pieced together the fragmented history of the area. Many of the summit's most valuable **remains** and important relics from across Jordan, can be found in the **Archaeological Museum** located on Citadel Hill.

Ascending to the Citadel, you pass the defensive **walls** that once encircled the L-shaped Citadel area. They largely date from Roman and Byzantine times, although later work was carried out in the early Islamic era. Remains of even more archaic barricades have been unearthed at the northern and eastern ends, possibly dating back to the Bronze Age.

The Citadel has three distinct tiers. The lowest spans out eastwards; the uppermost tier stretches to the north; the central tier, which contains the **car park, museum** and foundations of the great **Temple of Hercules,** can now be seen.

There is much evidence to suggest that the Ammonite settlement of Rabbath-Ammon once enshrouded the whole of the Citadel area. It is possible there was an earlier sacrificial altar where the Temple of Hercules was built.

Just to the north of the protective wall, at the northern edge of the Citadel, are the remains of an underground **water cistern.** Since it dates back to Ammonite times, it is reasonable to assume that it is the cistern mentioned by the Roman scholar Polybius. He narrated how Antiochus III had laid siege to Rabbath-Ammon in the early 3rd century BC, and forced the town to give in,

Above: Ornately carved relic in Amman.
Opposite: Legacy of Jordan's fabulous cultural and architectural heritage, ruins of the Ummayed Palace at Amman's Citadel.

Overleaf: Illuminated theatre at Amman hosts events for the citizens of Jordan's capital.

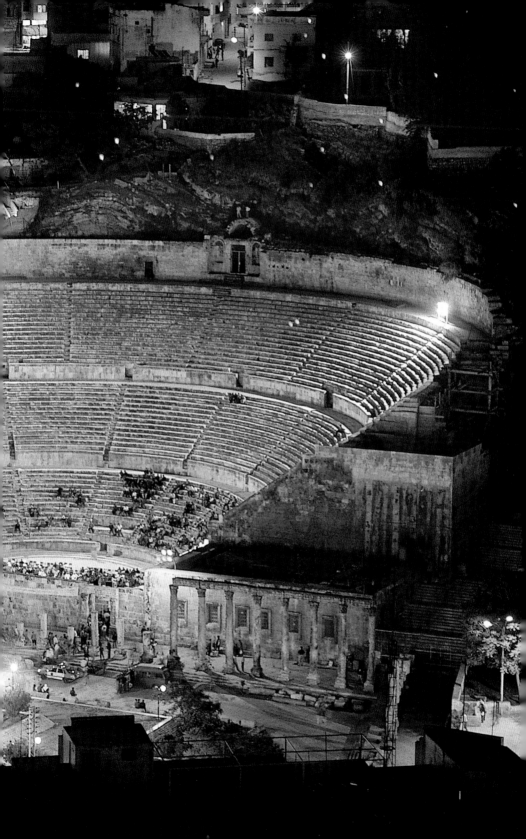

having prevented its inhabitants from getting to their water supplies through the hidden shaft. The grandest building on the Citadel is unquestionably the Temple of Hercules which has been reassembled as authentically as possible. It must have been massive. Observe the size of the blocks of stone, and the dimensions of its layout, to see how mighty it was.

The edifice, which was inscribed to the Roman empirical ruler Marcus Aurelius who reigned from AD 161-180, is similar to the Temple of Artemis in Jerash. A great staircase led down from the Temple of Hercules, reaching to the Forum area far below the Citadel.

Above: One of many Nabatean gods exhibited at the Archaeological Museum, Amman.

Opposite top: Five rare terra-cotta coffins in the Archaeological Museum of Amman.

Opposite: Priceless legacy from the past — the earliest known Hebrew texts, the Dead Sea Scrolls, were discovered in the cave of Khirbet Qumran overlooking the Dead Sea.

To the north of the Citadel area are remains of another **Roman temple,** but it is hard to distinguish what actually stood there. More easily recognisable is the debris of a 6th-century AD **Byzantine church,** which lay a little **east** of where the Museum now stands.

Perhaps the most extravagant of the Citadel complexes was the early Islamic (or Ummayed) **compound** which stood at the **north** extremity. It is thought to have been a governor's home and a centre for administration. The network of buildings would have been constructed during the 8th century AD, while Amman was the organisational nucleus for the **Balqa Province**.

Another example of the size of the Temple of Hercules is in Amman's Archaeological Museum on the Citadel. It contains the **fingers** of Hercules' **statue,** mounted on the stairs leading to the museum. They are so enormous, experts have estimated the statue must have been around 9 metres (29 feet) high.

The Archaeological Museum (admission free) is open every day except Tuesday from 09.00 until 17.00. It houses artefacts from all over Jordan, from the earliest times until the Islamic era. The size of the museum does not allow the whole collection to be displayed, but many exhibits are quite extraordinary. A **skull** discovered at Jericho, dating back to the Early Bronze Age, reveals that the cranium had been bored three times. The practice, known as *trepanning*, is thought to have been carried out to quell internal pressure, perhaps only a headache. Interestingly, one of the holes has partly repaired itself, indicating that the patient withstood at least the first of these horrific operations.

Other exhibits include an assortment of **Neolithic skulls** from Jericho and infant **corpses** still in their **funeral jars**. One area of the museum is given over to the reconstruction of a **tomb** dating back to the Middle Bronze Age that housed thirteen bodies. Note the wooden **table** and **pottery** vessels also found at the site.

There are few more precious artefacts than the fabled **Dead Sea Scrolls,** several of which are displayed in the Archaeological Museum of Amman. These priceless texts

were found in a cave in 1952 on the north-west shore of the Dead Sea. A shepherd named Mohammed Adh-Dhiba discovered them when looking for a goat. They are the earliest known Hebrew texts and relate to the book of *Isaiah*. They are older by a thousand years than anything known up to then. The scrolls, which recline in a box lined with purple velvet, tell of a treasure amounting to 200 tonnes in gold and precious objects, said to have been hidden in the area between Hebron and Nablus.

Also in the collection are **statues** of Nabatean deities. In particular the goddess *Al Uzza* is represented as a square block with a symmetrical — and strangely modern-looking — set of features.

Examples of Nabatean clay pottery are also on display. The pots and dishes, made from wafer-thin clay, and figurines are some of the finest made by ancient man.

One excellent example of early Islamic art is a limestone **capital,** decorated with superb Kufic script, that served as a water-level marker for the cistern in the palace of Muwaqqar. Below the Citadel's **southern rim** is a stream known as **Seil Amman**. It is on its **south bank** that most of the Roman city of Philadelphia was situated. This included the main forum, theatre, odeon, and various shops. Just north of the Seil was a large road that ran from west to the east.

This street, or **Decumanus Maximus,** gave access to the Citadel by a connecting path. It was 10 metres (33 feet) wide, bordered by Corinthian colonnades, and led, at its eastern and western extremes, to a set of monumental gates. The Seil has been fed since before Roman times, by run-off water from the mountain slopes. It pours into the low lying rivulet, causing flooding during heavy rains. The Romans ingeniously constructed a **conduit** to cover the stream for a considerable distance **south** of the main forum area.

A smaller main street, also lined with Corinthian columns, ran off the Decumanus Maximus called the **Cardo**. It branched off from the Decumanus in a north-west direction, about 200 metres (656 feet) **west**

of where the forum stood. Behind the junction of the two main streets was the site of the **Nymphaeum**. This sacred fountain, similar to the Nymphaeum at Jerash, was fed by water from the Seil Amman which ran to its southern wall.

Philadelphia was a favourite place for Roman soldiers and officials as — like Rome — the city was built on seven hills. The climate is also similar. Perhaps it was for these reasons that they went to such lengths to create lavish and elaborate monuments.

The great **forum** was encircled on all but one side by **colonnades** and had the theatre to its south. To its north ran the Seil Amman and one would have been able to see the Corinthian colonnade of the Decumanus above. Most of the forum is now concealed by the streets of modern Amman. Experts estimate that it encircled an area equal to over 7,500 square metres (80,700 square feet) — roughly that of a modern football pitch. The Roman Empire is not known to have constructed many fora of this size.

To its **north-east** lies the **odeon,** recently renovated to give an idea of how the original building would have looked. This odeon, or small theatre, would have been covered, and seated around 600 people. Directly behind where the forum once stood, it is an ideal place to wander. There is a bustle of traffic and everyday life, **stalls** selling *shish kebabs* or ice creams. **Souvenir shops** sell everything from bottles of coloured sand to miniaturised stuffed camels . . . on wheels!

The main **entrance** to the theatre is directly behind the stage. Entry is free. Amman's **theatre** is the largest in Jordan, with room for 6,000 spectators and is very similar in design to the South Theatre at Jerash. Thought to have been built between AD 138 and AD 161 by the Roman Emperor Antonius Pius, it was restored in 1970. The theatre is built into the side of the mountain and is still used for sport displays and cultural events.

In the **east wing** of the **stage** is the **Folklore Museum of Amman,** open from

Opposite: Amman's Roman theatre under restoration.

Above: The King Abdullah Mosque in Amman, constructed in honour of the assassinated king.

09.00 until 17.00 (except on Tuesdays). On holidays it is open from 10.00 until 16.00. There is a nominal entrance fee. The museum shows different insights into the traditional lives of the people of Jordan. Inside the door there is a **model** of a Circassian soldier in his black uniform, as still worn by the Circassian Guard at the Royal Palace. There is an assortment of **weaponry** including some 19th-century **revolvers**, but mainly weapons from the East, such as **swords** and **daggers**. One room houses a collection of **camel bags** and a large **treadle loom**, together with a **vertical loom**. Another displays **embroideries** on clothes from Jordan and Palestine. You can tell which community a person is from by the particular pattern of the needlework. Another set of steps lead to a makeshift Bedouin **encampment.** Under the black goat-hair canopy figures sip coffee, weave, or carry out other traditional activities. Particularly striking is the pair of model camels next to the tent. On the foremost sits a Bedouin man; behind, a Bedouin bride sits in the *hodatch*, a special carriage strapped onto the animal's back.

In the **western wing** of the stage is the **Museum of Popular Traditions**. There is a nominal fee, separate from the Folklore Museum, although they both have the same opening hours. Steps lead to a **gallery** of exquisite Byzantine **mosaic scenes** from Madaba. As you walk down, look to the **right** and you will see a wonderful assembly of

Above: Interior view of the King Abdullah Mosque shows the immensity of the central prayer chamber.

Islamic **battle standards.** The museum, which gives a sample of Jordan's rich costume heritage, has displays of all types of Bedouin and other national attires. The diversity of tribal jewellery is also shown in an outstanding collection of **bracelets, belts, earrings, headdresses, talismans, amulets** and the enormous **anklets** worn by Bedouin.

Amman is home to some of the grandest mosques in the Middle East. The newest is the **King Abdullah Mosque**, built between 1982 and 1989. Located **north-west** of the Citadel, it is capped by a magnificent blue mosaic **dome,** beneath which 3,000 Muslims may offer prayers.

The mosque, a memorial to assassinated King Abdullah, has a central area of 12,000 square metres (129,120 square feet). Features include a substantial **library** of **Islamic texts,** as well as a separate compartment for the king. Two **minarets** flank the main mosque, which has a separate area for women.

The huge main dome is surrounded by a cluster of eight smaller domes and is 35 metres (115 feet) in diameter and 31 metres (102 feet) high. It covers an area of 2,615 square metres (28,137 square feet).

Inside, the design follows an octagonal theme, extending from the shape of the main structure down to the **carpets.** A three-tiered **chandelier,** covered in gold and weighing eight tonnes, lights the great

chamber. Inscribed around the top are the ninety-nine names of Allah.

The most unusual mosque in Amman is the **Abu Darwwish Mosque,** situated atop the **Jabal Ashrafieh**. It is covered with an extraordinary black-and-white chequered pattern and is unique to Jordan. Two flights of stairs lead into the **main room,** whose **central dome** is supported by four **columns,** each surrounded by a row of outer pillars.

In contrast, the interior is almost totally free of the black-and-white theme. Instead there are light-coloured **walls** and **Persian carpets** on the floor. The **courtyard,** between the street and the mosque, features a central **washing area**.

Opposite: Exterior of the Raghadan Palace in Amman — residence of King Hussein and Queen Noor.

Above: Interior of one of the Raghadan Palace's many rooms.

Right: Throne room at the Raghadan Palace.

The bizarre religious building was erected by one of Amman's Circassian immigrants, named Hasan Mustafa Sharkas, known as Abu Darwwish, and the mosque has taken his name. It is not only one of the most unique buildings in the capital, but also in the Middle East. If you look by the **main gate** into the **courtyard** you will see that even the **water tanks** are striped.

The main areas of Amman gain their names from the seven hills on whose slopes they lie. Of these, **Jabal Amman** (*Jabal* means hill in Arabic) is the most fashionable, with **shops** and **office buildings**. The main **traffic islands** on Jabal Amman have numbers, which are referred to in addresses. They are numbered as 1st Circle, 2nd Circle and so forth. On Jabal Amman the biggest landmark is the **Jordan Tower Centre**, just below the **3rd Circle**. Most embassies and consulates are to be found at Jabal Amman, as well as the exclusive Shmeisani area, to the north-west.

At the far **north-western** extremity of Amman, past the **Shmeisani** area, is the impressive **Hussein Sports City**, formed in 1966 and run by the Al Hussein Youth and Sports Organisation. The great stadium seats 25,000 spectators and is used for sports, cultural events and national festivities. Three **swimming pools,** football and games **pitches**, **gymnasia** and **courts,** complement the excellent facilities.

Overlooking the Hussein Sports City is the **Palace of Culture**, also known as the Royal Cultural Centre, which houses theatres, cinemas and exhibition halls and is a regular host of exhibits, lectures, ballets, musical extravaganzas and conferences. The Centre attracts a great number of international celebrities and artists — forming a keynote in Amman's cultural identity.

The Sports City complex also houses the **Martyrs' Memorial** and, in it, the **Military Museum of Amman**. The museum is located inside an imposing edifice with an assortment of **armoured vehicles** at the front. It depicts the history of the Hashemite Dynasty and is open every day, except Saturday, from 09.00 until 16.00. Admission is free. Display cases line a **walkway** that spirals upward inside the great building.

Many exhibits are connected with the nation's recent historical events. The **ivory walking stick** carried by Sharif Hussein is displayed, as well as a dual **camel cane** and **swordstick.** Note the shape of the long, straight-bladed Circassian **daggers** with embroidered **sheaths,** still worn by the Circassian Guard at the Royal Palace. Other exhibits demonstrate aspects of the Arab Revolt. Yet another display is an incredible version of the Qur'an written on a single sheet of paper, measuring 30 by 90 centimetres.

The walkway which leads around the museum emerges into a **garden** on the **roof,** where the king and guests have the privilege of sprinkling water on an olive tree during distinguished visits. For art lovers the **Jordan National Art Gallery** is an important stop. It is near the **main park** on **Jabal al Luwaybida**. The collection of **paintings, sculpture** and **ceramics** is largely by contemporary artists from Jordan and the Arab World. Over 2,000 works have been catalogued, providing a reference centre for students and art devotees alike. It is a unique gallery that promotes Islamic art and increases cultural awareness. The gallery is open from 10.00 until 12.00, and 15.00 until 18.00 (except on Tuesday).

The 1990s have witnessed Amman's rise as a grand centre of art. A number of new galleries have recently opened, offering a wide range of exotic and traditional arts and crafts. One such — Darat Al-Funun — has been described as 'combining ornament and function in a valuable visual/academic melange of knowledge'. The gallery, which incorporates gardens, fountains, studios, and a Byzantine Church, provides an aura of tranquillity. The complex's staggering view of the city serves as a majestic backdrop for regular displays of performing art. Another fine Amman gallery, the Gallery Alia, can be found in a less expected spot.

Opposite top: The facilities of Amman's futuristic Sports' City are among the finest in the Middle East.
Opposite: Disused armoured vehicle stands guard in front of the Martyrs' Memorial in Amman.
Overleaf: Ancient ruins atop one of the hills of Amman.

Top: Contemporary art of Jordan on display in an Amman gallery.
Above: Traditional ceramic craftmanship at the Queen Alia Exhibition Centre.

The gallery — sponsored by Jordanian Airlines — fills two floors of the Insurance Building in Amman's First Circle. And, in keeping with its fellow studios, the Gallery Abad (at Mecca Street) provides frequent exhibits of Jordan's most prestigious artists. (See Listings for a complete directory of Amman's top galleries).

The soil around Amman can be quite fertile, but none more so than in the **garden** of **Ali Erar.** Digging one day in 1970, he stumbled across the ruins of an important **Byzantine church.** The building has one of the greatest **mosaic floors** in Jordan and is one of only a few Byzantine mosaic floors found in the capital.

The site, known as **Swafieh** (also spelt Sweifieth), is located between the **6th** and **7th Circles** of Jabal Amman. The main 46-square-metre (496-square-foot) mosaic, which is now covered by a protective roof, depicts the four seasons of the year. A Greek inscription, partly damaged, reads: 'In the time of the holy Thomas, Bishop . . . of the holy church, with zeal and labours'. The quality and state of preservation of the mosaic floor are superb. Experts are almost certain that it was laid during the 6th century AD. Archaeologists have unearthed fragments of **pottery** and **artefacts** from other civilisations at the same location, including Roman, Byzantine, and early Islamic.

Among the fascinating archaeological discoveries in Amman are the **Ammonite Towers,** which number more than two dozen. They once covered an area ranging from the beginning of the **Beka Valley** in the north, down to the southern-most extremes of Amman. These towers, known in Arabic as *Rjum el Malouf* (the round tower), were constructed from huge slabs of limestone and flint. In diameter they range from 8 to 22 metres (26 to 72 feet), with differing configurations of internal chambers.

The use of these strange edifices has been the subject of much debate. Some experts believe they date back to Neolithic times and functioned as watchtowers, storage houses for agricultural produce, or signal towers. It has now been widely established that they were built during the Iron Age, though many contain remnants of **pottery,** glass fragments and **jewellery,** from earlier civilisations.

Two towers, which largely escaped the ravages of modern construction, are situated in a central area. The round-walled **Rjum el Malouf** is easy to get to, and the best to visit. It is next to the **Department of Antiquities Registration Centre,** between the **3rd** and **4th Circles** of Jabal Amman. The tower, with a diameter of 22 metres (66 feet) and a height of 5.5 metres (18 feet), is one of several ancient constructions in the area. An intriguing feature is a primitive cooling system that circulated cool air beneath the floor. Roman **pottery** found during initial excavations indicates that the site was occupied well after the Ammonite era.

Craft shops

There has been a major revival of traditional crafts and art work in recent years. Many centres of crafts are sponsored by charitable organisations which benefit the poor, handicapped, and other disadvantaged members of society. They seek to revitalise the handicraft industry, and to foster awareness of Jordan's cultural heritage.

The **Jordan Design and Trade Centre,** in the **Shmeisani area** in **north-west** Amman, has an outstanding collection of **rugs, kaftans, furniture, pots, vases** and other ceramic works. It was established in 1989 by the **Queen Noor Al-Hussein Foundation** to produce and market a diverse selection of Jordanian crafts on a commercial basis. The project has made the production of Bedouin rugs economically viable once again and it has revitalised craft design and production while encouraging young people to continue these age-old practices.

The **Jordan Craft Centre,** also known as The Hand, is located near the **Inter-continental Hotel** between the **2nd** and **3rd Circles** of Jabal Amman. It houses examples of Jordanian and Middle East **crafts, tourist goods** and **Bedouin jewellery.** One room is filled with a colourful array of old and new **carpets,** under the canopy of a Bedouin tent.

There are few better **antique silver jewellery** collections in the Middle East

than that of **Hannah Saddiq**. By private appointment she will guide you around the glorious collection at her home. Her treasures encompass every area of the Middle East with examples from Iraq, Yemen, Saudi Arabia, Palestine, Jordan, Syria, as well as Circassian work. Most fascinating are the silver **amuletic canisters** worn for centuries around the neck or on the upper arm of Bedouin women. These contain the marriage contract. **Talismans** abound as well as large silver **anklets** and **belts.**

Only 20 minutes by car from the centre of Amman is the **Hebron Glass Factory**. To reach it you must drive out of the capital on the **south-west road** to **Na'ur.** There, on the **right**, after passing through Na'ur, come the premises which look like anything but a glass factory. It is run by the two Natcheh brothers who came from Hebron on the

Top: Amman's boutiques abound with an unending selection of brightly coloured tribal crafts.
Left: Weaver at work on traditional patterns on a modern loom.

West Bank and are now among the few
people commercially hand-blowing glass in
Jordan. The ancient tradition is dying out
across the Middle East, particularly in
Hebron which has been a major glass
blowing centre for centuries.

There are **racks** with **trays** of finished
glass works from bunches of **grapes** to
discs with lucky hands embossed, **bowls,
vases** and **jugs.** Traditional Hebron ceramic
work is now done at the factory where
young craftsmen display their skills. Prices
are competitive.

Silsal Ceramics on 4th Circle specialise
in traditional stoneware fired from local
clay and glazes.

Bani Hamida is the most established of
Jordan's small craft projects. Sponsored by
Save the Children and run completely
by women, this dazzling shop is on **Jabal**

Above: Assortment of glasswork at Hebron
Glass Factory on the outskirts of Amman.
Right: The Hebron Glass Factory produces
many different forms of glassware.

Above: Kan Zaman, which means Once Upon a Time, is a favourite spot for tourists.

Amman, below the 1st Circle. Essentially a weaving project, Bani Hamida involves 800 Bedouin women in over 300 families. Its aim is to help remove the discrimination against women which overshadows the Middle East. The weavers who create the rugs and textiles live 75 kilometres (47 miles) from Amman at **Jabal Bani Hamida,** just **south** of **Madaba**.

The project is based in the home and allows mothers and wives to weave while attending to household duties. Bani Hamida has concentrated also on reviving the dyeing craft which, until recently, had all but disappeared from Jordan. Both traditional and contemporary patterns are made to the highest standards. (See "Ain Mousa: The Springs of Moses".)

Most comprehensive of the other craft centres in Jordan, is the **Kan Zaman**, reached from the old part of the Desert Highway, which runs **south** from Amman towards Aqaba, about 16 kilometres (10 miles) from the capital. Kan Zaman, which means 'once upon a time' in Arabic, was built by the

powerful Abu Jabar family almost two centuries ago. It is a **walled village,** complete with **storage caves, stables,** winding **streets** and rustic **stone buildings,** all of which have been restored. Today, Kan Zaman revives the spirit of the settlement and its activities.

There is a **restaurant** in what used to be the stable, where cattle ate from their **manger,** which is still in place. The massive vaulted **dining-room** accommodates folk dancing, with live music every night, and serves traditional Jordanian and Western foods at a huge nightly buffet. Two **bars,** inside and outside, serve wine of Kan Zaman's own vintage, as well as offering *hookahs*, with a selection of original tobaccos including strawberry and apple flavours.

Kan Zaman is reasonably priced and popular with Jordanians as well as tourists. Shops offer a large selection of crafts, most of which are made on the premises. You may visit the production area and watch glass being blown and wood being carved in traditional ways. All the bread for the village is baked in the **bakery.** Beside it is

Above: Steam train of a bygone era at Amman.

a small **shop** packed with **coloured salts** extracted from the Dead Sea. Herbs and natural cures such as liquorice root, worm seed, camomile and Mary's Hand are available. Kan Zaman is open from 10.00 until 01.00, and the shops are open from 10.00 until 22.00. The most popular nights tend to be Thursdays.

Trains and the Hijaz Railway

The little **railway station** of Amman is situated **north-east** of the capital. No passenger trains run regularly within Jordan, except for the weekly diesel service to Damascus. The trip to the Syrian capital, which departs around 08.00 every Monday morning, takes 5 hours or more to complete. It returns from Damascus as a cargo train. It is sad that Jordan no longer uses the extensive railway lines which stretch the length of the nation. On occasion steam trains are laid on for visitors to the capital to take them around the locale.

The International Traders Company, based in Amman, promotes the use of the railway for tourists. In the past, it has worked to obtain backing for the great **Hijaz Railway's** revival for, like others, they consider it as a national monument.

The line was instigated when, in 1900, Sultan Abdul Hamid appealed to Muslims throughout the Islamic World to raise funds. Money was received from as far afield as Burma and China. The first tracks, which were to cover 1,303 kilometres (810 miles), were laid in 1901. The plan was to continue after Medina to Mecca, and to include a branch line to the Red Sea.

Completed in 1908, the railway became a target in the April 1917 Arab Revolt when three major attacks in the Ma'an area damaged the line. Several initiatives to begin new services ended in failure and there now seems little future for that once great Hijaz Railway.

Golf

Whether on business, or on holiday, there's no better way to pass some time than a game of golf at one of the kingdom's golf clubs. Golf is a game that's catching on fast in the Arab World. Greens and clubhouses are being planned around the country (new ones are on the drawing board for Jerash, Mafraq, Wadi Rum and Aqaba) and, as a result, the desert dust is being replaced by luxurious putting greens. Fifteen kilometres from Amman's 7th Circle is the kingdom's greatest golf course at the Bisharat Golf Club. Take the airport road out of the capital and turn into the Ghamdan National Park. Directions to the club are provided with intermittent signs. The club is located at the

Top: Traditional shop packed with everything from spices to canned soup.
Left: An Aladdin's cave of riches, one of Amman's numerous jewellery shops.
Opposite: Cave of the Seven Sleepers, whose tale is recounted in the Holy Qur'an.

far side of the Park, with its profusion of wild plants and pine trees and is a popular spot for picnics. Opened in the early 1990s, the Bisharat Golf Course is a favourite with Amman's business community, as well as with tourists to the kingdom. Its clubhouse boasts a fine restaurant (named 'The Cave'), with catering taken care of by the Marriott Hotel. Golf clubs can be hired for a nominal charge. Caddie and golfing fees are reasonable. Bisharat Golf Club (Tel: 079-20334).

Around Amman

The **Cave of the Seven Sleepers**, juxtaposed with Amman's green-domed **Mosque of Ahl el-Kahf** (the Mosque of the People of the Cave), is steeped in ancient tradition and fable.

It was known in ancient tales as *el Rakeem*, but in Arabic it is called *el Kahf*: 'the cave'. Myriad **tombs** with ornately sculpted covers are found at the site. These surround a quadruple-chambered underground tomb,

hewn from bare rock. An encircled **Greek cross** and other ornate **carvings** mark the entrance. The **cardinal chamber** is entered through a small opening, from which lead off four other chambers with arched caverns. Inside the **western** and **eastern chambers** there are eight **sarcophagi** cut from the rock. The ends of these, as well as areas of the walls, are ornamented with carvings, thought to be Byzantine or Islamic. A **shaft** through the roof allows light and fresh air to permeate the crypt. The aperture once led into a Byzantine church directly above, which was later turned into a small mosque during early Islamic times. It is still possible to make out the plan of the Byzantine church, with its rows of colonnades which once stood in the nave. The anterior of the cavern has a stone **band** designating where an olive tree was once positioned.

The legend surrounding the Cave of the Seven Sleepers, is told in the Qur'an in *Sura 18* (entitled The Cave), but there are numerous versions. The tale tells of seven Christian boys who, coerced by the pagan Roman empirical leader, were sentenced to death unless they exalted the pagan pantheon. The youths refused and fled to a cave which became shut tight. The boys, together with their dog, entered a deep slumber for somewhere between three and thirty decades. At length the young men stirred, finding themselves in the Byzantine period. On trying to shop in what was then Philadelphia, they were apprehended and locals took them to the ruler. After some time the seven boys and the dog returned to the cave, where God sent them once more into an endless slumber.

The keeper of the cave will allow you to peek through a **hole** into the partially open tomb in which are the **remains** of what certainly look like seven boys and a dog.

On the **northern outskirts** of Amman, the unearthing in 1983, and later, of a 7200-5000 BC **Neolithic settlement** near **Ain Ghazal**, produced the largest and best-preserved cache of busts and statues ever found in the Near East.

Quweismeh, a village in the **south-east corner** of Amman, is the site of a substantial **Roman crypt**, first unearthed in 1881, and later excavated in 1967. The **mausoleum** is square in shape, with walls 7.5 metres (25 feet) long. Inside is one oblong **compartment.** Four **steps** lead to the **doorway** in the **north wall**, above which is a **window.** C R Conder, the 19th-century excavator of the site, noted ten white limestone sarcophagi lined up against the walls of the crypt. In 1967 only four remained.

About 500 metres (1,640 feet) to the **north** of the crypt are the remains of a **Byzantine church** complex. Parts of the Corinthian **columns** are still present, and a fine **mosaic floor**, which dates from the early 8th century. There are also known Byzantine sites in the area, including a **mosaic floor** from yet another Byzantine church. The mosaic floorings can only be viewed on special occasions.

The most resplendent of all Roman tombs in Jordan, called **Qasr Nuweijis**, is situated 100 metres (328 feet) **south** of where the Tareq road meets the Amman to Zarqa motorway. It is worth the trip to tour such a well-preserved mausoleum of Roman design. The **square tomb**, which has been dated to the latter part of the 2nd

century AD, measures 12 metres (39 feet) along each wall. Within the crypt is a domed ceiling, above which rests a stone vase. You will notice that there is a substantial **parapet** atop the *Qasr*, and numerous sets of decoration chiselled into the stone.

A few minutes' drive from Jabal Amman's **8th Circle**, on the **south-western extremity** of **Bayadir Wadi Seer**, are the fragmented remains of the **Khirbet Sar Ammonite Tower**. With a great view across Wadi Seer, it would probably have been an important defence station for Amman's ancient forefather, Rabbath Ammon. Substantial Roman additions are still evident, such as the remains of a **courtyard.** The tower may well have been converted into a pagan shrine during Roman times. To the north the crests of six limestone arcs are visible, rising from the ground like a hump-backed sea monster. Khirbet Sar is said by some academics to be the biblical city of *Jazer*.

It is quite a contrast drive 24 kilometres (15 miles) **south-west** of the barren capital to the fertile tree-covered and steep-sloped valley of **Wadi el-Seer** where, about 10 kilometres (6 miles) further down the valley from the actual village of Wadi el-Seer, among the trees, fields and lush tropical fruit bushes, you come across the enormous ruins of **Qasr al-Abed: the Castle (Palace) of the Slave**.

The massive blocks carved from honey-coloured stone are thought to be the biggest in the Middle East. The place has been partially reconstructed, thanks to the work of a French archaeologist who spent three years piecing together the remains. His method was to make cardboard images of each fragment, and to work out the order of assembly before embarking on the actual reconstruction. Little is known about the history of this extraordinary edifice, but it is widely believed that the builder was Hyracanus, head of the prosperous Tobiad family, who lived during the reign of Seleucus IV (187-175 BC).

The estate was once surrounded by a wall and included a lake and a park full of luxuriant trees and shrubs. On the upper side of the **back wall** a giant **stone lioness** with huge fangs peers down at all beneath it. Under its belly is a small **lion cub**. One

Above: Aerial view of Iraq el-Amir, The Caves of the Prince.

reason for the building's collapse could have been an unstable design for, although the walls were up to 6 metres (20 feet) long, they were usually no more than 46 centimetres (18 inches) wide. During the Byzantine era the great castle seems to have been inhabited again and remodelled.

The Tobiad family was immensely powerful, and Hyracanus, at one time its leader, was nominated as governor of Ammon. This could explain the building's strange name. Some archaeologists believe that the title, *Castle (or Palace) of the Slave*, referred to Hyracanus himself who, as governor, was effectively a slave of the

people. Tourists rarely visit Qasr al-Abed, but the fact that it has been so neglected gives it an extra quality of tranquility.

As you drive back up the valley, stop about 500 metres (550 yards) from the Qasr where there is a **group** of **caves** cut from the rock, known as **Iraq el-Amir, the Caves of the Prince**. The caves, eleven in total, are arranged in two ranks at the actual cliff face and are thought to have been hewn by hand. At the front of one of the caverns the word *Tobiad*, engraved in Aramaic, gives more credence to the idea that Qasr al-Abed was built by that family.

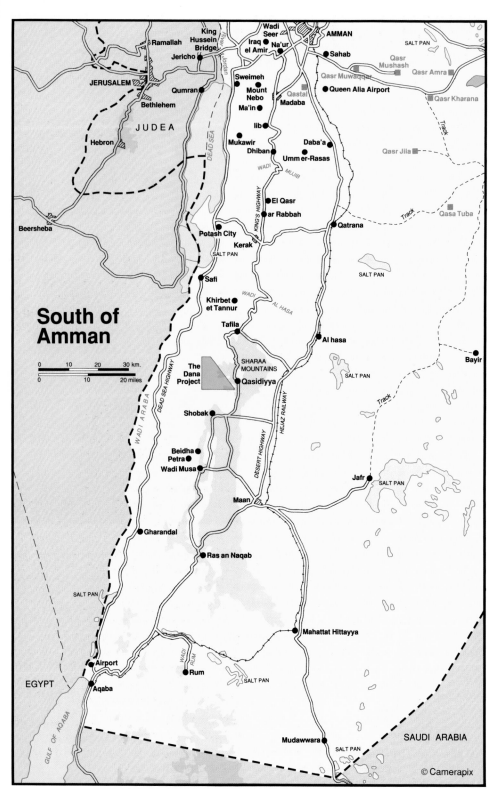

South of Amman

AMMAN

King Hussein Bridge
Ramallah
Jericho
Wadi Seer
Iraq el Amir
Na'ur
Sahab

JERUSALEM
Qumran
Bethlehem
Sweimeh
Mount Nebo
Ma'in
Madaba
Queen Alia Airport

Qastal

Qasr Mushash
Qasr Muwaqqar
Qasr Amra
Qasr Kharana

JUDEA
Hebron

lib
Mukawir
Dhiban
Daba'a
Umm er-Rasas

Qasr Jila

Beersheba

El Qasr
ar Rabbah
Qatrana

Qasa Tuba

Potash City
Kerak
SALT PAN

WADI MUJIB
KING'S HIGHWAY

SALT PAN

Track

Track

Safi

Khirbet et Tannur

WADI AL HASA

Tafila
Al hasa
Bayir

SALT PAN

DEAD SEA

The Dana Project
SHARAA MOUNTAINS
Qasidiyya

SALT PAN

Track

DEAD SEA HIGHWAY

0   10   20   30 km.
0   10   20 miles

Shobak

HEJAZ RAILWAY
DESERT HIGHWAY

Beidha
Petra
Wadi Musa

Jafr
SALT PAN

WADI ARABA

Maan

Gharandal

Ras an Naqab

Mahattat Hittayya

Airport
Rum

WADI RUM
SALT PAN

EGYPT

Aqaba

GULF OF AQABA

Mudawwara
SALT PAN

SAUDI ARABIA

© Camerapix

The Jordan Valley: Cradle of Man

Few regions of the world are blessed with such a diverse abundance of natural features as the expanse of land that lies between Amman and Aqaba. In a single afternoon one may venture from the Dead Sea — the lowest dry land on Earth — across the great desert plains to the crystal waters of the Red Sea, or the colossal Valley of Wadi Rum.

The Jordan Valley cleaves the length of the country, and forms a natural boundary to the west. It is actually part of the Great Rift Valley, which carves a passage further southwards through East Africa.

The valley gains its name from the river which runs along its contoured sides. It is from this great river that the modern nation has taken its name.

The valley's fertile lands have their history chronicled in the Old Testament. It was there, 10,000 years ago, that farmers planted crops — so beginning the legacy of agriculture that continues today. Like Neolithic Man, Jordan's modern farmers harness the valley's perennial water supply, and take advantage of its fertile soils. For centuries little changed, and agriculturalists persisted with methods passed down from father to son. In the last few decades, however, new methods of agriculture have been applied. These techniques, coupled with modern machinery, have maximised the valley's potential.

With the arrival of such expertise the valley's significance has entered a new phase. The latter years of the 1950s witnessed the construction of a canal to further irrigate the region. Known as the East Ghor Canal, the watercourse runs down the east bank of the Jordan Valley for 69 kilometres (43 miles). It has further exploited the valley's potential making the most of the short mild winters and long hot dry summers.

Throughout the year an endless cycle of fruits and vegetables ripen in quantities unparalleled in the valley's history.

The Jordan Valley is famous for its superb citrus fruits and recently installed portable greenhouses have boosted productivity of vegetables such as tomatoes and cucumbers sevenfold.

The Jordanian royal family and the government have worked relentlessly to ensure that the valley benefits the nation at large. The Crown Prince has taken a great interest in the needs and projects of its inhabitants. At the heart of the valley is one of earth's most extraordinary natural features: the Dead Sea.

The Sea of Lot

The Dead Sea, known in Arabic as *Bahr Lut* (The Sea of Lot), has a salt content of well over 20 per cent. Because the salt content is 8 times that of most of the world's oceans,

Above: High above the Dead Sea a stone monument indicates natural sea level.

you can float without even trying. The acute salinity arose through thousands of years of evaporation. The water is so salty it will sting your eyes. It has a film of oil on its surface apparently caused by marine life dying over the centuries.

Swimming in the Dead Sea is quite an experience, but be warned: an open wound — even a small cut — will be painful with the briefest water contact. It is best to swim only where there are showers nearby.

Getting there

The northern shores of the Dead Sea lie 55 kilometres (32 miles) from Amman. Further from the capital the sea's south-eastern shores can be reached via Madaba, Dhiban and Kerak.

When to go

As the lowest surface point on earth, the Dead Sea is always warm, often excessively hot. If travelling there in summer, be sure to take a wide-brimmed hat and water supplies. From May to September the Valley's heat can be suffocating.

Where to stay

At **Sweimeh** (often spelt Suweimeh) the newly-built **Salt Land Village** (nicknamed The Basement of the World) includes the Dead Sea Spa Hotel, assorted bungalows and the German Medical Centre which aims at helping skin-disease patients using the Dead Sea's natural healing powers. As well as the highly saline water, other therapies include black mud, highly oxygenous air treatment and filtered sunrays. Massage, gymnastics, mud packs and a private solarium with direct access to

Opposite: Dew-fresh oranges in a fertile valley of northern Jordan.
Above: Golden sunset over the Dead Sea.
Overleaf: Hardy flowers burst into bloom in the barren hills overlooking the Dead Sea.

the sea are advertised.

There is also a government-owned rest-house at Sweimeh with showers and modest facilities.

Another Dead Sea resort famous for its healing properties is the **Ma'in Spa Village**, situated between **Ma'in** and the sea. Reached by a spectacular winding downhill road the resort is set around a series of **hot springs**. One of the most popular treatments there is the body mud pack when Dead Sea mud is plastered on at between 40° and 50°.

Bathing there used to be enjoyed by all Jordanians but Spa Village now limits its access to guests.

Sightseeing

The Dead Sea has its own history and spiritual legacy from legends that tell of it being the site of it being the site of five biblical centres: **Sodom, Gomorrah, Admah, Zebouin** and **Zoar.** The journey

Above: Dead Sea Hotel illuminated at night.
Left: Laid-back tourist in the waters of the Dead Sea.
Opposite: Cascading falls at the health spa at Ma'in.

Above: Aerial perspective of Madaba, which has changed little since biblical times.
Opposite: Interior of the Chapel of St Theodore. The earliest known map of the Holy Land was discovered beneath its floor.

takes you through spectacular **landscapes** which could almost be of another planet and past a marble sign indicating sea level. A photograph of this against a backdrop of the sea more than 400 metres (1,300 feet) below is well worth stopping for.

The sea is lifeless due to its extremely high mineral content which gives the waters their curative powers, something recognised for over 2,000 years since the days of Herod the Great.

The sea's surface is usually extremely calm and, where sea meets shore, salt crystalises in thick, brilliant-white layers on every surface, giving the panoramic views an almost ethereal ambience.

Teleilat Ghassul

Meaning 'the small mounds of Ghassul' because of its surrounding terrain, the **fresco village** of Teleilat Ghassul was first discovered in 1929 by Father A Mallon who headed an archaeological team from the

Pontifical Biblical Institute. This resulted in a number of exploratory excavations between 1929-1938, in 1960 and 1967, and between 1975 and 1977. Subsequent to this, the area became a military minefield and was closed to the public until the 1994 Jordan-Israel peace treaty came into force. New excavations started almost immediately and were followed by three further seasons of work, the most recent in 1997.

The site's history began around 5100 BC as a farming village near the Dead Sea's north-eastern shores. Investigations suggest that the settlement was originally sited on the lush, thickly foliated banks of a river but was repeatedly affected, and even partly destroyed, by earthquakes which were then common due to regular geological activity in the area.

During the fifteen hundred years of its existence, between about 5100 and 3600 BC the village flourished to its eventual size of some 25 hectares. This unusually large size for a village of its time challenges preconceived ideas of what is now called

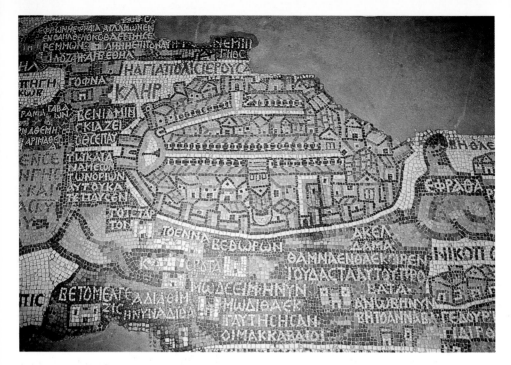

Above: The mosaic map of the Holy Land, with Jerusalem at its centre.

urbanism, which only began a millennium later.

An almost unique aspect of the village was that the plastered inside walls of many of the houses were painted with brightly coloured frescoes depicting human, geometric and naturalistic figures and symbols. The greatest mystery about the site, however, is its sudden desertion. The discovery of household implements on floors across the site indicates that on one normal day in the lives of the Ghassul inhabitants, something happened to make them drop everything and run for their lives, never to return.

Getting there

From Amman, drive toward the Dead Sea along the Na'ur road. Cross the Kafrein Junction toward the main army check-point 800 metres before this, turn left onto a dirt road. After 100 metres cross a paved agricultural road. Keep going and, after another 100 metres, you will be in the middle of the site.

Sighseeing

The **foundations** of some of the later **buildings** have been exposed by archaeological excavations, as have paved **pathways**. Of all the **frescoes** so far exposed, the most important, one of a **religious procession** of **three priests** approaching what might perhaps be a **shrine** or **altar,** is presently on display at the **Amman Archaeological Museum.** Restored with the assistance of **UNESCO** the **fresco's** sharply contrasting **colours,** created from mined blocks of coloured **ochres** and ground to **powder** by polished **stones,** are still almost as bright as when they were first mixed and applied to that particular wall.

Madaba: The City of Mosaics

Situated 30 kilometres (19 miles) south-west of Amman, the ancient city of Madaba is ideal for a half-day excursion. For anyone who has just arrived in Jordan it gives a splendid initial glimpse into biblical times. Madaba's history goes back 3,500 years. The earliest traces of human civilisation so far discovered there come from ceramic articles unearthed at the sites of ancient tombs near the city. These date back to at least the 13th century BC.

Madaba, referred to as *Medeba* in biblical texts, was the primary settlement vanquished by the Israelites on the Moabite plateau. (*Numbers 21:30; Joshua 13:9-16*). It was at Madaba that David's forces defeated the Ammonite and Aramean coalition. In the mid-9th century BC the Moabite ruler Mesha freed the city. Madaba was subsequently alluded to in *King Mesha's Stele*, a memorial inscribed with his greatest achievements.

Its strategic position meant that Madaba was constantly coveted over the centuries. The Nabateans governed the city during the 1st century AD having been awarded it by Hyracanus II, for their help in the battles against his brother Aristobulus II.

By the beginning of the 2nd century AD the Nabateans had been ousted by Trajan's army, and Madaba gradually became a provincial Roman city. Coins, minted during the Roman occupation, featured the emperor's head and grand phrases incorporating the city's name.

The Roman conversion to Christianity gave Madaba a new lease of life, and saw it enter its most affluent era. Grand provincial buildings were constructed. Colonnaded streets and other features such as the vast reservoir were built on the instructions of Emperor Justinian, on the north side of the community. In the 6th century bishops were assigned to Madaba, and buildings of religious importance were begun.

Getting there

Madaba is 30 kilometres (19 miles) south-west of Amman on an excellent well signed road that leads on to Kerak. If you are not travelling by car, the bus is quite reliable from Amman. It runs from the Wahdat Bus Depot in the southern part of the capital, to Madaba's bus station at the edge of town.

Sightseeing

The year AD 562 saw the laying of the **mosaic floor** at the **Chapel of St Theodore**, which nestles in the **atrium** of Madaba's **Cathedral**. Around this time much exquisite mosaic work was laid. The quality and quantity of the floorings has made Madaba one of the most prominent cities in the world for mosaics. But disaster befell in AD 614 when Persian forces ransacked the city. This single act of vandalism, together with the great earthquake of AD 747, led to Madaba's decay and gradual abandonment.

At the **southern entrance** to the city, nestled next to the road which wends its way down towards Kerak, is the **Church of the Apostles**. The **ruins** were discovered by the Roman Catholic parish priest of Madaba at the beginning of this century. They date to AD 578, and are adorned with beautiful **mosaic floors,** signed by a crafts-man named Salamanios.

The most significant section of the main floor is the **medallion,** inserted into the central portion of the nave. It is known generally as the Personification of the Sea, and is exactly that. The circular medallion, 220 centimetres (86 inches) in diameter, lies amid a theme of numerous pairs of birds. It depicts a woman emerging from the sea, half-clad, raising what is thought to be a rudder in line with her head. The Sea, concealing her left breast, suggests that the figure is part of the swirling waters; aquatic life surges around the figure, who stares out wide-eyed, with her right arm and hand positioned over her bare breast. Encircling the medallion is an inscription that reads: 'O Lord God who has made the heavens and the earth, give life to Anastasius, to Thomas, to Theodore and (to) Salamanios the mosaicist.'

A varied selection of creatures such as rams, bulls and parrots, as well as exotic vegetation, border the great floor's perimeter. You get the impression that the artist realised he had fashioned an unparalleled creation. Maybe this was why he signed the work so prominently.

Ten years after the main repopulation of Madaba, in 1890, the greatest, and most significant, of all the city's treasures was unearthed: the **Mosaic Map of Palestine**. The find was hailed as the oldest map in existence, and is located on the **floor** of the **Greek Orthodox Church** of St George.

Soon scholars were coming from far and wide to glimpse this singular discovery.

The century since this find has revealed an array of other mosaics. One can only wonder what other ancient feats of design and expertise await discovery.

The church is just **south** of the **Tourist Office,** on the opposite side of the road. Its central location makes it a good place to take a break from the bustling *souq*. Externally, the church belies its ornate, treasure-filled interior. It was constructed upon the foundations of an ancient Byzantine house of worship and only when the new church was having its floor tiled was the map revealed. The **eastern** section of the church, near the **altar,** is where surviving portions of the map may be seen. It measures 88 square metres (927 square feet), and extends between what are now the **central** and **south naves.**

The map represents the **Holy Land** and surrounding regions. The Mediterranean is the western margin; the deserts of Jordan the eastern border. Tyre and Sidon are depicted to the far north, with Egypt to the south.

It is thought that to lay the 2.3 million mosaics would have taken a workforce 11,500 hours. In 1965 experts from a museum at Trier in Germany restored the treasure.

Although embellished with features of wildlife, the map paints an extremely accurate and important picture of how the Holy Land and its surroundings looked during the 6th century. Great care was taken to give labels to those places represented. Indeed, different sizes of letters, and even different colours were used to give special prominence to certain settlements. It has been possible for scholars to identify most of the 150 named places, partly due to the meticulous depiction of natural features such as the **River Jordan,** the **Dead Sea,** or the **hot springs** at **Ma'in** where Herod is known to have bathed.

If you gaze into the collage, the map's true magic comes to life. Cities, such as **Jerusalem** in the centre, are represented by a gate flanked by two towers. A church represents a place of sacred retreat. But the most enchanting features are the details of vegetation, wildlife and people depicted everywhere. Lion are shown hunting gazelle, supporting the notion that until relatively recently such creatures inhabited the Middle East. Palm trees mark the sweet springs of the desert. A fish can be seen hurrying back from the Dead Sea in horror at what it found. Two boats on the Dead Sea have had their passengers erased — the supposed work of iconoclasts.

The most detailed section is that of Jerusalem. One can clearly make out the walls, streets and buildings of the ancient city, especially the colonnaded street which bisects the central area. The **Gate of Damascus** is still referred to in Arabic as **Bab el-Amud: the Gate of the Column**.

Leaving St George's Church with its heavily adorned walls, lines of chandeliers, and famed map is no easy task. Except for a few reminders of our century, life has changed little in this biblical town. **Carpets, camel saddle bags** and **tapestries** are crafted from dazzling hues of wool. Weavers, hard at their looms in the shade of their shops, are happy to sit and chat, over a glass of hot sweet tea.

The staff of the **Tourist Office** delight in recounting their town's heritage, and are always helpful. If you continue a few blocks **south** of the Tourist Office to the **Museum,** you pass a few small construction sites where **mosaic floors** have been unearthed. Madaba is an archaeologist's paradise, but poses enormous headaches for those in the construction business.

The museum was inaugurated in 1962 when it became home to a selection of fine **mosaic collages,** brought from different parts of the city. Some of those displayed are rare and in good condition. One of the most important is Jordan's oldest known mosaic frieze which comes from the Herodian fortress of Machaerus, dating back to the 1st century BC. The museum was established on the site of an ancient chapel so its own mosaics form the hub of the collection. An assortment of other ancient **artefacts** as well as traditional Bedouin and other **costumes,** complement the friezes. The museum, which is open from 9am to 5pm (except Tuesdays) charges a nominal entrance fee.

Madaba's **Archaeological Park** was established when the **Department of Antiquities** purchased a number of old

Above: The Monastery of Syagha, Mount Nebo, constructed in honour of Moses.

neighbouring **houses** built on **Byzantine mosaic** floors. The site, opened in December 1987, now houses numerous examples of **ancient mosaics** from **Hesban, Ma'in, Qastal** and **Mount Nebo**. Also on display are collections of **Ionian** and **Corinthian capitals, pottery, glass** and **metals,** and a number of **Byzantine colonnets** and **altars.** The adjoining **Folklore Museum** offers displays of **gold** and **silver jewellery,** cosmetic items, **traditional Jordanian costumes, rugs** and other traditional **household items.**

Mount Nebo: The Memorial of Moses

Less than 10 kilometres (6 miles) **north-west** of Madaba, towards the **River Jordan, Mount Nebo** soars above the great **eastern plateau** that stretches out to the **West Bank** and beyond. Nebo rises to about 800 metres (2,625 feet) at its apex and has, as its two most prominent crests, **Syagha** and **el-Mukhayyet**. Scholars have strong evidence that Mount Nebo has been inhabited since the earliest times.

An array of **prehistoric flint and stone tools** have been discovered in the region. The land, once abundant with rare creatures, valleys and sweet water springs, made the area perfect for habitation. It was there that Moses is said to have stood, forbidden by God to enter the Promised Land. On Nebo, Pisgah in the Bible, he was said to have lived out his days and, so legend has it, was finally interred.

From Syagha there is a matchless panorama of the **West Bank** stretching **westwards.** From this natural **viewpoint** one can make out the River Jordan, on the plateau floor, as well as **Bethlehem,** the **Mount of Olives** and, on a clear day, **Jerusalem.**

On the cusp of Mount Nebo, looking out towards the 'Promised Land', rises a **snake** fashioned from iron, curled around a cross. It represents the bronze serpent taken up by Moses when he was in the desert, as well as signifying the Cross on which Jesus was crucified.

Chapel

At **Syagha**, above the windswept plains, a **chapel** was erected in honour of the prophet Moses which drew many pilgrims. In the year 1864 the first modern illustration of Syagha was penned by the Duke of Loynes; but it was in the last two decades of the 19th century that two crucial accounts came to light which confirmed Nebo to be the resting place of Moses. The first was a 4th-century narrative by a traveller named Egeria, who recorded that the clergy there maintained the chapel had been sited where Moses had died, reputedly buried by angels. The second of the accounts was given by Peter the Iberian, Bishop of Gaza, who wrote of the chapel's divine pedigree.

The area of Nebo, Syagha and el-Mukhayyet were acquired by the Franciscans in 1934. A road was built to connect the sites to Madaba; and then began the daunting but important task of excavating the area.

The **monastery** at Syagha was constructed partly on the foundations of the early chapel, dating back to the 3rd or 4th century. The chapel is said to have been erected by monks from Egypt to commemorate the last moment of Moses' life. The monastery, which is protected by a synthetic roof, dates back to the 6th century. The original roof was probably wooden and was almost certainly held up by a series of internal columns, the **remains** of which can be seen inside the monastery building. Some of the most magnificent **Byzantine mosaic work** in Jordan is housed within its walls.

Entry into the antiquarian sites on and around Mount Nebo is free. To the **left** of the **main doorway,** parallel to the **central nave** of the monastery, a few **steps** lead down to the **baptistry.** This section, which was only discovered in 1976, comprises a **font** in the shape of a cross and, next to that, a superb **mosaic scene.** At the head of the tapestry in mosaic is a Greek endorsement stating when the work was completed: the month of August AD 531. A **walkway** allows you an overhead **view** of the scene.

A medley of exotic creatures fills the four main lines of the design. Two soldiers in the uppermost line thrust their lances toward a lion and lioness — providing yet further proof that these animals roamed the area. Below, a bear and wild boar are the prey of two horsemen. The third scene is of an assortment of sheep and goats grazing beneath bountiful trees. The fourth panel depicts a huge ostrich being led by one man, and a soldier beside him leading a zebra and a spotted camel.

At either end of the monastery light pours in through **stained-glass windows** which were added in modern times. They throw rich tints of blues and reds across the ruins, and are a welcome alternative to artificial lighting. At the **far end** of the central nave is the **altar,** pointing **east,** with the **apse** behind it. The original chapel is thought to have been primarily centred around the altar area.

Surrounding the monastery are the low-lying **ruins** of other ancient buildings. These, and the roof of the monastery probably fell victim to the great earthquake in AD 747. At the **east end** of the monastery's **outer wall** stands what is thought to be a gigantic **millstone,** though some locals maintain its purpose was more sinister.

As you arrive at the monastery up the hill path, a new **rest house** is on the **left.** It offers snacks, a wonderful vantage point and provides a cool place to shelter from the biting winds that howl across the mountain's face. The little rest house has its own **mosaic** proudly displayed on one wall. Inside the monastery on the **right** is a small collection of **souvenirs** and **booklets.**

Higher still above Syagha, just **east** of Mount Nebo, are the remains of the small village of **Nebo.** The place, now named **Khirbet El-Mukhayyad,** was mentioned in the Bible, as well as on the Mesha Stele. **Tombs** in the vicinity which have been excavated verify that the settlement has been populated since at least 2000 BC.

During the middle of the 6th century, when Byzantine mosaic work was at its height, a **small church** was built at el-Mukhayyet. It was apparently constructed by the native folk of the area, for their names feature in the Greek text alongside the mosaic work. The church, which was dedicated to the Saints Lot and Procopius, is carpeted wall to wall with mosaic scenes. Because of its location away from

Top: Byzantine mosaic frieze near the main nave at the Monastery of Syagha.

Above: Byzantine mosaic at Syagha depicts man encircled by a vine.

Opposite top: Ruins at Mount Nebo reach back to the pages of the Old Testament.

Opposite: Stone inscription at the Monastery of Syagha, where Moses is said to have died.

Above: Brightly coloured stained-glass window in the small church at Mount Nebo.

the monastery and up a mountain **track,** many visitors are unaware of its existence.

The trek to the site is rewarded by an unexpected scene. The Bedouin family who lived there for decades, and built walls around the remains of the church, were encouraged to leave in 1932. The large central panel, which fills the bulk of the room, remains almost perfectly intact, except for a black patch to the left of the doorway where bread was baked.

The family now look after the site. A worn **photograph** on a window ledge shows the now aged curator as a boy in the arms of his mother, who is greeting a young King Hussein.

The **mosaic tiles** depict myriad trees abundant with fruit, grazing creatures, wild animals and men. Vines wend and weave among the easternmost panel in an illustration of wine-making, hunting, music-making, and a bustle of activity. Raised up at the **altar,** just before the apse, are two sheep astride a fruit tree. As with most of

the mosaics of Mount Nebo and Madaba, the colours are vibrant yet soft, the shading so perfect that it seems as if the crafts-manship was done yesterday.

Ain Mousa: The Springs of Moses

Those well versed in the scriptures will recall how Moses struck a rock twice and water sprang forth. The site — complete with a running spring and reputedly the actual rock — has recently been renovated and housed in a new building. The site of **Ain Mousa** — in Arabic, The Springs of Moses — is a short distance **north** of Madaba. Look for three **white domes** by the side of the road which could easily be mistaken for a tomb or mosque.

The spring is now important in providing water for the town of Madaba. The area was surveyed by the Duke of Loynes in

1864, but it was not until 1984 that excavation began in earnest.

Within the small sturdily-built house a piece of **volcanic rock** rests, embedded in concrete. Beneath the stone, through a parting in the flooring, trickles crystal-clear water which is refreshing in the afternoon heat. Outside, a young boy hawking Bedouin coffee-pots and other wares tells the fable of how Moses made the water flow.

In the mid-1980s two highly significant discoveries were made near Ain Mousa. Two **churches** were revealed which have since been excavated. The first is the **Church of the Deacon Thomas,** which boasts superb Byzantine **mosaic floors.** The patchwork of colours and patterns depict animals, people, buildings and mixed motifs. The second is that of **Kayanos,** built in memory of Kayanos and John the Baptist during the early 6th century. The mosaic work has largely been removed for restoration. **South-west** of the **Madaba-Kerak road,** 25 kilometres (15 miles) from Madaba, are the ruins of a **Byzantine church** at **Mukawir.**

Getting there

Take the road west from Madaba towards Mount Nebo. About 1.5 kilometres (one mile) before the monastery, take the road right, driving downhill round sharp turns and through pine trees for about 2 kilometres (1.4 miles). You will notice the springs by their surrounding lush gardens and trees. The remains, to the left of the road, are in the process of being excavated.

Sightseeing

Look for the **well,** built in the Roman pear-shaped fashion, a style still used in the Middle East. You can easily make out the **apse** and **altar** area. The ruins overlook the hill on which Herod's fortress once stood, where John the Baptist was beheaded. A small **rest house** was recently completed at the site of the Byzantine church.

A stone's throw from the site stand two small **buildings** in which **Bani Hamida** textiles are made. (See "Amman: Great Seven-Hill Metropolis"). All around, Mukawir women can be seen spinning wool using nothing more than a bobbin, as those before them did for thousands of years. Others weave the long threads in the open, on a hillside, or outside their homes, in the ancient traditions of the Bedouin.

Thirty kilometres (19 miles) in the **south-east** of Madaba, almost equidistant between the **Desert Highway** and the **King's Highway,** you arrive at the spectacular ruins of **Umm el-Rassas.** The site, located in an elevated position, is seen some distance away.

Umm el-Rassas was an ancient encampment comprising an assortment of buildings, surrounded by a substantial stone wall.

The mid-1980s saw the beginning of an international excavation project in the area. The settlement of Umm el-Rassas was authenticated as the once-famed community of **Kastron Mefaa,** referred to in the Bible.

In the **northern extremity** of the area lies the **Church of St Stephen** which is itself one of a network of four churches that stood on the site.

St Stephen has probably the best example of an expansive 7th-century **mosaic floor** in pristine condition.

It is hard to imagine a more complex layout.

The combination of four churches interlinked in such ingenious manner is breathtaking. The northernmost **shrine** had its floor laid in AD 587, when Bishop Sergius was resident at Madaba. Sadly, many of the figures depicted were vandalised by iconoclasts in later years. Between the Church of St Stephen and that of Bishop Sergius, a **courtyard,** floored with flagstones, had an apse and roof added to transform it into another chapel. A set of stairs joined the two main churches, St Stephen's being a full metre higher than that of Bishop Sergius.

On either side of St Stephen's **altar** a passage of text indicates that the mosaic work around the altar was finished in AD 756, by two men: Staurachios and Euremios. However, it was not until AD 785 that St Stephen's floor was fully completed.

The mosaic is unusual for many reasons, among which are its double frame and extensive representations of Palestinian cities.

The spiritual community at Umm el-Rassas upholds the suggestion that an artistic colony remained active until at least the end of the 8th century.

Unexplained features at Umm el-Rassas make it fascinating for the visitor and archaeologist alike. The **watchtower**, 1,300 metres (1,422 yards) **north** of the settlement, crafted in the Byzantine period, stands 14 metres (46 feet) high. Some say that it was used to spy out intruders raiding the community's water cisterns or valuables. But in 1987 the **remains** of yet another **chapel** were unearthed at the column's foot. It gives some credibility to the idea that the tower was designed as a rostrum for meditative activities. The fact that there are no stairs leading to the **domed chamber** at the top further suggests the tower had an altogether more apocalyptic use.

Umm el Walid

South-east of Madaba and once a substantial fortified town, Umm el Walid lies 11 kilometres (7 miles) east of the Desert Highway, 8 kilometres (5 miles) south of Jiza. The well-preserved remains of a **walled enclosure** found there have been tentatively identified as a **caravan station.** This consists of a number of **rooms,** including **six suites** of two rooms each, built against an outer wall which surrounded a central courtyard. A number of small ruined buildings are adjacent, and several ancient cisterns, a few of which are still in use. A large open area paved with finely-worked slabs of limestone lies to the south.

Mukawir

To reach the **Mukawir** site which is now open to visitors, take the King's Highway south from Madaba. Turn right at the village of **Libb** and drive west for about 15 kilometres (9 miles) where there is a car park and some services 5 minutes walk from the site.

The old village of Mukawir has been partly renovated and houses an exhibition of the **Bani Hamida rug weaving project.**

Further west, just outside the village, is the site known locally as **Al Mashnaga** or **The Gallows,** believed to have been the location where **John the Baptist** was beheaded after the famous dance of **Saloumi** (Salome).

Humaima

North of Mukawir and 13 kilometres (8 miles) off the Desert Highway. **Humaima's** archaeological site covers an area of several kilometres. When the town was founded by the Nabatean **King Aretas III** in the 1st century BC, it was known as **Auara.** The remains can still be seen there of an aqueduct that once brought water from **Ain el Qana,** and the remnants of a one-complex water collection and storage system consisting of channels, cisterns and reservoirs.

The walls of a Nabatean house, reveal the remains of frescoes depicting **vines, clusters of grapes** and **human figures**.

More murals — which indicate the use of gold leaf in their detailing — can be found in the 2nd-century AD **Roman Fort** where the remains of a **metal-working forge** and traces of **weapons, helmets** and **body-armour** were found.

The ruins of five **churches** have been found at Humaima to date. In view of the town's size it is a number large enough to mystify archaeologists.

Ain Zara: Dead Sea Harbour

South of Humaima and 10 kilometres (6 miles) south of the Nazzal Dead Sea Hotel (200 metres from Ain Zara) thirteen sites dating from the **Hellenistic era** to the late **Byzantine,** have been recorded so far, though some have been badly damaged by agricultural, climatic or seismic disturbances.

It is thought that several archaeological remains are now either totally buried or too disturbed to be recognised. There are still numerous visible remains, however, one being the village boundary wall which also served to protect to the east.

Zara is also important for the ruins of a **villa** and the **harbour** which, being too large and complex for small boats, must have been used by larger **trading vessels**. Also to be seen are the remains of what is presumed to be a fort which once guarded the harbour. Due to the importance of this site it is now being kept as a **natural and archaeological park.**

Dhiban: Land of Treasures

Dhiban, about 65 kilometres (40 miles) south of Amman, has a history going back more than 3,000 years. It was there that King Mesha's fabled capital of Moab once

stood. The debris of the area spans three millennia, and encompasses remnants of all the Middle East's major civilisations from Nabatean to Roman, biblical to Arab, with each community built on the remains of the previous one.

Getting there
Dhiban is located just off the King's Highway, parallel with Umm el-Rassas, between Madaba and Kerak.

Sightseeing
Sections of the town's ancient **city wall** can still be seen. Iron Age and Byzantine **tombs** are just some of the relics at Dhiban.

But the town's most famous **antiquity** is probably the fabled **Mesha Stele**, the memorial to the exploits and achievements of King Mesha found by a missionary, Dr Kleen, in 1865. It recounted the battles between the Moabites and the Israelites around 850 BC. But the find was all the more important as the inscription on the stone, at the time, was the earliest example of Hebrew script.

It was fashioned from sheer black basalt 115 centimetres (45 inches) high, etched with 35 lines of script. Dr Kleen took the stele to Jerusalem where he informed Charles Clermont-Ganneau, an official at the French consulate, of his find. Clermont-Ganneau inspected the stone, made a mould of it, and returned to Jerusalem to raise the £60 he had undertaken to pay the locals for the treasure.

It was then that disaster struck. For while the Frenchman was collecting the necessary funds, the locals argued over who would get payment. In the ensuing hubbub a small fire was kindled beneath the Mesha Stone, after which water was poured on it. The result . . . a pile of shattered fragments.

The splinters were gathered up and taken to Paris where they were reassembled as well as possible. The stone is now on view at the Louvre in Paris. There are numerous copies, including one at the Kerak Museum and another in Amman's Archaeological Museum.

Just **south** of Dhiban on the King's Highway (in the direction of Kerak) you come to

El Qasr, which means literally 'the Castle or Palace'. This is the site of a small ruined **Nabatean temple** that dates from the first part of the 3rd century AD.

A few kilometres **south** of El Qasr you come to **Al Rabbath**, which was named *Areopolis* during Roman times. The community was mentioned in the Bible as Rabbath Moab (*Deut. 2:10-11*) and most of Al Rabbath's heritage is locked up in the pages of the Old Testament. There is not a great deal to see except the **remains** of various Roman and Byzantine **structures**.

Kerak: Mighty Stronghold atop a Precipice

Kerak, the ancient walled city steeped in history, has been known by many names during its long and eminent past. Variously entitled *Qir Heres*, *Hareseth*, and, in the Bible, *Qir Moab*, Kerak has been the prized possession of a multitude of forces. Its strategic position — almost a 1,000 metres (3,281 feet) above the plateau of the Dead Sea Valley, as well as on the main biblical trade routes — made Kerak the jewel in many conquerors' crowns.

Kerak was once set deep in the land of the Moabites and was witness to a bevy of bloody and brutal campaigns. The first part of the 5th century AD saw the arrival of Christianity in the city.

But it was not until the Crusaders arrived that Kerak attained true glory. In 1136 it is recorded that Payen, the Cupbearer, constructed the great fortress of Kerak on the instructions of Baldwin I, the monarch of Jerusalem. The Crusader fortress was erected at a strategically important point between Jerusalem and Shobak, forming part of a great line of other Crusader castles stretching from Aqaba to Turkey.

On the death of Baldwin III, a sole heir — a leper aged thirteen — was left. Being too young to rule he allowed a regent to do so on his behalf. But this regent died, leaving no successor but a widow named Stephanie. A nobleman, Reynaud de Chatillon, who had come to the Holy Land with the Second Crusade, rushed to the fortress where he proposed to — and wed

Above: One of the several vaulted subterranean passages under Kerak's fortress.

— Lady Stephanie, who was by this time one of the wealthiest and most powerful dowagers in the Holy Land.

Reynaud was at best merciless and, at worst, inhuman. As a result historians have painted him as a barbarian. There are numerous examples of his sadism, such as throwing captives from the battlements of Kerak's fortress — a drop of over 45 metres (148 feet) — with wooden hoods strapped over their heads to ensure that they remained conscious until they hit the ground.

When the young heir of Baldwin III reached the age of sixteen he saw little hope for the kingdom which was divided by internal disputes and the threat of war with the Muslim forces. So Baldwin IV appealed to Saladin for peace, and a truce was established.

Trade multiplied, as it was now safe for Christians and Muslims to travel in each other's lands. But then, as the ancient hostilities were curbed, Reynaud attacked and plundered a Muslim caravan heading towards Mecca. Saladin reciprocated by falling upon a Christian band of pilgrims en route for Jerusalem, and also by attacking Kerak itself. He withdrew, however, when additional support came to the Christians' aid from Jerusalem.

Reynaud again broke the armistice and Saladin responded with a massive bombardment of Kerak. At the battle of Hittin, Saladin overcame Reynaud, taking him prisoner and executing him. A year later, in 1187, Kerak was taken by siege and fell finally into the hands of the Arabs.

There could hardly be a more strategically placed fortress than Kerak. Its loss to the Christians marked the beginning of their decline of power in the area. They could no longer watch over the great plateau and send signals nightly to Jerusalem by beacon fires.

Kerak's significance returned with the uprising of the Mamluks and, after them, the Ottoman Empire. The city has gone through alternating periods of prosperity and stagnation. It is now a bustling and important city spreading far beyond the great walls into the surrounding area.

The fortress was built for defence rather than beauty and its critics have deemed it gloomy and morose. But to walk the battlements and the subterranean passageways gives one a true feeling of its formidable presence.

Getting there
Kerak is 129 kilometres (80 miles) south of Amman, and 88 kilometres (55 miles) south of Madaba. It can easily be reached by the Madaba-Petra road if travelling from Madaba. From Amman, take the Desert Highway south as far as Qatrana, then turn westwards to cover the short distance to Kerak.

Where to stay
The Government Rest House has an impressive view looking out to the Dead Sea and the West Bank. It is situated right on the lip of the escarpment and is built from Kerak's native stone. There are other small lodging houses, a bank and numerous places to eat. See Listings.

Sightseeing
A labyrinth of **passageways** interlink at several levels above and below the surface. The network of sheltered **storerooms** and **chambers** are lit by shafts of natural light.

Arrow-slits peek out towards the distant horizon.

Look for the geometric designs carved by the Mamluks into yellow blocks of stone. The Mamluks and the Ottomans after them built annexes to the main Crusader design. Some of the underground tunnels, with their rugged walls and ceilings, have been blocked by fallen rocks and it is easy to fantasise that there might be a secret treasure from the castle's golden age, waiting to be discovered.

In the **corridors** and some chambers you can still make out the remnants of an intricate earthenware guttering system. It would have been crucial, especially in times of siege, to collect as much rainwater as possible. Mud covering the walls of various underground areas perhaps suggests that they were used for water storage at some time. This would give even greater significance to the pottery pipes running the length of the walls.

As you tread through the deep cool passageways with the faint cries of the call to prayer echoing around the city, the practicality of the fortress becomes apparent. You can see the **millstone** used for pressing olives, the great **oven, basins,** and spacious underground **dining rooms.**

Kerak's **museum** is located within the fortress in a vast vaulted **hall** (open from sunrise to sunset). It is reached by a few **steps** that lead down from ground level, and displays many of the city's important relics. Among the artefacts are fine **glass bowls** and **flasks.** But you cannot avoid noticing the power-points on the walls. What would Saladin have thought of them? Another great vestibule is situated below Kerak's museum hall, covering the same area. It is reached by a separate set of steps and legend says that it was there, underground, that Saladin had his throne.

The Lisan Peninsula

Six kilometres (3.7 miles) west of **Mazra'a** and lying between supply pipes from the

---

Previous page: Ancient city of Kerak from the air, with the fortress in background.

Above: Potash Plant on the shores of the Dead Sea, one of the Middle East's most ambitious industrial projects.

Dead Sea to the **potash company,** are the ruins of a Byzantine monastery complex on the **Lisan Peninsula,** Lisan being the Arabic word for tongue.

The monastery is situated on a plateau with an open view of the surrounding landscape and the Dead Sea. The monastic activity covers a large area which includes a **Byzantine chapel** with partly preserved 6th- and 7th-century **mosaic** floors. Towards the summit of the site there is evidence of constructions from the Abbasid and Fatimid periods where materials from the Byzantine phase were re-used.

At nearby **Ghawr Haditha cemetery,** a kilometre east of the village of **Haditha** on the mainland, many differently-shaped stone tombs are attached to ancient terraces.

Safi: Where Old Meets New

At the south-east extremity of the **Dead Sea,** 110 kilometres (68 miles) south of Amman lodged between the **salt flats** and the **Dead Sea Highway** running between **Mazra'a**

and Safi, is an immensely ambitious solar **evaporation project** which presently reclaims around an annual 1.8 million metric tonnes of potash from the Dead Sea waters.

The project, aptly name the **Arab Potash Company,** was jointly funded by a number of Arab nations of which Jordan is the majority shareholder in this, the country's biggest industrial facility. The property extends over about 100 square kilometres (40 miles) of land which is covered with evaporation pools and processing plants, and there are plans to expand the factory to increase production by another 400,000 tonnes annually.

Potash, Jordan's foremost earner of foreign currency, is important for use in fertilisers. It has been known and used since biblical times when the ashes of burnt wood were boiled in huge pots — hence the name potash — to produce a solid mass of white potash salt, used a enrich the soil before planting new crops.

Deir Ain Abata: The Sanctuary of Lot

An international team of archaeologists, working on a site near Safi, have unearthed Jordan's most phenomenal discovery of recent times, at Deir Ain Abata: The Sanctuary of Lot.

Chapter 19 of *Genesis* describes how God destroyed the cities of Sodom and Gomorrah — to put an end to the perversions of their peoples. However, just before laying waste to the cities, He sent angels to lead Lot — the nephew of Abraham — and his family seeking refuge. With his two daughters, they found sanctuary in a cave near the ancient city of Zoar (modern Safi). Lot's wife was turned into a pillar of salt having turned to watch the destruction of Sodom. The find is of incalculable importance to Jordanian and Middle Eastern heritage. For it was at this cave, so legend says, that Lot's daughters gave birth to Moab and Ammon from whom the people of Jordan are descended.

For more than a thousand years the whereabouts of Lot's cave was unknown. Archaeologists spent years searching for the sanctuary — urged on by its description in the Bible, and its portrayal on the Byzantine map of the Holy Land at Madaba.

Getting there

Deir Ain Abata is situated about 2 kilometres (one mile) north of Safi on the hill overlooking the Dead Sea. Its discovery is widely regarded as the most important and exciting find in the Holy Land since the Dead Sea Scrolls.

The leader of the excavation, eminent Greek archaeologist, Constantinos Politis, battled against the phenomenal heat of the Dead Sea Valley during his seven year dig. The project, partly funded by the British

Top right: Entrance to the Cave of Lot at Deir Ain Abata, where Lot and his daughter sought refuge during the destruction of Sodom and Gomorrah.

Right: Pillar of salt beside the Dead Sea is said to be Lot's wife after she turned to watch Sodom being destroyed.

Above: Common mallow blooms in D'ana Reserve.

Museum in London, constantly surprises experts and local people alike. Each season tantalising new discoveries make the headlines. The recent removal of a partition wall revealed dozens of human skeletons — probably those of pilgrims and monks resident at the site in previous times. Also recently found were a wide variety of bronze age artefacts, as well as a number of new mosaic floors.

Sightseeing

The **Cave of Lot** at **Deir Ain Abata** looks out over the **Dead Sea.** Beyond that one can easily make out where Sodom and Gomorrah would once have stood. The Cave and **monastery's** position, halfway up a scree slope, is precarious; and has led to at least a third of the monastery tumbling down the mountain.

The site has revealed **relics** dating back as far as the Bronze Age (when Lot would have inhabited the cave) and an elaborate three-apsed **Basilica,** dedicated to him. One **mosaic pavement** in the **north aisle** is dated AD 606. This monastery obviously welcomed pilgrims to view Lot's sanctuary. Among the artefacts discovered within the basilica were the **pulpit, marble chancel screen,** and **chancel posts.** Other important finds include a number of unique Byzantine **mosaic floors; tombs,** presumably those of the monks who resided at the monastery; and a large once-covered **reservoir.** The list of Bronze Age, Nabatean, Byzantine, and early Islamic artefacts already excavated, is considerable. Kufic and ancient Greek **graffiti** have also been found.

The cave stands at the **apse** in the **north aisle** of the basilica. It is the site of the most recent and exciting excavations. The cave is paved with **marble floorslabs** and plain **mosaic,** which were certainly added during the Byzantine-Abbasid period. The floor was excavated to a depth of two metres (6.5 feet). Immediately below the floor level **Roman pottery** was discovered. Below this lay a complete **Bronze Age jug,** accompanied by several drinking bowls. Deeper beneath the floor a number of **flints** were found — as well as freshwater **mollusc shells** — indicating that the cave perhaps had a spring source of its own.

The monastery's **refectory, north** of the basilica, was also recently excavated, revealing a selection of Byzantine **cooking pots** and **jugs** — and some large pieces of **animal bone** and **chicken eggshell.** A large **oven** 3 metres (10 feet) in circumference and a large basalt **millstone** were also found. A **vault,** discovered in the refectory's proximity, revealed the **remains** of at least ten individuals. The far **south-east** corner of the refectory area houses a blocked, possibly secret, passageway into the cave.

To the area north of the main excavations at Deir Ain Abata, seventeen other important **sites** have been identified. Fourteen of these consist of round and oval vaulted cairn **tombs** with associated **pottery** belonging to the Middle Bronze-early Late Bronze Age.

It seems more than likely that the monastery was abandoned, almost certainly during the 8th century AD. The natural pressure of the mountain would account for the collapse of the basilica and other structures. Indeed, natural erosion has sent about a quarter of the basilica's remains

Above: Renovated building in the D'ana Reserve.

crumbling down the mountainside.

Further excavations will concentrate on the tombs, lifting the mosaics and re-laying them and excavating the Cave of Lot in search of evidence of early man.

It is planned to make Deir Ain Abata into a tourism centre. The site's location makes it perfect as a stop en route from Amman to Petra.

In the waters of the **spring,** after which Deir Ain Abata is named, **snails, crabs** and two species of **freshwater fish** have been found. These, and aquatic plants are believed to have survived since the days when the Dead Sea was a living lake.

The development of Deir Ain Abata as a viable tourist site has been slowed by lack of funding and by continuing excavations. A fine stairway now connects the site with the parking area below. In many ways, Deir Ain Abata is the best type of tourist site in Jordan. Visitors can see a major excavation underway, without the postcard sellers and ice cream stalls which tend to pop up at all established tourist sites.

Recently, an enormous burial site, just outside the small town of Safi, has been targeted by souvenir and treasure hunters. The burial grounds, some of which date back to Bronze Age (many others to the Roman era) are being ransacked on a daily basis for the loot interred along with the dead. Gold and silver jewellery as well as rare glass objects are finding their way onto the open market. Although Jordanian authorities are patrolling the area, the illicit trade is rife. If anyone offers you an ancient artefact near Safi, please do not buy it. Visitors to the kingdom are prohibited from taking abroad objects that are more than 100 years old. When an object is hacked from the earth, archaeologists' knowledge of it is destroyed forever.

Khirbet et Tannur: Temple of the Gods

To the west of Wadi Hasa — the steep-sided valley that runs south-eastwards from Safi — you come to the relics and debris of a great Nabatean temple. It could hardly have been built on a more precipitous bluff,

with access only from the southern flank. The steep path that leads up to the remains must have made building on the summit an exhausting task.

Getting there

Khirbet is a short distance from **Tafila** reached by a main road link from the Desert Highway but, if time is not a priority, take the King's Highway which continues from Kerak through Tafila and Shobak to Petra, on its way through valleys both lush and barren.

Sightseeing

The **temple** at **Khirbet et Tannur,** dating back to the 1st century AD, was supposedly that of Atargatis and Hadad. This solitary peak with its sacred temple is thought to have gone through several periods of re-structuring and renovation. **Relics** of many different Nabatean deities were discovered at the site, among them *Atargatis* (Artemis), the goddess of foliage and fruit; *Zeus-Hadad*, god of the thunderbolt; *Tyche*, a guardian goddess; *Tyche-Nike*, the goddess of fortune

and victory, and several others. Many of those recovered can now be seen at Amman's Archaeological Museum. Experts maintain that Khirbet et Tannur can be dated from between 25 BC and AD 125.

The surrounding area is littered with **remains** from other Nabatean periods, as well as items from Byzantine and Roman times. There are also a couple of **hot springs** nearby at **Burbeita** and **Afra.**

Tafila, a small but ancient town locked in the depths of a lush valley, has a ruined Crusader **fortress,** and gained importance at the beginning of this century as the site of the only set battle Lawrence of Arabia fought during his Arab campaign. The Crusader stronghold has a great **keep,** and it is interesting to browse among its 12th-century and Mamluk ruins.

Above: Building under renovation in the D'ana Reserve.

Above: Shobak fortress dominates the surrounding gaunt and rocky landscape.

The land running **west** between Tafila and Shobak is of great biblical importance. A region where early copper mining and metal smelting took place, it was home to the Edomites, and ensured extreme wealth for those who possessed it.

D'ana: Rugged Haven of Nature

It is hard to imagine a more dramatic and spectacular setting for a wildlife reserve than D'ana. The D'ana Reserve incorporates some of Jordan's most breathtaking scenery. It stretches from the peaks of the Sharaa mountains in the east, across gorges hewn by time through sheer rock walls, to the hills of Wadi Araba.

The region is known to have been inhabited since the late Iron Age, after which each civilisation left its mark. D'ana now is largely inhabited by Bedouin who came from Palestine during Ottoman times.

The natural diversity of D'ana and its environs is perfect for supporting wildlife.

From the Sharaa mountains, with their elevation of around 1,800 metres (5,906 feet) above sea level, down to the dunes of Wadi Araba, at sea level, is a full range of climatic conditions.

D'ana was chosen for a wildlife reserve study in 1976 to examine the vicinity's flora and fauna. In 1990 D'ana was established as Jordan's sixth wildlife reserve.

Getting there

Head for Qasidiyya, between Tafila and Shobak on the King's Highway. D'ana is located 25 kilometres (15 miles) south of Tafila, to the east of the King's Highway and Qasidiyya.

Sightseeing

The rugged habitat of the reserve has allowed the flora and fauna to continue largely unhampered by man. Today **ibex** are occasionally seen on the crags, as well as **mountain gazelle** which inhabit the lower rocky areas. In the scrubland **red fox, badger, porcupine,** and a variety of other creatures can be found. **Wolves, hyrax, striped hyena** and **jackal** roam the valleys.

A wealth of birdlife wings the gorges, nesting in trees and crags. Birds such as the **crested lark, chukar, partridge, great grey shrike** and **pale crag martin** make their home in D'ana. They share their habitat with the **common bulbul, mourning wheatear, black start, Tristram's grackle** and the **Sinai rosefinch.**

Archaeological finds in **D'ana Village** suggest that man has resided there for nearly six millennia. Evidence has revealed **remnants** of Palaeolithic, Egyptian, Edomite, Assyrian, Nabatean and Roman civilisations. Each community was drawn to the region by its lush vegetation, fertile land and natural springs. D'ana's small community has been largely unaffected by the 20th century. The zigzag **alleys** meander through the village and the **houses** are similar to those built hundreds of years ago.

In recent times the inhabitants of D'ana

have left the community for the nearby village of Qasidiyya, lured by electricity, modern communications and relative luxuries.

The D'ana Project was launched to revitalise the natural habitat and foster D'ana's growing numbers of wildlife. The project aims to combat overgrazing by cattle and goats, and cutting of trees for firewood.

The reserve is strictly protected against poaching and hunting. Species such as the ibex have been reduced to a mere handful in the last decades and the project hopes to increase their numbers, and those of other creatures. As well as boosting endangered species, the project is developing a designated camp ground and hiking trails. It is hoped visitors will appreciate the beauty of the D'ana Reserve and safeguard its future. D'ana Village has been renovated, returning it to its former charming character. In addition, a selection of cottage industries is planned to help revitalise the tiny community.

Shobak: Montreal of the East

Like Kerak, Shobak has a long and distinguished history that reached its peak in Crusader times. It too has a great fortress, constructed in 1115 by Baldwin I, as a link in the great chain of Crusader strongholds across Jordan. The fortress, known as *Mont Realis* (or *Montreal*) guarded the crucial Damascus to Cairo trade route below.

Getting there
The easiest route is to take the King's Highway south from Kerak through Qasidiyya and Tafila. The fortress becomes visible, high above the main road. An alternative route is to branch west to Shobak off the Desert Highway.

Sightseeing
If you approach the castle from the south you get a terrific view of its daunting position. It lies, prominent and supreme, on a knoll with its vantage point over the landscape, a bastion against the searing and relentless winds. Saladin besieged the stronghold several times before finally gaining it in 1189. At its height Shobak was home to about 6,000 Christians.

The 14th century saw a total restoration and rebuilding of Mont Realis by the Mamluks. The fortress is situated north-east of Shobak. There is a quantity of exquisite Mamluk lettering on the main square tower, between the arrow slits, but many of the rooms have fallen into disrepair and have even disintegrated into piles of rocks.

In one chamber on the first level two circular holes in the floor lead to a reservoir. Another of the rooms was probably a chapel. At its eastern end is an alcove and a set of steps to a chamber below, from which a tunnel leads to a spring in the valley. The shaft has 375 steps and is one of the deepest ever created by Crusader forces.

Wandering around the fortress you may find millstones for pressing olives, lintels from the great doorways and a few archways that have withstood the rigours of time.

From the crumbled walls of the fortress you can see just below the village of Al-Jaya: strangely unaffected by modernisation. There are no cars and no telephone lines — just a couple of old folk sitting in doorways enjoying the tranquillity. The ruins of such a castle as Shobak give insight into the anatomy of its structure. You can guess what was original, and what later additions were made by the Mamluks such as the rounder arches.

Top: Crumbling walls of Shobak fortress give an indication of the size of the stronghold.
Above: Crusader fortress at Shobak covered by a mantle of snow. Built in 1115 by Baldwin I, it finally fell to Saladin's forces in 1189.

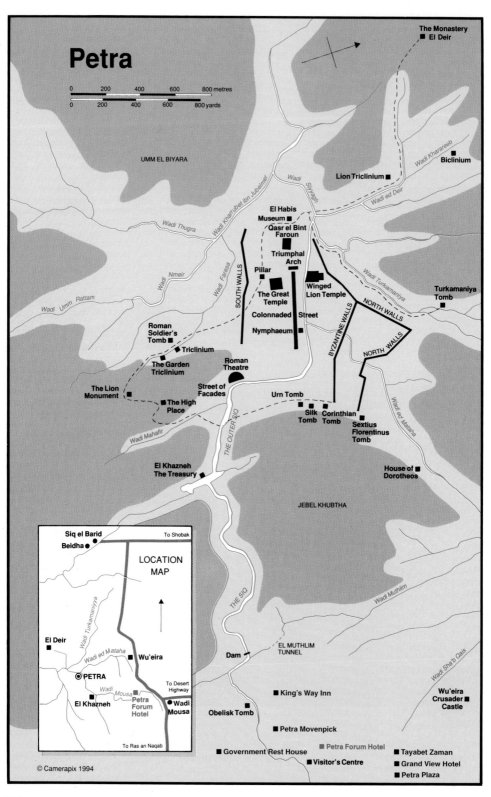

Petra

0   200   400   600   800 metres
0   200   400   600   800 yards

UMM EL BIYARA

Wadi Thugra

Wadi Kharrubet Ibn Jubeimet

Wadi Farasa

Wadi Nmeir

Wadi Umm Rattam

Wadi Siyagh

Wadi

Wadi ed Deir

Wadi Kharareeb

Lion Triclinium

Biclinium

El Habis Museum

Qasr el Bint Faroun

Triumphal Arch

Pillar

The Great Temple

Winged Lion Temple

Wadi Turkamaniya

Turkamaniya Tomb

SOUTH WALLS

Colonnaded Street

Nymphaeum

NORTH WALLS

BYZANTINE WALLS

NORTH WALLS

Roman Soldier's Tomb

Triclinium

The Garden Triclinium

Roman Theatre

The Lion Monument

The High Place

Street of Facades

Urn Tomb

Silk Tomb

Corinthian Tomb

Sextius Florentinus Tomb

Wadi ed Mataha

Wadi Mahafir

THE OUTER SIQ

El Khazneh The Treasury

House of Dorotheos

JEBEL KHUBTHA

LOCATION MAP

Siq el Barid

Beidha

To Shobak

Wadi Tuhamaniyya

El Deir

Wadi ed Mataha

Wu'eira

⊙ PETRA

Wadi Mousa

El Khazneh

Petra Forum Hotel

Wadi Mousa

To Desert Highway

To Ras an Naqab

THE SIQ

Wadi Muthlim

EL MUTHLIM TUNNEL

Dam

Wadi Shab Qais

King's Way Inn

Wu'eira Crusader Castle

Obelisk Tomb

Petra Movenpick

Government Rest House

Petra Forum Hotel

Visitor's Centre

Tayabet Zaman

Grand View Hotel

Petra Plaza

© Camerapix 1994

136

Petra: Rose-Red City Half as Old as Time

Petra is an enchanting place that captivates and excites the senses. Its overwhelming size, rich textures, and stunning surroundings create an ambience almost impossible to describe.

To understand how Petra evolved, travel back through time to the Old Testament. Part of Petra's magic comes from mysterious gaps in the region's history. Knowledge of the city's founders and their lives, although constantly increasing, is fragmented and only serves to compound the mystery.

It is certain that Petra has been inhabited from prehistoric times. Indeed, just north of the city at Beidha the remains of a 9,000-year-old civilisation have been discovered, making it as old as Jericho. The first residents in the region were the Edomites. It is thought they were at odds with the Judaeans and resided mainly in the mountains surrounding what is now Petra.

The city's beauty and charm have inspired artists and poets ever since its sensational rediscovery in the last century. John William Burgeon wrote of it:

> But rose-red as if the blush of dawn
> That first beheld them were not yet
>   withdrawn;
> The hues of youth upon a brow of woe,
> Which Man deemed old two thousand years
>   ago,
> Match me such a marvel save in Eastern
>   clime,
> A rose-red city half as old as Time.

The Bible tells of how David became king and subdued the Edomites, probably around 1000 BC. The remaining Edomites were enslaved, but at length won their freedom. However, there was a series of great battles between the Judaeans and the people of Edom. One of these saw the Judaean King Amaziah decimate the Edomites. He hunted them to their refuge at Sela and, as legend has it, cast 10,000 Edomites over a precipice to their deaths.

Petra burgeoned to its true glory with the arrival of the Nabateans. It is widely believed that they were a nomadic people from western Arabia who filtered into the Petra region and mingled with the remaining Edomites during the 4th century BC. It seems that the two peoples were not hostile toward each other. The Nabateans were a flexible race, formerly shepherds and random raiders of caravan processions, who adapted well to a more settled existence.

Scholars believe the Nabateans gave up their nomadic lifestyle because, by being resident in one place, they could enrich their lifestyle by levying taxes on travellers for safe passage through their lands. It is sensible to assume, however, that the nomadic Nabateans did not immediately launch into the construction of a vast city which, at its height, was home to more than 30,000 people.

Greek accounts in the annals of Seleucid talk of friction and battles between the Greeks and the Nabateans. Greek influence was strong at one time, indeed the city's name, Petra, derives from the Greek word meaning 'rock'. Records indicate that the Nabateans were prosperous and powerful and eager to remain on good terms with the Greeks in order to perpetuate their trading ambitions.

Nabatean society was greatly influenced by the advent of Hellenistic culture around 150 BC. The new ideas and concepts in art and architecture came at a time when the Nabateans were expanding their trade routes farther north to Syria.

Nabatean escalation as an economic and political power began to worry the Romans. Pompey, in 63 BC, dispatched a force to assail Petra and cripple it; but the Romans ended up being bought off and making peace with the locals.

The dynasty of Nabatean rule ended in AD 106 when Petra was assimilated into the fold of the newly formed *Roman Province of*

Overleaf: Snow-dusted mountains above Petra are stark contrast to the sun-baked facade of El Deir, the Monastery.

Above: Caves hewn from the sheer rock faces at Petra provided religious and living chambers for the ancient Nabateans.
Opposite: A mighty tomb at Petra with Roman stone additions below.

Arabia. The last Nabatean monarch, Rabbel II (AD 71-107), staved off Roman appropriation as long as he could until the order that the annexation must take place.

Much of what is known about their society is from the writings of Roman scholar, Strabo. He noted that their community was governed by a royal family, although a system of democracy prevailed. Their obsession with materialism led to the awarding of tributes to those who added to their assets, and fines on those who reduced their belongings. Strabo's words paint an idyllic picture of Nabatean life; a community without fortified walls, rich lands or luxuriant flora.

The fact that silver coins and possessions of any value are rarely discovered at Petra has led experts to suggest that the Nabatean withdrawal and evacuation was a methodical and unhurried process.

The virtual lack of inscriptions may be because they were removed before the departure. The best and longest example of Nabatean script at Petra can be seen above the doorway to the Turkamaniya Tomb. It is thought that the script was a form of Aramaic, and the precursor to Kufic lettering which, in turn, led to modern Arabic script.

Their religion is known to have had at least two major deities, those of *Al Uzza* and *Dusares*, as well as a host of minor gods. The Nabateans, like other peoples of their time, were opposed to portraying deities in graven form. The exception was Dusares, a god represented as a cube of stone. The deity has been found to be symbolised in areas far from Petra, and in forms more diverse than a mere solid block.

Nabatean accomplishments in the fields of architecture, engineering, pottery and calligraphy are hard to surpass even with today's technology, and were superior to almost all other contemporary civilisations. Alongside their fascination and obsession for money, there was one other compulsion — the collection and storage of water. It led to a system of earthenware pipes — the remains of which are evident around the city — which gathered water as it ran down the rock surfaces. Water was also brought into the heart of Petra through the Siq, and probably to the Nymphaeum, next to the Colonnaded Street, from Ain Mousa: the *Spring of Moses*.

Despite the general lack of water, freak rains in the winter months have been known to flood Petra, especially the narrow Siq. The Nabateans combated the problem by boring a tunnel from the Siq through the mountainside. Twenty-three tourists were drowned in 1963 when a flash flood turned the Siq into a raging torrent.

The Roman architectural additions to Petra after the annexation suggest that Petra certainly did not go to rack and ruin after occupation. Projects such as the Colonnaded Street do little to harm the character of the city. Indeed, it has been suggested that Petra went through a resurrection after the Romans arrived.

In his pivotal book, *Petra*, Iain Browning remarks on the comparison between the slender Roman colonnades and the stockier columns crafted by the Nabateans. The Romans had perfected such details which the Nabateans, and the Egyptians like them, could only strive to emulate.

Following a general stagnation of Petra in late Roman times, the final blow came to the city on the morning of Monday, 19 May AD 363. A massive earthquake brought freestanding edifices tumbling to the ground. Mercifully Petra's great constructions went largely unscathed as they were actually carved from the rock.

It is not clear whether the inhabitants had left their beloved city, before, or after, the great 4th-century earthquake. Reconstructing the damaged areas would have been a daunting task. It is known that, by the 6th century, Petra was almost uninhabited, just a memory of the once majestic capital.

Centuries passed and Petra slumbered in silence. The Arab empire sidestepped the region. And, except for a second great earthquake in AD 747 and a small Crusader community in Petra in the 13th century, the city was left relatively undisturbed for over a thousand years.

At the beginning of the 19th century a young Swiss, John Burckhardt, eager to travel in the Near East, disguised himself as a Muslim. He studied Arabic, grew a long beard, and made it known that he had ventured from the wilds of India. His journey took him from Damascus to Cairo. In 1812, Burckhardt heard rumours of the fabled city of Petra and, knowing it was in the vicinity, set out to find it.

The Bedouin who inhabited the area were sceptical of his claims, and their suspicions were raised further when he wanted to move off the beaten track. He said that it was his intention to make a sacrifice at the tomb of the Prophet Aaron, a mission that could not be condemned by the pious Bedouin.

After considerable exploits, recounted in his book *Travels in Syria* (printed after his death in 1822), Burckhardt, or *Ibrahim ibn Abdullah* as he was known, arrived at the Siq, the entrance to Petra.

What Burckhardt saw, those first glimpses of the rich colours and textures of sandstone, is essentially what is seen today. Then, as now, there was an almost supernatural silence about the place. The young Swiss man's venture into the forgotten capital was brief. Lingering, or overt scribbling of notes, would have branded him a spy and liable to execution. His observations were mainly of the Treasury and the Urn Tomb, before he concluded his sacrificial pledge.

News of Burckhardt's find raced through the Western world, and it was not long before audacious wayfarers began to venture to Petra. At the time, reaching the ancient capital was not only dangerous, but also, indeed until recently, entailed an arduous journey by horse across the desert for many days.

Burckhardt did not return to Petra, for he was involved in other travels. Among them expeditions to Mecca and Medina, which he entered as a Muslim. But he contracted dysentery while in Egypt and after eleven days died in October 1817. His last wishes

---

Opposite: Perhaps the most spectacular of all the rock-carved buildings in the majestic capital of Petra, El Khazneh, the Treasury, stands at the entrance.

Above: Brightly-decorated Bedouin camel. Opposite: Worn down by wind and weather, the mellow rocks of Petra enchant visitors.

were carried out and he was buried in the Muslim graveyard in Cairo. The epitaph above his grave gives his Muslim name: Ibrahim ibn Abdullah.

Present-day Petra

A lot has changed at Petra since Burckhardt's time. Indeed, the greatest changes at the ancient city have taken place in the last five years. The new climate of Peace in the Middle East has boosted tourism as never before. Westerners who, until recently, deemed the region too dangerous, and a vast number of Israeli tourists, flock to the city in droves on every day of the year. The deluge of tourism has had a deep-seated effect on the ruins and the surrounding area. New hotels and tourist facilities seem to sprout up daily, catering to the ever-expanding number of foreigners who make the pilgrimage to Petra.

The growth in tourism at Petra has recently led to a substantial increase in entrance charges. The price rise, say the authorities, is merely to put the city in line with other world-famous tourist destinations. The entrance fee, about JD20, may be included in the price of your tour, if you have travelled to Jordan as part of a group. If not, you can purchase the ticket from the Visitor's Centre.

Most newcomers to Petra pause at the Visitor's Centre before proceeding into the ancient metropolis. There you can stock up with film and necessary supplies. As well as the essentials, there seems to be an ever-increasing stock of souvenir bric-a-brac (all, of course, bear the image of The Monastery, or the Treasury). The Centre is open between 07.00 and 18.00 every day (including Friday). Next door is a bank where you can change foreign currency. The bank's hours are 08.30 to 12.30; 16.15 until 17.45.

Behind the Visitors' Centre a jumble of souvenir shops sell T-shirts and knicknacks displaying great monuments· of the city. Also behind the Visitors' Centre is a small Post Office. Until recently, tourists usually hired a horse to take them through the

Siq, the narrow gorge that leads into Petra. Cars are not permitted to enter Petra's ruins. A new ruling makes horse traffic impossible. The rapid growth in tourism led to an abundance of horse manure, pollution and erosion of the narrow passageway. Instead, you can still hire a horse but it will only take you as far as the entrance to the Siq. The Siq itself — a journey of about two miles must be made on foot (unless you are elderly, or disabled, in which case you will be transported by horse and carriage). If you hire a horse to the entrance of the Siq, hold on tight as the ground is extremely rocky. Before you claim your horse, look down from the natural vantage-point where you will be able to make out the Siq, the narrow gorge that leads into Petra.

Every year around 125,000 tourists head to Petra, making it by far the most visited attraction in Jordan and one of the most popular places in the Middle East. There are currently five archaeological sites within the city.

Getting there
Wadi Mousa, which lies 195 kilometres (122 miles) from Amman on the Madaba-Dhiban-Kerak highway, is the nearest main road point to Petra. Follow the signs from there. The turnoff may also be reached along the great Desert Highway by driving to Ma'an. From there take the road west for 35 kilometres (22 miles) to Wadi Mousa.

Where to stay
Many young travellers venturing to Petra, inspired by the surroundings, decide to camp out — sleeping within the ruined city. This is now illegal and, in any case, is not recommended. Since the Peace Treaty was signed with Israel, wave after wave of tourists have headed for Petra. As a result, a great variety of hotels has been built. A few years ago the only plush place to lodge was the Petra Forum Hotel (which has a camp site beside it, where tents can be hired). Since then, tourists have the choice of more than a dozen places. Among them are 5-star hotels and several of 3-2- and 1-star rating (See listings).

Very popular with travellers with modest budgets is the Government Rest House. Located just outside the Siq, it is a blend of ancient and modern, featuring its own dining area and Nabatean tombs.

If you are staying at Petra in the summer, be sure to enquire in advance whether your hotel has air-conditioning or, failing that, a ceiling fan. Similarly, if you are venturing to the ancient city in winter, check if heating is laid on. Petra is such a popular destination that lodgings — both inexpensive and less so — get booked well ahead.

Sightseeing
Before proceeding to the **Siq** most tourists stop just in front of the **Brooke Clinic** to hire a horse. You will see dozens of animals saddled up and ready to go.

The Brooke Clinic was opened by Princess Alia, eldest daughter of King Hussein, in March 1988. Its aim is to maintain the health of the horses. A full-time vet is now based at the clinic, which gives much more than medicine to animals and owners, ensuring, for instance, that worn-out saddles are replaced.

The Brooke Clinic oversees the breeding of horses, fostering 60 foals a year. Of the 500 horses in the immediate area, about 350 carry tourists regularly. A mobile clinic attends sick animals which cannot get to the clinic. Treatment is free and, if a horse has to be put down, the owner is compensated.

At various times of the year there are competitions for the best horse. Weddings at **Wadi Mousa Village**, the main modern village near Petra, are celebrated with horse racing and other equine activities. When you hire a horse or a two-wheel buggy, mounting platforms are provided.

The first important Nabatean monument you reach is the **Obelisk Tomb**, situated on the **left**. Below it is the **Bab el Siq Triclinium**. It is thought that the two structures, one atop the other, are not associated, the Obelisk Tomb probably being of an earlier date. The Tomb's great doorway, crowned by four gigantic obelisks, leads into a sole compartment, off which five **sepulchres** radiate.

Bab el Siq Triclinium, below the Obelisk Tomb, is a different design. It was constructed in the archetypal Nabatean mode and has a large **central chamber** which

Above: Petra's Roman Theatre and thirty-three rows of seats which held 3,000 spectators.

reaches back over 7 metres (23 feet).

As you enter the Siq, note a set of six obelisk-shaped **carvings.** Various inscriptions accompany each one. The most significant refers to a man who had resided at *Requem* — the antiquated Semitic name for Petra — and, after dying in Jerash, was returned to Petra. During Nabatean times the Siq, with 100-metre-high (300-foot) walls, was the only entrance into Petra. **Fissures** run deep on either side of the track.

Sections of the Siq's 1st-century Nabatean **paving** have been discovered by excavation. Look for the **remains** of a shallow **channel,** that once ran the length of the Siq on the **left. Guttering,** parts of whose earthenware pipes can still be seen, conveyed water into Petra from the Springs of Moses. A selection of Nabatean and Greek **graffiti** adorns the walls. Note the **niches** hewn at irregular intervals where Rock Gods are thought to have been placed.

The Siq's walls, smoothed by time, give a fantastic cross-section of the natural grain of the sandstone. At one point the passageway goes from a wide breach to a dark chasm not more than a few feet across. Suddenly,

in the space of a few footsteps, you get your first glimpse of Petra's most fabled achievement, **El Khazneh**, the **Treasury**, carved from the rock. Khazneh, sculpted so deeply from the stone, has defied the weathering of time. It is largely due to its sheltered position, enclosed in the extension of the Siq. But the Treasury, as it came to be known, if not defiled by nature, was defiled by man. Iconoclasts have smashed the sculpted forms on the mighty façade, obliging us to guess at what the figures once depicted. Other vandals spent their time attacking the **urn** on top of the Treasury.

A myth circulated for a thousand years that the great urn housed the Pharaoh's treasure. He had allegedly filled the urn with his wealth, positioning it far from any man's grasp. Dozens of other hoards were said to have been concealed around the ruins making the locals distrustful of visitors. You will notice many **bullet holes** have peppered the upper reaches of the great monument. The Treasury thus gains its modern name from the legend, *Khazneh al Faroun*, which is translated as 'the Treasury of the Pharaoh'.

The building measures 28 metres (92 feet) across and, at its highest point, is almost 40 metres (131 feet) tall. Within the edifice there is a vast **chamber,** some 12 metres square. As you enter the room, with its blood-red walls, notice the **bowl** carved from the **top step.** A run-off **channel** leads to the **left,** giving credibility to the idea that El Khazneh was once a temple and the bowl was created where sacrifices were made.

There are conflicting views among scholars as to when, and by whom, El Khazneh was constructed. Discussion always returns to the building's style for evidence. Some say it was erected in the 1st, or even 2nd century AD; others argue that it was carved much earlier.

The Treasury bewilders travellers and experts, both by its great dimensions and by the enigmas which surround it — mysteries such as the purpose of niches on either side of the monument's doorway, arranged in a vertical design. They may have been carved during construction of the Treasury. Petra's mood changes with the light and can only be truly savoured by spending many hours or days roaming its splendour.

As you follow the **Outer Siq** you will notice the earthenware **gully** running the length of the craggy **wall,** which would have taken water further into the city. The Outer Siq widens to become much more than a mere gorge and, as you pass through it, you come across numerous **façades** in the steep passage walls. On the **left bluff** you soon arrive at the first of many immense **tombs.** Notice how only the tops of many **doorways** can be seen at ground level, a reminder of how the gorge filled with sand during the last millennia. Some façades have doorways, but no cavity or chambers behind. At the Outer Siq's widest point a **gully** runs abruptly off to the **south** (peeling off to the **left**). The **path,** which leads up an acute incline, takes you to **the High Place:** an ancient sacrificial site with an altar cut from the rock.

For those who can stand the strenuous climb the sweeping **view** of Petra is well worthwhile. The track leads firstly southwards to the **Lion Monument,** a **fountain** crafted in the form of a lion which once spurted water from the mouth.

Note, too, the remains of a stone **altar** adjacent to the **Lion Fountain.** Past the altar the track continues, leading to the **Garden Triclinium,** or the **Garden Temple Complex.** There are two free-standing **colonnades** still intact, a rarity in Petra, which form a portico, in front of which are the **remnants** of a **shrine.** As you look towards the Triclinium's portico you will notice a substantial **stone wall,** which braced a patio area on the upper level, the remains of which can still be seen.

Continuing on, one passes dozens of **wall niches** and a host of other minor signs of habitation, before arriving at the **Roman Soldier's Tomb,** and a further **Triclinium.** The Tomb's façade is certainly Roman and quite different from the classical Nabatean styles. The **entrance** leads into a substantial **chamber** which, in turn, has another **room** leading off to the **left.**

On the **opposite side** of the Roman Soldier's Tomb is the Triclinium. It is unique in that its **walls** are intricately sculpted with numerous **alcoves.** The site is all the more spectacular for the glowing seams of colour which meander about the walls. The Tomb and the Triclinium made up a much larger complex that experts are certain was encircled by a **colonnaded verandah.**

Petra has dozens of sacred sites, chosen by the Nabateans and those before them, as places of devotion and sacrifice. But perhaps the most important is the fabled **High Place,** known as *El Madbah* in Arabic. It was there that the sacred observances of the Nabateans were performed. On a windswept ridge, high above their city, the Nabatean people extolled their gods at the **platform** where immolations were made, although whether such sacrificial offerings were of beast or human is disputed. The **altar,** and indeed the whole site of the High Place is well-drained, allowing spilled blood to run away. Years of sandy wind

Opposite: El Deir, the Monastery, is one of Petra's most magnificent sights.

Top: Nabatean god carved into blood-red stone.

Above: Wind worn stones stand as monuments to the vanished civilisation of the Nabateans.

churning up the Outer Siq have caused havoc to its wondrous carvings, eroding the soft textured stone. Dozens of classical Nabatean **ruins** can now be seen on the **left** in an area that has come to be known as **The Street of Façades**. Some rock-hewn **chambers** whose **ceilings** are little higher than about 1.5 metres (5 feet) were probably used to house coffins.

The Outer Siq makes a sudden turn **northwards** and leads to the **Roman Theatre** on its **western wall.** It was built in typical Roman style, yet experts have suggested that it was actually constructed before the Roman annexation of Petra in AD 106. This is quite possible when we remember the considerable Roman influence on Nabatean society during the 1st century AD. The thirty-three **rows** of **seats** were capable of holding around 3,000 people. The audience peered down from their vantage carved from the rock to a **stage** almost 40 metres (131 feet) in diameter. The Theatre marks the last span of the Outer Siq; like a river running into the sea, it expands into Petra's great open area.

A number of residential and other buildings would have been packed together around the slopes of Petra. The Nabateans, famed for their carved constructions, were certainly capable of building free-standing structures as well.

It is well worth spending a few minutes exploring the formidable collection of **Royal Tombs** which are reached by a path from the Theatre. They exemplify the excellence in rock carving attained by the Nabateans.

The first of the group reached is the **Urn Tomb.** Dating it is a daunting task. Its characteristics flaunt both Nabatean and Roman idiosyncrasies. It is quite possible that the tomb was constructed during the latter Nabatean period for one of the royal leaders. Other than the building's great height, the most staggering element is the gargantuan **chamber** within. The room is 17 by 18 metres (56 by 59 feet) and is the largest of all hollowed cavities constructed by the Nabateans. It was redesigned as a place of Christian worship around AD 447 when it is thought that various internal partitions were removed.

During a recent excavation of the church,

the single largest collection of **written material** from ancient Jordan found to date, was discovered in the form of **papyri,** or **papyrus** scrolls. The 6th-century AD Greek documentary papyri — in all about 150 scrolls to date — shed new information on many aspects of ancient Jordanian culture and its relationship with foreign lands.

Just north of the Urn tomb is the **Silk Tomb**, which seems almost as if a great bucket of coloured inks had been cast across its façade. The rich hues of red have become all the more prominent as the sand in the wind has ravaged the front.

Beside the Silk Tomb lies the **Corinthian Tomb** in all its splendour. The upper section reminds one of El Khazneh, yet the lower segment is of a different architectural heritage. It has been suggested that the Corinthian Tomb is that of the royal leader in whose reign El Khazneh was carved.

The **Palace Tomb**, situated just to the north of the Corinthian Tomb, is yet another surprising example of Petra's architecture. Constructed in three distinct storeys, its sheer size must have impressed even its builders. It was so ambitious that the uppermost storey ran out of rock from which it could to be carved and had to be constructed with supplementary masonry. Within the Palace Tomb four mammoth **chambers** lie side by side with only the innermost pair interconnecting.

Activity in Petra, especially during Roman times, centred on the **Colonnaded Street** area. It is now reached from the extremity of the Outer Siq's continuation. The precinct would have been central to a variety of Roman shops and markets. As well as shopping areas there was a **Nymphaeum**, a public **fountain** at the **eastern end** of the Colonnaded Street and a conglomeration of temples, gates and royal buildings. Although some colonnades were recently restored, Colonnaded Street today is a far cry from the street the Romans built.

At the **western end**, with the Great Temple on the left and the **Winged Lion Temple** on the right, you find the **ruins** of the **Temenos Gate**. Although largely destroyed, one gets an indication of its original size and elegance by the amount and quality of the stones strewn about. The

gateway, constructed in the common Roman three-arched style, has fascinated architects and archaeologists who know it also as the **Monumental Arch**, or the **Triumphal Arch**. Experts have ascertained that the ruins were those of an **entranceway** that led into the expansive piazza of the mighty **Qasr el Bint**. The gateway was endowed with great doors. The Temenos forecourt to Qasr el Bint was covered with **flagstones,** some of which remain.

The substantial building *Qasr el Bint Faroun* — in Arabic 'Palace of the Pharoah's Daughter' — was first thought to be Roman. New evidence suggests it was put up by the Nabateans in the last years of the BC era. **Plasterwork** and **remnants** of another building on the site have led to the suggestion that the Qasr succeeded an earlier construction. The Qasr, which must have been awesome, demonstrates the Nabatean use of plaster and fresco work. More importantly, it demonstrates to the sceptical that the Nabateans were capable of creating free-standing buildings. Its original **portico** of four distinguished **columns** has tumbled. The large internal **arch** which remains looks as if it might collapse at any minute.

It seems that the Qasr was in use up to Roman annexation. Then the great edifice was set alight. What fire did not damage two immense earthquakes in the 4th and the 8th centuries did.

Guides point out the wooden **beams** that run horizontally along the **walls**, which may have been incorporated to absorb the stress of an earthquake. Whether this is true or not is uncertain. From Qasr el Bint Faroun it takes less than an hour to scale the **path** that leads to Petra's second most spectacular construction — after the Treasury — **El Deir, The Monastery**. For a feeling of Petra's true immensity and the sheer power of the rock, the trip is essential.

The path leads **north-west** up the hillside past numerous Nabatean monuments and sites. On the **left** you will see the **Lion Triclinium**. The structure, whose **lion figures** are just discernible, is said by some to be Roman because of the ornate carving. Lions are known to have been a powerful symbol of the Nabateans. The path lures you on round its steep bends and weaving

Above: The Urn Tomb, was perhaps the burial place of a Nabatean ruler. It was turned into a makeshift church in Byzantine times.

chamber into which light floods through the central **portal**. The Monastery, which is thought to have gained its name through the distinct **crosses** on the **back wall,** provides a superlative view. To the **south-east** Wadi Mousa nestles below, and the Wadi Araba can be seen wending its way between the Dead Sea and Aqaba. On the **south-west side** you will be able to make out the **white dome** of the **Tomb of Haroun,** the site where Moses' brother Aaron is said to have been interred.

Across from the Qasr el Bint a jumble of **steps** lead up to Petra's **Museum.** The room housing the small collection is the most monumental exhibit of all. Rich hues of sandstone dazzle the eyes and provide a spellbinding setting in which to browse. The room houses an assortment of Nabatean, Roman and Byzantine **objects** gathered around Petra. There are fragments of **pottery, glass** and **metal** excavated from digs about the ancient city, as well as a series of earthenware **water pipes** and **jewellery.**

The museum **walls** are so fragile that the slightest touch causes them to crumble. The museum is located on a ridge that proceeds round to the **left**, forming a natural parapet. High above the ground you glimpse hundreds of caves peppering the rocks, where you might see goats grazing.

Four hundred metres (1,312 feet) **west** of the museum is **El Habis** (which means 'The Prison'), also known as the Citadel. It takes no more than a few minutes to reach the spot, to the **south** of which a Crusader **fortress** once stood, looking down directly onto Qasr el Bint. The castle, now in ruins, probably never saw much action. Perhaps, more importantly than the Crusader ruins at El Habis, is the existence of a sacrificial area with **altar** and **basins.**

One of the single most important sites in Petra from an archaeological standpoint, is the **Turkamaniya Tomb,** to the far **north** of the city in what is known as **Wadi Turkamaniya**. The tomb, on the **west side** of the valley, is hollowed from the rock. Its soft stone façade has split leaving only the upper portion hanging. It has two large **chambers** (one behind the other), and was once the central part of a much larger complex. Yet its most important feature is the rare **inscription** in Nabatean script adorning

turns past many relics of the Nabateans. As you climb higher and higher, and your legs begin to tire, you get a superb view of Petra below. There are few sights so treasured by travellers to the Middle East.

For those not exhilarated by the magnificence of the landscape, the sight of El Deir, The Monastery, is certain to delight. Its façade, measuring over 46 metres (151 feet) wide and 40 metres (131 feet) high, gives it the edge over even the Treasury. Unlike El Khazneh, its crowning urn is not backed against the rock. This is the easiest way of telling the two buildings apart. The sweeping plain in front of the Monastery, flattened presumably in Nabatean times, indicates that great masses of people once flocked to the site. Within El Deir there is a single vast

Above: A marvel of ingenuity — supposedly the shrine in which Aaron, Moses' brother, was buried.

the façade. It is amazing that the words have not been erased by erosion. They tell of how the tomb, its contents and surroundings, are the undeniable property of the god Dusares. A pledge to this deity is followed by a statement that no man other than the one contracted to be interred in the tomb, can be buried at the site.

One kilometre (half-a-mile) **north** of the **Petra Forum Hotel** are the **ruins** of a **Crusader castle** at **Wu'eira**. You can just about see the site from the road that continues from Petra to **Beidha**. The fortress, built during the early years of the 11th century, seems to have been deserted before Saladin's army captured it in 1189.

The castle, which was the primary Crusader stronghold in Petra, was known to the Christians as *La Vallee de Moise*, a name echoed in Wadi Mousa village. The fortress is impressive even after the marvels of Petra. Entry is across a **bridge,** spanning a **moat,** before continuing to a **gate-room** sculpted from the rock. Water **cisterns, towers** and vaulted **ceilings** can be seen.

The **apse** of what was almost certainly a Crusader **church** still remins although little

else of this once grand structure. **Siq el Barid**, just a short distance further **north** from Wu'eira, has been called a Nabatean *suburb*. Its importance came from its strategic position on the confluence of several major caravan routes. The wealth that the small community achieved is reflected in its buildings. A great deal of water was collected in giant cisterns, less than a kilometre (half-a-mile) east of the settlement.

Siq el Barid gains its name from the modest **gorge** that leads into the area. The most interesting features are the temple's **portico**, with two renovated free-standing **pillars,** and the **Painted House**, which contains remains of ornately-decorated **plasterwork.** It is seen best on the **ceiling**, where cupids fly with their bows and arrows amid a profusion of vines and fruit.

A kilometre (half-a-mile) further from Siq el Barid, to the **south-west,** is one of the Petra region's most important archaeological sites known as *Beidha*. Rare **pottery** dating to about 6800 BC have been discovered among the ruins of this Neolithic community. No less than six levels of Neolithic construction have been identified.

Aqaba: Harbour from the Desert Sands

What greater contrast to the scorching desert lands of eastern Jordan, or to the lifeless waters of the Dead Sea, could there be than Aqaba? Where deserts part, nature has formed a paradise, framed by mountains, bathed in rustling palms, its waters teeming with fish.

It was not until the last decade, or so, that archaeologists were able to fill in some of the details of Aqaba's past. Recently discovered ancient sites have encouraged new theories as to who once inhabited the area, but there still remains one intriguing mystery. Why, during the course of the last five millenia, have the historical settlements at Aqaba moved steadily from the north-west to the south-east — finally stopping at the surviving castle just north of today's port?

For more than five millennia man has settled on these shores, providing a vital link in the chain of trading posts through the ancient world. Ships ventured from Africa, Asia, and the Mediterranean. It is this rich cultural broth which has shaped Aqaba.

Vessels from across the world's great oceans still ply the azure waters of the Red Sea to Aqaba. But this city is more than just a port. Known as Ezion Geber in biblical times, its age is evident in the winding streets and a Crusader fortress; its charm permeates through shops and cafés where generations of locals sip their bitter-rich Arabian coffee. And Aqaba is also an aquatic sports playground, offering scuba diving, snorkeling and waterskiing.

Getting there

The main road into Aqaba approaches the city from the north-east. This is the extension of the great Desert Highway that heads southwards from Amman and Ma'an.

Amman is 335 kilometres (208 miles), and Ma'an 121 kilometres (75 miles) to the north. Another road arrives at Aqaba from the Dead Sea and the occupied territorial frontier along Wadi Araba. A short stretch of highway links Aqaba to the Saudi Arabian border directly to the south. Aqaba's recent boost in tourism is partly due to the opening of a border crossing between Jordan and Israel nearby. The crossing — known as The Arava Crossing — permits reasonably free access between the two countries. If you plan to make use of this route, make sure well in advance that the checkpoints are indeed open. They are usually operational from Sunday to Thursday (inclusive) from 08.00 to 18.00. On Muslim New Year and on the Jewish festival of Yom Kippur, the crossing is closed. A bus leaves Aqaba bus station for the border on a frequent basis. Having actually crossed into Israel, one takes another bus to the neighbouring town of Eilat. A nominal fee is levied for passengers travelling across the border via the Arava Crossing. Ensure that you have the necessary entrance (or return) visa if you are crossing between Jordan and Israel. Remember also that many Arab countries will not permit the owner of a passport bearing an Israeli stamp into their country. The Israelis, of course, will refrain from stamping your passport should you request it. But, if your passport bears the stamp of a Jordanian border post adjoining Israel, an Arab country is likely to put two and two together.

Where to stay

There is a range of hotels, clubs and resorts to choose from. The mid-1990s has seen the establishment of new hotels and serviced apartments. See Listings.

Sightseeing

On the road which now leads to **Aqaba's International Airport** there came to light a small but crucial site which archaeologists have dubbed **Tell Maquss**. The remains date back to about 3500 BC, from the Chalcolithic era. It is thought that the community specialised in copper smelting. The **remains** of brick-built **furnaces** were unearthed, as well as fragments of **copper, slag heaps** and **ingots**.

Dr Lutfi Khalil, an eminent Jordanian archaeologist in charge of the Tell Maquss excavation, believes smelted copper was brought from other areas. The smelters

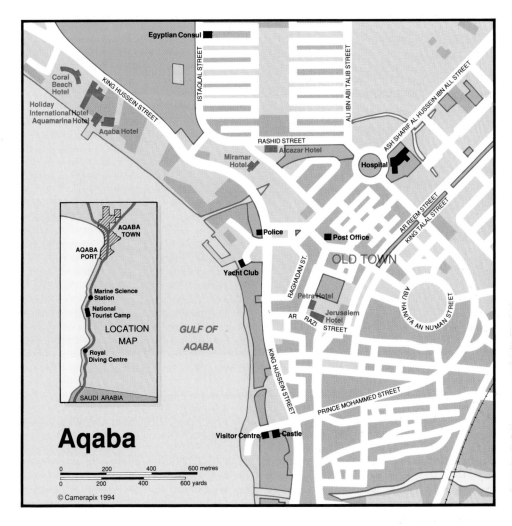

Coral Beach Hotel
Holiday International Hotel
Aquamarina Hotel
Aqaba Hotel
Egyptian Consul
ISTAQLAL STREET
ALI IBN ABI TALIB STREET
ASH SHARIF AL HUSSEIN IBN ALI STREET
KING HUSSEIN STREET
RASHID STREET
Miramar Hotel
Alcazar Hotel
Hospital
AR REEM STREET
KING TALAL STREET
Police
Post Office
OLD TOWN
Yacht Club
RAGHADAN ST.
Petra Hotel
Jerusalem Hotel
ABU HANIFA AN NUMAN STREET
AR RAZI STREET
KING HUSSEIN STREET
PRINCE MOHAMMED STREET
Visitor Centre
Castle

AQABA TOWN
AQABA PORT
Marine Science Station
National Tourist Camp
LOCATION MAP
Royal Diving Centre
SAUDI ARABIA

GULF OF AQABA

Aqaba

0   200   400   600 metres
0   200   400   600 yards

© Camerapix 1994

were possibly those of King Solomon, who had such sites in the area.

Another important site nearby known as **Tell el Kheleifeh** dates to the first millennium BC. A great conglomeration of square-shaped buildings nestle together, some built on top of the remains of others. The settlement was certainly inhabited by the Edomites and would have been an important base on the major trade route.

At a site 2 kilometres south of the Tell el Kheleifeh and just north-west of the ancient **Islamic town** of Ayla, a 1996 archaeological excavation identified significant urban remains of a **fortified** city called **Aila** in the Nabatean-Roman-Byzantine era. In the 2nd century AD Aila's strategic importance at the south-eastern frontier of the **Roman**

Empire was supported by: the building of the **Via Nova Traiana,** a road linking **Damascus, Amman** and **Petra** with the Red Sea; the construction of a Roman **Fort** just north of present-day Aqaba at a place called **Qaa'es Sa'adiyeen;** and, at the end of the 3rd century AD, the transfer from **Jerusalem** of a thousand-man garrison, the **Legion X Fretensis.** Different areas of this site have the remains of houses with 2-metre-high **mud-brick walls,** numerous **bread ovens,** existensive **ceramics, baking** and **metal** industries and the remains of part of the **fortification wall.** One of the most exciting finds was the discovery of a 4th-century AD **double-storeyed building** which has been tentatively identified as **a church.** If confirmed, it makes it the earliest-known church

Above: Aquamarina Hotel in the Red Sea town of Aqaba, one of the many ideal resorts along a glorious coastline.

in Jordan and one of the oldest in the world.

Of various Arab descriptions, the most significant is that penned by geographer Shams ad Din Muqaddasi. He ventured from Jerusalem to Ayla in the 10th century and described it as 'a city on a branch of the China Sea. Great in prosperity with its palms and fish, it is the port of Palestine and the storehouse of Hijaz.'

Muqaddasi noted that Ayla was not the true settlement, which he referred to as lying in ruins close by. For this reason he called the settlement **Wayla**.

The medieval town that Muqaddasi would have stayed in is now situated just **north** along the shore from the modern city. It was unearthed in the mid-1980s by a joint American-Jordanian team of archaeologists. In the medieval settlement a vast **wall,** complete with **turrets** and a large **gateway,** was excavated.

Over the main **arch** where the great gate was once positioned, the Qur'anic *Ayat al-Kursi*, commonly known as the *Throne Verse,* was inscribed. The town was constructed in the classic Islamic axial plan. Two **walls** of

a merchant's house remain, where once fine frescoes existed.

The 12th century saw the construction of Aqaba's **Crusader fortress** which remains largely intact today. The Crusaders, who called the settlement Helim, housed a relatively small garrison of troops at the fortress, at the **southern** end of the town.

One main **gate** leads into a **vestibule** that, in turn, proceeds into the central **courtyard.** Look above the main doorway before entering, there is a rather grand **coat of arms** straddling the area between the two front **towers.** It is the crest of the Hashemites, placed there after the First World War, on the spot from where boiling oil may have once been poured down.

On the sides of the front towers are two Mamluk circular **panels.** The brick-red paint that once covered the Mamluk **vestibule** inscriptions coats the magical lettering. **Steps** lead down to **dungeons** from the two rooms astride the vestibule.

If you enter the fortress and climb the **battlements** you can actually stand behind the **Hashemite crest**. Endless **chambers**

Above: The Hashemite Coat of Arms engraved into the outer wall of Aqaba Fort. The capture of the fort during the Arab Rebellion opened a supply route for freedom fighters.

and **antechambers,** perhaps used as storage rooms, are dotted about. After visiting the great fortresses of Kerak and Shobak, Aqaba's castle seems much more modest. In various first floor chambers you will see that the ceiling timbers are nothing more than the sawn-up trunks of palm trees. A sprawling eucalyptus tree gives the central courtyard welcome shade, its leaves rustle in the breeze which streams off the gulf.

Behind the fortress, almost on the water's edge, is Aqaba's **Visitor's Centre** and **museum.** Brochures with comprehensive information on the city are available. The museum was once home to the Sharif Hussein bin Ali (King Hussein's great-grandfather). It is well laid out and houses many interesting artefacts unearthed at Aqaba. The *Ayat al-Kursi* **lintel** from the main gate of medieval Aqaba is displayed there, and Nabatean, Roman, Byzantine, and Egyptian **articles** as well as items from across the Arab World. A selection of early Islamic Stealite **lamps** are unusual and look curiously modern.

Aqaba's small size means that in just a few minutes you can go from quiet white beaches and blue waters to the commotion of the modern **port.** There, **containers** are piled high beside the great loading **gantries** which look out like sentinels down the Red Sea. Ships docking at Aqaba have rust-covered bows after months at sea.

Near the **port** is the new **ferry terminal** for the **vessels** crossing to **Nweibeh,** in Egypt, twice daily. The first ferry leaves Aqaba at 12.00 and you have to be there a couple of hours beforehand to clear passport control and other formalities. At the same time its sister ferry leaves Nweibeh, and the two pass halfway. The second departure leaves Aqaba — and Nweibeh — at around 18.00. During the pilgrimage season more boats are laid on. The Jett bus company has a bus which leaves Amman each morning for Cairo by way of the Aqaba-Nweibeh ferry. An Egyptian bus travels the route via Aqaba to Amman, and on to Damascus.

The public **aquarium** is by the ferry terminal. An unusual feature is that water is pumped directly from the gulf to the aquarium, and then out again. This means corals can be grown, a rare development in

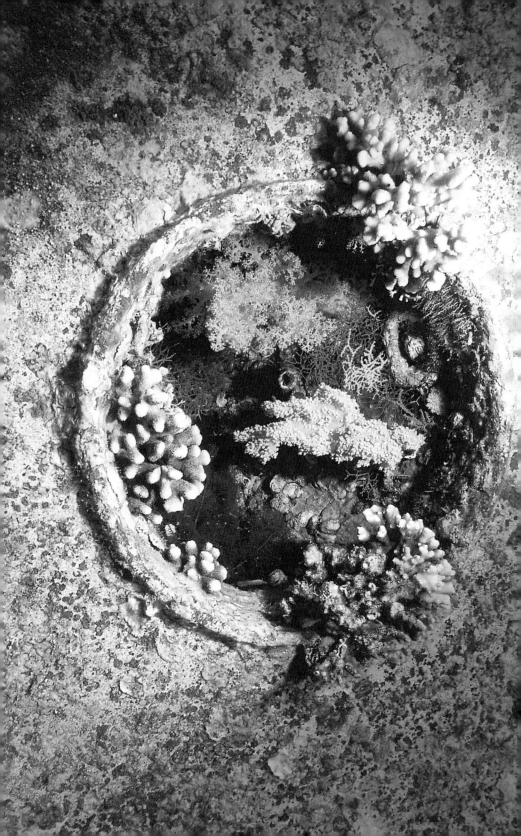

aquaria. The tanks, with their glistening fish and plentiful plantlife, give an insight into what lies beneath the Red Sea's surface. The aquarium is open every day from 08.00 to 15.30 (except Thursday when it is open from 09.00 until 16.30). There is a nominal entry fee.

Near the aquarium is the **Royal Aqaba Yacht Club** with its lines of pristine **yachts**. The club, which has a total of 150 berths in its **marina**, offers superb facilities as well as a good vantage point for the Red Sea.

By far the most enthralling area of Aqaba for exploration is the **old town**. Little has changed there since medieval times and the tempo is that of a bygone age. People wander the winding **alleyways,** or sit in **cafés** eating humus and sipping sweet tea, waiting for evening. The markets are filled with a wealth of different shops. Many are

Above: The waters of the Gulf of Aqaba give life to countless species of marine plants.

Right: Weird growth spins a crimson fantasia from a coral head.

Opposite: Spectacular array of bright corals flourish in the porthole of a wreck off the coast of Aqaba.

laden with **gold jewellery**, their windows lined with thousands of glinting **bracelets.**

In the **southernmost** corner of the **main square** an opening leads into the vegetable and fruit market. It is like peeping through a keyhole into the pages of *A Thousand and One Nights* with heaps of giant **water-melons,** piles of **tomatoes, pumpkins** and mounds of exotic **spices.** Continue down past the small hotels and shops, and follow the smell of baking **bread.**

As one alley interlinks with another you will encounter the bakeries. You can watch the production line that produces steaming round pittas. One man rolls out balls of dough, another places them on wooden palates. Then they are shovelled into the open oven for three minutes before coming

out crispy brown. All manner of other pastries are stacked about.

Diving Paradise

Few places can match Aqaba for diving with its unpolluted and tranquil waters. Because the **Gulf of Aqaba** is almost an inland sea means that, although the water is deep, it stays warm and calm. Aqaba's air temperatures range from 20°C in winter to a pleasant 24°C in summer, though it can soar to 40°C. The water is even warmer, with temperatures ranging from 20°C in winter to 26°C in summer. Prevailing winds from Wadi Araba to the north keep the surface clean. The water around Aqaba is free from strong currents which also helps keep it crystal clear, ideal for underwater photography. The profusion of exotic fish and plant life makes the region unbeatable for serious divers and snorkelers. Over 140 species of **coral** have been identified, among them numerous species endemic to the region.

The four main diving centres at Aqaba are: **Aquamarina**, **Sea Star**, **Red Sea** and the **Royal**, which is the only government-

Above: Colourful example of the complexity and shape of living coral.

Opposite top: Clownfish among the tentacles of its host anemone.

Opposite below: Scuba diver mixes with marine life a few metres offshore at Aqaba.

run diving organisation. You may be asked for documents to confirm your level of competence. Most major diving certificates are respected. Minimum age for restricted diving is twelve years, and full unrestricted diving can begin at the age of fifteen.

There are many other aquatic activities: **paddleboats, sailing boats, windsurfers, rowing boats** and **canoes** can be hired. Try waterskiing on the glass-surfaced gulf. Fishing from the shore is excellent due to deep water near the edge, but fishing by boat can be arranged.

A new **diving area** called **Yemenia** is being developed **south** of the main shore-line in the direction of the **Saudi Arabian border**, about 20 kilometres (12 miles) away. With an assortment of watersport facilities, **hotels**, and **restaurants** the complex is generally known as the **South Coast**.

Much of the coastline now in Jordan was a gift to the country from Saudi Arabia during the 1970s. It became vital to the Hashemite Kingdom following the loss of the West Bank.

The Gulf of Aqaba, like its big sister the Red Sea, is actually a vast water-filled cleft and a part of the Great Rift Valley. This rift extends through the Middle East from the very north of Jordan, through eastern Africa to join Lake Malawi. The fact that the Red Sea — and the Gulf of Aqaba — are part of the rift, means that they are both extremely deep. The Gulf of Aqaba alone plunges down more than 1,900 metres (6,234 feet).

This gives rise to a unique situation. Wind blows gently across the surface, forcing the top-most water to head southwards while, at the same time, cooler water rises upward from the deep. A cycle of cool currents is formed, enhancing the marine life. Temperature variation between the summer and winter months is so negligible in real terms that the coral grows very well indeed.

Aqaba's diving is classed as tropical, and as there are no cities pumping sewage into the water, marine life is unspoilt.

Opposite: Chorus of red and yellow beneath the Red Sea.
Overleaf: Sunset bids golden farewell to a glorious day in Aqaba.

Above: Youngster plays in the dazzling waters of the Gulf of Aqaba.

Coral reefs at Aqaba are protected from spear-fishing and human destruction and the area in front of large tourist hotels at the extreme **northern end** of the gulf is generally reserved for watersports other than scuba diving, to protect divers from power boats and paddleboats, and vice-versa.

Work is being done to further enhance the environment of Aqaba's marine life. Prince Abdullah pioneered a project in 1985 to sink a **cargo ship** in the Gulf, to form an **artificial coral reef.** It lies some 30 metres (98 feet) below the surface, with the top **deck** only submerged by 12 metres (39 feet). The wreck created one of the finest artificial reefs on the Red Sea. The Royal Family, who are deeply committed to the preservation of the Gulf's aquatic life, have ensured that strict controls are kept on ships which dock at Aqaba. Many of the Royal Family are keen divers.

The birthday of King Hussein on 14 November, is marked each year by a **Water Festival**. The king usually attends the event which involves water-sport competitions. Other festivals are held throughout the year.

Wadi Rum: Valley of the Moon

The main route to Wadi Rum, and the village of Rum, branches east off the Aqaba to Ma'an road, about 5 kilometres (3 miles) south of Quweira.

To the Arabs Wadi Rum is known simply as The Valley of the Moon. To travellers who have roamed its vast landscape, Wadi Rum seems more akin to the surface of a distant planet than to anything on earth. The combination of its immensity, colour and awe-inspiring shapes creates an atmosphere that is almost supernatural.

Lawrence of Arabia, who held Wadi Rum in high esteem, wrote: 'Our little caravan grew self-conscious, and fell dead quiet, afraid and ashamed to flaunt its smallness in the presence of the stupendous hills . . . . Landscapes in childhood's dreams were so vast and silent.' (T E Lawrence: *The Seven Pillars of Wisdom*).

Getting there

When driving to Wadi Rum from Aqaba, you will notice the tan-coloured landscape, devoid of vegetation, with thick veins of copper ore running along the low-lying hills. (King Solomon's copper mines were not far off). A few goats forage in their endless quest for grass. Then the road to the village of Rum divides off to the east. Alongside it runs the Aqaba to Mahattat Hittiyya railway which joins up with the Hijaz line. This line is a freight line only.

Sightseeing

As you near Wadi Rum, look to the **left,** or **north,** and you will see the **Seven Pillars of Wisdom**, where T E Lawrence had his camp. These natural **columns** are huge, and vary in height. The true size of the **mountains** is only realised when a human or animal form gives the vastness a perspective. If you stop to look at the Seven Pillars, the tiny **settlement** of **Rum** is visible on the horizon.

Above: The Seven Pillars of Wisdom en route to Wadi Rum made famous by T E Lawrence, who pitched camp there.

Opposite: Sheer rock faces, many hundreds of metres high, attract mountain climbers to Wadi Rum from across the globe.

Above: Rock carving near Wadi Rum.

The perfect way to see Wadi Rum is by hot air balloon. Flights take off at sunrise for a one hour ride during the 'ballooning season' (March-November). For more information, call Balloons Over Jordan, on 825224.

Life does not seem to have changed in Rum for a long time. The pace is slow, and tourist activities tend to centre on the **rest house.** No more than a cluster of Bedouin **tents** and basic **houses** make up the village. The rest house has no rooms for visitors but offers good food, including the most excellent humus and salad.

As Jordan's cities, towns and tourist sites continue to bustle with visitors from every land, one can seek solace and unknown tranquillity at Wadi Rum. This place, whatever one's interests or foibles, offers an Arabia of long ago. This is an Arabia which has not changed in ten thousand years. For all his conquest, man has hardly dented the surrounding landscape. Although rumours constantly abound that Rum is to have a hotel at its core as yet it does not seem likely.

It would be a waste for anyone to visit Rum and not venture far into the *wadi* (valley). There is no feeling to compare with being in the wilderness, with pinkish sand beneath your feet and no sound but the wind cutting across the surface of the rocks. Daybreak at Wadi Rum must surely be one of life's greatest experiences.

As the first rays of morning light sear the horizon, they bring life to a landscape whose likeness seems more lunar than earthly. With its rosy, yet pallid, complexion, the sky is vast and seems as forbidding as the wilderness beneath it. Dragging unending shadows in their wake, three specks of life can be seen between a range of vast flat-topped pinnacles heading in your direction.

An hour later the sky has changed, to an ocean of indigo, yet the travellers are still distant. By the time they have arrived, a fire in the Bedouin encampment is kindled and a pot of steaming coffee brewed. Leaving their camels outside, the **riders,** venerable warriors of the **Desert Patrol,** sit for refreshment.

The camels become camouflaged in the backdrop of the giant, square, tooth-like

Above: Bedouin camp in the vast landscape of Wadi Rum.

mountains (each of which is known by its own name). By noon the sun is extremely hot and gnaws at the skin. Cover the head with a scarf for protection.

The Bedouin who make their home in Wadi Rum have endless tales of how it came to be. They speak of a full moon, not so long ago, so bright that they had to cover their eyes from being blinded. If possible, take your own vehicle or you will have to beg a lift, and won't have much freedom.

You can hire a camel, or even a Land Rover in the village. If you ride a camel, you might want to take along an extra blanket as your thighs can get sore from rubbing. Beware of the sun. When you set out it might not seem hot, but as it gets higher it is capable of burning your neck and face in seconds. There are no mosquitoes but the flies will hunt you down mercilessly.

Some distance the other side of Rum there is a considerable quantity of **Thamudic carvings** in the **rock faces** of various fissures. The main ones are a couple of kilometres out of Rum. But as wondrous as the Thamudic carvings are, the natural grains of

the rocks themselves make a stunning sight.

During shooting of the film *Lawrence of Arabia* at Wadi Rum, director David Lean insisted that every piece of scrub be plucked from the landscape so as to give a sense of wild, unbroken desert. Look around and you can imagine what a daunting task this must have been.

As you enter Rum you will pass the small **fort** which looks perfect for Beau Geste. It is home to the elite **Desert Patrol**, whose corps watch over and protect much of Jordan's **eastern deserts**. Visitors are always welcomed and, in the ritualistic fashion of the desert, offered a cup of cardamom-flavoured coffee, hot sweet tea — or both.

Wadi Rum's immensity is hard to leave. The longer you stay, the more attached you become — and long for it when you have gone. The Valley of the Moon makes man tremble at nature's power and majesty.

Overleaf: Cliffs and mountains of Wadi Rum, Valley of the Moon.

The Desert Palaces

Stretching east from Amman is a desert region bewildering in its size and ruthless climate; a place of sand and barren basalt landscapes which bear witness to ancient glories. Nomadic man has roamed these desolate wastes for thousands of years and as they moved across the landscape of what today is eastern Jordan, they left in stone a reminder of their presence.

The Ummayed Caliphs of the Early Islamic era, who cherished the hard desert life, built a string of palaces, hunting lodges, baths, meeting places, caravanserais and fortresses, in what were then the farthest reaches of the desert. Known collectively as the Desert Castles or Desert Palaces, the constructions demonstrate the best of early Islamic ingenuity. Their water-harnessing devices and reservoirs made it possible for man to travel through, and live in, one of the most austere environments on earth.

Some buildings, such as Qasr Kharana look like castles — hence the generality of Desert Castle — but were almost certainly intended as palaces. Indeed, the Arabic term *Qasr* means *Castle* or *Palace*.

Getting there

Many of these monuments of Ummayed design are located directly east of Amman, and can be reached easily from the capital. Others, such as Qasr Tuba or the ruins at Bayir, involve a much lengthier expedition. If you are travelling to remote castles take plenty of water and petrol, and use a 4WD vehicle with a guide. There is no greater feeling than arriving at Tuba after the long dusty trip over the bumpy desert trail. In a single day several sites can be visited. One suggested route is the road south-east from Amman to Azraq. It will take you past several castles including Kharana and Amra. After lunch in Azraq, you can continue either on the road via Hallabat to

Above: Crumbling elegance of Qasr Mushatta beside the international airport of Amman. The palace was never completed.

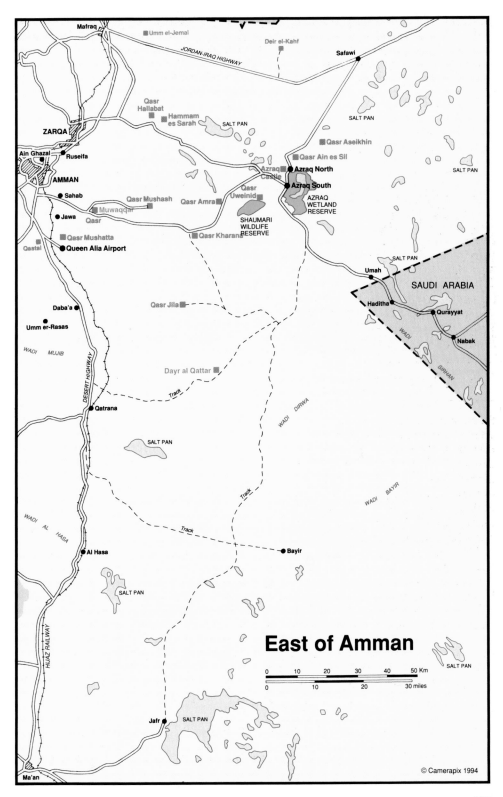

Mafraq
Umm el-Jemal
Deir el-Kahf
JORDAN-IRAQ HIGHWAY
Safawi
SALT PAN
Qasr Hallabat
Hammam es Sarah
SALT PAN
Qasr Aseikhin
ZARQA
Qasr Ain es Sil
SALT PAN
Ain Ghazal
Ruseifa
Azraq Castle
Azraq North
AMMAN
Qasr Uweinid
Azraq South
Sahab
Qasr Mushash
Qasr Amra
AZRAQ WETLAND RESERVE
Muwaqqar
Jawa
Qasr
SHAUMARI WILDLIFE RESERVE
Qasr Mushatta
Qasr Kharana
Qastal
Queen Alia Airport
SALT PAN
Umah
SAUDI ARABIA
Daba'a
Qasr Jila
Haditha
Qurayyat
Umm er-Rasas
Nabak
WADI MUJIB
DESERT HIGHWAY
WADI SIRHAN
Dayr al Qattar
WADI DIRWA
Track
WADI AL HASA
Qatrana
SALT PAN
Track
WADI BAYIR
Track
Al Hasa
Bayir
SALT PAN

East of Amman

HIJAZ RAILWAY
SALT PAN

| 0 | 10 | 20 | 30 | 40 | 50 Km |
| 0 | | 10 | | 20 | 30 miles |

SALT PAN
Jafr
SALT PAN

Ma'an

© Camerapix 1994

173

Zarqa, and then Amman: or proceed north from Azraq to the Jordan-Iraq highway. This takes you past Deir el Kahf and Umm el-Jemal to Mafraq from where you can continue south to Amman.

Qastal

Although the **palace** of **Qastal** would once have been many days' travel from any town of significant size, now it is probably the easiest of all the desert palaces to get to. While it lay dormant over the centuries, the surrounding development steadily encroached. The palace complex is now no more than 100 metres **west** of the multi-lane **Amman** to **Ma'an Desert Highway**. The capital is 25 kilometres (15 miles) to the **north**, with **Queen Alia International Airport** a stone's throw to the **east**.

Qastal, which gives its name to the **modern village** adjacent to it, is one of the oldest of Ummayed palaces. What's more, it is still almost complete. Walking around the site, you get a sense of the community which existed there. The **remains** include a complete range of buildings and facilities, such as a **mosque, central palace, cemetery**, small **houses, baths,** a **reservoir** and even a **dam**.

Scholars suggest that its name *Qastal* comes from the Latin word *castellum* meaning fortress or castle. This possibility becomes all the more intriguing when you note that Qastal's layout is similar to that of a Roman stronghold.

The palace, which was lavishly decorated with fine stone **carvings**, measured almost 70 metres square. Along the **walls** were a total of 12 semi-circular **turrets** with round **towers** in each corner. The **central courtyard** housed a substantial subterranean **water tank,** around which were located a large assortment of **chambers.**

As in many of the desert palaces, the decorative work in Qastal was extravagant. Stucco **plasterwork,** mosaic **panels** with elaborate illustrations and ornate **carvings** embellished the interior of the palace. The rooms themselves were well appointed, and anything but ordinary. An upper auditorium was designed with three apses.

The Ummayed Caliph Abd el Malik ibn Marwan, one of the most formidable builders of the Early Islamic era, probably had Qastal constructed. Among his other feats of architecture was the magnificent Dome of the Rock in Jerusalem.

Gravestones at Qastal indicate that the complex was in use at least into the Abbasid era (which spanned from AD 750 to 969).

A little **north** of where Qastal's palace stands is the community **mosque**. Strangely, it is not orientated exactly eastwards toward Mecca. Of particular importance is the shrine's **minaret** which is certainly one of the oldest built during the Early Islamic era.

Another notable feature of Qastal is the rare Early Muslim **graveyard**, located **south-west** of the palace. It is the oldest Muslim cemetery in Jordan, and some of the tombstones are positioned in the direction of Jerusalem. Several gravestones from Qastal are now exhibited in the Archaeological Museum in Madaba, together with some of the palace's mosaics.

Like the other desert palaces, Qastal only survived through accumulating water. Over the Desert Highway, about one kilometre east of Qastal, is the vast stone **Ummayed dam**, constructed to retain rainwater. With a capacity of around two million cubic metres, the dam is about 400 metres (437 yards) in length. Ummayed ingenuity becomes apparent when you realise that the dam area was formed from the quarry which itself supplied the stone for Qastal's palace.

Qasr Mushatta

Qasr Mushatta is extraordinary because of its grandeur and construction, its colossal size and its amazing location. Like Qastal, Mushatta was once a long way from any-where. Now it could not be more on top of things, as it is situated right at the end of **Queen Alia International Airport's** north runway.

To get to Mushatta, you have to drive around the 13-kilometre (8-mile) perimeter of the airport. Do not be put off by the army sentry boxes and road checks; you will be waved through. Few visitors make it to

Above: Desert Palaces demonstrated remarkable early architectural ingenuity.

Mushatta these days and, ironically in view of its new central location, it is rather ignored. The great lamps, used until recently for the Sound and Light display, are broken.

Mushatta is square in shape, with its immense yellow **brick walls** stretching 144 metres (158 yards) in each direction. At least 23 **round towers** nestled along the walls. The palace is usually attributed to the Ummayed Caliph Walid II, who would have constructed it between AD 743 and AD 744. It was never completed. A single entrance led through the **south wall** into the palace, which must have looked delightful.

It is worth visiting Mushatta at sunset as the last rays illuminate the exquisite brickwork. These fired bricks form **vaulted ceilings**, which seem almost as if they were built yesterday. And although Mushatta is not in a good state of repair, much of the brickwork is still standing after over a thousand years of wear and tear.

Another page in Mushatta's history was added in 1904, when the magnificent carved geometric designs and floral patterns were removed and presented by the Turkish Sultan Abdul Hamid to German Kaiser

Wilhelm. The relics were taken to Berlin, where they were damaged during World War II.

Qasr Muwaqqar

From **Amman,** take the **Sahab** to **Azraq** road **eastwards** past the **industrial area**. As the highway presses into the desert, leaving the clustered city buildings behind, you enter the small town of **Muwaqqar** after about 25 minutes of driving. It is no more than about 14 kilometres (9 miles) **north-east** of Qasr Mushatta.

You may have to ask the friendly people of Muwaqqar exactly where the remains of the Qasr are. The palace once stood on a peak above the crossroads of several ancient desert tracks. We know, from the Kufic-inscribed **water gauge,** once in a huge water **cistern** nearby, that Muwaqqar was constructed by the Ummayed Caliph Yazid II ibn Abd el Malik (AD 719-724). Little now remains of the palace. Close to where it was built are the even more archaic **ruins** of a **Byzantine settlement** which has been partially excavated. Fragments of **mosaic flooring** and a few decorated **lintels** have been unearthed. Many of the **wells** still used at Muwaqqar are of Roman origin.

On the plain below, the capacious **water cistern** is still used when there is rain. The reservoir indicates, by size and design, Muwaqqar's importance during the Ummayed period as a caravanserai. This cistern, which has two flights of **steps** leading down to it, was excavated in 1952 by a joint Jordanian-American team.

The Mayor of Muwaqqar tells of the 1930s when his father built a house in the town. He used an ancient Ummayed lintel above the door, inscribed in Kufic writing with the *Throne Verse* from the Qur'an. He remembers also when the stone water gauge still stood in Muwaqqar's water cistern, before being taken off to the Archaeological Museum in Amman.

Qasr Mushash

Less than 20 kilometres (12 miles) **north-east** of Muwaqqar are the **ruins** of the **Ummayed settlement** of **Mushash**. A small **road** leads to the remains, which are just **north** of the **Sahab** to **Azraq road**. There, the Department of Antiquities discovered the remnants of **18 buildings**, fashioned from **stone blocks**.

The largest of the edifices that once stood at Mushash may have been a palace. It was square in shape with walls over 25 metres (27 yards) in length. The **central courtyard** was encircled by 13 square **rooms**, the largest of which were to the **right** of the **main entrance** and on the **west wall,** opposite the entrance. The sheer size of the Mushash complex is perhaps its most significant feature. The remains are sprawled over an area of more than 2 kilometres (one mile).

Qasr Kharana

Kharana is located **south** of the **Sahab** to **Azraq road**, forming a line with Mushash and Muwaqqar. It is 55 kilometres (34 miles) **east** of Amman, and in good condition. An assortment of tall **radio pylons** on the other side of the highway mark the spot. These create a bizarre contrast to the ancient **Ummayed palace.**

Qasr Kharana, with its imposing **walls, arrow slits** and panoramic **views,** looks like a castle, but experts think that it was built as a palace. A painted **Kufic inscription** above a **door** on the upper level is dated September AD 711, though the building is older. A variety of **stones** in the **main entrance,** inscribed with Greek letters, may well indicate that Kharana was erected on a Roman or Byzantine site.

Although the main walls of the palace are no more than 35 metres (38 yards) long, the impression is of substantial size and strength. This is created partly by the second storey, but more because of the lack of other structures on the open plain. A **circular tower** is constructed at each corner, and a **semi-circular tower** marks the centre of each wall. A pair of semi-circular towers flank the only **entrance,** which is to the **south.** The upper storey of the outer wall is adorned with a kind of herring-bone brick design, as are the towers. The outer stones are still covered with plaster.

American explorer and adventurer Gray Hill was one of the first Westerners to write about Kharana, in 1896. He was sure it was a Crusader fortress, rather than a palace. More recently, in 1979, Kharana was surveyed and excavated by American archaeologist Stephen Urice.

The towers at Kharana are not large enough to have been effective defence and may have been built as buttresses against the walls. The arrow slits are cosmetic, as their inside edges are not wide enough to allow an archer sufficient visibility. They are also too high from the floor.

The ground and upper storey have an impressive 61 **chambers** between them. Lavish plastering, of particularly the upper halls and rooms, some of which have been restored, again raises the question of whether Kharana was a fort. The splendid vaulted **ceilings** and attention to decorative detail are unlikely in a solely functional building. Stephen Urice maintains that Kharana was probably not a caravanserai as there was no substantial water source or major trading route passing by. Instead, he suggested, Kharana was conceived as a lavish meeting place for Ummayed leaders.

Qasr Amra

Amra is **north-east** of **Kharana,** just **north** of the **Sahab** to **Azraq highway**. It is 85 kilometres (53 miles) **south-east** of Amman and 30 kilometres (19 miles) **south-west** of **Azraq**.

Of all Ummayed buildings in eastern Jordan, Amra is the most loved, and charming. It is exemplary in that it was built as a **bath house**, a luxurious place for soaking off the desert grime. Its existence adds to the theory that these 'Desert Castles' were built mainly as places of leisure, rather than as fortresses.

Amra gains its fame from the outstanding **frescoes** adorning its **interior walls** and **ceilings**. They are thought to be the earliest

Above: The mighty fortress at Kharana is one of Jordan's strangest anomalies — built in the form of a castle, experts maintain that it was really a palace in disguise.

Opposite: Qasr Kharana is perhaps the best surviving example of Ummayed architecture in the eastern section of Jordan.

Above: The yellow bricks of Qasr Tuba have been baked so dry by the sun they crumble at the touch.

example of pictorial art made in the Islamic era, having been painted during the middle years of the 8th century AD if not earlier. The designs have stood the passage of time remarkably well.

During the early 1970s a Spanish group of archaeologists carried out a painstaking restoration of the frescoes. Damage had been done to the walls by the fires of Bedouin and travellers who, over the centuries, stayed at the Qasr.

Amra, which looks bigger from the outside than it really is, consists of three long **aisles,** lying parallel to each other, with vaulted **ceilings.** At the end of each is a windowless dark room. Directly in front of the **main doorway,** at the end of the **central aisle**, is a **fresco** of the Caliph sitting on his throne. On the **south wall** another fresco depicts the enemies of Islam: Roderick the Visigoth, the Byzantine Emperor, the Sassanian ruler Krisa, the Negus of Abyssinia, and two others — thought to be the leaders of China and the Turks.

The **auditorium chamber,** used for feasting, meetings and cultural events, leads through an **antechamber** into the **baths.** The antechamber's **walls** are adorned with a rich **tapestry** of vignettes and **panels** depicting athletic scenes, hunting scenes, and illustrations of wildlife and fantastic images such as a bear playing a lute.

The two **bathrooms** consist of a warm room, known as the *tepidarium*, and the hot steam room, the most famous in Amra, known as the *caldarium*. It is capped with a **domed ceiling** whose **fresco** depicts the heavens, showing the constellations of the northern hemisphere and signs of the Zodiac. The chamber is naturally lit by four **shafts** at the base of the dome.

Outside the **main entrance** to the baths is an extremely deep **well,** now dry. The well was sunk to 40 metres (131 feet) to reach the natural water table of the area. Water was raised by animal power, the harnessed beast walking in a circle to operate a lifting mechanism.

Amra's prosperity depended on water, but its absence today is evidenced by hoards of flies.

Above: Interior of the fabled baths at Amra in Jordan's eastern desert.

Qasr Uweinid

Uweinid is the **site** of a **Roman stronghold,** rather than a palace built in the Early Islamic era. Located about 15 kilometres (9 miles) **south-west** of **Azraq,** you get there by turning **right** off the main road heading **south** from Azraq, and then **right** again.

It was conceived as an outpost to oversee the important **Wadi Sirhan** and was constructed during the 3rd century AD. Asymmetric-shaped, with a **tower** jutting out on the **south-west corner,** the fortress was constructed from the local black basalt. Numerous chambers enclosed the **main courtyard** on each side.

An **inscribed lintel,** and another **panel** of inscription found at the site, date to the first years of the 3rd century AD. Later, during early Arab times, Unweinid is known to have been used as a caravan stop en route from Arabia to Amman.

Azraq Castle

Reached either by the south-east road out of Amman via **Sahab,** or the north-east road via **Zarqa, Azraq Castle** is located just west of **Azraq North.** Crafted from the region's black basalt rocks, the town's ancient **fortress,** with its ominous ambience, has taken advantage of Azraq's important strategic position. It is thought to have been initiated by the Romans during the last years of the 3rd century AD. Numerous remodellings and rebuildings continued as the castle changed hands. Its location protected the town's key water source. The stronghold was redesigned by the Mamluks in AD 1237, and was also used by the Byzantines, Ummayeds and Mamluks. It is almost square-shaped, with **walls** 80 metres long encircling a central **courtyard.** At each **corner** is an **oblong tower.** The primary **entrance** is through a small **doorway,** protected by a basalt hinged door. Inside is a cool **chamber** that leads into the central courtyard. Various **rocks** in this

Above: Qasr Amra was used as a remote but elaborate bathing complex and was installed with a sophisticated heating system.

vestibule are inscribed with Greek and Latin and you can make out the name of Constantine on one stone. Within the main courtyard is a **mosque,** probably erected during the Mamluk era, and beside it is the main **well.**

The curator is an old man, whose father served under Lawrence of Arabia, who was stationed at the fortress during the 1917 Arab Revolt. The chamber directly above the main entrance was where that famous warrior plotted his strategy.

The curator is proud to show a few old **photographs** of Lawrence, including one of him wearing British military dress rather than his usual flowing Arab robes.

Qasr Ain es Sil

Like several of the *Qasrs* of Jordan's eastern desert, Qasr Ain es Sil was never used as a palace. It was a farming estate with a bathing complex attached.

Getting there
From Azraq Castle, take the road north-east for a further 1.5 kilometres.

Sightseeing
It is not certain whether the complex was built on the site of an earlier Roman estate, although this is probable. The **main building** is asymmetric, no more than about 17 metres (18 yards) along each of the four walls. It was constructed, like all the other structures at the site, from black basalt.

A **central enclosure** was encircled by **seven rooms.** Another chamber to the **north-east** housed two clay **ovens** for baking bread. A couple of **olive presses** were also discovered during a series of excavations in 1984. One of the presses made use of a Roman millstone dating back to the 3rd century AD.

At the **west wall** are the remains of a small **bath house** which, like those at Amra, would have had a changing room as well as hot and cold baths. The hot tub would have had a hypocaust — the Roman heating system in which hot air was circulated under the floor and between double walls — similar to that at Amra although not nearly as elaborate.

Qasr Aseikhin

Some distance out of Azraq, on the **Azraq** to **Safawi road** towards the Iraq Highway, a turn-off leads east to the **remains** of the Roman **fort** of **Aseikhin**. From the main road there is an 8-kilometre (5-mile) drive to the **hill** on which the fort is perched. Although the stronghold is in a sorry state of repair, you can still see a number of **arches** and **entrance ways** between the remnants of the fort's main **walls**. The castle was built in a square shape around an inner **courtyard.**

There are no exact pointers to the fort's age: early or mid-Roman. The site was probably occupied earlier by the Nabateans. The fort's importance was never great, but it would have allowed a watch to be kept on Azraq and surrounding areas.

Qasr Hallabat

One of the easiest of all the Desert Castles to reach from Amman is situated north-east of the capital, just off the main road that links Zarqa with Azraq.

Getting there
Drive through Zarqa and once north of the city take the right turning towards Azraq. A minor road signposted Qasr Hallabat leads to the left after a few kilometres.

Sightseeing
The **fortress** is the most ostentatious and complete of all the Ummayed compounds in Jordan. Its traditional square shape with square corner **towers,** was constructed on the site of an earlier bastion of 2nd century AD origin. Some scholars have suggested that this fort was erected by the Nabateans. An **inscription** reveals that the main fortifications were put up during the rule of Caracella (AD 198-217). However, the Ummayed overhaul of the site tore down much of the Roman and Byzantine craftsmanship, replacing it with ornate frescoes and decorative carvings. You can still make out hints of decoration and fancy details which once covered the stronghold.

A few metres **east** of the castle is a ruined **Ummayed mosque.** You can see its **alcove** pointing **eastwards.** Other features of Hallabat included **enclosed areas, meeting places, dams, reservoirs** and a **bath complex.** The main bathing area was situated 2 kilometres (one mile) **east** of the fortress, next to where the main road runs today.

The complex is called **Hammam es Sarah,** and was once adorned with lavish **marble** and mosaic work.

Umm el-Jemal: Mother of Camels

Drive **north-east** out of Amman up the main northbound highway to **Mafraq,** a distance of 72 kilometres (45 miles). At Mafraq take

Above: Traditional Ummayed bath house.

Above: Crust of black basalt in the Black Desert of east Jordan.

the **major highway** to the **east** (heading for the Iraqi border) for a further 15 kilometres (9 miles). At the first **desert police post** turn **left** and go **north** for another 3 kilometres. It should not take more than 90 minutes from Amman to Umm el-Jemal.

Umm el-Jemal provides an ideal example of how Jordan is a country of constant surprises. In this quiet backwater, almost touching the **Syrian border,** you come across a vast **black city** built more than 2,000 years ago. The **ruins**, fashioned from sombre chunks of **black basalt rock**, lie scattered across an immense area. The founders of this vast city are best known for their other constructions for Umm el-Jemal, it is thought, like the mighty metropolis of Petra, was built by the Nabateans.

At Umm el-Jemal is yet another reminder of the ingenuity of these people who used the materials which were to hand. The landscape, then as now, provided little more than the harsh dry basalt plains. The Nabateans used basalt to build everything from ceilings to doors, and from walls to shrines. In fact, the absence of wooden

supports and beams means that the ruins have lasted extremely well.

The city was only 6 kilometres (4 miles) **east** of the great **Via Nova Traiana,** the Trajan New Road which linked north and south, stretching all the way from Syria to Aqaba. But before this important Roman highway was constructed (AD 112-114) Umm el-Jemal had taken advantage of the ancient trading routes for many decades. Its importance as one of the great caravanserais is given credence by the ancient Nabatean city's name, for Umm el-Jemal, translates in Arabic as Mother of Camels. The large vacant area in the centre of the town was reserved for visiting caravan corteges that trekked across these ancient lands. But the city's original name is still a matter of some debate.

Umm el-Jemal was inhabited from at least the 1st century AD, for about 700 years. What was probably started by the Nabateans was carried on by the Romans. Gravestones reveal Nabatean and Greek lettering, suggesting a convergence of the two societies. It seems, however, that the 3rd

century AD brought a stretch of instability causing the inhabitants to resort to drastic measures for protection. Tombstones and other available blocks of basalt were used to construct a fortifying wall.

This wall surrounding Umm el-Jemal was rebuilt, or refortified, during the 4th century AD. It had six gates, situated on the south, east and west walls. One of these, the Gate of Commodus, was decorative, having been erected during the reign of Marcus Aurelius and his son Commodus.

Most buildings at Umm el-Jemal were constructed as residential houses in a design that has changed little in 2,000 years. After the Roman occupation had come and gone, the city was hit by a series of catastrophic

Above: The fortress at Azraq which T E Lawrence made his base during the Arab Revolt of 1917.

Opposite: A sketch of T E Lawrence in his familiar desert attire is on display at the fortress of Azraq.

Overleaf: Bird's eye view of the great basalt fortress of Azraq with a tiny mosque at the centre.

events such as the Persian invasion, plagues, and the string of great earthquakes that brought havoc on an unprecedented scale to the Middle East from the 8th century.

The buildings were practical, and certainly never as glamorous or ornate in design — or materials — as Roman and Nabatean structures elsewhere. The basalt, a stone that is very hard to dress, still retains the rough appearance which must have characterised the city. One feature is noticeable: there was clearly little predetermined planning. **Houses** lie in an array of randomly placed sites, in complete contrast with Jerash.

Umm el-Jemal, covers an area measuring about 800 by 500 metres (875 by 547 yards). Despite the host of predetermined walks or routes around the ancient metropolis, it is just as much fun to roam about mapless on your own. If you have time, Umm el-Jemal is worth a few hours, perhaps with a picnic lunch. As you wander, take care not to fall on the hard basalt. Look out for the **remains** of the 15 or so **churches** and the **cathedral,** some of which are dated. There are subterranean **chambers, reservoirs, storehouses, gateways, barracks** and a multitude of other buildings which once made Umm el-Jemal the fabled 'black gem of the black desert'.

Deir el-Kahf

The great basalt fortress of **Deir el-Kahf** is located on the **north side** of the highway that stretches from **Mafraq (north** of **Amman)** to the **Iraqi border.** It is about 45 kilometres (28 miles) **north** of Azraq travelling from Mafraq. It is reached by turning **left** after 63 kilometres (39 miles). A 13-kilometre (8-mile) drive along a rough road takes you directly to the Roman stronghold. Deir el-Kahf is certainly off the tourist routes, but if you happen to be passing it is well worth a visit.

The fort was about 60 metres (65 yards) square, with corner **towers** rising three storeys high. Its name means The Monastery of the Caves, and a large number of chambers were built mainly on two levels. As well as what is thought to be a **church,** there was at least one water **cistern, stables,** and a variety of other functional

buildings. After some of the Ummayed palaces, Deir el-Kahf seems to have been a very practical fortress that served as a large defensive garrison. The original construction was built in the early years of the 4th century AD.

Qasr Tuba and Qasr Jila

There is only one way to achieve the sensation of elation and endurance that must have been felt by the Ummayeds on reaching one of the great palaces in the desert — get off the beaten track. And there is no better Ummayed construction, or one more off the beaten track, than the glorious **Qasr Tuba**, a hermitage cut out of a 40-metre-wide sediment column

To get there you need to venture **south** from **Kharana** into the **desert**. The path ploughs across rocky terrain for about 46 kilometres (29 miles). Halfway between Kharana and Tuba is the site of **Qasr Jila** (some distance **west** of the track). **Another track** also leads **east** from the **Desert Highway**, near Qatrana. This is about 70 kilometres (44 miles). If you decide to set out for Tuba, which is in a small wadi approximately 3 kilometres **west** of Dayr al Qattar, it is advisable to go in a high clearance, 4WD vehicle with a reliable guide. Take a compass, a lot of water, and make sure you have sufficient petrol.

Tuba was similar in construction and brickwork to Qasr Mushatta. It consisted of a rectangular structure which enclosed a number of vaulted brick **chambers**. As with Mushatta, the brickwork is of the highest standard and its beauty helps you imagine the grandeur Tuba once enjoyed. The palace was almost certainly built by Caliph Walid II, in the year AD 743. Like Mushatta it seems never to have been completed and was probably a caravan station rather than a military stronghold.

The **central arena** was a rectangular 140 by 73 metres (152 by 80 yards). A gateway on the north side would have led into the palace. Like Mushatta, most of the brickwork rested on a foundation.

You get an idea of why Tuba is disintegrating from the yellow fired bricks, which

Above: Byzantine carvings decorate the walls of Qasr Hallabat, one of the most complete of all the Ummayed compounds in Jordan.

crumble at your touch. There are **holes** in the ground of the **inner chambers** where the Bedouin and adventurers have dug for treasures. The ground is littered with ceramic-like pebbles, volcanic and brittle in composition.

Bayir

If you reach Tuba and are still keen to continue, you can go a further 70 kilometres (43 miles) or so to **Bayir**, which remains in splendid isolation 85 kilometres (53 miles) **east** of the **Desert Highway**.

Bayir (which means *wells*), is the **site** of an ancient **Nabatean fortress,** that was adapted during the Ummayed era. Little remains now of the stronghold, which is located next to a contemporary bastion. Two notable **wells** are situated at Bayir.

Continue **west** from there and you will link up with the **track** that heads from Azraq to Ma'an, via **Jafr**. At Jafr lies the **old fortress** of Sheikh Auda Abu Tayi, one of Lawrence of Arabia's allies.

Above: Three onagers roam the plains of Shaumari Wildlife Reserve.

Azraq: Oasis in a Desert Land

Azraq is located at the convergence of various main roads that intersect the Middle East.

Getting there

From Amman, take the Sahab to Azraq road, which leaves the capital from its south-east. Alternatively you can drive north-east from Amman and, after Zarqa, take the road via Hallabat to Azraq. The major highway leading to the Iraqi border is linked to Azraq by the Azraq to Safawi road. Azraq is 115 kilometres (71 miles) from Amman. Another road leaves Azraq south, linking it with Ma'an, before continuing to the Saudi Arabian border.

Sightseeing

Azraq, which means blue in Arabic, gets its name from the waters that gush to the surface from the region's four main **springs**. For at least 2,000 years its **oases** have been

the most important, and fertile, **east** of the **Jordan River**. Today there are two main **villages** at Azraq, whose citizens live simple lives. They have managed to avoid the hustle and bustle of modern times. Azraq depends on high-quality salt harvested in the region, and a small agricultural programme. The district's fortunes have declined in recent years, primarily due to the pumping of Azraq's water supply to Amman and Irbid. This syphoning of the crucial water reserves has begun to devastate the ecosystem once supported by the area, resulting in the destruction of some of the marshlands. The consequences, which have only recently become apparent, have been ugly and far reaching.

To the **north** of Azraq North, the land is covered with hard chips of **black basalt**. It makes a contrast to the sandy **desert plains** to the **south**, or to the white **limestone flats** to the **east**.

Above: The Arabian Oryx was on the verge of extinction a few years ago. Shaumari now boasts a herd of over 130.

Two of the main springs are found in **Azraq South**, known as **Shisan**, and a further two are located in **Azraq North**, which is called **Azraq Druze**. These springs gush forth millions of litres of water every day which, until recently, have sustained the fragile ecosystem of the **marshland.** Millions of migrating birds visit Azraq each year, sheer numbers at times obscuring the sun. When a project began to channel water to the thirsty capital, birds which had always stopped in Azraq began to change their migratory routes, bypassing the marshlands.

Only now, following an intensive international effort, are the lush wetlands returning to Azraq once again. Plans to develop small scale ecotourism are on the cards. One hopes that this will help preserve the valuable waterlines for generations to come.

Remnants of past societies hint of a time when Azraq enjoyed bountiful wildlife and flora. **Flint tools** have been unearthed in the region, signifying that Stone Age man lived on the flat plains of the oasis at least 200,000 years ago. Indeed, scholars have suggested

that less than 8,000 years ago Azraq and the surrounding area had a much more temperate climate. Only in the last sixty years has Azraq's game been decimated by poachers and hunters, using modern transport and automatic weapons.

Azraq's existence on ancient trading and migratory routes has produced a society with different communities. The majority of Azraq North's people are **Druze**. They are the ancestors of the people who fled during the 1920s from Jebel Druze in Syria, during the uprising against the French.

The Druze sect is found mainly in southern Syria, Lebanon and parts of Jordan. Their society, which dates back to the 11th century AD, has its own scriptures and closely guarded beliefs. It believes in one God, and professes the divinity of the 6th Caliph al Hakim (AD 996-1021) of the Egyptian Fatimid dynasty. Inhabitants of Azraq South (Shisan) are Muslims, both of Arab and Circassian stock. The Circassians came to Azraq during the 19th century, having been brought by the Ottomans after persecution in their native Russia. (See "The People:

The Circassians", Part One.)

Azraq has an atmosphere like that of a border town. Although the **Iraqi border** is a long way to the **east** there are no other major settlements at which to stock up with supplies. Despite the great lack of water, Azraq still has a copious amount of shady **date palms.** There are **cafés** and a selection of small **hotels.** Between North and South Azraq is the spotlessly clean **Government Rest House** complete with a **restaurant, bar, bedrooms** with en suite bathrooms and — most surprisingly — a **swimming pool.** It is a welcome sight in such hostile land.

Azraq Wetland Reserve

The Azraq Wetland Reserve is situated east of Amman, across from the point where the **Amman road** leads into **south Azraq,** A handful of years ago this region seemed doomed forever. By 1993, Azraq's famous marshlands — once teeming with creatures of all types — were dried to a cinder. The future looked bleak: the oases were parched. The ecosystem seemed to have entirely collapsed. But then, at the eleventh hour — in 1994 — an emergency national and international committee began a campaign to save Azraq. A conservation project was established, charged with the great task of breathing life back into Azraq's waterlands. The Azraq Oasis Conservation Project (AOCP) oversaw the pumping of million of gallons of water to the parched areas. This, coupled with a cleaning project of the area, gradually restored precious life. Day by day flora returned; followed by birds and other animals. The AOCP's work was hindered severely by the Middle East drought of 1995. But weathering the drought year so early in their campaign gave the supervisors of the project great morale to continue.

Sadly, some of the unusual species which were once found at Azraq have died out. But plans are afoot to reintroduce wild horses and buffalo again. At present, the main focus is on nurturing the rare strains of aquatic life which are cherished in this,

Jordan's favourite oasis.

Those who live and work at Azraq hope that modest ecotourism in the area will help to safeguard the lush waterlands. A Visitor's Centre at Azraq, based upon the design of Qasr Amra, will boast lecture and exhibition halls, an outdoor amphitheatre, a handicraft centre and, most importantly, a staggering view of the oasis.

It is hoped that — in the not too distant future — the Reserve which covers 12 square kilometres (5 square miles), will boast over 300 species of bird, as well as snakes, lizards, foxes, and striped hyena once again.

Shaumari Reserve

Situated 12 kilometres (7 miles) due south Azraq and reached by following the track to the Wildlife Reserve's western side, the park is open every day from about 07.30 until around 16.00. This is a barren land which at first seems blessed with little more than an occasional dust swirl and parched scrub. The Reserve has yet to benefit from the regeneration of its sister — Azraq Wetland Reserve. Water is severely short, making one realise what a miraculous liquid it is. When visiting this part of Jordan ensure that you take your own provisions of water along.

Across the vast plain — stretching out in all directions — the road ploughs on into the desert. Just as you begin to wonder whether the reserve actually exists, the route stops at an enclosure. There, at the main office, the warden of the park greets visitors with a smile.

Sightseeing

The **Shaumari Wildlife Reserve** covers 22 square kilometres (8 square miles); an area completely encircled by a **mesh fence.** Since its inception in 1975 the main focus of the reserve has been to increase numbers of animals once indigenous to the vast plains of the Azraq region.

Creatures such as the **Arabian oryx,**

Opposite: Ruins of a once elegant Roman aquaduct at Umm el-Jemal.

Above: Ostriches are bred in captivity at the Shaumari Wildlife Reserve.

ostrich, wild ass, as well as various species of gazelle, have been encouraged to procreate in the park's protected enclosure.

Despite the great work achieved by the staff of the centre, the lack of water in the region — and the resulting loss of habitat for wildlife — is causing concern.

At the Visitors' Centre, next to the main gate, a small exhibition on the reserve's history and wildlife has been set up. Together with the preserved exhibits of wildlife is an assortment of fossils and remnants of Roman pottery. As a ranger leads you round you begin to understand the devastation caused by the lack of one vital element: water. Several important and renowned projects implemented at Shaumari are represented at the Visitors' Centre. Sadly many birds displayed in the natural history room no longer venture to Azraq, their ancient migratory routes having changed over just a few seasons. Shaumari's tourist numbers have dwindled

along with the wildlife. At its height Shaumari recorded some 3,000 visitors in one weekend alone. Today the picnic tables are empty, the large children's playground is silent. Amman's immense thirst has brought decline to Shaumari and the surrounding wildlife reserves. But, with the renewed international interest in the region, there is hope. Eco-tourism may hold the key to sustaining the desert's fragile flora and fauna in the future.

Of all Shaumari's projects, the most famous and successful is Operation Oryx. Its aim, to increase the population of the almost extinct Arabian oryx (Oryx leucoyx) has been realised. The white oryx, with its two straight horns and black face markings, once roamed the deserts of Arabia, Jordan, Palestine and Iraq.

Well suited to arid lands, the oryx is a resilient animal requiring a low intake of water. To the hunter however, the animal was a worthy foe, providing meat as well as elegant horns and a soft hide. Although it survived the passage of history, it was almost annihilated when hunters began using vehicles.

Indeed, the motor car and high-powered automatic weapons decimated much of the Middle East's wildlife. Cheetah, wolves, gazelle, wild ass and ostrich, vanished over a few short years.

Operation Oryx was launched in 1962 by the Fauna Preservation Society and the World Wildlife Society. Three oryx were caught in Aden and six others were soon provided from Saudi Arabia and Kuwait. These nine Arabian oryx, known as the *World Herd*, were taken to Arizona's Phoenix Zoo to breed.

By careful management a 'miracle' was achieved and numbers increased substantially in a short time. The first release into the wild of the Arabian oryx in Oman took place in 1982. Now Shaumari boasts a herd of about 135 Arabian oryx. The reserve has also fostered twelve ostrich from a single pair. Their enclosure, close to the two tall **watchtowers**, has allowed the giant eggs to hatch without poaching by man or predation by beast.

Above: Delicate bloom flowers in harsh desert landscape.

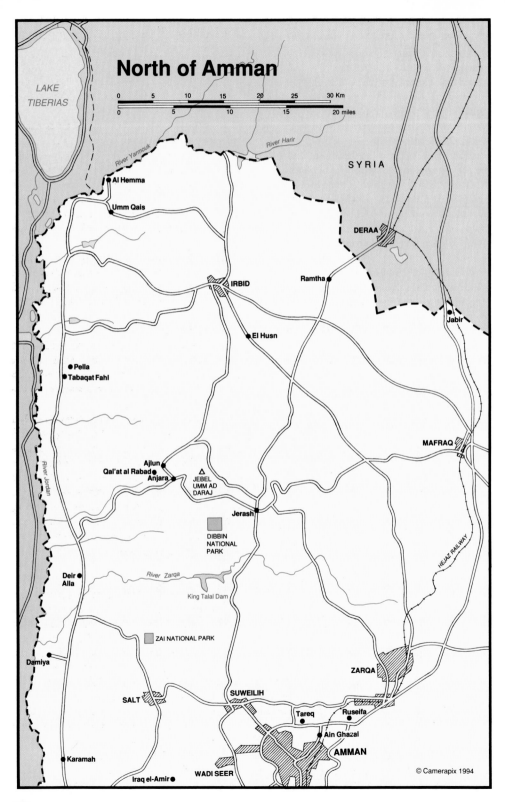

North of Amman

LAKE TIBERIAS

0 5 10 15 20 25 30 Km
0 5 10 15 20 miles

River Yarmouk

River Harir

SYRIA

● Al Hemma

● Umm Qais

DERAA

IRBID

Ramtha ●

Jabir ●

● El Husn

● Pella
● Tabaqat Fahl

Ajlun ●
Qal'at al Rabad ●
Anjara ●

△ JEBEL UMM AD DARAJ

MAFRAQ

Jerash ●

DIBBIN NATIONAL PARK

River Zarqa

King Talal Dam

Deir ● Alla

HEJAZ RAILWAY

ZAI NATIONAL PARK

Damiya ●

ZARQA

SALT

SUWEILIH

Tareq ●

Ruseifa ●

● Ain Ghazal

AMMAN

● Karamah

WADI SEER

Iraq el-Amir ●

River Jordan

© Camerapix 1994

194

North of Amman: Silent Peaks, Lush Valleys

Jordan's northern extremities are deep in the melting pot of history. From Neolithic times man has trod this land. Civilisations and empires have come and gone, leaving their stamp on everything from the tiniest vestige of a ceramic fragment to the great remains of Jerash.

The northern reaches of Jordan today are still the most populated regions of the nation. Their towns and villages, though strangely up-to-date, preserve the age-old ways. An excursion northwards will take you to Jerash, the most sublime of all Roman provincial cities; to the luxuriant fertile slopes of the Jordan Valley; and to the highlands from which you can look down on Lake Tiberias (the Sea of Galilee) and Syria.

There are sights all the way, such as Crusader and Saracen castles, Roman hot baths, Byzantine mosaic work, and Bronze Age settlements. Northern Jordan's wonders are never far from Amman, and so a very pleasurable day trip can be made by visiting several sites.

Salt: Enchanting Capital of the Past

Salt is one of the most charming and charismatic of all Jordan's towns. History has spared it from industry or modern bureaucracy. Salt, which is the administrative centre for the Balqa Province, probably gleans its name from the Latin word *saltus*, meaning a wooded valley.

Various ancient tombs in the area indicate that Salt was founded on an Iron Age site which, later in Byzantine times, was known as *Saltos Hieraticon*. Its gleaming white buildings cover the slopes of a cluster of hills. On the crest of one of the hills lies the stronghold of the Mamluk Sultan al Malik al Mu'az.

Built in AD 1220, the fortress had a short life, as it was devastated during the Mongol assault of AD 1260, although it was partially reconstructed the following year.

The 19th century again saw the castle being destroyed before the existing buildings were erected as Ottoman barracks in 1870. Salt was of great strategic and administrative importance to the Turks. They ruled over what is now Jordan using Salt as their headquarters. For this reason the town is filled with wonderful Ottoman architecture in the classical style. Recent times saw Salt as the initial capital city of Jordan where, at the beginning of his reign, King Abdullah ruled before moving to Amman.

In Salt there is a growing selection of tourist centres, but the city's main attractions are its charming layout, the buildings, and its extremely warm and hospitable people.

Getting there
Salt is 29 kilometres (18 miles) north-west of Amman on a drive which takes about half an hour. Another road links the town to the Dead Sea, and yet another to the Jordan Valley at its east.

The new road leading from Amman makes visiting easier than ever. Suddenly, as you approach the town, a sharp bend reveals the dazzling buildings. You immediately notice the Ottoman houses with their long-arched windows. An array of tall minarets look down on Salt, as if standing guard. It is well worth spending a morning or afternoon walking through the narrow and picturesque streets.

Sightseeing
Just before you enter the main part of Salt (from the direction of Amman) you will pass, on the **left,** Salt's **Department of Antiquities Museum** and **Tourist office.** Although small, the museum has a number of fascinating **early photographs** which help to explain how rapidly the town has grown. Panels of Byzantine **mosaic work** adorn the walls, as well as Chalcolithic **pottery** found at Salt, **gold Byzantine coins** and **Bronze Age bowls** and **pots.**

Roman and Early Islamic artefacts are also on display, such as a superbly calligraphied and damascened deep bronze **bowl.**

A most eerie exhibit is a small **stone sarcophagus** next to the **door**, which contains the bones of an infant.

Just off the **main street** is the new **Salt Cultural Centre**. Its complex houses another **museum, library, handicraft school,** and the town's main **hall.** The **museum** is on the upper street level. This complex, opened in 1989, is the pride of the town.

The museum displays traditional life with a selection of **models** weaving, grinding coffee, milking sheep, or just sitting around in a large Bedouin tent. Note that female models are wearing the traditional headdress of Salt. The museum is open from 08.00 until 14.00 every day except Friday. Entrance is free.

Next door is the **public library** which has acquired a large **collection** of **antiquated** and very interesting **English books.** The librarian welcomes visitors to chat and drink traditional cardamom-flavoured coffee.

Downstairs is the **Handicraft School of Salt.** Its projects are sponsored by the Queen Noor Foundation and the Salt Development Foundation. Among the various departments are those teaching ceramics, weaving, silk-screen printing and dyeing.

A tour of the **workshops** gives an insight into traditional crafts, but at the same time shows how these ancient skills have been adapted and modified with contemporary techniques. Handicrafts made by the students are sold, making the project self-financing.

Behind the Cultural Centre is Salt's **Weaving Centre**. Set in an exquisite **Ottoman house,** the centre oversees and teaches the making of typical Jordanian textiles using wool coloured with natural dyes.

Spend as much time as you can roaming the winding streets where you will find **small cafés, barbers' shops, jewellery** and **gold stores,** and others purveying local

Opposite: Brightly-coloured railings on one of the charming buildings in the old capital of Salt.

Top right: Elegant minaret stands sentinel over the streets of Salt.

Right: One of many examples of Ottoman architecture in Salt.

Above: Serene interior of the Church of the Assumption of the Virgin Mary — one of many old churches in Salt.

crafts. The main **market area** in the oldest part of town is reserved for pedestrians, the streets being too narrow for cars.

Jerash: Magnificent Gateway through Time

Jerash, located 48 kilometres (30 miles) due north of Amman, is the finest example anywhere of a Roman provincial city. Its colonnades, streets, theatres, buildings and mosaics have been preserved in good condition for almost 2,000 years.

As you walk about the ruins you can almost hear the shouts, and feel the bustle of Roman life. Look for the grooves worn by chariot wheels in the Colonnaded Street. Numbers etched into seats at the South Theatre are visible and the Nymphaeum's

Left: Old men enjoy an al fresco game of *Mengalah.*

Opposite: Jordanian girl in the traditional dress of northern Jordan.

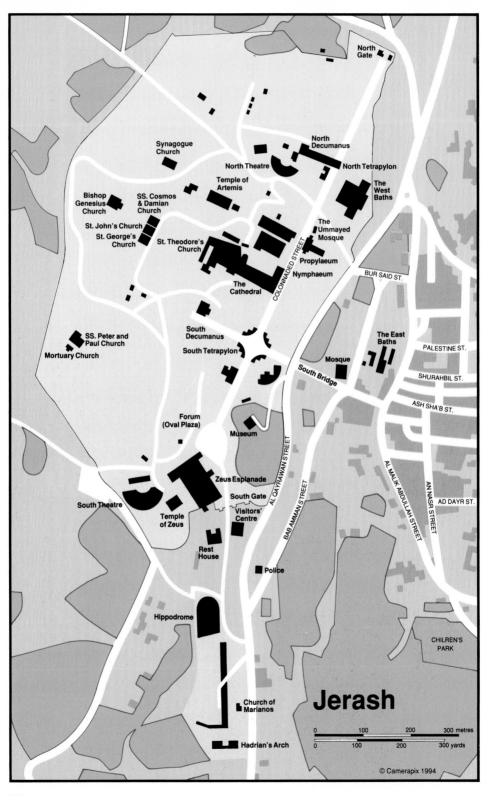

Jerash

North Gate

North Decumanus
North Theatre
North Tetrapylon
The West Baths
Synagogue Church
Temple of Artemis
The Ummayed Mosque
Bishop Genesius Church
SS. Cosmos & Damian Church
St. John's Church
St. George's Church
St. Theodore's Church
Propylaeum
Nymphaeum
BUR SAID ST.
The Cathedral

COLONNADED STREET

SS. Peter and Paul Church
South Decumanus
South Tetrapylon
The East Baths
PALESTINE ST.
Mortuary Church
Mosque
SHURAHBIL ST.
South Bridge
ASH SHA'B ST.

Forum (Oval Plaza)
Museum

AL QAYRAWAN STREET
BAB AMMAN STREET
AL MALIK ABDULLAH STREET
AN NASR STREET
AD DAYR ST.

Zeus Esplanade
South Gate
South Theatre
Temple of Zeus
Visitors' Centre
Rest House

Police

CHILREN'S PARK

Hippodrome

Church of Marianos

Jerash

| 0 | 100 | 200 | 300 metres |
| 0 | 100 | 200 | 300 yards |

Hadrian's Arch

© Camerapix 1994

carved lion heads have not withered with time. These small points, and more, give Jerash its immeasurable charm.

Excavations around the southern area of the city, where the Temple of Zeus was constructed, have unearthed Bronze and Iron Age relics. It came as no surprise to find such ancient tokens at Jerash, as the region is ideal for habitation. It is fed with water year-round by a creek that passes through the city centre. Its altitude of over 500 metres (1,600 feet) gives Jerash a temperate climate and excellent visibility across the lower lying areas. Its position on major trade routes has fostered a rich economic environment since the earliest times.

Even before the Hellenistic era, the area where Jerash now stands was known locally as *Garshu*. This evolved over the years to become the Roman *Gerasa*, from which *Jerash* (also spelt Jarash) derives. Long before the elaborate Roman buildings graced these hills there was a substantial Hellenistic settlement at Jerash. It was about the time that Alexander the Great stormed the territory in 332 BC that Jerash began to rise in prominence.

With the collapse of the Seleucid Empire, and a period of fighting between local chiefdoms, Pompey led his Roman cohorts through Jerash in 64 BC. The town was assimilated into the Roman province of Syria, and later named as one of the great cities in the Decapolis. Pliny mentioned this federation in his work *Natural History*, saying that ten communities within the union were: Damascus, Philadelphia (now Amman), Gerasa (Jerash), Scythopolis (Beisan), Gadara (Umm Qais), Hippos, Dion, Pella, Canatha and Raphana.

During the decade between AD 50 and AD 60, the Romans began work on the city which grew as the Roman Empire expanded and, as time passed, both flourished. Trade thrived under the benefits of the *Pax Romana* and Jerash's buildings and riches escalated. Emperor Trajan's conquest south in the year AD 106, in which he annexed Petra, brought even more prosperity to Jerash through the excellent lines of communication between the cities. Jerash became part of the Roman province of Arabia and, along with Petra and a conglomeration of other cities, was overseen by the Roman governor at Bostra, in southern Syria. The Via Nova Traiana, the Trajan New Road, sped southwards, linking Jerash to Petra, Aqaba and cities across the Eastern World.

Much of what we now know as Jerash was constructed during the early years of the 2nd century, under the aegis of Emperors Trajan and Hadrian. By the middle half of that period Jerash had reached its peak, after which there was a time of stabilisation, slowdown, and inevitable decline.

It is thought that, at its height, Jerash was home to some 25,000 people.

Taxes were levied on traders bringing foreign goods to Jerash, much as happens with customs now. These tariffs would have been applicable on everything from dried dates to slaves. One interesting point is that dozens of small inscriptions about Jerash note general philanthropic deeds by citizens to build new monuments or maintain existing ones. The Temples of Zeus and Artemis, the South Theatre, and other buildings were erected mainly from funds donated by residents. The names of individuals are inscribed for eternity, honouring such people as Titus Flavius, son of Dionysius, who financed an area of seats at the South Theatre. Others gave funds as a guild, such as the potters, smiths or weavers.

The political unrest that started in Rome and permeated through the great empire took a long time to hit Jerash. As the city was located on the eastern extremity of the empire its region prospered from areas far to the East, and Jerash was not troubled until the beginning of the 3rd century AD.

In AD 330 Emperor Constantine announced that Christianity would be the new religion of the Roman Empire's eastern half. Jerash fell into this newly-formed Byzantine segment and a spate of building, as well as remodelling, began. Some temples were transformed to become churches and many

Overleaf: Corinthian colonnades of Artemis Temple in Jerash — a fine example of Roman architecture.

Above: Detail of the splendid colonnades that dominate much of Jerash.

new churches were erected, with mosaic floors, similar to those laid at the same time in Madaba. Jerash flourished under the Byzantine umbrella for 300 years.

The 8th and 9th centuries AD saw no new fortunes for Jerash, only the disaster of several earthquakes that seriously damaged buildings. Under Islam, which reached Jerash with the Persian invasion of AD 614, the city hardly grew. From then on, except for a short-lived habitation by the Crusaders, Jerash slept for a thousand years. In 1806 the German traveller Ulrich Jasper Seetzen stumbled across the city and broadcast his findings to the world.

Getting there

Jerash is situated among the Hills of Gilead, on the road due northwards from Amman in the direction of the Syrian border. The journey takes about 40 minutes.

The city is perfect for a day visit. As you drive from Amman, you are immediately aware of the change in vegetation. Instead of barren ground, there are low-lying hills with olive groves and stalls lining the road selling tomatoes and fruit.

Sightseeing

When you approach **Jerash** from the **south** you arrive first at the **Visitors' Centre**, on the **left**. It is worth looking at their large three-dimensional **plan** of the **ruins**. Free **maps** of Jerash are supplied at the centre as well. If you study the large plan you will notice that the tourist centre is just **south** of the southernmost gate into the **old city.** This is **Hadrian's Arch** and to the **left** of it is the **Hippodrome** where horse racing was held. The plan clearly shows that the old city is situated on the **east banks** of **Wadi Jerash,** while on the **west side** — although the map shows a deserted area — is the new community. The plan reveals the original walls of Jerash in their entirety, although few sections remain.

Around the Centre are **souvenir stalls** selling **guidebooks** and **trinkets**. At the Arch of Hadrian, you must buy a ticket to enter. The ruins are open from 08.00 to 19.00. **Sound and Light shows,** from May to October, at 20.30 last until 22.30.

Hadrian's Arch, which was built during AD 129-130, stands at the **southernmost end** of Jerash. It was constructed to mark

Above: Student group enjoys an afternoon exploring the architectural wonders of Jerash.

Emperor Hadrian's visit. Strangely, the elaborate gate was never connected to the city **walls**. The design is of a **central arch,** flanked by two smaller ones. You will also see that **chambers** have been built into the **left** and **right** sides of the edifice, and that some of the original, highly decorated stones still remain. On the **left** of Hadrian's Arch are various **ruins**. **Steps** lead down into a **pit** below where you will see a large **millstone** used for pressing olives.

Just **north** of Hadrian's Arch are the **ruins** of the **Church of Bishop Marianos,** constructed in AD 570. The floors have been buried, following the recent excavation, to protect them. The church was supposedly in use until the 8th century AD.

A short walk from Hadrian's Arch leads to the **Oval Plaza**, or **Forum.** The plaza is extremely rare in that it is oval-shaped. It measures some 80 by 90 metres (87 by 98 yards) and is surrounded by a series of **Ionic colonnades,** typical of the 1st century AD, upon which is laid a continuous architrave, or line of lintels. These have been reconstructed in parts. The forum, which is paved, has at its centre the **remains** of a

podium which was originally the base to a statue. The statue was later removed, and following a remodelling, a **fountain** or water trough took its place.

You will notice that the columns radiating off the Oval Plaza are Corinthian, whereas the plaza's columns are Ionic. The lower halves of the forum's columns are lighter in colour than the upper sections, indicating that they were buried beneath the sand for centuries. You can also see that the columns still have bumps on their sides which were used in erecting and positioning the columns and were then usually filed or chiselled off.

In the **south-west corner** of the forum is a **staircase** that once led to the great **Temple of Zeus** and its surrounding buildings. The stones flanking the steps have images of grape vines carved into them. Beneath the lowest steps is an **arch** and further **stairs** that lead down into a long vaulted **passageway,** running **west-east.** There are rounded **niches** in the walls of the vault, which is naturally lit by shafts of sunlight. Towards the **western end** of the vault a 'secret' set of **steps** leads up to the Temple of Zeus.

The original Temple was almost certainly constructed in the Hellenistic era, during one of the first two centuries BC. The initial Roman temple on the site was built during the first half of the 1st century AD. Inscriptions of the financiers' names, together with dates, provide valuable clues as to when the great temple was constructed. Most of what is now visible was put up in AD 162. There is a **grand staircase** leading to a large **platform** above the Oval Plaza. **Fragments** of an **altar** on the **north** side of the **terrace** still exist. Another **great stairway** led from the patio, via another higher paved area, up to the Temple of Zeus. The temple would have been immense, for the columns encircling it were 15 metres (49 feet) high.

Today the temple is filled with the giant **blocks** that once formed the walls, testimony to the severity of the earthquake that knocked them down. On the outer sides of the temple, in walls still standing, are a series of alcoves where figurines stood. Many of the bases of the Corinthian columns are still in place.

The **South Theatre,** located to the **northwest** of the Temple of Zeus, was finished during the early part of the 2nd century AD. Of the three Roman theatres at Jerash the South Theatre was the largest, with more than 3,000 seats. The theatre, which is in almost perfect condition, was not submerged in sand like the **North Theatre** at Jerash. You will notice the Greek **seat numbers** below many of the seats, especially those to the **right** of the **stage.** Also to the right of the stage is a lengthy inscription in Greek.

Two main **entrances** lead into the South Theatre through **doorways** to the **left** and **right** of the stage. The acoustics of the theatre are excellent even now, 2,000 years since its construction. The brilliant design took every conceivable factor into consideration, such as the sun's brightness and

Opposite: Exquisitely carved colonnades in the Temple of Zeus.

Top right: Ruins of the gateway into the ancient city of Jerash.

Right: Lone column, crowned by a carved summit, towers over Jerash.

direction. For this reason the orientation of the theatre is north-westwards, so as to allow the least amount of sunlight to disturb spectators.

A path runs parallel to the **Cardo** (the main **Street of Columns**) along a **ridge** linking the Temple of Zeus with the **Temple of Artemis**. To the **west** of the ridge is a cluster of three Byzantine churches of **St Cosmas and Damian, St John,** and **St George**.

Jerash had all the ingredients for a spectacular revival during Byzantine times, components that led to the construction of many classical Byzantine churches. There was the know-how of mosaic laying — what is now the northern half of Jordan was at the time the world centre of mosaic work. Alongside were many carved stone blocks left from the Roman era, waiting to be cannibalised into churches.

Since the 1920s excavations have unearthed 15 Byzantine churches, mostly dotted about Jerash's central region. But archaeologists are certain that many more churches could exist beneath the top-soil, still awaiting discovery.

Of the 11 Byzantine churches excavated on the **west side** of the Cardo, few walls still stand. Some of the great **mosaic floors** are still in place, while others have been removed to museums at Amman or Jerash, or have been covered again for protection.

Above: Detailed carvings surround a window in Jerash.

The three churches of St Cosmas and Damian, St John and St George, which lie alongside each other, are thought to date back to the early part of the 6th century AD. **The Church of St George** is the **southernmost** of the three, that is, the furthest from the Temple of Artemis. It was probably the first to be completed, being constructed between about AD 529 and 530. Evidence suggests that the church was still used after the tremendous earthquakes of the 7th and 8th centuries AD, whilst the other two in the line were destroyed. Although fortunate that it was largely spared from the earthquakes, it fell prey after the Byzantine era to the work of iconoclasts. Ironically, the other two churches were so badly demolished by natural circumstances that the iconoclasts had no way of moving the rubble covering the mosaics to damage the designs.

The central church of the three is that of **St John the Baptist**, erected during the dominion of Bishop Paul in AD 531. The **mosaic frieze** that once covered the main **nave** is today in quite a bad state of repair. Yet you can still clearly see the remnants of exquisite images of flora and fauna, as well as depictions of various sacred cities, such as Alexandria and Memphis. Leading from the unusual horseshoe-shaped **apse** is an entrance into the **baptistry** of the **Church of St Cosmas** and **St Damian**.

This church, **northernmost** of the three, was constructed in AD 533 in the name of twin brothers who were known for their medicinal skills. The church's **mosaic floor** is certainly the best preserved in Jerash. It is well worth inspecting, if only for the sheer brilliance of its mosaic floor. As well as birds, animals, mathematical and other designs, there is a series of images of the church's benefactors and religious leaders. A **path** leads from the three Byzantine churches to the **south side** of the Temple of Artemis.

It is a larger temple and in better condition than the Temple of Zeus. It was dedicated to Artemis, patron Goddess of the city of Jerash. An immense podium area formed its base with a large **courtyard** surrounded by colonnades encircling it. You can enter the temple from the courtyard which leads down a monumental **staircase** to the Cardo far below. No grandeur was spared for what is thought to have been one of the finest temples constructed in any provincial Roman city. On the **south-west** side via a **path** from the sanctuary's main entrance, you enter the **vaults**.

Three main underground **naves** are accessible, running **east-west**. The most central of these barrel-vaulted passageways is the longest and leads into another complete **chamber** at the **east end**. The vaults were originally reached from inside the temple itself.

So great is the number of closely-packed Corinthian columns, which formed the portico, that it would have given the impression of a grove. Sadly, none of the marbles that once adorned the walls of the *cella*, or internal section, remain. The **west wall's recess** would probably have been

Above: A cluster of colonnades at Jerash.

Above: Spring flowers surround the great Temple of Zeus.

graced with an elegant statue of Artemis. The goddess, who was of special importance not only in Jerash, but throughout the Decapolis at large, was the daughter of Zeus and sister of Apollo. It is believed that the temple, the most impressive building of ancient Jerash, was never completed by the Romans. Continued excavation brings to light new material adding to the shrine's history.

The Byzantine era saw the site used for pot baking, evidenced by **kilns** unearthed in front of the temple. Arabs later used it as a fortress, adding to its walls for increased defence. It was subsequently bombarded and seized by the Crusader monarch King Baldwin II.

A few metres north lie the **remains** of Jerash's **North Theatre**. Although not as well preserved as the South Theatre, you gain a good idea of the amphitheatre's original design from the fallen **lintels,** heavy with inscription. The theatre, which is undergoing extensive reconstruction, was excavated initially during the early 1980s, and is of similar design to the South Theatre.

The fact that Jerash had two theatres and an odeon underlines the city's importance as a municipal and cultural centre in Roman times.

On the **north side** of the theatre runs the **North Decumanus,** leading off the Cardo at right angles. This was the route by which spectators arrived at the theatre, whose front portico faced the Decumanus.

During the latter half of the 2nd century AD the theatre was completed, perhaps initially as an odeon. It may well have been covered and used for general recitals and community meetings before being enlarged during the 3rd century AD. Some of the lower seats, nearer the stage, still bear inscriptions in Greek of the *phylai*, or polling groups, which went to make up the community council. One derives its name from Emperor Hadrian, the others from the Olympian deities. The existence of these names substantiates the notion that the theatre was used at one time or another as a meeting place for regional or municipal officials. With the later addition of the upper seating area, the theatre could have held around 1,600 people. Like the Temple of

Above: The remains of the Nymphaeum at Jerash — the city's formerly magnificent fountain complex.

Artemis the North Theatre was, during the 7th and 8th centuries, used for pottery manufacture. Following the theatre's collapse due to earthquake, the perfectly carved stones were carted off and used by the Byzantines for their own churches and houses.

The North Decumanus runs from its right-angled intersection with the Cardo known as the **North Tetrapylon**, to the city's **western wall** and the **north-western gate** that cut through its perimeter. The north-west gate, which no longer stands, was built between AD 75 and 76.

The Cardo was the main artery of Jerash, stretching in a **north-east** direction from the Oval Plaza in the extreme **south-west,** to the **North Gate** of the city at the **City Wall,** in the north-east. It was an interesting mixture of pedestrian walkway and traffic thoroughfare. Its importance becomes obvious when you consider how the Temple of Artemis, the Cathedral complex, the Western Baths and a host of other central areas were positioned to take full advantage of this key street's access.

The Cardo was originally 800 metres (874 yards) in length, flanked by Corinthian colonnades. The sight of so many columns lining a straight route must have been impressive. The Cardo was originally bordered with Ionic columns but the street was redesigned during extensive renovations in the latter half of the 1st century AD. The Ionic columns were replaced by those of Corinthian design, in line with the ancient city's growing status as an important Roman provincial metropolis.

The **northern part** of the Cardo, which is generally called the North Colonnaded Street, was not widened or bestowed with Corinthian columns, and gives you an idea of how the whole thoroughfare once appeared. Much of the Cardo was lined, to the **right** and **left,** with a variety of shops which are rejuvenated every summer during the **Jerash Festival** celebrations.

This North Colonnaded Street leads to the North Gate, which was erected in AD 115. It is worth walking up the overgrown **North Colonnaded Street** to see the North Gate, even though little of it remains today. From the simple single-arched gateway leads the important road linking Jerash to Pella, another town of the Decapolis.

A stroll down the Cardo brings Jerash to life. You get a sense of power from the monumental buildings that line the route, and the tiny details peppering the street add a truly human dimension. Look at the **ruts** running straight up the street, created by the hard-wheeled chariots almost two thousand years ago. You can still see the stone **manhole covers,** positioned down the centre; a reminder of the street's advanced subterranean sewerage system.

Across from the Tetrapylon junction are the remains of the **West Baths** — the **East Baths** are situated on the **east bank** of **Wadi Jerash**. The West Baths were a substantial complex, constructed in the 2nd century. They have yet to be properly excavated and are in a sorry state, but they do give an idea of the importance of bathing during Roman times.

The complex was characteristic of 2nd-century Roman baths design. There was a *Frigidarium* (cold bath), a *Caldarium* (hot bath), a changing room and a pair of splendid pavilions. The **domed roof** of the **northern pavilion** is in superb condition. The **West** and **East baths** at Jerash are thought to have been the largest complexes ever built by the Romans in what is now Jordan.

Just south of the West Baths, a few metres from the Cardo, are the lasting remains of the only **Ummayed Mosque** known to have existed in Jerash. It was built during the 7th or 8th centuries and was only discovered in 1981. It was curiously constructed inside the column-bordered **atrium** area of a Roman house. Only the **bases** now remain of the columns which once supported the roof. The **mosque,** whose floor is still paved, used an existing alcove from the Roman house for the *mihrab* recess in the **south wall.**

About 25 metres (27 yards) south of the Ummayed mosque the Cardo is reached on its **west side** by the substantial remains of where the Temple of Artemis' gateway once stood. Everything about the temple was enormous; no expense was spared to ensure that the maximum impression was made on citizens and visitors alike.

Four massive **columns,** and 13 of more modest size, mark where the great entrance or *Propylaeum* leads onwards and upwards

to the mighty temple. Much of the gateway, as well as the steps, have stood the test of time and are in remarkably good condition.

On the same side as the temple's Propylaeum, and a few more metres **southwards,** are the remains of another of Jerash's most important and ornate constructions, **the Nymphaeum**. The very building of this Nymphaeum, or fountain system, bears out yet again the height of prosperity that Jerash achieved. As the name suggests, the Nymphaeum was consecrated in dedication to the Nymphs. Scholars believe it was erected at the height of Jerash's opulence during the latter years of the 2nd century AD. Another **four** vast **columns** soar up at the point where the Nymphaeum's outer portico once stood.

The Nymphaeum's frontage is over 20 metres (66 feet) wide and is offset from the Cardo's west side. It consisted of a main semi-circular alcove embedded in the hillside, that was itself lined with smaller alcoves in which figurines stood. A partial dome hung over the central alcove, echoing the sounds of gushing water and the cries of the admirers of this astonishing structure. Notice the exquisite **carving** still in place within the **central alcove.** The lower tier of the Nymphaeum's alcove was encased in a layer of green Aegean marble, and the top tier was painted gypsum.

Water poured through the lower tier's figurines, flowing into the central pool. From this basin the gleaming waters passed through a number of carved lions' heads and ran along a **central trough,** which can still be seen. The carved spout in the middle allowed water to stream into a red circular granite reservoir in front, which was added in the Byzantine period.

Just south of the Nymphaeum is the **Cathedral Gateway** that leads onto the Cardo. What is spuriously called **the Cathedral** has its remains directly behind the Cathedral Gateway. No one is sure if it was ever a cathedral; what is certain is that the complex was erected on the **site** of the 2nd century AD **temple** dedicated to Dionysus. The cathedral's stonework was acquired from Jerash's earlier Roman remains and the gateway's imposing blocks date back to the 2nd century AD.

Above: Aerial view of the colonnaded streets of ancient Jerash.

Stairs were built on the foundations of those that led to the Temple of Dionysus. The cathedral, together with the **Church of St Theodore** beside it, form part of an extensive sacred area which was the most important of Jerash's Byzantine sections.

One hundred metres (109 yards) **south** of the Cathedral Gateway stand the remains of the **South Tetrakionion piazza**, marking the bisection at right angles of the Cardo by the **South Decumanus**, which stretches to the city's **west wall**, parallel with the North Decumanus.

The piazza was a late addition, built during the latter part of the 2nd century AD. Continuing on **south** down the last stretch of the Cardo takes you back to the Oval Plaza.

Ajlun: Home of Qalaat-al-Rabad

To experience some of Jordan's most fertile scenery, continue north-west from Jerash. The road to Ajlun carves a path across hillsides lined with olive groves whose trees' dark green leaves are blanketed with a coating of chalky white dust.

Getting there
No more than 25 kilometres (15 miles) from Jerash, 73 kilometres (45 miles) from Amman, lies the sleepy town of Ajlun.

Sightseeing
Ajlun is easy to get to and is well worth the trouble. After some 20 minutes of driving from Jerash, as the road wends its way out of the village of Anjara, you catch first sight of the mighty Saracen **stronghold** of **Qalaat-al-Rabad** on the apex of the hill above Ajlun. Many visitors to Jordan neglect Ajlun's fabled fortress, which provides a fascinating comparison with the country's Crusader castles.

In AD 1184-85 the nephew of Salah el-Din al Ayyubi (Saladin) built a small fortress on the **summit** of Jabal Beni 'Awaf, on the site of what is now Qalaat-al-Rabad. Its

Overleaf: Poppies and thistles burgeon in northern Jordan's fertile soil.

Above: Qalaat-al-Rabad, the hilltop fortress at Ajlun in northern Jordan.

dominating position, some 1,200 metres (3,937 feet) above sea level, allowed an extraordinarily wide vantage over the surrounding lands, affording protection against the Crusader forces, permitting Saladin to concentrate on the iron mines at Ajlun without hindrance.

The original core of the fortress had four corner towers, with narrow arrow slits and a moat some 16 metres (17 yards) wide. After the death of 'Izz ad-Din Usama, Saladin's nephew, the castle was enlarged in the year AD 1214-15 by a high-ranking Mamluk officer named Aibak ibn Abdallah. He added a new tower in the south-east corner and constructed the main one. Soon after, in AD 1229, the castle fell to the Emirate of Kerak.

Later, in AD 1260, the Tartars captured the stronghold before being driven out in the same year by the Mamluks. The battlements, which had been destroyed by the Mongols, were restored together with a host of other renovations. It was at this time that the south-western tower was constructed.

Qalaat-al-Rabad was a strategic message post for carrier pigeons and a point for fire beacons, one in a chain of stations that enabled messages to be relayed between Cairo and Baghdad. The castle's colourful history continued until the Swiss traveller, Burckhardt, visited the fortress in 1812. He wrote that forty members of the Barakat (meaning *blessing*) family were based there.

Qalaat-al-Rabad's **view** is one of the best in the Middle East. High above sea level it looks down on the **Dead Sea**. On a day with little haze you can make out the water, stretching southward, as well as the **Jordan Valley,** the **West Bank** and **Lake Tiberias** (the Sea of Galilee). Just before you reach the fortress the road becomes steep, and the higher you climb, the better the view.

The curator will be happy to give you a **brochure** detailing the castle's rich history. There is no entrance fee. You have to walk over a **bridge** straddling a dry **moat** to gain access through the **main entrance.** The walkway leads to a **doorway** which has replaced the drawbridge. Inside this outer entrance on the **left,** next to the first **arrow slit,** is a fine **Mamluk stone inscription** taken from a **mosque** situated near the castle.

Steps lead up to the body of the castle.

Above: Ajlun fortress — one of the finest examples of Arab military architecture in the the Middle East.
Opposite: Impenetrable hilltop fortress of Ajlun lies half-hidden by heavy winter snows.

You pass through a larger **doorway,** over which there is a series of **carvings** of pairs of birds symbolising the carrier pigeons used throughout the stronghold's history. If you look upwards, just above the main door, you can see a **gap** in the stonework through which boiling oil would have been poured on invaders. Inside the main doorway a **chamber** is filled with roughly-shaped **boulders** for hurling at assailants, probably by **catapult**.

The bulk of the castle is in good condition. Most of the high-vaulted **ceilings** are still intact. Several **wells** are dotted about, which ensured the soldiers got enough water. The most striking aspect is the contrast in design with the Crusader castles. The shape is not only different, but so are specific architectural details, which seemed important to the Arabs but not to the Crusaders.

Deir Alla: The House of God

A short distance **south-west** from Ajlun, with the **River Jordan** just a few kilometres

to its **west,** lies **Deir Alla**, which means The House of God. This is deep in biblical country where each community's history is embedded in the Bible's pages. It was at Deir Alla, just south of the River Zarqa, named *Jabbok* in the Bible, that Jacob was said to have wrestled with the angel. It is uncertain whether a large community ever existed at Deir Alla, but it is likely that the religious community there was isolated from nearby towns and villages, such as Safi. Deir Alla was supposedly where Esau was reunited with Jacob. (The events are recounted in *Genesis* chapters *32-33).*

Excavations in the area uphold the suggestion that a civilisation dating back to at least 1600 BC was in existence. A **temple** was discovered with a **shrine**, as well as **incense burners, figurines** and a number of other ancient **artefacts**. A selection of fragments, probably coming from sacred vessels used in various early Christian rituals were also unearthed. Eminent Dutch archaeologist, Dr Franken, found three **clay tablets** at the site inscribed with a curious system of writing, similar to Phoenician.

Above: Pink flax bring a splash of colour to the hillside rocks near Deir Alla.

Later **tablets** were also unearthed, bearing Aramaic inscriptions. It seems that the shrine was never reconstructed. Numerous other societies came and went.

Continuing on from Deir Alla you come to the historically important remains of **Damiya**, mentioned in the Bible as Adam (or Adama): 'That the waters which came down from above stood and rose up upon a heap very far from the city Adam, that is beside Zaretan: and those that came down toward the sea of the plain, even the salt sea, failed, and were cut off: and the people passed over right against Jericho.' (*Joshua Chapter 3, Verse 16*)

A **Roman bridge** which can still be seen was constructed over the **ancient ford** across the River Jordan.

Pella: A Million Years of History

Pella, and the modern village of Tabaqat Fahl, lie nestled in some of the country's most luxuriant scenery, less than 5 kilometres east of the Jordan River. The drive to the city reveals Jordan's beautiful woodland, cradled among undulating hills and thriving with flora and fauna.

Pella is thought to have been continuously inhabited for over 6,000 years and signs found in the surrounding area suggest that even earlier man tramped the dewy grass and fished in the sweet waters of the abundant streams. The area's tranquillity, superb natural resources, fertile land and ideal climate allowed man to thrive.

Strategically placed, Pella straddled numerous important trading routes which linked Europe and the Near East with Central Asia and the farthest reaches of China and Mongolia. It developed financially from trade and was influenced by the great diversity of transient cultures. Within what is now Jordan, Pella was well connected to other Decapolis cities as well as being linked by the Via Nova Traiana or New Trajan Road to the crucial trading port of Aqaba in the south.

A great proportion of Pella's remains are still to be excavated, making it all the more alluring. The area's rich heritage is reflected in the way that the local Bedouin children greet tourists with a few ancient gold and silver coins they've found while playing around the site.

Getting there

From Deir Alla, Pella is a 30-kilometre (19-mile) drive due north on the road that runs from Amman, through Salt, north to Deir Alla and beyond. It is a 95 kilometre (59 mile) drive from Amman.

Pella can easily be visited en route to Umm Qais. Look out for the Department of Antiquities' blue signpost at the site of the ruins of Pella, or you may not realise you have arrived.

Sightseeing

There are a few Bedouin tents, a flock or two of black goats chewing at the bright green grass, a stream meandering through the valley below and, at a first glance, little more than a jumble of colonnades. Despite this, **Pella**, Decapolis city of the Roman Empire, is an archaeologist's paradise. The **array** of **fragments** left by past civilisations span the chronicles of history.

Things have changed considerably since the area was home to Stone Age hunters during the Palaeolithic era. A couple of kilometres **north-east** of Pella, at **Wadi el Hammeh**, **remains** of a primitive civilisation, existing almost 20,000 years ago, have been located. A variety of **stone weapons** and **tools** have been unearthed for killing gazelle, wild boar and perhaps even elephant which once roamed the savannah lands on which Pella was later built. Although ancient and extremely primitive, the so-called **Natufian site** near Pella has revealed relatively sophisticated and artistic **implements** and **tools.**

Pella's remnants provide examples of man-made artefacts from the Palaeolithic, Neolithic and Chalcolithic eras and Bronze and Iron Ages. Yet it was not really until the Hellenistic era (332-63 BC) that Pella began to experience its most monumental development. Some scholars maintain that when Alexander the Great marched through the site of Pella en route to Egypt, he laid the city's foundations. But it is more likely that Pella was founded by one of the

Seleucid rulers and burgeoned shortly after Alexander's death in 332 BC.

Extensive remnants dating back to the 2nd century BC indicate that Pella reached a height of prosperity during the 2nd and 1st centuries BC. Local **coins** struck in the city have been unearthed along with **coins** and **fragments** originating from across the East. These relics demonstrate the sophistication of the Ancient World. The two **Hellenistic castles,** constructed on the outskirts of Pella, emphasise the city's strategic and commercial importance during the later BC era.

But disaster came in 83 BC when the Hasmonean leader of Judaea gave the people of Pella an ultimatum to embrace Judaism, which they refused to do. In consequence Pella was raided and ransacked by soldiers under the command of Alexander Jannaeus, the ruler over Judaea. It was one of several Hellenistic communities on the **east banks** of the River Jordan, targeted by Jannaeus. Evidence of destruction from this brutal assault has been unearthed.

It was not until 64 BC that Pella, and a host of other Hellenic cities, were liberated from the grip of the Hasmoneans when Pompey forced his way **southwards** to take control. It was then that Pella formally entered the Decapolis.

Once out of the clutches of the Judaeans, Pella's fortunes revived again. The earliest **Roman coins** to be struck in the city date to about AD 83. Pella's history is enriched by all kinds of events, such as the influx of Christian refugees from Jerusalem, fleeing from the Romans in AD 66. Remnants of the Christian inflow have come to light during excavations. One dig unearthed a **sarcophagus** made of **stone**, believed to have been carved for a Christian commander, interred under the **floor** of what is now the **West Church.**

A Roman **odeon** to hold 400 spectators was erected during the 1st century AD on the banks of the Wadi Jirm, which runs through the settlement of Pella. With its pink and yellow blocks of stone it later became part of the temple and forum complex. The **shrine,** alongside the **stream,** was the largest of the temples built at Pella and on its site a large **Byzantine church**

was constructed. In the **remains** you can make out the sanctuary's **apse** pointing **eastwards** where the **altar** once stood. The fact that the complex was so near to running water suggests that the odeon was capable of being flooded for special performances.

This was a popular feature of Roman theatres, the Colosseum in Rome itself was flooded for mock sea battles and it has been suggested that Amman's own theatre had the same facilities. The close proximity to the stream would also have enabled fountains to spout water around the forum and other areas. Numerous **earthenware pipes** have been excavated which were used for this purpose. Coins struck in Pella portray a great temple and Nymphaeum which must have stood at the site, and is perhaps still awaiting discovery.

The Byzantine era once again restored Pella's flagging fortunes. Industry developed as trade routes to the area strengthened. By the late 5th century AD 25,000 people made Pella and environs their home. A large number of the **remains** visible today come from the Byzantine period, including **domestic houses, churches, shops, barracks, baths** and **tombs**.

On the **left side** of the **main site** of Pella three **columns** stand in a line where the 6th-century **West Church** once stood, repositioned there by the Department of Antiquities in recent years. Just **north** of the church an immense **water tank** has been excavated, built by the Byzantines to hold some 300,000 litres of water.

On a natural **balcony** overlooking the valley you can see what is left of the **East Church**. It is the earlier of the two, erected during the latter part of the 5th century AD. An impressive staircase once led down to the Wadi below. Like most of the other buildings at Pella it was probably brought crashing to the ground during the earthquake of AD 747.

Despite friction between the Byzantine and early Islamic peoples, Pella seems to have passed into Islamic times with relatively little bloodshed. The city's Semitic name of *Fahl* was reinstated, and again it entered a new era. Its contact with international trading routes was reduced after it became Islamic but, as always, the city adapted. This time it increased agricultural activities to compensate for loss of funds through commerce.

The Ummayed era, which lasted almost 100 years from the mid-6th century, was built on Byzantine foundations to form yet another civilisation. The grandeur and sophistication of these dwellings is apparent. One at least was known to have had 17 rooms. With the end of the Ummayed era, Abbasid control began, after which the Mamluks came and went.

As you tour the ruins it is exciting to speculate what lies deep beneath your feet. Next to the **main ruins** the Department of Antiquities compound has a collection of **relics** found during excavation work. Fine pieces of **mosaic,** taken from the lower church on the stream's edge as well as various white **marble slabs** with Byzantine lettering, **crosses** and **carved animals**, are found still being found in the compound.

Umm Qais: Frontier of the North

There is no better vantage point in northern Jordan than where the crucial Decapolis city of Gadara stood. Today the site is known by the name of the new town adjacent to it: Umm Qais. Situated 518 metres (1,700 feet) above sea level, the view reveals, to the north, Lake Tiberias (the Sea of Galilee), the Yarmouk River canyon and the Golan Heights.

Gadara was well known for its buildings during the period of the Roman Empire, but is perhaps more eminent for the orators, artists, poets and philosophers who originated there and rose to fame. Men such as Menippos — the liberated slave who became well-known as a satirist — and the philosopher, Oinomaos, were just two of the scholars who hailed from Gadara.

Like Pella, its sister Decapolis city, Gadara was blessed with fertile soils,

Opposite: Golden sunset behind the ancient Roman ruins at Pella.

Above: Roman ruins at the city of Umm Qais once formed part of ancient Gadara.
Opposite: Verdant hillsides surround Umm Qais with views to the north over Lake Tiberias.

abundant waterways and, most import-antly, an assortment of passing trade routes that crisscrossed Asia and Europe. Gadara was watered by numerous springs, amongst which were Ain Gadara, and Ain et Trab. The latter, although some 12 kilo-metres (7 miles) **east** of the Roman town, was connected to it by a man-made furrow.

Gadara comes from the Semitic word for a stronghold. The town reverted to Umm Qais during the Middle Ages, the name deriving from the ancient Arabic *mkes*, meaning a border station.

The Seleucid ruler Antiochus III overran Pella and beseiged Gadara in 218 BC, having forded the Jordan River. Pompey later over-whelmed the region as he marched south in 63 BC, emancipating Gadara, as well as Pella and a host of other towns, from the grip of the Jewish Hasmonean ruler Alexander Jannaeus.

Following Pompey's annexation of the city there was a run of prosperity, with coins being struck for local use. Soon after, in 30 BC, the town and its vicinity were awarded to King Herod of Judaea. This was an unpopular move with the people of Gadara, who protested vehemently.

When Herod died, Gadara was absorbed into the Roman Province of Syria. Jesus is alleged to have visited the town. A story, recorded in the New Testament, tells how he healed two men possessed with devils by forcing the demonic spirits to enter a herd of swine, which then ran violently into the Sea of Galilee and drowned:

'And when he was come to the other side into the country of the Gergesenes, (Gadarenes) there met him two possessed with devils, coming out of the tombs, exceedingly fierce, so that no man might pass by that way.' (*Matthew* Chapter 8, 28).

The prosperity of the Decapolis' was only truly attained in the latter part of the 1st century AD. *Pax Romana* allowed wide-spread trading and a good deal of building work to be carried out. Much of what can be seen today was actually constructed during the 2nd century AD.

The city's proximity to the hot springs of Al Hemma meant that the settlement was visited by people from across the Roman

Above: Impressive colonnade at Umm Qais.

Empire seeking refreshment and the therapeutic waters. It seems plausible that the numerous theatres and community edifices were put up, as Strabo tells us, because visitors would like to relax in Gadara after bathing.

The Byzantine era saw Gadara slip into relative obscurity. Earthquakes destroyed many buildings and, when the early Islamic era dawned, Gadara was nothing more than a village once again. However, discoveries at Umm Qais have led to speculation that the city of Gadara might have been as vast and prosperous as Jerash, the foremost city of the Decapolis. More excavations are needed to glean a greater understanding of Gadara's curious past.

Getting there

Two main routes lead north to Umm Qais. The first is the Jordan Valley road that runs up the western flank of Jordan, to the Syrian border.

The other road makes its way from Irbid

(north of Ajlun) in a north-west direction to Umm Qais. The ruins are some 110 kilometres (68 miles) north-west of Amman, a journey that takes around 2 hours. From Irbid the distance is 30 kilometres (19 miles). Extremely fertile lands stretch northwards as you drive from Irbid or Pella.

Plantations of banana trees, date palms and fig trees stretch in all directions. There are lemon and orange groves and a profusion of farm life mixes with the infrequent traffic. You begin to wonder whether you are really in Jordan, especially if you have already visited the desert regions.

Sightseeing

Situated in the **south-east** of the settlement, the **acropolis** was the most important part of **Gadara**. A quantity of square-shaped low-lying buildings on the **acropolis hill** were part of the Ottoman village. On the **north-east** flank of the acropolis is the **North Theatre**, one of three constructed during Roman times. This theatre was the largest but is today little more than a jumble of **stone blocks.** Many stones were subsequently used to build houses.

The North Theatre, like its western counterpart, is also thought to have been built in the years straddling the 1st and 2nd centuries AD. Its **seats** point due **west** and, at sunset, are brought to life by the direct sunlight. A considerable number of the seats are still intact and as basalt is harder than sandstone, the blocks have not worn as badly as at many Roman theatres. Note the seats still have their rounded edges, and how the lower seats (probably reserved for honoured guests) have higher **backrests**.

Until recently a headless **white marble statue** — now in Umm Qais' small **museum** — sat at the foot of one of the theatre's internal **staircases.** You can see the space where she made a strange contrast with the black basalt seats. It seems likely that the goddess, thought to be **Tyche**, was the patron goddess of Gadara and was once positioned above the theatre.

Just **north** of the West Theatre an assortment of black, almost charred-looking basalt **Corinthian columns** stand in memory of the great **Basilica** of **Gadara**. The spectacular view from the Basilical Terrace has only added to its downfall for winds have eroded them. A little further **north** of the Basilica are the contrasting profiles of white limestone **columns** which were designed as part of a colonnaded courtyard.

The **west flank** of the Basilica was once bordered with a row of shops. Of the 14 barrel-vaulted chambers, little remains today to indicate that they were ever shops at all. At right-angles to where they stood runs what remains of Gadara's **main road**. This rather forlorn **Decumanus Maximus**, only surfacing in a few places now, was designed to merge into the road to Tiberias, passing the stadium and various important mausoleums en route.

On the Decumanus Maximus, just to the **west** of the colonnaded courtyard, were situated one of Gadara's main sets of **baths**. You can still make out the remains of the well-built *hypocaust* (underground heating system). The city is thought to have had two or three public baths reflecting its theme of relaxation and recuperation. From the baths, directly across the Decumanus Maximus, is the **site** where the **Nymphaeum** was located. **Fragments** of statues and the fine **floor tiles** that would have adorned the building have been discovered during recent excavations.

Umm Qais' modest museum is located in one of the old Ottoman buildings on the acropolis area. It was inhabited until 1985 when the Department of Antiquities took it over. A covered **walkway** houses some of the relics discovered at Umm Qais that were bestowed in Gadara's rich legacy. Of these, the best is the headless statue of goddess Tyche, from the West Theatre. Also displayed is a **mosaic frieze,** taken from a stone-lined tomb in the Byzantine crypt of the **western mausoleum.**

An impressive lid and base of a **marble sarcophagus** are also under the covered walkway. The lid had been reused as a marble screen for a Christian church. Various other **sarcophagi** and **panels** of **mosaic work** are also exhibited, hinting at Gadara's extraordinary heritage.

The museum is open in summer from 08.00 until 17.00, and in the winter from 08.00 until 16.00. It is closed on Tuesdays.

Al Hemma: Fiery Water from the Earth

Ten kilometres (6 miles) **north** of Umm Qais on the **main road** — which now is little more than a tarmac track — you arrive at **Al Hemma**. It was there that the famous **Roman baths** were situated at the **hot springs** which are still used. If you make it to Umm Qais it would be a pity not to drive on for the few extra minutes to Al Hemma. As you proceed **north** you may need to check with locals that you are still on the road to Al Hemma as various other roads fork off it. Do not be put off by the numerous military **checkpoints.**

Al Hemma is tucked away in a **valley** filled with fruit trees. The tiny village has an unspoilt charm due, no doubt, to its position at the end of the road, with no through traffic. **Steps** lead down to the baths from the road. A large murky pool fed by four springs stretches out in front, ranging from 2 to 17 metres (56 feet) in depth. The manager of this complex notes that the water is cloudy with beneficial minerals, not dirt. The main hot spring, whose waters are around 57°C, pours into an **indoor pool**. Men and women take alternate two-hour shifts to bathe in the hot mineral waters. The indoor environment is rather stifling due to the high sulphur levels in the water. Twenty-five **chalets** can be rented in the complex, which is open between 06.00 and 20.00 daily. The baths can be hired by the public from 20.00 until midnight.

Irbid: Majestic City of the North

The 88-kilometre (55-mile) drive from Amman to **Irbid** takes about 90 minutes. From Jerash the distance is about 40 kilometres (25 miles). The town is linked by a network of roads, leading in all directions, including the **Syrian and Israel borders.**

Irbid is a pleasant town with wide **roads** and narrow **alleys,** lined with **fruit trees.** In recent years it has emerged as an important

Above: Bustling street in Irbid, north-west Jordan.

provincial administrative town. Although there is not a great deal to see, the shops are worth a browse, as is the Friday *souq*. Irbid has a good selection of **cafés** serving traditional Jordanian food. There are several small **hotels** and **banks** where you can change foreign currency.

Irbid's importance as a key trading centre en route to Haifa ended in 1948. However, the town has continued to prosper, despite a lack of natural water, which is pumped from a **spring** 18 kilometres (11 miles) to the **north-east.** The town's industries are a big employer for the region and the early 1980s saw the completion of a large **city university.**

Modern Irbid is located on the site of an Early Bronze Age settlement. A **city wall,** built like so many of the houses of black basalt, once encircled the town, although very little now exists. The location of Irbid is thought to be mentioned in the Bible as *Beth Arbel*. Scholars have debated whether the site was the burial place of Moses' mother and four of his sons. During Roman times the city was named *Arbila* and was one of the crucial Decapolis cities. Almost all of the ancient heritage is hidden beneath the new city.

South of Irbid, on the road to Jerash, you pass the **ruins** of **Tell el Husn.** The site probably dates back to the Early Bronze Age, but came to prominence during Roman and Byzantine times when it was almost certainly Dion, one of the cities of the Decapolis.

Zarqa

It is worth mentioning briefly that **Zarqa**, Jordan's second-largest city, is located 23 kilometres (14 miles) **north-east** of Amman. There is little of tourist interest in modern Zarqa, which depends on industrial activities. At the turn of the century it was nothing more than a small Circassian village but after 1948 it mushroomed. As well as being an administrative centre for the surrounding area, and a headquarters for the Arab Legion, Zarqa has a number of **factories, tanneries, breweries** and — most significant — the **oil refinery** on the **north side** of town.

The **main highway** leading to **Syria**, via **Mafraq**, passes **east** of Zarqa. The site of most interest is the ruined **Arab fortress, Qasr Shibib**, built on the foundations of an earlier Roman stronghold, situated above the **Zarqa Spring**.

Mafraq

Located 72 kilometres (45 miles) **north-west** of Amman, **Mafraq** is an administrative centre of relatively small importance. It stands at the crossroads of the great highway leading to Syria, and the other monumental motorway that stretches to the Iraqi border and beyond. Until 1920 Mafraq was no more than a crossroads of two tracks but, during the 1930s when work began on the oil pipeline from Iraq to Haifa, it escalated in size. An **Arab fortress,** as well as various Roman and Byzantine **remains** and even Nabatean **relics**, have been discovered in the locality. But, like Zarqa, there is little chance of excavation because of modern construction.

Ramatha: Border with Syria

The border crossing between Jordan and Syria is at the small town of Ramatha. Many tourists visiting both countries traverse this point. Communal taxis, buses and private cars haul tourists and their belongings from Damascus to Amman, **and**

vice versa. If you are thinking of leaving Jordan for Syria, be sure to have a Syrian visa before you reach the frontier. Syrian visas are not issued at the border. Remember, if you will be returning to Jordan, that you should get a multiple entry visa for Syria. Although one can usually get a Syrian visa from the Syrian Consulate in Amman, it is advisable to get it in your home country before travelling to the Middle East since this will tend to be cheaper. When applying for a visa, bear in mind that — if one puts 'journalist' or 'writer' under 'occupation' — the decision to let you enter the country will come from the Ministry of Information . . . in Damascus, a long process. One is also advised not to put 'yes' when you are asked whether you have entered the West Bank or Occupied Territories. JETT buses run a 5 hour service between the two capitals. The train connecting Jordan with Syria is, unfortunately, unreliable. A train leaves for Syria with passengers each Monday morning, returning only with cargo. The service is subject to change without notice.

Above: Railway station in the old town of Mafraq.

The West Bank: Sacred Rocks and Holy Shrines

The West Bank encompasses many of the greatest cultural, religious, and historical sites, not only of the Middle East, but in the world. The names of its cities — such as Bethlehem, Jerusalem, Jericho and Hebron — form the cornerstone of Christianity, and are also of great consequence to Muslims. The jewel in the crown is Jerusalem with its historical and religious eminence.

The Israeli occupation of the West Bank in 1967 was disastrous for Jordan. The occupation not only robbed the country of many of its most prized historical sites, but created innumerable other problems. The influx of Palestinian refugees onto the East Bank, the loss of crucial fertile farming land in the Jordan Valley, and a loss in tourist revenue, were obstacles with which the country had to contend.

Getting there
As of 1998 there is only one crossing point from Jordan to the West Bank and vice versa, but two into Israel proper. Conditions change as time passes, however, and it is always best to check.

The King Hussein (Allenby) Bridge crossing is a 30-minute drive from Amman and is the only crossing for those with permits to visit areas under the Palestine National Authority (PNA). The bridge is open Sunday through to Thursday from 07.00 until midnight and between 07.00 and 13.30 on Fridays and Saturdays.

If coming from the East Bank you will probably be heading for Jerusalem but it is worth stopping in Jericho en route. Provided you clear the formalities for the West Bank early, Jericho is a delightful place to have lunch.

Many tour groups in the Middle East take the opportunity to visit both the East and West Banks on the same trip.

(For crossings into Israel see Part 5 'Crossings to the West Bank and Israel')

Jericho: Oldest City on Earth

Jericho, known as *Ariha* in Arabic and meaning Moon, is revered by all peoples of the Middle East. Some say it is older than time itself. If not as old as that, it is certainly archaic. The city is also renowned for being the lowest urban settlement on earth, situated at a remarkable 250 metres (820 feet) below mean sea level. In her book *Jordan*, Christine Osborne wrote, 'Jericho sits like an emerald in a bowl of barren hills' — an apt description indeed.

Sightseeing
Jericho is one of the world's oldest continuously inhabited cities. It has a history that dates to about 9000 BC. Numerous **excavation sites** are dotted about the city and its environs. **Tel-es-Sultan**, for instance, illustrates the myriad communities which have inhabited the region. Tel-es-Sultan, like many sites in Jericho, dates back much further than Joshua's fabled attack on the city around 1250 BC when the priests blew their horns and made the walls collapse *(Joshua 6:20)*. The site is open from 08.00 until 17.00 and is home to a fascinating **Neolithic watchtower.**

Jericho's **oases** are fed by many **springs,** making the area exceptionally fertile. Almost anything grows in the semi-tropical environment. One famous spring (*Ain* in Arabic) is that of **Elijah**. It was there that the Prophet Elijah is said to have made the waters sweet by throwing in a handful of salt *(Kings II 2:21)*.

About 5 kilometres (3 miles) **north** of Jericho are the remains of the **Hisham Palace**, an Ummayed palace probably constructed by the Hisham, the 10th Ummayed Caliph, who reigned from AD 724 until AD 743. Like so many of the great Ummayed palaces it was never completed, and was ultimately devastated by an earthquake.

The palace complex boasts two **mosques,** an **audience hall, baths** and a **colonnaded court.** Its greatest asset is the **mosaic frieze**

Top: Gleaming white Saleh Abdul Mosque in the ancient city of Jericho.
Above: Sunlight on the courtyard of the Hisham Palace, north of Jericho.
Overleaf: The majestic caves at Qumran, where the Dead Sea Scrolls were discovered in 1947.

on the floor of the Caliph's own chamber. The work depicts a Tree of Life which is popular as a carpet design: beside the tree laden with fruits, a lion is depicted devouring a gazelle.

West of Jericho stands the infamous **Mount of Temptation**, where Christ is said to have withstood the temptations of the Devil for forty days and forty nights *(Matthew 4:8-9)*. A **steep path** ascends the slopes of the mount, advancing past the **Greek Orthodox Monastery** halfway up. On the summit's crest are the **remains** of an **ancient fortress**. The trek to the top might be tiring but it rewards the determined with a spectacular view of the **Dead Sea**.

A very popular stop for visitors is the **caves** at **Qumran**, some 30 kilometres (19 miles) **south** of Jericho. These became famous in 1947, and then only by accident.

Opposite: Twinkling lights illuminate the skyline of Jerusalem.

The most significant is **Cave 4,** with its keyhole-shaped entrance. It might not look impressive, but within its rock walls was discovered the single most important biblical find ever.

A Bedouin shepherd boy looking for a goat stumbled upon the concealed entrance of the cave. He thought that he may have unearthed a haul of hidden contraband, but he had found much more . . . a manuscript of the ancient book of *Isaiah*. This copy, a thousand years older than any other document ever discovered, became known as the **Dead Sea Scrolls**. The most authoritative book on the scrolls is John Allegro's *The Dead Sea Scrolls: A Reappraisal*.

A monastery of the Essenes, a Jewish sect, was sited at Qumran from the 2nd century BC onwards. But they inhabited an earlier site, dating back to the 8th century BC. The sect's library was situated in caves chosen to be inaccessible to intruders.

In the upper storey of one **room**, long **tables**, narrow **wooden benches,** and two large **inkwells**, were found. This seems to have been the chamber in which the Dead Sea Scrolls were written.

Other **rooms** and **chambers** of all kinds have been discovered (such as **kitchens, audience halls, workshops** and so forth). The site appears to have been evacuated when the Roman legion brought an end to the first Jewish Revolt in 68 AD. It was only then that the scrolls were stored in the caves at Qumran.

Jerusalem: Holy City of Three Creeds

Jerusalem is a city known by many names and adored by many peoples through time. In Arabic it is called *Al Khodz*; in Hebrew, *Yerushalayim*, and in ancient epochs it was called *Urusalimu*, and *Salem*. Whatever its name, no other city can match Jerusalem's historical and religious significance.

Above: Cave 4, with its keyhole-shaped entrance, is where the Dead Sea Scrolls were found by a Bedouin shepherd boy.

It is hard to say when habitation first occurred. About the year 1000 BC it was captured by Israelite forces under the command of King David. Elevated to capital of the Israelite kingdom, it grew in stature, primarily in the reign of David's son, Solomon. Temples, including the great one on Mount Moriah or the Temple Mount, as well as walls, palaces and other edifices were erected and Jerusalem quickly became a formidable metropolis.

Yet on Solomon's death in 922 BC, the Israelite kingdom was split north from south. The north was proclaimed the kingdom of Israel and the south the kingdom of Judaea which had Jerusalem as its capital.

Four centuries of warring battered the kingdom of Judaea, as one ancient power after the next — among them Egyptians, Philistines and Arabians — sought to overrun the city. The Assyrians, who had managed to storm Jerusalem, were replaced by Nebuchadnezzar in 587 BC.

The Babylonian rule of Nebuchadnezzar did not last as long as the great monarch would have hoped, for the city was conquered by the Persian, Cyrus I, in 539 BC. Many of the buildings destroyed by Nebuchadnezzar were rebuilt.

Alexander the Great conquered the metropolis in 332 BC, after which the Seleucid Empire, under Antiochus, swept in victorious around the year 170 BC.

But one of the most important conquests was that of the Roman Empire, which took Jerusalem in 64 BC. The years of Roman rule, under the fabled Roman potentate Herod, saw the building of splendid palaces and public buildings.

With the end of Herod's rule in AD 4 and the relinquishing of control by his son, Archelaus, after less than a decade, the stage was set for the era of the New Testament.

The Roman commander Pontius Pilate was in control when Christ was crucified. His reign became increasingly autocratic and contributed to the Jewish Revolt of AD 66. Hostilities were extremely fierce, forcing the Roman legions to pull out of Jerusalem. But after regrouping, the Roman battalions, under Vespasian, returned.

It is said to have been Vespasian's own son, Titus, who took control of Jerusalem after a siege which lasted four months. Sadly, many of the archaic parts of Jerusalem were razed to the ground, including the Great Temple.

Much of the Old City was reconstructed around AD 130 by Hadrian, under his construction and development programme named *Aelia Capitolina*. Emperor Constantine, the first Roman Emperor to convert to Christianity, was eager to construct buildings of Christian significance on sites of ancient importance to Christianity.

The 7th century, with the advent of Islam, saw Jerusalem's transition to a holy city of Islam. It was in AD 688 that one of the greatest and earliest shrines of Islam was constructed: the Dome of the Rock.

As the centuries passed, one power continued to supersede another in Jerusalem. The Fatimids of Egypt were succeeded by the Seljuk Turks in AD 1077. And then began the legendary era of the Crusades. Forces from Europe set out for the Holy Land, storming Jerusalem in AD 1098. They constructed and renovated various sites of Christian importance and made it possible for pilgrims to venture to Jerusalem. But the great Saracen leader, Saladin, retook Jerusalem in 1187, returning the city to Islamic rule.

Jerusalem remained a prize, and any empire of stature fought to gain control of it. The Ummayeds ruled it from Damascus, and later came the Mamluks, after which the great Ottoman Empire took the city, holding it until 1917.

After World War I, a British Mandate (approved by the newly-formed League of Nations) led to British rule over Jerusalem in 1922. Later, after the United Nations agreed to the partition of the city, Zionist fervour led to the 1948 war between Jews and Arabs. A no-man's land through Jerusalem left the Arabs with no more than the Old City and Arab East Jerusalem. The remaining area was turned by the Israelis into the capital of their new state.

In 1967 the second Arab-Jewish conflict saw the Israeli invasion of the Jordanian West Bank and remaining parts of the city of Jerusalem. This situation still prevails with the city annexed by Israel as the eternal capital of the Jewish state, although it has never been recognised under international law.

The Old City

Most sites of great archaeological, religious and cultural importance are in an area of about one mile square, known as the **Old City**. This **sector** of **Jerusalem** was occupied by the Israelis in 1967. The Old City is loosely subdivided into four segments and is largely as it was arranged during the 2nd century AD by Emperor Hadrian. In the **south-west** is the **Armenian Quarter** and **east** of that, in the **south-east,** is the **Jewish Quarter. North** of the Armenian Quarter, in the **north-west,** is the **Christian Quarter** with the **Muslim Quarter** in the **north-east.**

Most of the **walls** surrounding the Old City were constructed during the 16th century. They have **eight gates. Herod's Gate** is at the far **north-east** and clockwise, the others are: the **Gate of St Stephen,** the **Golden Gate** (which has been closed since 1530), the **Dung Gate,** the **Zion Gate,** the **Jaffa Gate,** the **New Gate** and the **Damascus Gate.** Tourists can walk the **wall** between the Damascus and Jaffa Gates or around the city on the ramparts.

Entering the Old City through the Gate of St Stephen, you will see on the **left** the **Haram esh-Sharif,** the sacred enclosure that covers some 12 hectares (30 acres). It is there, at the apex of **Mount Moriah,** that the sacred shrine of the **Dome of the Rock,** as well as the **El Aqsa Mosque,** are situated. The Dome of the Rock, at the centre of the enclosure, is much as it was when built in the 7th century, a masterpiece of octagonal design.

The Dome of the Rock is not a mosque, but a **shrine** housing the **actual rock** from which the Prophet Mohammed ascended to heaven. After the holy shrines of Mecca and Medina, the Dome of the Rock is next in importance. The sacred rock inside is said to be the threshing floor of Araunah

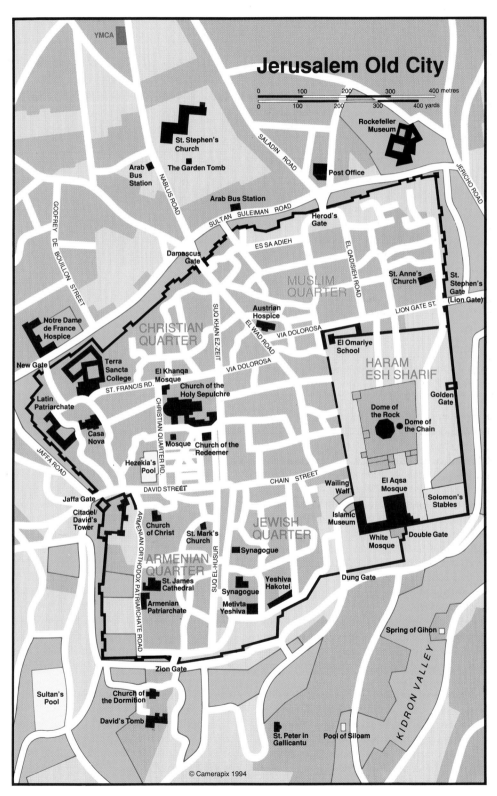

Jerusalem Old City

0 100 200 300 400 metres
0 100 200 300 400 yards

YMCA

Rockefeller Museum

St. Stephen's Church

The Garden Tomb

Arab Bus Station

Post Office

SALADIN ROAD

JERICHO ROAD

NABLUS ROAD

Arab Bus Station

SULTAN SULEIMAN ROAD

Herod's Gate

ES SA ADIEH

Damascus Gate

MUSLIM QUARTER

EL QADISIEH ROAD

St. Anne's Church

St. Stephen's Gate (Lion Gate)

GODFREY DE BOUILLON STREET

Notre Dame de France Hospice

CHRISTIAN QUARTER

Austrian Hospice

SUQ KHAN EZ-ZEIT

EL WAD ROAD

VIA DOLOROSA

LION GATE ST.

El Omariye School

HARAM ESH SHARIF

New Gate

Terra Sancta College

El Khanqa Mosque

VIA DOLOROSA

ST. FRANCIS RD.

Church of the Holy Sepulchre

Golden Gate

Latin Patriarchate

CHRISTIAN QUARTER RD.

Dome of the Rock

Dome of the Chain

Casa Nova

Mosque

Church of the Redeemer

JAFFA ROAD

Hezekia's Pool

DAVID STREET

CHAIN STREET

Wailing Wall

El Aqsa Mosque

Solomon's Stables

Jaffa Gate

Citadel/ David's Tower

Church of Christ

St. Mark's Church

JEWISH QUARTER

Islamic Museum

ARMENIAN ORTHODOX PATRIARCHATE ROAD

Synagogue

White Mosque

Double Gate

ARMENIAN QUARTER

SUQ EL-HUSUR

St. James Cathedral

Synagogue

Yeshiva Hakotel

Dung Gate

Armenian Patriarchate

Metivta Yeshiva

Spring of Gihon

Zion Gate

KIDRON VALLEY

Sultan's Pool

Church of the Dormition

David's Tomb

St. Peter in Gallicantu

Pool of Siloam

© Camerapix 1994

235

Above: Detail of the fabulous ceramic decoration on the 7th-century Dome of the Rock, the third holiest shrine of Islam.

on which King David constructed the altar of the Lord.

In 1966, under the guidance of King Hussein, the dome of the shrine was replaced with a dome fashioned from aluminium bronze alloy. The early 1990s saw further gilding and restoration work. An inscription mentions the Prophet's ascension into heaven. This event is mentioned in the Qur'an, *Sura 17*, verses 1 to 7, and is entitled The Night-Journey.

The inside of the dome is no less magnificent than the outside. Oriental **carpets** adorn the floor, and **stained-glass windows** — many dating back to the time of Suleiman the Magnificent — delicately filter the light. A huge earthquake during the 11th century brought the original dome thundering to the ground.

The sacred **rock** has an **indentation** which looks similar to a **footprint.** Islamic lore maintains that this was left by Mohammed as he sprang to heaven. The story goes that the rock tried to ascend after the Prophet, but was held back to earth by the Angel Gabriel. The **other imprint** is asserted to be the Angel Gabriel's handprint — embossed forever as he held the mighty rock down.

Just **east** of the Dome of the Rock is the **Dome of the Chain**. Smaller in size, it is said by some to have been a prototype for its larger counterpart. **South** of the great Dome of the Rock is the **El Aqsa Mosque**, the fourth holiest shrine in Islam, on whose steps in July 1951 King Abdullah was assassinated. El Aqsa, which means 'the distant place', has been replaced several times. The present mosque dates back to the 11th century. During the Crusader occupation of Jerusalem, the El Aqsa Mosque was turned into the headquarters of the Knights Templar. The greatest destruction has come through earthquakes, but any damage has always seen the rebuilding and reconstruction of this crucial shrine of Islam. A flight of steps leads from the mosque to the Dome of the Rock.

One eminent writer of the Arab World during this century, John Grant, wrote about Jerusalem in his acclaimed work *Travels in the Unknown East*, just before World War II:

Above: The magnificent Dome of the Rock is a shrine housing the rock from which the Prophet Mohammed is said to have ascended to heaven.

'Unlike any other town, Jerusalem does not seem to suffer the ups and downs in its ordinary life caused by the occurrence of such ceremonies at Christmas and Easter, for the devout atmosphere is always present — it is part of the everyday.

'Perhaps that is why a considerable number of worshippers follow the Franciscan fathers on their procession every Friday along the Via Dolorosa.

'If you have even the slightest religious feeling, seeing these venerable men take the Way of Sorrow on which Jesus walked bearing the Cross will bring home the fact that, this majestic age notwithstanding, men can yet suffer eagerly for their conviction: only a short way from immortality and the hilarity of vice and wine.

'There are fourteen stations where white-bearded monks, wearing sandals, sun-helmets, and thick blanket coats, kneel and recite prayers on this Way of Agony under the intense heat of the midday sun. The procession is led by Muslim mace-bearers, through bazaars, up and around the cobbled streets of Jerusalem.

'Later, see also how a Christian Arab salutes his Muslim fellow-countrymen, how they greet each other — "Good morning" — they call with a smile, and feel love of good neighbourliness. Here more than in any other part of the world, they appreciate that both are *People of the Book*.

'A Muslim's heart, however, goes out to the Holy Place which encompasses the Aqsa, *the Farthest Mosque* mentioned in the Koran itself, and the Rock which was the scene of the Prophet's night-journey to the Celestial Throne.

'On entering the gigantic quadrangle, you see an edifice surmounted by a golden dome about seventy feet high. This is the Dome of the Rock. Standing on a raised platform, it dominates the landscape.

'Discarding my shoes as I went in, I beheld a thing, the like of which my eyes had never seen.

'Light fell upon a gigantic grey-red rock below, on a stone which ripples and twists in undulations. All in a piece, some sixty feet long, it lay there like something living.

'The hoofprints in the rock left by *Buraq*,

Above: A section of the old city walls around Jerusalem beside the entrance to the 14th-century citadel.

the Prophet's steed, were pointed out. I prayed in a crypt under the rock, reached by descending eleven steps. It is surrounded by a railing almost my own height, and I am a tall man.

'The effect of the light entering the interior through the coloured glass windows was marvellous. The ceiling is painted with dull gold; the floor is of marble mosaic. The richness of decoration inside brings home to the worshipper how little sacred things need man's hand to beautify them.'

The **Via Dolorosa** (Road of Sorrows), is said to be the route that Christ took when carrying the Cross, from the Praetorium to Calvary. It leads from the **Lion Gate** (Gate of St Stephen) to the **Church of the Holy Sepulchre**. This church is thought to be built on the **site** where Christ was crucified.

There are **fourteen stations** along the route where significant incidents happened to Christ while he was bearing the Cross. These range from where he fell for the first time to where he was nailed onto the Cross. Each is marked; some by a **chapel,** others by a **column,** and at these sites pilgrims to

the Holy Land stop for a moment to pray. This tracing of the Cross ceremony is performed every Friday by the Franciscan Fathers and pilgrims alike.

If you walk from the Gate of St Stephen, you will see the **Church of St Anne** on the **right** of Via Dolorosa. This is supposedly where Mary was born and is thought to have been erected in Crusader times.

The **Church of the Holy Sepulchre** is the most revered site in Christianity, marking the spot where Christ was not only crucified but buried as well. Following various earlier churches on the site (the first, constructed in AD 335 by Emperor Constantine, was ransacked by the Persians in AD 614), the Church of the Holy Sepulchre was erected by the Crusaders in the 12th century.

The mélange of styles and influences inside are due to the fact that the Ottoman Turks distributed various sections of it to the six main Christian communities (such as the Copts and Armenian Orthodox). You can visit the stations between numbers **ten** and **fourteen** — the final one — all of which are in various parts of the Church of the Holy Sepulchre in chapels such as the **Latin Chapel** or the **Greek Chapel**.

One of the great descriptions of a visit to Jerusalem was given by the American writer Mark Twain, in *The Innocents Abroad* (1869): 'And so I close my chapter on the Church of the Holy Sepulchre — the most sacred locality on earth to millions of men, and women, and children, the noble and the humble, bond and free. In its history from the first, and in its tremendous associations, it is the most illustrious edifice in Christendom.

'With all its clap-trap side-shows and unseemly impostures of every kind, it is still grand, reverend, venerable, for a god died there; for fifteen hundred years its shrines have been wet with the tears of pilgrims from the earth's remotest confines; for more than two hundred, the most gallant knights that ever wielded sword wasted their lives away in a struggle to seize it and hold it sacred from infidel pollution.

'Even in our own day a war, that cost millions of treasure and rivers of blood, was fought because two rival nations claimed the sole right to put a new dome upon it. History is full of this old Church of the Holy Sepulchre — full of blood that was shed because of the respect and the veneration in which men held the last resting place of the meek and lowly, the mild and the gentle, Prince of Peace!'

At the **West Wall,** located right by the Jaffa Gate, is the **Citadel**. Also known as **David's Tower**, it was erected in the 14th century on the foundations of another tower, which itself was built on foundations dating back to the 1st century AD. The top of the tower gives an unparalleled **view** across the Old City of Jerusalem and out to the Mount of Olives. The Citadel houses the Jerusalem **City Museum**. Another important museum is the **Rockefeller Museum**, outside the Old City's wall, just **north** of Herod's Gate.

The Old City of Jerusalem is crammed with remnants of religious and cultural activity spanning well over 2,000 years. In addition to the twenty-nine **mosques** and dozens of **churches** and **chapels** of every sect and order, there are hundreds of places with special significance.

Above: Interior of the Church of the Holy Sepulchre — the most revered site in Christianity. It marks the spot where Christ was crucified and later buried.

The best way to see the Old City is just to roam, and not worry about getting lost. You will soon get to know where and what the main landmarks are. You will come face to face with a bustle of religious and commercial activities. Wherever you look people pray, barter, think, muse, chat or simply wander about.

The *souq* of the Old City is resplendent with a feast of goods on offer. The labyrinth of alleys interwind, but reveal a hidden world, redolent of biblical times.

Just **north** of the Old City you will find **East Jerusalem** where there are many of the cheaper **hotels** as well as the two **Arab Bus Stations.** East Jerusalem reaches down to the Gate of Damascus.

The **New City** of Jerusalem, which encapsulates most of the commercial facilities, sprawls out from the Jaffa Gate.

The main thoroughfare, **Jaffa Street,** runs from Jaffa Gate to the **bus station.** In the downtown zone you will find the usual features of a modern city, including **cinemas** and **restaurants.**

The main **tourist office** is located at 24 **King George Street.** It is open every day. The other branch, just inside the Jaffa Gate, has many tourist **maps** and **brochures.** A free weekly booklet with a diary of events and advertisements is available at tourist offices, entitled *This Week in Jerusalem.* The **Christian Information Centre,** also inside the Jaffa Gate, has a great deal of information but is not open on Sundays.

Above: Fourteenth-century David's Tower stands over the Wailing Wall and the Jaffa Gate and is a vantage point for stunning views across the city to the Mount of Olives.

Bethlehem: Birthplace of Christ

Mentioned in the pages of both the Old and New Testaments, **Bethlehem** is renowned as the town in which Christ was born. Although Bethlehem has almost become a suburb of Jerusalem, located 17 kilometres (10 miles) to its **south,** it retains much of its age-old charm.

The centre, with its **Manger Square,** overlooking the **Church of the Nativity,** is at the hub of endless bustle and commotion. As one tour bus leaves, another ten arrive. Souvenir shops sell every imaginable

Above: Steps leading up to the bell-tower of the Church of the Nativity, considered to be the oldest church in the world still in use.

trinket; the Nativity scene is sculpted from wood, etched into metal and assembled from cloth-covered pegs.

Keepsakes are available on every corner, in every shop. In all this commercial bustle it would be easy to forget the town's prominence, which began in Old Testament times. The marriage of Ruth to Boaz took place there, and it was where David spent his youth.

It was at Bethlehem, during the 4th century, that St Jerome translated the Bible from Hebrew and Greek into Latin.

The Church of the Nativity stands on the site of an earlier church, erected in the 4th century by Emperor Constantine. The design of this initial church seems to have been similar to that of the Holy Sepulchre in Jerusalem. Having been ravaged by fire during the 6th century, the replacement was put up under Justinian's guidance in the same period. It is thought to be the world's oldest church still in use. A cave within was said by Constantine to be the actual birthplace of Christ. It is located under the high **altar.**

The **ceiling** is fashioned from English oak, a gift from King Edward IV of England during the 15th century.

In the 17th century the Ottoman Turks stripped the lead from the roof to melt it down for ammunition. This action, together with neglect during the Mamluk regime, led to the virtual dereliction of the building which was only restored to its former glory last century.

The Church of the Nativity is shared between three denominations: Roman Catholic, Greek Orthodox, and Armenian, which vie for ascendancy. Each has its own **altar** and **chapel** in the rather austere-looking church, but the strict allocation of Mass times remains a source of friction.

Stairs lead down into the **Grotto of the Nativity** from either side of the **main altar**. It is there that the manger was supposed to have stood.

A **silver star** indicates the place where Christ was born. Various altars are dotted about in the **grotto,** including one to mark where the three Wise Men stood to pay homage to the infant.

Catholics are prohibited from praying at the **Altar of the Nativity**, although they are permitted to burn incense over the silver star: they are requested to pray at the **Altar of the Manger** instead.

The greatest festivities take place at Christmas, when pilgrims come from all over the world to pray and pay homage.

There are three quite different celebrations of Christmas. Those of Western Christmas — and most of the world — on 25 December; Orthodox Christmas on 6 January; and the Armenian Church's Christmas on 19 January.

The atmosphere is festive in the days that lead up to Christmas on 25 December, but the true celebrations begin on the afternoon of 24 December.

A **tourist information office** at the **western** extremity of Manger Square provides visitors with a map of Bethlehem.

Above: The Grotto of the Nativity is revered by Christians the world over as the birthplace of Christ.

Above: Pilgrims come from all over the world to pray and pay homage in the old city of Bethlehem.

Hebron: City of Four Hills

Hebron, which is called **Al Khalil** in Arabic, is located at a height of 914 metres (3,000 feet), some 45 kilometres (28 miles) **south** of Jerusalem. It is the ancient **Valley of Ephron**, a place mentioned time and again in the Bible.

The focal point of Hebron is the extraordinary **Haram al-Khalil Mosque**. This immense building is sacred to both Muslims and Jews alike. It is constructed over the **Cave of Machpelah** and a **synagogue** is also housed there, as well as a mosque. The primary section of the building was originally a Crusader Church, which itself was constructed on the foundations of an earlier religious edifice.

In the **southern wall** is the *mihrab* (prayer niche) which faces towards Mecca. It is crafted from multi-coloured marble and mosaics. Beside the *mihrab* is the *minbar*, a pulpit carved from walnut, crafted without nails, supposedly during the 11th century. **North** of the *mihrab* are two free-standing **cenotaphs** in black and white marble, dedicated to Rebecca and Isaac.

A subterranean **cave** can been seen through an opening in the floor, through which an oil lamp lightens the dimness. The bodies of those whose cenotaphs are above are said to be interred below.

Around the Haram al-Khalil is an assortment of the usual **souvenir shops** and **stalls**. Some of these purvey examples of Hebron's famous **glass work**. The old *souq* in Hebron is certainly worth visiting and its selection of ·**glass work** is superlative. This hand-blown glass is shaped and crafted using techniques that date back thousands of years.

PART THREE: SPECIAL FEATURES

Above: Dazzling embroidered items on display in the Jordan Design Centre.
Opposite: Scuba diver explores the submarine waters of the Gulf of Aqaba.

Above: Yellow and blue angel fish with companion reef fish find shelter in a coral garden.

Marine Life: Underwater Paradise of the Middle East

At the innermost part of the Red Sea's long expanse, the Gulf of Aqaba juts northwards with the Sinai Peninsula as its western bank and Saudi Arabia to the east. The gulf gets its name from the Jordanian town at its head.

The Gulf of Aqaba is home to some of the finest marine life in the Middle East. Its coral reef is unmatched, as is the serenity of its waters. Unlike other areas of the Red Sea, in which diving is hindered and marine life hampered by the busy shipping lanes, the gulf is a haven of tranquillity.

Aqaba, whose history stretches back more than 3,000 years, has been an important trading port throughout Middle Eastern history. With the Arab-Jewish conflict of 1948 Aqaba's significance increased as it became Jordan's only port. Its use for shipping phosphates to the international market is of particular importance.

The Gulf of Aqaba lies along the Great Rift, which runs from Lake Tiberias (the Sea of Galilee) down to eastern Africa. The gulf is very narrow and its waters extraordinarily deep. At the **northern end** it is no more than 5 kilometres wide, yet its depth ranges between 1,000 and 1,800 metres (3,281 and 5,906 feet).

The climate is hot and dry, with less than 20 millimetres rainfall a year. High levels of evaporation mean that the salt content is unusually acute. Salts make up over 4 per cent of the water content.

The **northern stretch** of Jordan's **coast,** between Aqaba and the **port,** has a sandy shoreline, broken by intermittent areas of stone. The strip has a gently sloping shore leading to expansive submarine **grasslands**. Beyond the port, where diving is not possible, the shoreline has much steeper sides. These rock faces sheer down into the water, sinking thousands of feet. Deepwater **corals** and **fish** are sustained, even at the low depths of the region. Indeed, the profusion of marine life at the **southern** area of Jordan's coast, known as the **South Coast**, is outstanding.

On the sandy shores it is hard for some

Above: Lionfish in the sparkling waters of the Gulf of Aqaba.

creatures to survive. Those with soft frames can be crushed by the drifting sand, which tends to dry out during the day. Yet creatures such as the **ghost crab** (*Ocypode saratan*) are found there. **Sandhoppers** and the small **mole crab** (*Hippa*) are also evident.

The depths and diversity of submarine terrains provide for differing kinds of underwater life. In shallow waters, where the shore slopes gently into the gulf, a plethora of creatures live buried under the sandy bottom. These include the **acorn worm** (*Ptychodera flava*), the **fan worm** (*Sabellastarte*), the **terebellid** (*Loinia medusa*) and a host of **polychaete worms**, which live in burrows or under stones.

A great deal of submarine life has adapted itself for survival while confined to the bed of shallow waters. For instance, the **sea cucumber** has a mass of threads, coated with a gluey blanket, with which to tangle up predators. Several types of **sea star** (such as *Linckia* and *Asterina burtoni* as well as *Astropecten polyacanthus*) live on the bottom of shallow waters of lagoons.

Other creatures resident in lagoons are **crabs**, **shrimps** and a number of the **sea**

urchin family, of which the *Diadema setosum* is frequently found, as is the rarer *Echinometra mathaei*. In the shallow waters camouflage is a necessity for fish hoping to lurk undisturbed for prey, or to avoid becoming the prey of others. Many of these have flat bodies which are easily concealed among the stones and sea grasses.

Fish such as the **leopard flounder** (*Bothus pantherinus*), **lizard fish** (*Synodus and Trachinocephalus*) and many others, are found.

Many varieties of **sea grasses** are present in the waters of the Gulf of Aqaba. Among the more common varieties are the *Halophila stipulacea, Halophila ovalis* and *Halodule uninervis*. Their long strands tend to blanket the sea bed and can exist from the shallowest of waters to about 40 metres (130 feet) in depth. Their presence is of great consequence as they create carbohydrates and other organic chemicals with the help of sunlight. They are also the

Overleaf: Dazzling display of tropical fish dart through the azure waters of Aqaba.

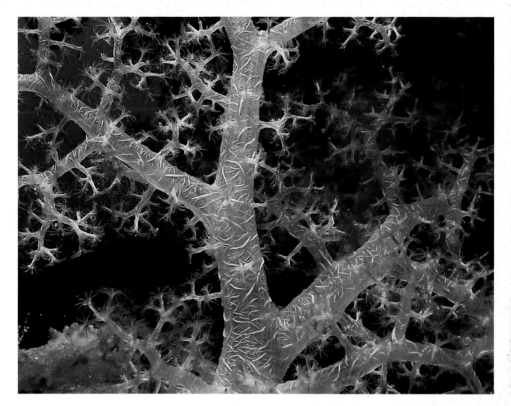

food of many herbivorous marine creatures while other denizens use them as breeding grounds.

When diving around these fragile grass beds look carefully for the many creatures which make themselves almost inconspicuous. You may see not only **sea horses** but **pipe-fish** (*Syngnathidae*) and the infamous **ghost pipe-fish** (*Solenichthys*).

The **creamy-grey moray eel** (*Siderea grisea*) and several other varieties of **eel** can also be found in the gulf's grass beds. Of these, the **garden eel** (*Gorgasia sillneri*) is only found in the Gulf of Aqaba. Growing to about 60 centimetres (2 feet) long, it lives in holes burrowed into the sand.

For most divers **coral reefs** provide an endless source of delight, and Jordan's are no exception. The most important of these stretches lie in the **southern** waters

Above: Delicate corals grace the sea bed at Aqaba.

Opposite: Clown fish dart between the tentacles of an anemone.

of Jordan's coast.

There are around 100 varieties of **stony coral**. Their abundance is partly due to their symbiotic relationship with **microscopic algae** which live within the coral tissues photosynthesising the light. Although this leads to a profusion of stony coral, it only occurs where there is enough light.

Corals develop according to conditions around them and the reef is by no means unbroken. When you dive you will see pockets which have managed to develop in favourable surroundings. Note that collecting corals and the use of spearguns are forbidden.

Up to about a thousand species of fish are thought to inhabit these waters. Each survives through its own particuliar adaption. Some, such as the **damsel fish** of the *Pomacentridae* family, or the diminutive groups of ***Dascyllus aruanus*** seek shelter in the corals. The latter rely on the **coral Stylophora** in shallow waters for survival. **Clown fish** (*Amphiprion bicinctus*) depend for their existence on a lifetime spent among the tentacles of **giant sea-anemones**.

Above: Water skiier displays adroit skills at Aqaba.

Butterfly and **angel fish,** of the *Chaetodontidae* and *Pomacanthidae* families respectively, dart among the corals. They move with graceful motions, enabling them to negotiate their path between even the narrowest of crevices. Like butterfly fish, **parrot fish** also eat live coral, scraping off its surface as best they can.

Many other species of fish have also adapted to living off the coral. These include **trigger-fish** (*Balistidae*) and the *Acanthuridae* family which are **surgeon fish** eating not the coral, but the algae which grows on it.

The climate is equable all year round, which makes it possible to dive at least twice a day. Only when you venture beneath the surface can you begin to comprehend the Gulf of Aqaba's wealth and diversity of submarine life. (See "Aqaba: Harbour from the Desert Sands", Part Two).

Aqaba's Aquatic Playground

In biblical times Aqaba was a great port, from whose shores all the luxuries of the age were transported across the known world. Peacocks and ivory, frankincense and myrrh, gold and silver, were loaded aboard vessels, which then plied the ancient waterways to distant destinations. But, with the collapse of the Roman Empire, the trade routes and trading posts fell into disrepair. And, for many centuries, Aqaba and many such communities hibernated.

Not until recently did Aqaba awaken, shedding its slumber to become the bustling centre for watersports that it is today. Its phenomenal geographic location — boasting unpolluted, placid waters — transformed what until three decades ago was little more than a sleepy fishing village.

Virtually an inland sea, the Gulf of Aqaba, on which the town sits, provides the perfect ingredients for some of the best watersports activities in the Middle East. Water temperatures range from 20°C in winter to 26°C in summer; with air temperatures ranging from about 20°C in winter to a very hot 40°C in summer.

The gulf's prevailing winds, which sweep down from the north, keep the surface clean. And, as the surface water is

Above: A catamaran speeds over the still waters of the Gulf of Aqaba.

pushed southward, the gulf's unique water circulation comes into play, letting deeper waters forge upward. This allows the gulf to spawn a wide variety of marine life.

The Gulf of Aqaba is actually part of the Great Rift Valley which plunges to depths of over 1,800 metres (5,906 feet). Most astonishing of all is that the waters thrust downward hundreds of feet within a few feet of the shore. For scuba diving this presents a great advantage: that no lengthy, costly, shuttles out to dive sites are necessary. And for the novice this provides a superb range of diving near to the safety of the water's edge.

Aqaba's aquatic facilities are comprehensive: ranging from **scuba diving** and **waterskiing,** to **windsurfing** and **parasailing**. Several **aquatic centres** provide all the necessary equipment and instruction where appropriate. Whether you are an expert, or an enthusiastic amateur, Aqaba's pleasures should be sampled by all. For those reluctant to try the challenge of scuba diving or waterskiing, Aqaba's gentler sports — such as **snorkeling** and **paddle-boating** — are a wonderful way to relax and unwind.

But if you are ready to taste the thrills of Aqaba's pristine waters, try out its waterskiing, windsurfing, or scuba diving in its enchanted waters.

Four main dive centres providing fine facilities and expert instruction are located at Aqaba. They are: **Aquamarina Diving Centre**, **Sea Star Diving Centre**, **Red Sea Diving Centre** and the **Royal Diving Centre**. The latter is the only government-run organisation. The minimum age for restricted diving is generally 12 years, and full unrestricted diving begins at 15 years of age. Qualified divers may be asked to produce their official documents. Most international diving certificates are respected at Aqaba.

When hiring the necessary equipment for scuba diving, waterskiing, or windsurfing, make sure that you have checked it at the place of hire, and that you understand how to use it competently.

Visitors will find that Aqaba's hire shops maintain the highest standards of quality; and that the staff are willing to answer any questions about local conditions or the equipment. Also make sure that you

are well briefed as to the currents and areas of the gulf in which you can move about.

Aqaba's coral reefs are protected from spear-fishing, which sadly has destroyed many of the world's great diving regions. Apart from the natural seclusion of the Gulf of Aqaba, the most rigorous standards are applied to ensure that the waters remain crystal clear.

The port of Aqaba is some distance away from the aquatic activities. Several projects in recent years have attempted to enhance the natural abundance of coral reefs. Prince Abdullah's pioneering project — launched in 1985 — arranged for a cargo ship to be sunk in the Gulf of Aqaba, which formed a superb **artificial coral reef.** It lies some 30 metres (98 feet) below the surface, with the top deck only submerged in about 12 metres (39 feet) of water.

Aqaba's glass-like surface, with slight cross currents, provides excellent wind-surfing opportunities. Similarly, the gulf's waterskiing is considered second to none. King Hussein, and many members of the Royal Family, excel in waterskiing and other aquatic sports.

The king has from the time of his youth pioneered the development of watersports at Aqaba, ensuring that the town stays as charming as ever, and its facilities remain pre-eminent.

Above: Youngster enjoys playful afternoon in the warm waters of Aqaba,

Opposite: Tourist gazes out over the Gulf of Aqaba into a golden sundown.

Wildlife: Struggle to Save a Rare and Ancient Heritage

Although the 20th century has seen the greatest and most encyclopaedic documentation of Arabia's fauna, it is the progeny of a much earlier zoological heritage. As early as the 9th century, Arabs were writing authoritative works of zoology. Perhaps the greatest of these is the treatise entitled *Al-Hayawan* by Abu Othman al Jahez, who studied the behaviour and habitats of animals.

Al Jahez was the forerunner of another great Arab zoologist, Kamal ei-din el-Dumeiry, whose magnificent work entitled *The Great Animal Life* was written during the 15th century. The work was an alphabetic classification and reference guide which interlinked not only zoological information but matters regarding superstition as well.

In recent years the habitats of Jordan's birds, mammals, reptiles and even insects, have altered immeasurably. The consequences of widespread drought, damming and other changes have been devastating. Ancient migratory bird routes, which have always included a stop at the **Wetland Reserve** at **Azraq**, have been altered following the almost total draining of these vast plains.

Amman's great thirst for water has sucked oases such as Azraq nearly dry. Where a few years ago there were hundreds of species of birds, now just a few dozen remain. This unquenchable thirst came as modern methods of hunting had just about annihilated herds of **white oryx, gazelle, ostrich** and other great creatures. Thankfully the government, with Royal support, is now protecting and promoting Jordan's precious wildlife.

Birdlife

Birds have always been held in high regard in the Middle East. Their forms adorn ancient frescoes, such as those at the *qasrs* of Hallabat and Amra, and are found on pottery and manuscripts. Jordan is occupied by two distinct groups of avifauna: resident species and migratory visitors. The last few years has seen a sharp drop in birds stopping at Jordan, especially at **Azraq**, traditionally the nation's greatest site of ornithological importance.

Jordan's proximity to Europe, North Africa and Asia, made it a crossroads for birds of many types. Around 300 species are known to have visited the **Azraq Wetland Reserve** before its water levels were so radically depleted. Of these, there were fifteen species of **duck** alone. So many birds were there that it created a visual effect similar to an infestation of locusts. Two hundred thousand birds at a time congregated at Azraq: everything from **spoonbills, white pelicans** and **egrets,** to **sandpipers, terns** and **gulls.** They used the oasis en route to and from Africa, having flown from Russia and Europe.

Indigenous species, however, seem to have survived the great drought of the 1980s reasonably well. The Jordan Valley and the Dead Sea area have many species. Such birds as the **Dead Sea sparrow** (*Passer moabiticus*) are found nowhere else.

Arid conditions have forced indigenous avia to adapt, in order to survive. In the desert, where there are no trees, nests are constructed on the ground. This poses problems of shade, so parent birds stand over their eggs to keep them from baking.

As with all desert residents, birds have learned interesting survival techniques. The **sandgrouse**, for example, will fly

Opposite top: Long-legged buzzard
Opposite left: Purple heron
Opposite right: Common snipe

Above: Arabian oryx at Shaumari Wildlife Reserve.
Opposite: Usually wary of visitors, ostrich thrive at Shaumari Wildlife Reserve.

miles each day in order to collect water for its chicks. By soaking its specially adapted belly feathers in cool waters, it can transport enough liquid to sustain its offspring.

Other native birds have adapted their mating habits, feeding procedures and nesting arrangements to suit the country's harsh climatic conditions.

Mammals

Features in the **Byzantine mosaic** at **Madaba** and **Mount Nebo**, and in the magnificent **frescoes** at **Qasr Amra** in the **eastern desert**, show that in the land of what is now Jordan, there was once an abundance of creatures. Mosaics, such as on the floor of the Church of the Deacon Thomas at Ain Mousa, dating to the 6th century, clearly depict lion and cheetah. The **Asiatic lion** survived until the end of last century when, along with many other mammals, it was made extinct by the hunter's gun. **Roe deer, Syrian bear, Addax antelope** and **Jordanian crocodile** have also disappeared. Strenuous multinational ecological efforts have managed to save the **Arabian oryx** from extinction.

Devastation hit Jordan's forests and woodlands, which once covered the entire north earlier this century. They were cut down to provide grazing land and fuel for the **Hijaz Railway**. As a result, small creatures robbed of their shelter and food had little chance of survival. Now the harsh conditions of the wilderness, which covers four-fifths of Jordan, allow only an assortment of nature's hardiest, yet most diffident creatures, to survive. These include the **Asiatic jackal, red fox, striped hyena, wolves** and **wild cats**. Along with the **white oryx**, which came close to extinction due to hunting on the open plains, are the great **mountain ibex**. Their stealth and superlative rock climbing ability have

allowed them to evade hunters.

Driving, especially on the **Desert Highway,** tends to be fast and furious, resulting in the death of a substantial number of mammals.

But thanks to the work done in Jordan's wildlife parks and sanctuaries, some endangered species have been given the chance to increase their numbers in natural surroundings once again. Such parks as the **Shaumari Reserve** (at Azraq) whose name is synonymous with Operation Oryx, are working under incredibly severe — almost waterless — conditions. Tourist facilities at Shaumari are all but neglected.

Dibbin National Park, just off the **old road** to Jerash, is one of Jordan's most lovely areas, its **rivers** fed by the melted **snows** of the mountains of **Gilead,** and its **trees** and **flowers** glorious in the spring.

The **D'ana Reserve**, located in **southern Jordan** with its famous D'ana Project, is also seeking to revive the natural ecological balance of the region. Like so much of Jordan, D'ana has been set back in recent years by drought.

Above: Camel train in the Jordan Valley.
Opposite: Camels with young.

Camels: Venerable Ships of the Desert

Camels are held in higher regard in the Middle East than any other creature. For the Bedouin, in particular, a camel is a ticket to survival. Yet it is more than a mere method of getting from A to B: it is a friend and companion, a source of hair from which to make tents, clothes and more. It is also a provider of meat, milk and dung, which can be used as fuel.

Camels of **Arabia** differ from those of Asia and within their own species. Those in the **north** are larger, with heavier, bigger bones than those in the **south**. Different tribes roaming Arabia have always favoured their own particular breed, and spend hours debating an individual's qualities.

The best of all Arabia's camel breeds is said to be the *Batiniyah*. It originated in **Oman** and has fine features. Its head is small, forehead wide, nostrils small, ears long and eyes large. Its body is sleek and its movements are as graceful as those of a gazelle. But its most important asset of all is its extraordinary stamina.

Camels generally graze whilst the Bedouin are camped and contrary to popular belief have been herded for milk and provisions throughout history. Only a few are used for riding or transport.

While in the desert, camels have an extraordinary ability to find water. Where water can only be drawn from a well, the Bedouin fill containers and water the camels from them. Salt has to be provided as well, especially in the heat of the summer. With good nourishment and salting the camel's hump increases in size as the animal builds up a strong deposit of fat.

The Bedouin take great care of their camels and, in freezing conditions, are known to cover a weak camel's back with blankets. In icy winds they are brought to lie in the shelter of the tents.

Camels not only have the ability to find water, but also possess the skill of being able to retrace their steps through the desert, even during sandstorms.

At celebrations such as *Eid,* weddings and births, camels may be slaughtered. The meat is coarse, yet nourishing, the hump being the most favoured part. Camel milk is also nourishing, but low in cream and not good for making butter.

At walking pace, a riding camel covers about 6 kilometres (4 miles) an hour; its speed is doubled when trotting. At high speed some camels run about 16 kilometres (10 miles) an hour, and have been known to cover about 160 kilometres (100 miles) in a single day. When a camel is laden the pace is reduced to about 4 or 5 kilometres (2 or 3 miles) an hour. In the extreme heat of the summer, travelling is generally done at night; in winter a caravan will plod on during the day and rest at night.

Each group of Bedouin traditionally brands its camels. A brand, known as a *wasm,* is only used on camels, not on horses. If a camel dies in the desert and the Bedouin have to leave its load while they continue, they mark the load with the sign of the *wasm.* No other Bedouin will touch it. The *wasm* is placed on the camel's thigh, cheek, shoulder or neck.

Camels are ridden from about four years of age. Both sexes are used, though females are preferred. In desert conditions they can go up to a week without water.

A small peg, known as a *khezam,* is tied through a small hole in the camel's nose and a string is attached to it. The cord is held with the reins and gently used to direct the animal when riding.

The saddle for camel riding used in Arabia is different from elsewhere. It is known as a *khorj,* has two stumps called *ghazal al-shidad* and is made from wood. The rider straddles the area between the stumps, sitting on a layer of padding. Fixed to it are a number of pouches and bags. The harness, known as the *rassan,* which includes the reins, has no bit. In Arabian camel riding there are usually no stirrups: instead, the feet dangle or can be placed upon the saddle.

A camel drinks between 60 and 100 litres of water in about fifteen minutes. On average they need to be watered every three or four days. They suck water rather than lapping at it.

Camels are loved by the Bedouin in a way difficult to describe. Theirs is a comradeship fostered by endurance of mutual hardship. Bedouin tales and proverbs tell of their inimitable companions, sometimes in jest, but always in respect. One such proverb goes: *'Araj al jamal min shiffatu'* — The camel limped from its split lip.

Arab Horses

Horses, like camels, are held in high esteem by Arabs, companions of the Bedouin — never failing on that most rugged of journeys — but camels are shabby, foul-smelling, arrogant creatures, while Arab horses are sleek and graceful in the extreme.

Arab lore is rich with proverbs and anecdotes about the Arab steed — widely regarded as the finest in existence. A Turkish couplet says: 'Care for your horse as though he were a friend, but ride him as though he were an enemy.'

The Prophet Mohammed's own steed, which was called Buraq (meaning *The Bright One*), is famed throughout the Islamic World. It was on Buraq — a mighty white horse with wings — that the Prophet ascended into heaven on his Night-Journey. Some people believe that it is none other than Buraq's hoofprint on the great rock — within the Dome of the Rock — created as the steed pushed his way upward into the sky.

Hughes (in his *Dictionary of Islam*) cites Anas, who said that the Prophet Mohammed held women and horses in unparalleled favour. Abu Qatadah (continues Hughes) affirms that the Prophet said that 'the best horses are black with white foreheads and having a white upper lip.'

Bedouin tradition holds stallions in less regard than mares. The sale of Arab stallions to countries outside the Middle East took Arab horses far afield. With their elegant looks, Arab stallions were always popular for pulling carriages and, later, racing.

Traditionally, Arab mares are so valuable in Arab eyes that a group of people within one tribe would together own a single mare. This meant the sale of a particular mare was unusually complex — as each part-owner was required to give his consent.

A perfect Arab horse has big nostrils, long ears, a wide forehead, large ribs, a long neck and round croup, muscular quarters, and a stride of twelve feet at full gallop.

There are many thoroughbred strains of Arab horse (known as *asil*, meaning 'noble'). Five pedigrees are regarded as more worthy than the rest. Throughout the Arab World, they are known as *Al Khamsah*, 'The Five' (or, *Al Khamsat al Rasul*, The Five of the Prophet). These thoroughbreds are: *Kuhailan, 'Ubaiyan, Sagawi, Hamdani,* and *Hadban.*

The Bedouin say that the first mare that ever existed was caught by Ishmael — in the desert of Nufudh south of Jauf. From her foal, Al Kuhaila al Ajuz, there came 130 families.

Enormous status is bestowed on the owner of a particular Arab horse; just as in the West racehorses are sometimes accredited with gigantic values.

Traditionally, a Sheikh would keep one or more fine mares, known as *rabat,* for breeding. A particular strain would be guarded from jealous neighbouring tribes — and given as a gift to the highest ranking guest.

The qualities of an Arab steed in battle are manifold. Their dexterity, speed and, perhaps most importantly, their stamina, ensured that they were never far from the centre of a battle. Hardy stallions, kept by Sheikhs for breeding, were traditionally kept away from the mares in iron hobbles, known as *hadid.*

As with camels, Arab horses have always been imbued with superstitious beliefs. Added luck will attend the creature if it is born by day, if it is of a reddish-brown bay colour, and if it has a circular spot on the forehead — formed by hair growing in a round pattern from one centre (called *sa'ad*).

An ill-fated horse, however, will have a white near hind leg, and a white off foreleg (this is called *shukaili*); or have white stockings (*lattamat*) on two of its legs; or a line of hairs growing towards each other on its throat (*shaq zij*). A particular line of hair behind the ear on the horse's neck (known as *fattalah*) is unlucky, indicating — some say — that the rider will be stabbed while riding.

Traditionally an Arab steed's stamina and performance in conflict was considered to be related to superstitious circumstances. The Evil Eye — known to most societies at one time or another — is linked in the Arab World to the horse.

Amulets and charms are fixed to a horse to dispel malevolent forces. *Surah CXIII* of the Qur'an is sometimes inscribed on a horse's bridle, or concealed in an amuletic pouch. Or, a blue bead — often of turquoise

Above: Flower-filled meadow near Amman provides a grazing horse with a hearty meal.

— is attached to a horse or its saddle bags, in the belief that it will ward away *Isabatu 'l 'Ain*.

Additional talismans ensured that a steed would pull through battle unscathed. These magical charms might be in the form of a hidden pouch, a geometric sign, or a single word or phrase etched into the horse's protective armour.

As the empire of the Arab world spread, and horses were used increasingly in conflicts, equestrian armour developed to an unprecedented level. Many of the finest chamfrons (protective plates of steel for the horse's face) were crafted. Saddles (*ma'arag*) — some made from gold, silk, and leather — halters (*risan*), and horseshoes (*na'al*), reached new levels of excellence: spurred on by growing understanding of metallurgy.

The Royal Family of Jordan have been keen equestrians since the time of King Abdullah — the present king's grandfather

— and Crown Prince Hassan is a keen polo player. Their stables boast some of the finest Arab stallions and mares in the world.

But the Royal Family's attention is not merely limited to the most exquisite. They have campaigned to improve the living and working conditions of Jordan's horses. The most challenging scheme, centred at Petra, has aided hundreds of horses which carry tourists through the city all year round.

Under the guidance of the Brooke Foundation — sponsored by Princess Alia — the Princess Alia Clinic for Horses was established at Petra. It ensures that each horse is registered and, more importantly, is carefully looked after. Equipment such as an X-ray unit for horses, modern surgical facilities, and an on-site veterinary surgeon, are available free to all the horses at Petra.

In the Arab world few deeds are considered more venerable than treating a horse with clemency. It is recorded that the Prophet Mohammed said: 'He who loves

his mare and treats her kindly shall have God's bounty, and he who ill-treats his mare shall be cursed of God.' Another couplet, also said to have been spoken by Mohammed, says: *The expression in a horse's eye is like a blessing on a good man's house.*

Top: Crown Prince Hassan in action during a match.

Left: Colt owned by Princess Alia.

Flora

Spring is an exhilarating season in most parts of the world. Jordan, although predominantly a desert land, is no exception. During the months from February to May many regions are carpeted with a dazzling variety of flowering plants, which sometimes cover acres at a stretch.

This wealth of flora stems from the variations of climate and topography that exist in Jordan. Geographically, the kingdom is divided into three main, disparate regions. These are: hilly terrain stretching from the mountains of Ajlun in the north to Ras en-Naqb in the south; the vast desert, which extends from north to south in the east; and Jordan Valley (*Al Ghor*), which runs from Lake Tiberias to the Dead Sea.

From tropical regions lying 392 metres (1,250 feet) below sea level to temperate mountain zones rising more than 1,250 metres (4,000 feet) above, there is ample variety of climatic conditions to produce a unique cross-section of plant life. The amount of vegetation in these regions also depends on rainfall. A warm, dry winter may cause a substantial reduction in the growth of wild plants. In 1984, when temperatures rose as high as 30°C and no rain fell in January and February, some flowers failed to appear or were considerably reduced. However, Jordan's variations of climate lead to a remarkable variety of flora. There are more than 2,000 species, some of them rare and many unusually fascinating to study.

Despite the topographical differences, a number of plants are widespread. One of the best examples is the popular **crown anemone** (*Anemone coronaria*); its flowers are predominantly red, but white and mauve can also be found. The latter are at their best in the northern hills. This anemone is often confused with the scarlet **turban buttercup** (*Ranunculus asiaticus*), as the flowering period of the two plants overlaps and they sometimes grow together.

Another prolific plant found in many regions is the tall-stemmed **pink asphodel** (*Asphodelus aestivus*). Common on rough over-grazed ground, it is already in flower by the end of January.

The wild **cyclamen** (*Cyclamen persicum*) can be seen clustering among rocks in the hilly regions as early as December, the flowers ranging from near-white to deep pink. Often in the same locality is found the little dark blue **grape hyacinth** (*Muscari commutatum*), and on grassy slopes are groups of the miniature lily-like **gagea** (*Gagea reticulata*). Conspicuous along roadsides, creating a haze of blue, is the tall, prickly **alkanet** (*Anchusa strigosa*). Equally striking are strands of **red-topped**

Above: Refulgent bloom of the ever-popular zinnia.

Above: A crimson hibiscus blooming in the springtime.

Above: Flora of many colours blanket the fields in the north of Jordan.
Opposite: Jordan's meadows bloom in spring with powerfully-scented flowers.

sage (*Salvia horminum*) that crowd the verges.

A handsome perennial is the **horned poppy**. Both the scarlet (*Glaucium aleppicum*) and the orange-flowered (*Glaucium grandiflorum*), with their attractive blue-green leaves, can be seen clinging precariously to the sandy precipices.

Of the many flowers that inhabit cultivated fields, some of the prettiest are the **field gladiolus** (*Gladiolus italicus*) and the violet-blue **ixiolirion** (*Ixiolirion tataricum*), which are frequently found side by side among the corn.

The bane of farmers, because of its deep roots, is the sharp **Syrian acanthus** (*Acanthus syriacus*). The design of its leaves can be seen on the capitals of many ancient Roman columns. Another prickly customer that grows widely on rocky hillsides is the striking **green thistle** (*Gundelia tournefortii*). The large mottled leaves and orange-purple florets can be dried, sprayed and used as indoor decoration over the winter months.

Many visitors to Jordan are familiar with the famous **black iris** (*Iris nigricans*), which

is the national flower. What they may not know is that this particular iris is not found on either the islands or mainland of Europe. It grows fairly extensively and, in a good year, can be seen in masses not far from **Madaba**, a town about 30 kilometres (19 miles) south-west of **Amman**.

Besides the flowering plants, there are several beautiful trees. Harbinger of spring is the sweet-scented **white broom** (*Retama raetum*), a real hardy that grows almost anywhere, as does the popular **blue-leaved wattle** (*Acacia cyanophylla*). In April and May, many picnickers drive home with their car bonnets decorated with sprigs of the sweet-smelling yellow flowers. Imported from Australia and not strictly indigenous to Jordan, this acacia has become an integral part of the landscape. Because it germinates easily and is extremely drought resistant, it is planted in considerable number on hillside terracing.

More specific to the **Jordan Valley** is the **Jerusalem thorn** (*Parkinsonia aculeata*), a tall graceful tree with feathery leaves and orange-yellow flowers clustered along its

Above: The pungent aroma of thistles and crown daisies fills the air throughout northern Jordan.

Above: Flowering trees in abundance can be found throughout the northern meadows of Jordan.

Overleaf: A thornbush in blinding yellow.

spiny branches.

Grown as an ornamental plant is the colourful **Judas tree** (*Cercis siliquastrum*), which dots upper hillsides. Less showy is the small **hawthorn** (*Crataegus aronia*) which is smothered with white flowers in late spring.

The most spectacular tree by far must be the **royal poinciana** or **flamboyant tree** (*Delonix regia*), which requires year-round warmth. A native of Malagasy that spread to the Caribbean, it is named after M. de Poinci, who was a governor of the French West Indies.

Through June and July the tree is seen in all its glory. Beautiful scarlet flowers — each with five large petals, one of them marked in white — are grouped at the ends of the branches and set amidst the bright mimosa-like leaves.

Among the eye-catching plants are the **giant fennel** (*Ferula communis*) and the **common mallow** (*Malva sylvestris*). The fennel frequently attains a height of 2 metres (6.5 feet). It grows widely and its large, yellow flower heads and feathered leaves immediately catch the eye. The dried pith of its mainly hollow stems can be used as tinder, but its leaves are eaten in salads and known locally as *shomar*.

The common mallow, in contrast, is much shorter. Growing abundantly along many roads, the attractive rose-purple flowers are a pretty sight.

Of dandelion clocks, there is ample choice. Distinct from the more mundane varieties is the **mauve salsify** (*Scorzonera papposa*), with its large daisy-like petals. The tubers of certain species of this plant are cooked and enjoyed as a tasty vegetable, especially in Europe.

During the spring months, thick green shoots are offered for sale along the roadsides. These are the succulent young sections of the **milk thistle** (*Silybum marianum*), which makes a favourite Arab salad.

Shrubs of **rock roses**, both the vivid pink (*Cistus creticus*) and the white (*Cistus salviifolius*) bring one right into the realm of Mediterranean flora. It is in the calcareous hilly regions of the north, especially above the **Zarqa River** and around the **Dibbin** woods, that these plants flourish.

Mingling with them are yellow-green bushes of **Jerusalem spurge** (*Euphorbia hierosolymitana*) and the red-berried **thorny burnet** (*Sarcopoterium spinosa*). The latter is used in rural communities as a protective fence for animals. Beware when walking, as the thorns are vicious.

One of the loveliest sights during spring is the panorama of many wild flowers, large and small, fused together in a wonderful display of color. The creamy **carmel daisy** (*Scabiosa prolifera*) and **golden pallenis** (*Pallenis spinos*) are prolific growers. The charming **pink sun rose** (*Helianthemum vesicarium*) and its relative, the **yellow sun rose** (*Fumana arabica*), will also be seen. Blooming a little earlier are the **scarlet tulips** (introduced, tradition has it, by the Crusaders) and, in the open woodlands, the **pink butterfly orchid** (*Orchis papilionacea*).

The **northern region** is one of the finest sites for **blue lupins** (*Lupinus varius*), which are massed across the grassy slopes. Looking at these sturdy plants, it is hard to imagine that they germinate, grow, flower and seed all in one season.

In contrast, but as striking, are the purple flowers and spikes of the **Syrian thistle** (*Notobasis syriaca*), adorning the roadsides and mixed here and there with a very tall **pink hollyhock** (*Alcea setosa*). This *Alcea* is the commonest of several species found in Jordan.

As spring progresses, a gradual change occurs with the emergence of such plants as the dazzling yellow **crown daisy** (*Chrysanthemum coronarium*). At times growing in masses and varied with the blue-mauve **bugloss** (*Echium judaeun*), the combination presents a stunning sight.

Bindweeds, too, appear. One of the most attractive is the **leafless bindweed** (*Convolvulus dorycnium*), a maze of angular leafless stalks and dainty funnel-shaped flowers that give the effect of ice-pink clouds. They are particularly noticeable as they bloom in early summer when many plants have already died down. With an extended season appears the **golden henbane** (*Hyoscyamus aureus*). Sprouting from walls and crevices, the bright yellow flowers with their saucy purple 'eyes' would never suggest that this plant contains the alkaloid hyoscyamine, a narcotic known and used since ancient times.

Wadi Shueib, a winding sheltered valley between the town of **Salt** and **South Shuna**, is home to numerous other plants. There, the shrubby grey-leaved and aromatic sage (*Salvia graveolens*) flourishes with the **pitch trefoil** (*Psoralea bituminosa*), so called because of its faintly tarry smell. The shrub **trichodesma** (*Trichodesma boissieri*) at first glance appears dull and dusty; but it is worth taking a closer look, for the pale blue flowers are large and very pretty. On the higher slopes, the tall **Lebanese fritillary** (*Fritillaria persica*) is easily identified by its yellow-green bells. Rather rare **Indian sage** (*Salvia indica*) and the common **cerinthe** (*Cerinthe palaestina*) also inhabit this valley.

In the late autumn, when the cliffs look quite bare, the brilliant **yellow crocus** (*Sternbergia clusiana*) appears — at first without leaves, so it seems simply stuck into the ground.

Spring seems to awaken earlier in the very **north** of Jordan. By early February, the dainty short-lived **Barbary Nut** (*Cynandriris sisyrinchium*) already is in flower. The olive groves are carpeted with rosy-pink **catchfly** (*Silene aegyptiaca*) and often, too, with the ubiquitous **yellow groundsels** (*Senecio vernalis*). In the **hills**, where winter temperatures are low, **virgin's bower** (*Clematis cirrhosa*) twines over small trees. This is a most attractive *clematis*, the large creamy flowers hanging down in clusters.

A little later, the **woodland glades** will attract the eye with their special beauties. Chief among them is the **anatolian orchid** (*Orchis anatolica*). Flourishing against rocks or in large groups, the bright magenta flowers and spotted leaves are very distinctive.

Jordan's **desert flora** is of equal interest: months, at times years, without water in a sandy wasteland cannot be inducive to plant survival or growth. Yet, one of the most fascinating regions is the desert floor. An area easily explored on foot lies between **Wadi Yutm** and the base of **Ras en-Naqb**.

In Wadi Yutm the rocks are alive with plant growth. **Pink fagonia** (*Fagonia mollis*) is common, and what looks like an ordinary **sorrel** could be the very rare *Rumex*

vescarius. Found by the road in moister soil, but easily overlooked, is the delightful tiny yellow-mauve **toadflax** (*Linaria haelava*).

In the desert itself, there is the tall **Sinai fennel** (*Ferula sinaica*), the very pretty dark-eyed **purple geranium** (*Erodium hirtum*) and shrubs of pink **spiny astraglus** (*Astraglus spinosus*). The name of the latter derives from the Latin word meaning vertebra, which aptly describes the leaf formation of this plant. Several species grow in Jordan.

The delicate **Arab gypsophila** (*Gypsophila arabica*) also thrives in the desert, as does the showy **broomrape** (*Cistanche tubulosa*), a parasite living off its *tamarix* host plant. The large yellow and purple-tinged flowers form a very dense spike, virtually hiding the stem from view.

Bright **yellow salsify** (*Scorzonera schweinfurthii*) can also be found. And perhaps the easiest of all the desert flora to recognise is the **zilla** (*Zilla spinosa*), which blooms profusely between April and May in a good season, its spiny bushes massed with lilac flowers.

Certain trees are well adapted to the inhospitable desert climate, among them another acacia (*Acacia radianna*). It has reddish brown bark, up to twelve pairs of comparatively small leaflets and exceptionally long, straight thorns. Around **Qasr Amra**, a desert hunting place of the Ummayed period situated in the **northeast** of Jordan, there are some very fine wild **pistachio** trees (*Pistacia atlantica*). The tree is deciduous, grows up to 20 metres (65 feet) and has an edible fruit.

Away from the desert, on hills and waste ground in what can be a hostile climate, is the **holly oak** (*Quercus calliprinos*). Instead of extreme heat, these trees have to combat frequent driving winds. The evergreens can attain a height of 15 metres (50 feet), but with an exceptionally slow rate of growth and adverse conditions, they take years to reach maturity. Unlike European oaks, the acorn cup is bristly and holds a smooth cylindrical acorn, each with a sharp tip. The tree is common and its wood is used for charcoal.

Another species of evergreen is the **Phoenician juniper** (*Juniperus phoenica*). It is a dense tree with tortuous branches. The minute grey-green leaves give off a strong aromatic scent when crushed. There is a nice **forest** of these junipers not too far from **Tafila**, a town **south** of the **Dead Sea**.

Finally, there are some rather strange plants. The **love apple** or **mandrake** (*Mandaragora autumnalis*) grows from a taproot and spreads its rhubarb-like leaves flat on the ground. Violet flowers rise from the centre and later form orange fruits. It is slightly poisonous and has long been used for various medicinal purposes and as an aphrodisiac.

Another unusual plant is the highly poisonous **thorn apple** (*Datura innoxia*), whose leaves and seeds contain toxic alkaloids. The Greek naturalist Theophrastus wrote of it along these lines: 'three-twentieths of an ounce, a patient becomes sportive; double the dose, he goes mad; treble it for permanent insanity; and one final dose to kill him off.' In contrast with its dangerous potential, the plant is attractive, with large, white trumpet flowers and heart-shaped leaves. It grows in wastelands and desert regions.

The **Dead Sea fruit** (*Calotropis procera*) is an untidy shrub found throughout the Dead Sea area. The leaves are large and the stems milky. Its mauve-white flowers are inconspicuous, but not so its fruits, which resemble green balloons, soft and filled with fleshy fibres. Animals do not touch it.

Commonest of these floral oddities in Jordan is the quaint **sea squill** (*Urginea maritima*), an unmistakable plant both during spring and late summer.

Early in the year, fleshy tulip-like leaves appear from the thousands of very big bulbs that grow on the bare hills. Then the leaves die down completely and, in August and September, tall spikes appear from the dry ground, bearing many small white flowers.

Above: Ancient craft of glass blowing survives in workshops around Amman.

Arts and Crafts

Jordan has become famous for the high standard of crafts available to tourists and local people alike. The influx of Palestinians from the West Bank, as well as that of Circassians and Armenians, during the Ottoman time, has increased Jordan's already rich artistic heritage.

A wide variety of crafts fill the shops of Amman and the bustling bazaars of the smaller towns and villages, far from the capital. Whatever you are looking to purchase, be careful to compare the prices and products of different shops before committing yourself.

With the inundation of Jordanians from the West Bank, after hostilities with Israeli forces, some of the West Bank's most illustrious artists and craftsmen shifted east of the Jordan River.

The craft of glass-blowing — which has been perfected over 2,000 years — is a dying art in the Middle East. Ironically, some of the finest of all Hebron glass-blowers

(traditionally one of the centres of glass-blowing) can now be found around Amman.

At the Hebron Glass Factory, south-west of Amman, the two Natcheh brothers continue to create fabulous glass objects in styles typical of the region.

Clear glass is melted down from old bottles and glass jars, to which is added coloured powders — which give the glass its particular hue. Only when the furnace is heated to over 900°C does the glass become malleable.

It takes years for a craftsman to master the skills of plying the toffee-like substance. With a hollow pipe he scoops up a ball of oozing glass and, while continually turning the glowing orb, begins to blow. When the piece is complete it is put in a cooling chamber, as the chill air temperature would crack the delicate object.

The shelves of the Natcheh brothers' shop, adjoining the factory itself, are crammed with fragile glass masterpieces. Everything from full dinner services fashioned in a rich blue glass, to tall vases, lampshades, and mysterious glass *Hands of*

Above: Young Jordanian weaver practises skills on traditional loom at a handicrafts school.

Fatimah — averters of the Evil Eye.

Traditional Hebron ceramic work has also found its way across the River Jordan. Coarsely-fired pots, vases and plates are placed on a rotating wheel. Then, in a manner that has not altered in centuries, an artist chooses the thinnest of brushes, the right colour . . . and then he begins to paint. The designs are extremely intricate, as historically each artist would try to out-master the next: the result is plain to see.

The nomadic Bedouin's flocks of sheep are fine providers of wool. Spun by both men and women, the wool is dyed in brilliant colours, woven on small looms and made into all manner of goods. The tools of the Bedouin seem not to have changed since biblical times. They are simple and have been refined through generations. The basic spindle, *meghzal*, is twisted and turned (usually by women) as they wander in the fields or sit in the cool shade of a doorway.

When the wool has been crudely spun, it is dyed. A wide variety of colours were traditionally obtained from ordinary plants. Mulberries, onion skin, pomegranate, sumac, and the dried, crushed cochineal beetle, are some of the typical ingredients used to produce dazzling colours. Now chemical dyes have replaced many of the traditional ones. These are more permanent, and their shades are consistent from one batch of dyeing to the next.

Simple ground looms, which can be collapsed when it is necessary to move on, are typical in Jordan. The weaver sits astride the loom, which spans out in front. A number of recently established craft projects in Jordan, such as the famous Bani Hamida scheme, have been assisting communities to carry on with traditional methods of weaving.

One of the most rewarding, but sometimes tricky, purchases to make is that of an Arab or Oriental carpet. A handmade carpet is as much a piece of furniture as a fine desk or a loved bookcase. Even a simple carpet can give colour to a drab room, creating a warmer ambience. Every carpet has its own intrinsic character, its own special feel and unique design.

Various kinds of carpet find their way to

the shops and markets of Jordan. There are two distinct types: one is made with the *Turkish* knot, and the other with what is known as the *Persian* knot. Hundreds of thousands of knots are tied side by side to form a tufted pile. Generally speaking the closer the knots are together, the higher the quality.

The designs also fall into two categories. Tribal rugs — such as those traditionally made by the nomadic Bedouin — are quite different from those manufactured in cities. Though the two types of rug produced are dissimilar in style, there is not necessarily a difference in quality. The designs of tribal rugs tend to be more angular than those of city carpets. Historically they are made to be used by the members of the clan or tribe. Only in times of economic hardship would a carpet have been sold out of the tribe.

Carpets manufactured in a city are crafted to a much more rigorous system of specific designs, using measured motifs and regular colours, in more rounded patterns. The weavers are paid by the hour, or by the week: a fast weaver can tie somewhere in the region of a thousand knots an hour, yet a medium-sized carpet still takes up to eighteen months or more to complete.

A well made carpet's pattern will be clear on the underside; and the knots will be tight. Most machine-made rugs do not have the pattern on the underside. If you are buying a silk carpet take especial care, as it is extremely hard to tell the difference between silk and polyester. Make sure that the warp and weft threads, which form the skeleton of the carpet, are strong. If you bend the carpet over face inwards, twisting delicately, and hear snapping or cracking sounds, the carpet is probably no good.

Remember that buying old rugs is different from buying new. Generally the older it is the more it will cost. Check that it has not been repaired by running your fingers gently across the surfaces as you may not be able to see a good repair. Be wary if a dealer draws your attention to a date woven into a carpet, these are easily, and all too frequently, added later.

Above: Intricately woven handcrafted Jordanian rug.

Opposite top: Master weaver at work on his loom.

Opposite: Potter spins a masterpiece from a lump of clay.

Arab Weaponry: Wicked Beauty, Abounding Grace

At the height of the Arab Empire, which lasted almost a thousand years, craftsmen brought new meaning to the word *excellence*. They perfected techniques in design, metalwork, chemistry and calligraphy. They implemented these skills in architecture, art and many other fields. But perhaps the greatest achievements were made in their mastery of weaponry. Swordsmiths devised methods of making steel malleable, yet strong; they conceived designs that turned the most deadly objects of the day into masterpieces of elegance.

Although there has been profound advancement in weapons throughout history, styles tended to evolve rather than change. Thus the same designs and patterns were employed and refined by one generation after the next, steadily growing in perfection and detail. Indeed, swords and daggers still used in the Middle East, albeit ceremoniously, are not so different from those crafted a thousand years ago. Islamic weapons are fascinating to study, for their surfaces are adorned with stanzas from the Qur'an, amuletic verses designed to protect the warrior in battle, or simple patterns.

Jordan has long been at the centre of international trade and military routes. This has meant that the vast number of trading parties, and armies, which passed through over the centuries left their own indelible impression on the region's military constitution. Invading forces and traders, who were always well armed, influenced Jordan's own production of weapons with new styles. Innovations in weapon making, such as the fabled Arab 'watered steel' blades, were conceived in nearby Syria and developed there, as well as in Palestine, Jordan, Iraq and Arabia.

Many countries of the Middle East had distinct styles in swords and early firearms. After a brief examination anyone can tell the difference between a Turkish *Yataghan*, a Circassian sword, or an Indian *Talwar*.

When the Persians swept through the Middle East during the early years of the 7th century, their unique weapons were used against people who later copied them.

Great advances in metalwork were made in the early years of Islam, which resulted in the crafting of weapons sharper than ever before. Their blades were more flexible and did not blunt so easily. Armour became stronger, lighter and, importantly for stealth, more silent when worn. Early helmets were dipped into molten iron to provide an impenetrable surface.

Later, Islamic swordsmiths developed the method of creating the fabled 'watered steel', from metal ingots transported to the Middle East from Kona Samundum in India. Metal was heated at great temperatures (made possible by a development in forging), and by slowly cooling and reheating the metal many times it acquired the peculiar 'watered' surface. Zigzag and other patterns could be made in this fashion. The most famous centre for sword making was Damascus, and Jordan as its neighbour also became important.

As with Islamic swords, the range of Islamic daggers reflects the preferences and capabilities of each craftsman. Some are heavily ornate or extra flexible, some were straight and others rounded. Of all the daggers crafted in Arabia, probably the most famous is the *Jambiya* which, although traditionally manufactured throughout Arabia, is now found mostly in Yemen. Its long, double-edged and heavily curved blade, with a central ridge running along it, is often found with a rhino horn handle. The scabbard is distinctive in that it tends to bend in a 'U' shape, back on itself.

Throughout the era of the Arab Empire and beyond, skilled master craftsmen were held in great respect. Their work was regarded with reverence and fascination by peasants and kings alike. Such artisans were rewarded with fortunes, and their names are still spoken with awe. When monarchs ventured to distant lands on conquests they took their best swordsmiths with them. Tamurlane is known to have taken armourers and swordsmiths from Damascus to his new capital at Samarkand, in the year 1400.

Arab alchemists first acquired gunpowder

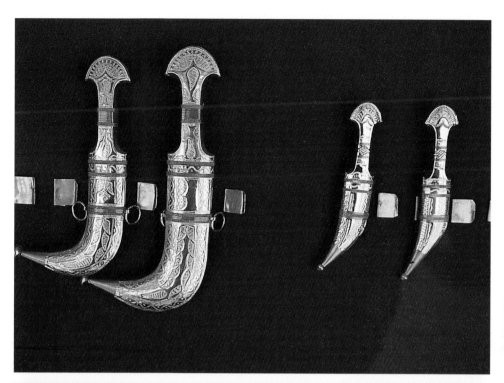

Top: Fine detail of traditional Arabian daggers and scabbards on display in Amman.
Above: Tourist souvenir and deadly weapon all in one.

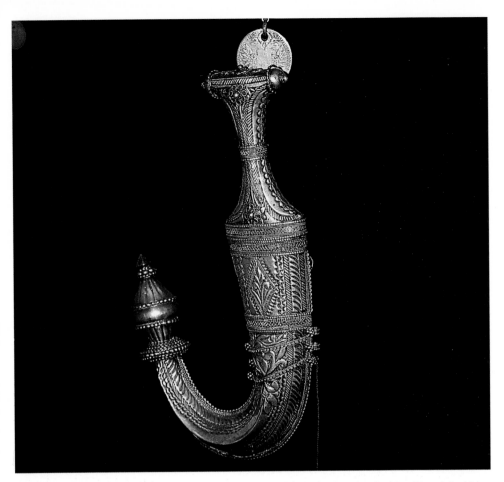

Above: Exquisite craftsmanship shown in the extreme detail of a handcrafted traditional Arabian dagger, the *Jambiya*.

during the initial half of the 13th century. It came from China, where it seems generally to have been used for fireworks. The alchemists designed primitive firearms from barrels hollowed in wood: capable of firing only arrows or the most rudimentary of bullets. These were known as *midfa*.

Before the Ottoman Empire, the Turks had understood the true potential of firearms and, by the year 1453, cannons had been effective at the seige of Constantinople. Scholars maintain that by the year 1500 Turkish soldiers had a relatively advanced selection of firearms at their disposal.

From Turkey, guns began to filter into Arabian lands. Before long, distinct Arab guns were in production. Of these, perhaps the first was the long-barrelled gun produced in the Maghreb. Thus Arab excellence known in sword making was transferred to the fashioning of firearms.

The barrels were crafted from watered steel, damascened with gold, while ivory, steel and bone adorned the stock. For the wealthy, precious jewels were an added option for decoration.

With the advent of the firearm, various accessories became necessary. Powder flasks were fashioned in every conceivable way. They were made out of different metals including silver and gold; others came from the horns of rams or from sea shells. Ramrods, such as the distinctive Turkish *suma*, also became fashionable.

Arab Costume and Jewellery

Many things inherent in a society's culture are easily affected by change; and this is particularly true of fashions. Over the last thirty years Western attire has spread like wildfire across the globe. Just as in Central Africa, South America, and China, people are now accustomed to Western dress, so the people of the Arab world are losing this valuable part of their heritage.

Fifty years ago the Middle East was inhabited by people clothed in a style that had altered little in the last two thousand years. It was possible to tell at a glance which town or village a particular person was from.

Numerous organisations in Jordan have embarked on pioneering schemes to ensure that the traditional methods of costume-making, embroidery, and so forth, do not die out. Projects such as the Bani Hamida scheme have looked long and hard at the fundamentals of a fading legacy. Bani Hamida, and a few others, provide the necessary logistical assistance and raw materials, and let the experts (usually the women) do the rest.

Raw materials used in Palestinian and Jordanian dress were typically cotton, wool and linen. Syria, particularly during the time of the Ottoman Empire, was a large producer of silks, satins, and fine brocades. Further woven materials came from Egypt and Europe. Wool generally was produced locally — as it still is. Men, children, but mainly women, account for the weaving of wool on small hand bobbins. Even in the villages outside Amman one finds women taking shade from the midday sun fumbling with a bobbin and a lump of shiny fleece.

One begins to understand the significance of costume to the people of the Middle East, when looking at the extensive vocabulary of clothing. Each article, however small and seemingly unimportant, had a name.

Chemical dyes have brought a standard-isation of colour, and with it customers have come to expect this. But when chemical dyes were still unknown, that is before World War II, indigo (nileh) was perhaps the most common of colours. There are numerous records of the indigo crop along the Jordan Valley. Burckhardt, who 'found' Petra in 1812, for instance, noted the indigo production in the area.

For women, various hues of red have generally been preferred. Prepared from the dried and crushed cochineal beetle, the female kermes crocus, or the root of the madder plant, they were used with enormous skill to create wonderful patterns. Anilin (synthetic) dyes — developed in Germany during the 1880s — had almost completely put an end to natural dye production in the Middle East by 1918.

The giving of a trousseau — usually in the form of cloth — has always been a part of the marriage ritual. This trousseau offering, presented by the husband to his bride-to-be, is known as kisweh.

The long, generally unembroidered, shirt in Jordan and Palestine was traditionally the thob. Worn by both villagers and nomadic Bedouin, the thob was generally plain undyed cotton, or an indigo blue. Worn by villagers, it tended to have long tight sleeves — tied back, while working, with a cord (shmar). That worn by the nomadic Bedouin generally had baggy triangular sleeves (called irdan).

Sheepskin coats or jackets (farwah) — with the wool facing inward — protected the wearer in the severest of winters. Coarse handwoven wool capes were also worn (abayeh); these were usually indigo blue or left the natural colour of the wool. Few items were more useful than a trusty abayeh. They could be used as a blanket, a prayer rug, a sack, a feeding bag for one's animals, or as a piece of clothing in the cold of winter.

A wide variety of jackets and waistcoats have been worn in Jordan during the last century. As the population increased in prosperity, they yearned for finer fabrics, and a wider range of colours.

The most important clothing accessory of traditional male attire was the plain leather belt (sherihah), to which anything, it seems, could be attached. From this was worn a dagger, or some other weapon. Belts are a good indication of the wearer's origin. Woven cloth belts (known as kamr) — generally red or brown — with leather

Above: Dance troupe demonstrates traditional Jordanian dances.
Opposite: Headdress fashioned from silver coins.

trimmings and fastenings, varied from region to region.

In the Islamic world feet are deemed to be unclean and, accordingly, shoes made for contact with the outside earth enjoyed fairly minor attention. Until cheap imported sandals and other shoes began to flood into the Middle East, locally made shoes (*wata*) were worn by those who did not go barefoot. Horsemen were the exception. They wore red boots known as *yezmeh*.

Since World War II most civilisations with some dealings with the West, have begun to lose their traditions of headdress. As, in the West, the trilby, bowler or Panama hat are now relatively rare, the headwear of the Middle East has altered significantly. Headdress gave a clear indication of the wearer's origin, social class and status. In *Palestinian Costume*, Shelagh Weir mentions the ritual of male headdress: 'First was a white cotton skull cap (*taqiyeh* or *'araqiyeh* meaning "sweat-cap"). Over this was placed a white or grey felt cap (*libbadeh* or *kubb'ah*), and over that in turn a red felt hat (*tarbush maghribi*) with a floppy black or

navy blue silk or cotton tassel (*dubbahah* or *sharbush*) attached to the crown.'

A powerful symbol of the Bedouin people is the distinctive square head-cloth (*keffiyeh*), with its head-ropes (*'aqal*) to hold it in place. Beneath the cloth can be worn a cloth skull cap (*taqiyeh*). The wealthier Bedouin would, and still do, wear *'aqals* interwoven with gold thread (*'aqal mqassab*). The black and white *keffiyeh* — adopted by Yasser Arafat — the Chairman of the Palestine Liberation Organisation — has become a strong symbol of the Palestinian cause. Despite being clothed in Western business suits, it is now common to see people in Amman — and other cities in Jordan — wearing traditional headdresses.

The costume of Palestinian and Jordanian women has tended to be more elaborate than that of their male counterparts, possibly because women have traditionally attended to the embroidery and the making of clothes.

The first real festive garments given to a girl, or made for her by her family after puberty, were normally connected with

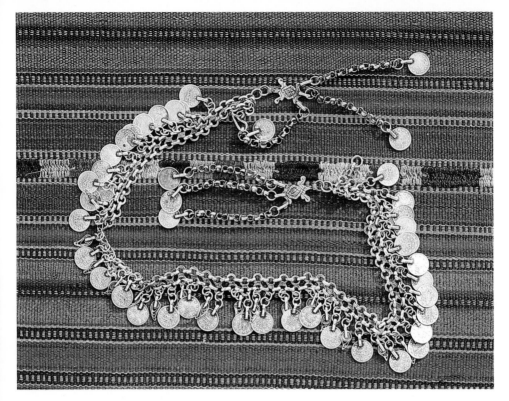

Above: Traditional Jordanian necklace fashioned from silver coins.

marriage. An elaborate trousseau (*jihaz*) was traditionally presented to a bride by her fiancé. This generally included a number of bright dresses for ceremonial and festive occasions (known as *thob al-tal'ah*), as well as jewellery, and garments for everyday use. The bride would also contribute a number of heavily decorated garments for the trousseau, made in the particular style of her village.

The traditional festive dresses of women in Jordan and Palestine are elaborately decorated. Few other costumes of the Middle East can match them for their stylish embroidery, and lavish colours.

A professional embroiderer would take an already decorative garment and embellish it further with appliqué patches, trimmings of taffeta, velvet and satin. The more elaborate the design, and the more expensive the materials, the fewer the customers. So, the wealthiest brides of all wore the most richly adorned costumes.

The distinctive *qabbeh* (chest panels) of women's dresses in Jordan and Palestine, are famous throughout the Middle East. From the rectangular panel one can tell exactly where the garment originated. Innumerable designs were created — each one slightly different from the next.

Every region of Jordan has its particular pieces of jewellery. As with costume, the craft was easily influenced by passing masters, or by those trading new designs.

The influx of Circassians and Armenians into what is now Jordan, during the latter years of the last century, brought a wave of distinctive jewellery from their homelands.

Generally, Bedouin and village jewellery of Jordan and Palestine, has been made of silver. As people have become more prosperous there has been a trend to buy small gold pieces. The wealthier the customer, the higher the quality of the silver used, the more of it and the greater the number of semi-precious and precious stones. Coins (such as the Maria Theresa dollar) were melted down and transformed

Above: Finely worked jewellery on display in Amman craft museum.

into silver jewellery; or the coins themselves were simply sewn onto the garment — particularly the chest panel.

Traditionally, jewellery has complemented a fine outfit, especially those of women. But the combinations of precious metals, such as silver, and stones, like turquoise, are known to have had a deeper importance originally. Much as clothing once identified the wearer's social group, jewellery also had specific significance. Many types of Arab jewellery are known to have been created partly (if not completely) for the purpose of warding off malevolent forces, for protection in conflict and to engage various cryptic powers. Talismans and amulets were produced throughout the Middle East for centuries.

Many originated in a deep-rooted belief in secret sciences such as alchemy and numerology. Their strength was gleaned from the exact combination of stones, metals and colours. Only when each component was present was the charm activated. Sadly,

these traditions are slowly being lost, although the signs and symbols of a once-powerful body of knowledge are all around.

Today few can unlock the hidden meanings of these sleeping charms. Instead, ancient talismans of all kinds are worn across the East and West as no more than fashion accessories, while their hidden powers remain unharnessed.

The words *talisman* and *amulet* slipped into English from Arabic. There is a subtle difference in their meanings, which is often overlooked. The talisman comes from *talism*, meaning something that causes a change. *Amulet* is thought to be derived from the Arabic root *hamail*, meaning something that is suspended, affording its wearer protection and sustenance.

Amulets and talismans have been fashioned across the Middle East since the earliest times. Early charms were made from stone, wood or bone, and were not necessarily inscribed. The mostly unadorned

Above: Smiling model displays traditional dress and jewellery.

amulets of more recent times consisted of a scrap of paper with a spell, magical word, or symbol, inscribed. A person with the necessary magical powers would mark the surface with special ink. Amulets written on paper were thought to have magical properties.

The scrap of parchment was folded, then slipped, perhaps, into an ornate silver canister or leather pouch, depending on the purpose of the charm. Then, if designed for protection in battle, for example, the amulet would have been tied to the upper left arm. Only when the magical fragment of parchment was inserted into the container, was the spell activated. The container and its contents formed the spell — without one or the other there would be no harnessing of magical power.

An understanding of numbers is at the root of deciphering many talismans and amulets. Each number has its own cryptic meaning. In the Islamic world, number one stands for God. It cannot be used in the fabrication of charms as it would be too profane.

Number two represents *Jinns*, unearthly spirits, whose assistance the charm might be seeking. Three stands for riches and wealth; a talisman, for instance with clusters of circles in threes, might well be committed to the accumulation of wealth for its wearer. Number four represents guardianship. It is very common especially in battle amulets, or for shielding an infant against disease or illness. Number five has a mystical significance that must never be discussed in words.

Six is resigned to augmenting one's position in a hierarchy. Seven denotes life itself, and all that is sacred to it. It is very powerful and must be used with prudence. Number eight deals with the stabilisation of something: whether a financial situation, a relationship, or whatever. Nine represents movement: of the planets, of our own position in life, and our interaction with those around us.

The orchestration of the numbers holds as much significance as the numerals themselves. One of the most forceful methods of organisation is that of numerical squares. Each digit is influenced, and strengthened, by those next to it. One common magic square consists of nine numbers. When added up in any straight line, the total always comes to fifteen. The sum of the line is then tallied up. That is, the one is added to the five, to create the new total of six. Six, in this case, represents an increase in rank or status — so the actual purpose of the square has been discovered.

Anything can be broken down to a mathematical formula. The number of letters in a word, the number of words, number of stones, the sides of an object, the sum of the number of metals used to create an object: all bear direct relevance to the charm's intentions. Jewellery, boxes and plates, often crafted from three metals, such as copper, brass and silver, are made to provide paramount effectiveness.

Above: Handcrafted Jordanian bracelets.

The eight-sided *Muthamman* is a very forceful figure in the fabrication of talismans and jewellery. This octagonal emblem is seen everywhere across the Middle East. To the layman this might appear purely decorative, but to the master, it is far more significant. Specific instructions on how to activate the spell are often based on numeric formulae (revealed only to the user). Many mathematical formulae have roots in the classic texts of Al-Buni and bin al-Hajj.

Numerous stones, colours, and metals are identified with certain planets, sentiments, months of the year, and so on. Gold is equated with the sun, silver with the moon and iron with Mars. Topaz is identified with November, cornelian with August, and turquoise with the month of July. Yellow and orange are seen as unfavourable in the Middle East, and consequently are rarely used in the fabrication of charms. Blue, rose-red, and lilac are auspicious colours.

Certain stones hold special qualities. Agate, for instance, protects its wearer from the Evil Eye, as does alum. Amber's uses are extraordinary. Beads carved from it are thought to protect the wearer from rheumatism, headaches and internal ailments. For centuries amber, ground into a fine power and swallowed with water, has been taken to prevent miscarriages. When placed beneath a pillow at night amethyst supposedly gives the sleeper refreshing dreams. Jade was thought traditionally to bring rain during drought and quench one's thirst in the desert.

Known as *Ain al-Hasad*, the *Evil Eye* is found in diverse societies across the world. The ancient Egyptians knew it as Iri-t ban-t; in Germany it is known as Uebel Augen; in Spain as Mal de Ojo; in China as Ok Ngan. From Sumatra to Greenland it has been felt, and feared, and warded off, since the earliest times. The Evil Eye's power is said to be transmitted by certain men, women, reptiles and other creatures — even inanimate objects — causing injury by a single look.

Two main types of devices used for averting the Evil Eye from an individual or a community are prolific in the Middle East. The first is a symbolic portrayal of an eye, made from coloured (blue and white) glass. The other is the Hand of Fatimah. The hand, either in a stylised drawing or crafted from metal or glass, is said to represent the right hand of Fatima, the Prophet Mohammed's daughter. Such hands hung above doorways, or in cars, are thought to have the power to protect against this most sinister of forces.

The Dead Sea Scrolls

One day in the summer of 1947 Mohammed Adh-Dhiba, a shepherd from the Ta'amireh tribe, was searching for a stray goat. The boy climbed up a craggy rock face overlooking the Dead Sea near Qumran. He rested for a moment in the extreme heat and, as he sought a welcome patch of shade, Mohammed noticed a hole, no more than a few inches wide, in the limestone rock.

Fascinated, he went over to investigate. He picked up a pebble and cast it through the aperture. The stone struck something that sounded like a ceramic pot, and the noise resounded as though his pebble had landed in a cave. Mohammed put his eye to the hole, and peered into the darkness. He spied lines of standing amphora in a large cave. This was the first glimpse in recent times of the Middle East's most important archaeological site.

Mohammed hurried away from the scene — terrified that it was the lair of a mighty jinn. But the next morning an older friend coaxed the boy to lead him to the site.

As the sun rose high above the Dead Sea, the pair managed to squeeze through the tiny hole, into the cave. They had hoped to find gold, but there was none. What they did discover must have seemed very dreary by comparison. Yet the find of jars and what seemed like bundles of rags had a far richer value.

They took some of the booty back to the camp and examined it. In the secrecy of their goat-hair tent, the boy unwound one of the scrolls (now thought to have been one of the two long manuscripts of Isaiah). It stretched the length of the tent.

The passage of what became known as The Dead Sea Scrolls, from the hillside at Qumran overlooking the Dead Sea to the academic libraries of the world, was long and troubled.

The discovery was made at a time when the political climate of the Middle East was anything but cordial. Fearful of being branded for carrying out illegal excavations, the early players in the Dead Sea Scrolls affair acted with enormous secrecy and, looking back on it, stupidity. Without realising the extraordinary research value of the hoard, it is miraculous that anything survived intact: having been left with a cobbler (who considered using the parts of the 'rags' for making shoes); sold for the grand sum of £24; and finally hidden in a domestic garden at Bethlehem.

The first scrolls were sold at Jerusalem in 1947 — and so began the academic study of them. The site at Qumran was fully excavated in 1949 by the Jordanian Department of Antiquities and the French School of Archaeology at Jerusalem. The excavation produced hundreds of new fragments. Still more fragments were bought up from the Bedouin people of the Qumran region — and from dealers, into whose hands they had subsequently fallen.

Three years later, in 1952, ten further caves, each containing fragments of manuscripts, were discovered in the immediate area at Wadi Qumran. Yet more fragments were unearthed in the Valley of Murabbaat and at Khirbet Mird.

It seems that the community at Qumran had been established around the time of Alexander Jannaeus (103-76 BC). Following a significant earthquake in 31 BC, the site was probably abandoned. It is thought that the caves were re-inhabited around 4 BC, for a further seventy years or so.

Relatively little is known of the ancient community at Qumran. Most of what can be deduced has been done so through its written legacy. Known to themselves as The Covenant, the sect was led by a Teacher of Righteousness. This leader ensured that a rigid framework of communal life was maintained.

The bulk of the Dead Sea Scrolls have been identified as manuscripts of the Old Testament texts. The most important of the texts are the two manuscripts of Isaiah, discovered in the first cave. Although one is incomplete, the other is intact, and is one of the oldest of all the manuscripts. It seems to have been finished during the 2nd century BC — perhaps even before the community at Qumran was established. The true importance of these texts is that they reveal forms of the Hebrew Old Testament older by a thousand years than those already known and used.

This important scroll was composed by an Essene, it is an interpretation of Isaiah, one of the books in the old Testament. The interpretation or Pesher, seeks to demonstrate that the prophet Isaiah was prophesying about the time of the Essenes.

: ۱ التوراه القديمة ، أو فـي زمـن الأسـنيين.

لـه كتبت من قبـل أحـد الأسـنيين ، وهي تفسير لأنـبيا

As well as the Old Testament manuscripts found at Qumran, a considerable number of sectarian manuscripts was also discovered. These non-biblical texts cover a phenomenal range of subjects. Works of a legal nature, commentaries referring to the sect's own history and doctrines, hymns and prayers, have also been deciphered.

The extremely dry conditions of the Dead Sea region allowed the scrolls (and other relics unearthed around Qumran) to be preserved almost intact. Experts maintain that the region may well conceal further texts from the biblical era. Indeed, some believe that complete libraries may still be awaiting discovery. Since the 1967 war in the Middle East excavations in the Qumran area have slackened.

With advances in technology, however, such equipment as Subsurface Interface Radar (SIR) can now be used for investigating the Qumran region. SIR has the ability to reach depths which were previously inconceivable; what is more, they reduce unnecessary and destructive excavations. Who knows what further treasure these new methods will discover in the hills overlooking the lowest point on earth?

Above: Living history from the Dead Sea — section of one of the priceless and irreplaceable Dead Sea Scrolls, one of mankind's oldest surviving manuscripts.

Tastes of Jordan

Feasting is a preoccupation not only of Jordan, but of the Middle East as a whole. Whether you are in a Jordanian home, a Bedouin encampment deep in the desert, or in your hotel restaurant for that matter, you may be sure that vast platters of food will be produced. Eating rituals are very important in the East and, as a guest, it is rude not to gorge yourself to the point of bursting.

Jordan's cuisine, although unique, is part of the Middle East's distinctive culinary heritage. Dishes which have been savoured for well over a thousand years are sure not only to tempt, but to delight.

Great feasts of the past are spoken of years afterwards. Songs have been sung, poems penned and tales told of impressive banquets given by kings for their people. Favourite recipes are handed down by mother to daughter, from father to son. Traditionally each clan has its own secret recipes.

The national dish of Jordan is *mensaf*: lamb seasoned with aromatic herbs, sometimes lightly spiced, cooked in yoghurt, and served with huge quantities of rice. Feasting on *mensaf* is taken seriously, and hours are spent in its preparation. At a large feast, such as a wedding or birthday, several animals may be slaughtered.

Other occasions, such as the safe return of a traveller, or the healing of a sibling's illness, are celebrated by the sacrifice of a goat. To make the meat *halal*, the throat of the animal is slit.

Women generally prepare *mensaf* which is cooked in *jameed*, a dried yoghurt, which is then mixed with water in a tray to produce a creamy sauce which is poured into a large stewing pot with chunks of meat. The pot is put over an open fire. In the desert, this is fuelled by dry camel dung (or charcoal, if available). As the stew begins to warm it is stirred to prevent the yoghurt from separating. The secret of *mensaf* is in the preparation just before serving. Large

Opposite: Fresh produce of many varieties has made Jordan's culinary inventions a gourmet delight.

Above: Golden confection — syrup-sweet dish rounds off a typical Amman banquet.

Overleaf: Coffee is served in a Jordanian coffee house.

trays are covered with the doughy flat Arab bread and dampened with yoghurt. On top of this a layer of rice is heaped. Then the mutton or lamb is piled on top, sometimes with the actual head of the animal at the centre. Almonds, pine-kernels and other nuts may be sprinkled over the dish, which is then ready for serving.

Besides *mensaf*, a wide variety of other foods and specialities are popular in Jordan. These include *mahshis* meaning stuffed, which are vegetables stuffed with meat and rice. All types of vegetables are prepared in this way, including onions, potatoes, courgettes and tomatoes. They are very popular at midday, the time when the main meal of the day is served. Steamed vine leaves, also stuffed with rice and meat, are a delicacy.

As a visitor to Jordan you may be surprised by what seems to be an excessive use of oil. It is put into every manner of dish, as well as being poured liberally on humus and salad. Meat and fish are often fried before being turned into a stew.

As in the West, a particular sauce made by a family can be a closely-guarded recipe. Sauces and other Jordanian dishes, depend on flavour rather than on spices for taste. Garlic is used liberally.

Of great importance in Jordan, and the East, is drinking coffee and sweet Bedouin tea in a ritual steeped in desert tradition. Coffee is often served only a few drops at a time and is heavy with the fragrance of cardamom seeds. A few drops of this powerful elixir revive the senses. If you are served coffee in a restaurant, or in a Jordanian home, it will be poured from a long-handled copper coffee-pot into your cup. When a guest's cup is empty, it is automatically refilled. Only when the guest has tipped the empty cup from side to side, does the host cease offering.

There is no greater honour nor more pleasurable experience than to receive refreshment in a Bedouin encampment. Guests, greeted with a courtesy that only the contrasting desert harshness could have bred, are invited to sit and relax. Cushions are brought and, beneath a goat hair canopy, everyone waits while a fire is rekindled with dry twigs. A number of thimble-like cups are washed carefully using

a few beads of clean water so as not to waste a single drop. Then, as the host converses, an old box is produced. A handful of powdered leaves is taken from it and sprinkled into the pot.

When the pot has steamed for a few moments it is removed from the heat with mathematical precision and the straw-coloured liquid is poured into tiny cups, one by one. The tea, flavoured lightly with mint and heavily sugared, is invigorating.

Amman has numerous restaurants to cater for all tastes from Arabic to international and from à la carte to snack and takeaway.

Most restaurants frequented by visitors accept credit cards.

Above: Garden-fresh produce from Jordan's fertile plains add zest to national recipes.

Opposite top: Master chef prepares dishes for an evening buffet.

Opposite: Mouthwatering dish of lamb seasoned with aromatic herbs and served with mounds of rice.

Al-Hashemi: The Royal Family of Jordan

In the Islamic world — where a family's lineage is unparalleled in its importance — one line is revered above all others: that of *Al-Hashemi*, the Hashemites. Tracing their unbroken chain of ancestry from the Prophet Mohammed himself, the Hashemite Family has produced men and women of prominence since the dawn of the Islamic Era. The Hashemites have founded and administered nations, led armies into battle, excelled in science, literature, the arts, and philosophy. No other family has contributed so much to almost all areas of Islamic society and culture as *Al-Hashemi* — often known as *The People of the House*.

The royal family of Jordan, which belongs to the Hashemite line — led by King Hussein, has its ancestry through Fatima, the daughter of the Prophet. Fatima had two sons: Hassan and Hussein. Descendants of Hassan are known as *Ashraf* (the plural form of the Arabic word *Sharif*, meaning *honourable*). The royal family of Jordan is descended through the line of Ashraf.

King Hussein — son of King Talal bin

Abdullah and Queen Zein — is the thirty-ninth in direct line to the Prophet. For centuries his ancestors were masters of the Hijaz region of Arabia. Known as the *Sharifian House of Aoun*, they rose to great distinction during the 19th century. It was then that the House's founder — Mohammed bin Aoun — held the renowned title of Amir of Mecca, the holiest of all Islamic cities.

King Hussein's great grandfather, Sharif Hussein bin Ali (known as *Al Munquiz Al A'zam* — meaning 'The Grand Saviour'), led the Arab Revolt of 1916-1917. Waged against the Turkish Ottoman Empire, the movement succeeded in bringing to an end Ottoman rule in Arab lands. Sharif Hussein's own son, Amir Abdullah bin Hussein, actually established the Emirate of

Above: King Hussein with his brother, Crown Prince Hassan bin Talal.

Opposite top: King Hussein, (left) with Prince Mohammed (centre) and Crown Prince Hassan bin Talal.

Trans-Jordan in 1921: so becoming the first monarch to preside over the newly-formed Hashemite Kingdom of Jordan.

With the assassination of King Abdullah in 1951, on the steps of the Al Aqsa Mosque in Jerusalem, the King's son — Talal bin Abdullah — was installed as monarch. Unfortunately King Talal abdicated in 1952 due to ill health. He died in 1972.

The present monarch — King Hussein bin Talal — was crowned as King on 2 May 1953, aged eighteen. Before Prince Hussein assumed his responsibility as monarch, his mother — Queen Zein el Sharaf — played a significant role in ensuring the orderly transfer of power. Queen Zein, who was ever popular with the people of the country, passed away in April 1994. For more than four decades King Hussein has steered Jordan through the turbulent waters of the Middle East. He has sought peace and economic prosperity for all Jordanians, even though faced with adversity.

King Hussein's leadership has influenced and inspired not only the people of Jordan, but all peoples of the Islamic world. But, as in any family, the leader draws from the inspiration of those around him. In all the Middle East, if not the world, there is no leading team as unique as that of Jordan. For Hussein's most valued advisor and confidant in matters of state is none other than Hassan bin Talal, his own brother.

Together Hussein and Hassan share the work load, directing Jordan's course, and complementing each other's work impeccably as they do so.

As well as Prince Hassan, a number of other prominent members of Jordan's royal family have initiated dozens of worthy projects, and give patronage to many more.

Her Majesty Noor Al-Hussein: Queen of Jordan

Queen Noor — born Lisa Najeeb Halaby on 23 August 1951 — comes from a prominent Arab-American family. She attended schools in various parts of the United States before entering Princeton University — to study Urban Planning — from where she graduated with a BA in 1974. Following her studies, Queen Noor participated in a number of design projects in the United States, Australia and the Middle East. Then, in 1976, she contributed in the research of an Arab Air University — set to be established in Jordan. She subsequently joined Royal Jordanian Airlines as Director of Planning and Design Projects.

King Hussein and Queen Noor were married on 15 June 1978. They have two sons and two daughters: Prince Hamzah, born on 29 March 1980; Prince Hashim, born on 10 June 1981; Princess Iman, born on 24 April 1983; and Princess Raiyah, who was born on 9 February 1986. Queen Noor is also the stepmother to Princess Haya and Prince Ali — both born to the King from his marriage to Queen Alia — and to an adopted daughter Abir Muhaisen. Queen Noor directs and sponsors various projects within Jordan, focusing on many areas, from social welfare to environmental protection.

In 1981 Queen Noor founded the Jerash Festival — an annual festival of cultural and artistic activity held amongst the ruins of Jerash. The Noor Al-Hussein Foundation was established in 1985 to consolidate the various projects and programmes headed by Queen Noor. Holding a number of important national and international decorations, Queen Noor has travelled widely, and speaks English, French and Arabic. She enjoys watersports, skiing, riding and tennis.

Queen Noor is the fourth wife of King Hussein. The King's first marriage, in 1955, was to Princess Dina. She bore him a daughter, Princess Alia. The marriage was later dissolved. In 1961 King Hussein married for the second time. His bride, Princess Muna Al-Hussein (née Antoinette Gardiner), gave birth to two sons, Princes Abdullah and Feisal, and twin daughters, Princesses Zein and Aisha. King Hussein's marriage to Princess Muna was also dissolved and, in 1972, he married again. His new wife, Queen Alia, bore a son and daughter. Tragically, Queen Alia was killed in a helicopter crash in February 1977.

Prince Mohammed bin Talal

The younger brother of King Hussein, Prince Mohammed bin Talal was born in Amman on 2 October 1940. Although less prominent on the international stage than his brothers, he is well-respected throughout Jordan for his work and achievements in areas such as the military, tourism and sport.

Following his primary education at the Islamic Scientific College in Amman, Prince Mohammed attended the École Beau Soleil in Switzerland, before completing his secondary education at Bryanston College in England. On his return from the Military Academy in Baghdad, where he spent a year between 1956 and 1957, Prince Mohammed joined the Jordan Arab Army, serving in the Royal Guard Regiment. After which he became Aide-de-Camp to King Hussein.

Prince Mohammed has served Jordan in an official capacity on numerous occasions. He held the distinguished role of Crown Prince between 1951 and 1962, after which Prince Hassan assumed the position.

King Hussein appointed Prince Mohammed as Head of the Tribal Chiefs in 1971; and chose him as his Personal Representative in 1973, a position which he continues to hold. In addition to serving as Regent and as Head of the Regency Council on various occasions, in the absence of the King, Prince Mohammed has had the honour of heading the Supreme Committee for Tourism in Jordan.

Decorated with numerous national and international awards, Prince Mohammed holds the honorary rank of Full General in the Jordanian Armed Forces. In his role as president of numerous sporting and benevolent foundations in Jordan, he seeks to encourage the nation's youth in participating in sports as diverse as shooting, Karate and chess. He himself excels in a wide range of sports, having been awarded a first Dan and an honorary fifth Dan in Koyokoshinkie Karate.

Prince Mohammed married Princess Taghrid, daughter of the late Hazza Basha

Opposite top: Queen Noor of Jordan with His Majesty King Hussein.

Opposite left: Princess Sarvath el Hassan, wife of Crown Prince Hassan.

Opposite right: Crown Prince Hassan bin Talal.

Above: Princess Basma bin Talal.

Al-Majali, former Prime Minister of Jordan, on 28 June 1981. He has two sons from a previous marriage: Prince Talal, the Military Secretary to King Hussein (born 26 July 1965), and Prince Ghazi (born 15 October 1966).

Hassan bin Talal: Crown Prince of Jordan

On 1 April 1965, King Hussein proclaimed his youngest brother — Amir Hassan bin Talal — to be Crown Prince. For almost thirty years Prince Hassan has played a key role in not only advising his brother, the King, but also in establishing a great variety of educational, academic, cultural and economic projects. Few men have such an encyclopaedic knowledge of the Arab world, its traditions, history and cultures.

Born on 20 March 1947, Prince Hassan was educated at Harrow School in England, before attending Christ Church, Oxford. On 28 August 1968, he married Princess Sarvath, the daughter of an eminent states-man from the Indian subcontinent. Prince Hassan's interests — which are extremely wide-ranging — have induced an enormous variety of notable and important projects to

be established. He has worked relentlessly in pioneering programmes ranging from humanitarian causes to those concerned with economic issues. In sponsoring such initiatives, and in acting as patron of a large number of organisations, both in a national and an international capacity, Prince Hassan has succeeded in giving a voice to many groups, both Jordanian and otherwise, who are usually unrepresented.

Prince Hassan, author of several books and many articles, is polymathic in his interests — which span fields as diverse as economic planning, geo-politics, education, science, technology and development, multilateral dialogue, Islamic civilisation, humanitarian issues and the welfare of Jordan's youth.

On the international stage, Prince Hassan is ever active. He addressed the 36th Session of the United Nations General Assembly in 1981, proposing the establishment of a New International Humanitarian Order. This led, in 1983, to his founding and co-chairing the Independent Commission on International Humanitarian Issues, whose final report he presented in 1987 to the Secretary General at the 42nd General Assembly.

At home in Jordan Prince Hassan is constantly occupied with directing and establishing institutes and committees, as well as attending to important matters of state. The catalogue of projects to which he has devoted his time within the last three decades is extensive and ever growing. Since the early 1970s he has chaired National Development Plan Committees; in 1972 he founded the Royal Scientific Society; in 1978 the Bilad Al-Sham Conference; in 1980 the Aal Al-Bait Foundation; in 1981 the Arab Thought Forum; in 1982 the Forum Humanum (later renamed the Arab Youth Forum); and in 1987 the Jordanian Higher Council for Science and Technology.

In addition, the Prince established and directs his nation's Islamic Scientific Academy; the Biannual Conference on the History and Archaeology of Jordan; the Hashemite Aid and Relief Agency; the Centre for Educational Development; the Centre on Refugees in Yarmouk University; and the new Aal Al-Bait University in Mafraq.

The Crown Prince, accompanied by

Princess Sarvath, has travelled throughout five continents on official invitation. He has received the highest decorations from over twenty countries, as well as being awarded the Al Hussein bin Ali Medal, Jordan's highest accolade. He is fluent in Arabic, English and French; and has a working knowledge of German, Spanish and Turkish.

Prince Hassan has promoted many kinds of sport including squash, scuba diving, swimming, mountaineering and skiing. In addition, he holds a 5th Dan in Taekwondo, and a black belt in Karate.

Princess Sarvath el Hassan

Princess Sarvath comes from an eminent family of the Indian subcontinent, and was born on 24 July 1947. Her late father, Mohammed Ikramullah, was Pakistan's first Secretary of State for Foreign Affairs, Ambassador to the United Kingdom, France, Canada and Portugal. Her mother, Begum Shaista Suhrawardy Ikramullah, is a writer, former member of parliament, several times delegate to the United Nations, and former Ambassador to Morocco.

Prince Hassan and Princess Sarvath have four children: Princess Rahma (born 13 August 1969), Sumaya (born 14 May 1971), Badiya (born 28 March 1974), and Prince Rashid (born 20 May 1979).

The Princess heads a range of projects, many of which seek to benefit the women and youth of Jordan. She heads the Ladies Branch of the Jordanian Red Crescent Society — under whose supervision fall the Hilal Hospital and the Red Crescent Clinics. Princess Sarvath is also the President of the Young Women's Muslim Association.

In 1981 she was instrumental in the establishment, of the Amman Baccalaureate School and continues to chair its Board of Trustees. This independent non-profit co-educational school aims to offer an education of the highest international standards. It has over 900 students of whom over fifteen per cent are on assisted places for merit.

Princess Sarvath is a member of the Council of Foundation of the Geneva-based International Baccalaureate Organisation. She is also a member of the International Board of the United World Colleges, and heads the Jordanian UWC. Committee. In

Above: Prince Mohammed bin Talal.

addition, she is a member of the Voluntary Services Overseas Council, a charity dedicated to helping the developing world; as well as being patron of the Centre for Phonetics Research at the University of Jordan. UNICEF and others have called upon her to give talks focusing on areas such as the role of Muslim women and education.

Princess Sarvath, who was the first woman in Jordan to receive a black belt in Karate, also enjoys swimming, walking and skiing. The Princess, who is fluent in Arabic, English, French and Urdu, is a keen gardener.

Princess Basma bin Talal:

Born in Amman in 1951, Princess Basma — the only sister of King Hussein — was educated in Jordan and England. She completed her education at Oxford University, where she studied languages and is fluent in Arabic, English and French. She is patron to more than two dozen individual charities and foundations — most of which seek to benefit women and children, the needy, and the handicapped. Like other female members of the royal family she has initiated training programmes for women, with the aim of enhancing their lives and the opportunities open to them.

With the creation of the Jordanian Save the Children Fund in 1974, the Princess was elected President: it was to be one of the first charities with which she became involved. In her role as representative of Jordan's women, Princess Basma chairs the Arab Association for Women and Development, which was established in 1989. With its membership open to both women and men, the Association seeks to enhance the role of Arab women in society. In addition, she chairs the national Committee for Women's Affairs which, established by government decree in 1992, aspires to strengthen women's role in development.

In May 1993 Princess Basma continued her work in the field of development, having been appointed as an Honorary Human Development Ambassador by the United Nations Development Programme (UNDP).

Her association with the United Nations continues — as a member of the International Advisory Group. The Group, established by the United Nations Secretary General, advised on the preparatory process for the Fourth World Conference on Women held in Beijing in September 1995.

Princess Basma is married to Walid Al-Kurdi. She has four children: Farah, Ghazi, Saad and Zein. She enjoys skiing, riding, walking and reading.

Royal Foundations

The Royal family of the Hashemite Kingdom of Jordan sponsor many worthy charitable foundations, some of which are described as follows:

The Crown Prince Award Scheme
Many of Prince Hassan's initiatives have sought to inspire the youth of Jordan. Through projects such as The Crown Prince Award Scheme, Prince Hassan has worked to foster qualities such as teamwork and leadership in Jordan's new generation.

Derived from the Duke of Edinburgh Award Scheme — itself established in 1956 — The Crown Prince Award Scheme has given thousands of young Jordanians the opportunity to find adventure, as well as developing their own personalities, and working within a team framework. When started in 1984 as a pilot project at the Amman Baccalaureate School, the Scheme proved remarkably successful.

Most of all, the Scheme provides challenges. As these are met and overcome, participants achieve levels of proficiency and skill which merit specific awards. The Scheme maintains an atmosphere of freedom, justice and cooperation, in which the young Jordanians gain a sense of national pride and social responsibility.

The Noor Al-Hussein Foundation
Sponsored by Queen Noor, the Foundation was established in September 1985 by Royal Decree, with the intention of meeting developmental needs throughout Jordan. It supports cultural and educational programmes, as well as handicraft and other community projects. The main focus is generally geared to the needs and well-being of Jordan's women and children.

Specific projects spearheaded by the Noor Al Hussein Foundation include: Al Noor Project for the Development of Rural Areas — seeking to improve the quality of life in rural communities; Women and Development Programme; National Handicrafts Development Project — which seeks to revive traditional crafts, create employment and increase income, particularly among women; Health Communication for Child Survival — aimed at furthering overall health objectives through better communication.

The Noor Al-Hussein Foundation — which works alongside existing public and private organisations — heads projects throughout Jordan from the biggest cities and towns to the nation's smaller communities.

The Jerash Festival
No place in Jordan could be more perfect for hosting a cultural gala than the ancient Roman Provincial city of Jerash. Forty-eight kilometres north of Amman, Jerash hosts an annual summer Festival of Culture and Arts.

This Festival, which usually takes place from the second week in July onwards, is designed not only for tourists but primarily for the benefit of Jordanians. The Festival, which is administered by the Noor Al-Hussein Foundation, focuses on a great variety of events, many of which take place in the evening. These range from folklore groups to poetry readings, dramatic plays (both modern and traditional) and orchestral recitals, complemented by dancing groups, choirs, folk groups, acrobats and even tango extravaganzas from around the world.

The Young Woman's Muslim Association
The YWMA has branched out in many directions since Princess Sarvath was asked to take over the patronage of the Association in 1970, the new projects revolving largely around education. The YWMA relies entirely on the generosity of its sponsors, private, corporate or governmental.

The Centre of Special Education was founded in 1972, and has been in its present purpose-built facility since 1980. It is a non-profit-making school catering for moderately handicapped infants and children.

The administration of the Centre is frequently called upon to hold courses and workshops in the field of special education, both in Jordan and abroad.

The Sheltered Workshop was established in 1987 in the industrial city of Sahab, on the outskirts of Amman. Over sixty mentally handicapped young men and women are employed there, supported by a trained staff. The workshop is recognised as a regional model by the ILO. In addition to the goods mass-produced in the workshop, there is a showroom in Amman where individual items are for sale. The aim of the workshop is to create a safe working environment for the handicapped as well as to generate an income towards the running costs of the other YWMA projects.

The Sheltered Workshop and the school benefit from the presence of American and Japanese volunteers.

The Princess Sarvath Community College was founded in 1980. It aims to help girls from financially disadvantaged backgrounds to acquire the skills to earn a living. Initially, through technical assistance offered by the German GTZ, the College concentrated on the teaching of what were new fields for women at the time — architectural drafting, computing skills, bi-lingual secretarial skills, marketing and business administration. Now, in co-operation with the government of Canada and the Ministry of Education, the College has been concentrating on Early Childhood Education and the development of a national Learning Disabilities programme, with the long term aim of becoming a regional Centre of Excellence in the field.

The YWMA also run a small hostel for women. Residents are either students or professional women. In the summer months there are occasionally beds available for transit guests.

The Queen Alia Fund
Established in 1977 as a non-governmental organisation concerned with social development, The Queen Alia Fund for Social Development is headed by Princess Basma, the King's sister.

It was King Hussein himself who assigned Princess Basma with the founding of the Queen Alia Fund for Social Development. Under the aegis of the Fund, the Princess has established and administered numerous projects, such as the National Population Committee — aimed at studying demographic changes in Jordan.

The Fund, which seeks to help people revitalise their rural and urban communities, has established Community Development Centres across Jordan.

Often run by women, these centres hold regular educational workshops and seminars, covering issues as wide-ranging as literacy and child health.

Although the Centres are small, they reach a great many Jordanians — estimated at around 750,000 people a year. In addition to the lectures and seminars, each Centre fosters projects, such as sheep raising and date cultivation, to improve local life.

Other projects concentrate on supporting crafts such as ceramics and weaving. In particular, these ventures offer women the chance of administering and directing programmes which will benefit the community as a whole.

Royal Jordanian Airlines

With aviation a keen interest of both King Hussein and the Crown Prince of Jordan, it is no wonder that the nation boasts one of the finest airlines in the Middle East.

But despite its remarkable track record and extensive network, Royal Jordanian had humble beginnings. When operations began, on 15 December 1963, the fleet was modest to say the least: then boasting a single DC-7 and a pair of Handley Page Heralds, acquired from the Royal Jordanian Air Force.

The introduction of a Caravelle 10-R in 1964 enabled the establishment of the Jeddah and Rome routes. Within the airline's first three years of service, its traffic trebled. From the beginning, those at the helm of the company understood the importance of long-haul routes to and from the Middle East.

Tragedy came to the fledgling airline in the shape of the June war in 1967. The destruction of two RJ DC-7s — and the loss of the routes to Jerusalem — was seen by sceptics as a death-knell for the airline. But Royal Jordanian acquired new aircraft and added several new routes to the network. These included Dhahran, Doha, Nicosia and Benghazi. The year 1969 saw further expansion for Royal Jordanian with the addition of routes to Munich, Tehran and Istanbul.

In the early 1970s, problems arose with the closing of air spaces, and the October 1973 war. At this time the airline became independent of government assistance and a wholly public corporation.

Undeterred by the uncomfortable Middle East climate during the early 1970s, the airline introduced a pair of long range Boeing 707-320C jets to its fleet in 1971. The routes were extended to Karachi in the East, to Madrid, Casablanca and Copenhagen in the West. At the same time Royal Jordanian cooperated with Pakistan International Airlines, under a three-year management and technical assistance programme.

In addition to the Boeing 707s acquired in 1971, two Boeing 720-B aircraft were procured in 1972, with a further three Boeing 727s in 1974. By 1977, with Royal Jordanian carving itself a firm place in the world aviation market, the decision was taken to acquire two Boeing 747-200B jumbo jets.

The early 1980s saw further expansion, with eight more aircraft. In 1984 Royal Jordanian began services to Chicago and Los Angeles. Four years later, in 1988, Miami and Montreal were added to the network.

The late 1980s witnessed continued growth and several Airbus A310-300 and A320-200 aircraft were acquired at the beginning of the 1990s. The introduction of the Airbuses allowed the old Boeing 707s to be used solely as cargo carriers.

For the administrators of Royal Jordanian, the ever-changing emphasis on specific destinations is constantly monitored. During the latter years of the 1980s, the decision was made to relinquish the more costly medium- and long-haul routes, such as Copenhagen, Bucharest, Los Angeles, Chicago and Miami. Other routes, such as New York, Kuala Lumpur and Singapore, had the frequency of their services reduced.

In 1996, Royal Jordanian served forty-six cities spread over five continents — covering some 145,915 unduplicated route kilometres (91,200 miles) extending to Singapore in the Far East and New York in the West.

Royal Jordanian looks forward to a long and prosperous future as we head toward the new millennium.

Opposite top: At the hub of the Middle East, Amman International Airport is one of the busiest in the region with flights leaving and departing around the clock to and from all parts of the world.

Opposite: One of the jewels in the Jordanian crown — sleek bird of the Royal Jordanian jet fleet leaves Amman International Airport. Following page: Jordanian girls dressed in their country's national colours took part in festivities to mark the Fortieth Anniversary of their Monarch's accession to The Throne.

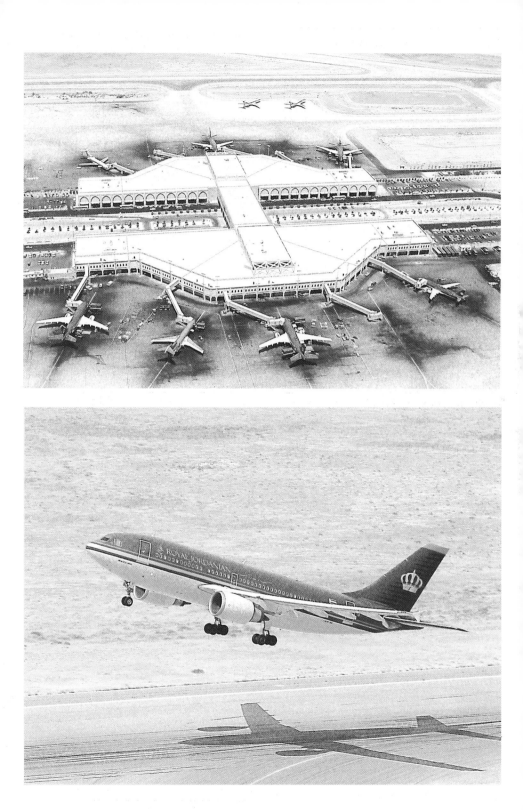

PART FOUR: BUSINESS JORDAN

The Economy

Jordan is a country that has not only survived against all odds, but indeed has prospered in the face of adversity. Its government has managed to turn disadvantage into advantage and, with assiduous toil, has transformed the small Middle Eastern nation into an extraordinary economic success. The catalogue of obstacles that Jordan has overcome since independence after World War II is daunting. Two wars with Israel, diplomatic dilemmas with other Arab nations and those of the West, as well as water and oil problems, seem only to have driven Jordanians on to greater achievements.

The new climate of Peace in the Middle East has provided unprecedented stability, permitting new businesses and entrepreneurial ventures to rise and flourish. The age of communication seems to have come into its own in the Middle East, with Jordan's capital, Amman, constituting a formidable hub of international business. Jordan is now linked to emerging markets and well respected financial centres through cyberspace. With the surge of recent foreign investment, the kingdom's role as a key bastion of economic success seems set for many years to come. In the past decade the GDP has achieved a growth of 135%.

Jordan's economy is primarily based on agriculture, industry and services. Agricultural production, boosted by expansion of irrigation and technological advancement in farming methods, especially drip irrigation and the cultivation of fruits and vegetables, contributes 5% to the GDP and employs 10% of the workforce. Large-scale industries, which include the mining of mineral resources and the manufacture of cement, fertilisers and refined petroleum products account for 18% of the GDP.

The services sector, which consists mainly of government, tourism, transportation, communication and financial services, contributes 80% to the economy and absorbs approximately two-thirds of the country's labour force.

Over the past two decades, Jordan has developed into an active business centre reflecting its strategic location in the region. Amman has attracted a large number of regional offices since 1975-76, when the first major movement of foreign companies to Jordan took place. By 1998 over 8,500 firms were registered with the Amman Chamber of Industry.

Theoretically speaking, Jordan has adopted a policy of a free economy. Ownership and management of factors of production are supposed to be held by the private sector. Therefore saving, investment and management of producing units are mainly undertaken by the private sector. The government, however, plays a moderately active role. For example, the sole airline, the postal service, telecommunications, water services and electricity generation are all owned and operated by the public sector. Further, the government is a shareholder in several large corporations in the country.

Mineral resources

Jordan's natural resources are scarce. So far, no minerals other than potash and phosphates have been discovered and exploited. Potash is abundant in the Dead Sea which has an estimated 45-billion tonnes of salt reserves.

The major players on the heavy industry scene, the Arab Potash Company (APC) and the Jordan Phosphate Mines Company (JPMC) continue to expand and diversify. In 1996 JPMC was the world's sixth largest exporter of phosphates and around 25% of Jordan's 1996 exports were of phosphates and potash.

By 1997 potash production was in the region of 1.8-million tonnes putting Jordan among the world's top three potash exporters and plans were put in hand to bring capacity to 2.2-million tonnes before the end of the decade.

Two joint ventures in this sector began operations in 1996 with exclusive export rights to the Indian and Japanese markets; a US$ 160-million Indian-Jordanian venture (with 52% Indian ownership) to produce phosphoric acid, and a US$ 24-million Japanese-Jordanian venture (with 60% Japanese ownership) to produce fertilizers.

In addition to phosphates, potash and gypsum mining, the search continues for new mineral resources and new methods for extracting existing deposits. Limestone, kaolin, glass sands, marble and granite are also mined. Other minerals being surveyed include copper and uranium.

The late 1980s saw a renewed exploration for oil with the view to reducing Jordan's dependency on foreign imports. Gas was discovered in 1987, as were considerable quantities of oil shale, especially in the Lejjun region. However, these reserves of oil shale and oil sand are expensive to process and extract.

One of the most significant developments in the future will be the formation of the country's first National Oil Company, which will be run on a commercial basis, with the directorate of petroleum at the Natural Resources Authority

(NRA) acting as the core of the new company. New emphasis is also being put on renewable energy sources — wind and solar power. Four wind generators were erected in the late 1980s with an output capacity of 80KW each, and the Jordanian government is looking to expand this energy source by attracting foreign investment for larger wind farms.

Agriculture

Jordan is somewhat self-sufficient in some agricultural produce and exports limited quantities of certain crops especially citrus fruits and vegetables. There are three quite different physio–graphic regions, each with its own distinct climate:

(1) The Highlands: mountainous and hilly regions ranging in altitude from 600 to 1,600 metres (1,969 to 5,250 feet) above mean sea level. Fruit trees, vegetables and cereals are grown in these areas.

(2) The Rift Valley: marks the west flank of Jordan, reaching a depth of about 400 metres (1,312 feet) below mean sea level at the point of the Dead Sea. Soil is fertile, generally well irrigated and ideal for growing fruit and vegetables. It is an extremely temperate climate ranging between 14.9°C in January, to about 40°C in July. About 60% of Jordan's agricultural produce is grown there.

(3) The Semi Arid region: forming the eastern two-thirds of Jordan. The climate is inhospitable with low rainfall. Little is grown; but herds of goats and other livestock are tended.

While agriculture contributes 8% of the GDP, fewer and fewer Jordanians are depending on it for their livelihood. Many are turning to other forms of labour, because of the limited returns of farming the country.

Tourism

At last Jordan seems to have come into its own as one of the Middle East's prime tourist destinations attracting more than a million visitors a year. Amman, Aqaba and Petra have seen the development of a spate of luxury hotels in the last 20 years.

The kingdom, which boasts magnificent remnants from past civilizations, unspoilt woodlands and superlative beaches, welcomes visitors like no other country. And, as we approach the next century, new hotels and tourist facilities are being developed to provide luxury and value for all.

Making a decisive step towards positioning Jordan as a unique tourism destination on the international map, on 25 October 1997 Jordan's Council of Ministers approved the Charter of the Jordan Tourism Board (JTB) thus setting up the kingdom's first national tourism organisation.

Jordan's rich archaeological heritage has been a boon to the tourism industry which, by 1996, accounted for US$ 750 million and 15% of the gross national product.

Amman and Aqaba saw a spate of luxury hotels develop during the 1980s and throughout the 1990s, catering for businessmen and tourists. Although the 1967 war with Israel and the occupation of the West Bank devastated Jordan's tourist industry, it has improved considerably since that bleak period, and is now the country's most valuable earner of foreign currency after potash. The volatile state of Jordan's neighbours, and particularly the 1991 Gulf War, caused an uncertain period, but by the end of 1993, many of the traditional tourists had started to flow back.

There are several major archaeological attractions. Petra is one of the few sights in the world that surpasses all expectations. Much of Petra, or the Rose City as it is called, is only a three-hour drive south of Amman. Most of the ancient city has yet to be uncovered. The existing buildings are tombs cut in the rock face; they appear to have outlasted the civic buildings of what was once a grand city of huge proportions built 2,000 years ago.

Other main tourist attractions in the kingdom include the splendour of Wadi Rum, close to Petra, where adventurous tourists can try rock climbing or camel safaris. Just north of Petra is Shobak, one of the earliest Crusader castles, in a striking position on a small hilltop guarding the gap between the two ranges of mountains.

In the north are several beautiful places, including the pine-clad hills of Ajlun, with its Crusader castle, and the Hellenistic city of Jerash. With its colonnaded streets and oval plaza, and the magnificent South Theatre with bank after bank of steeply raked stone seats, Jerash still retains much of its original city walls as well as the imposing Hadrian's Gateway.

In the far South, for watersport lovers, Aqaba is Jordan's highly-prized 'window to the sea'.

Business etiquette

The East boasts hospitable and warm people who treat their guests with much respect. This might intimidate Western visitors who may expect more rigid rules between business partners. The Jordanian businessman can be expected to exchange a lot of niceties and try to gain your friendship before actually getting down to business. You should be ready to be invited to the home of your Jordanian counterpart before any business deals are concluded.

Other than this element of Eastern hospitality, a visitor to Jordan can expect to conduct business largely along the Western standards for similar occasions. Jordanian businessmen pride themselves on being sensitive to the needs of their guests. They will not impose their own traditions and will avoid embarrassing situations.

Devout Muslims are not likely to make you aware of their need to conduct prayers at a certain time nor will they bring up subjects such as drinking alcohol and male/female relationships unless they are specifically asked. Many will buy alcoholic beverages for their guests, but will stick to soft drinks themselves.

Experienced executives doing business in the Middle East attest that knowing a few Arabic words can make all the difference. Simple words and phrases — such as *shukran* (thank you), *min fadlak* (please), *kaifa halak* (how are you?) — are always appreciated. It is worth spending a few moments making sure of the correct pronunciation of the host's name and title. Errors in such pronunciation by foreigners are so common that getting it right makes an immediate impression.

In the Arab world, people are generally referred to as so-and-so the son of so-and-so; with the family name often omitted. For instance, *Yussef bin Ali* equates with "Yussef the son of Ali (note that *bin* is the same as *ibn*). The family name may be present, for instance: *Yussef bin Ali Al-Qassim* (note that in this case *Al* is a long sound and denotes "the family of"; it is not to be confused with *al*, the Arabic word for "the".)

A growing number of women are directly involved in business and have high places in some government departments and ministries. Being a Third World country, businesswomen are unlikely to follow the same standards of social interaction with male guests. They will keep a businesslike manner and will probably not suggest business over lunch or a visit to their homes. However, this may be changing with women assuming top government posts.

Business advantages

There are at least nine major advantages Jordan possesses over other nations in the Middle East:

(1) **Political stability:** in an environment with a constitutional monarchy guaranteeing freedom of religious belief, speech, press association and private property.

(2) **Central location:** at the crossroads of the Middle East where three continents merge, offering easy transportation and communication through the Middle East. Swift transport to Syria, Iraq and Saudi Arabia by road between two and five hours, as well as a offering a major port right into the heart of the Middle East.

(3) **Special trade link:** providing the largest body of skilled manpower in the area and 250,000 traders, entrepreneurs, technicians and bankers working in other countries of the Middle East.

(4) **Quality of labour:** with a workforce of some 500,000 men and women dedicated to high quality and efficiency. A workforce well-versed in English and, to a lesser degree, French.

(5) **Education and technical training:** with national literacy at 70%. A student population of over one million, benefiting from free compulsory education until the age of 16 — ensuring skilled, well-educated labour for years to come. There are 18 universities and many community colleges, both public and private, which have a student body of over 100,000. A further 74,000 students study abroad.

(6) **Monetary stability and services**: good balance of payment situation, with the Jordanian Dinar a fully convertible currency. At least 16 major banking institutions offer a full range of facilities with promise that more will probably emerge during the next few years.

(7) **Infrastructure**: transportation facilities consist of modern highways leading to all parts of the Arab world; deepwater harbour facilities at Aqaba; freight railway system linking the country to Syria, as well as international airports at Amman and Aqaba; communications to high international standards; satellite systems linking Jordan to the world, facilitating easy communication with other parts of the Arab world in particular; excellent telephone, electricity, water and sewage systems throughout the country.

(8) **Good climate**: fine weather throughout the year with long sunny days, and mainly extremely dry. The difference between the four seasons can be felt and preparations for a visit should take account of the season. It snows in winter, is hot in summer, is cool and fresh in spring with the occasional chilly nights and in the autumn there is a cold breeze during the afternoon and evening.

(9) **Investment guarantees and incentives**: generous incentives to new companies. Special benefits include between 25% and 75% tax exemption from income and social service taxes on net profits for ten years; 100% exemption from all customs duties and import fees on equipment and machinery for three years; tax free salaries for non-Jordanians working for non-Jordanian companies; 100% exemption from property tax for five to seven years; guaranteed repatriation of capital and free transfer of interest and profits; government-owned land outside the governorate of Amman granted free of charge to approved projects.

Other benefits are also available to foreign companies with regional headquarters in Jordan, including 100% tax exemption on profits earned outside the country, as well as on the salaries of foreign managers and employees.

Ramadan

This, the ninth month of the Muslim calendar, commemorates the revelation of the Qur'an to the Prophet Mohammed and is respected by abstention from food or drink during daylight. Ramadan is observed throughout the Islamic World.

Be patient if you are on a business trip during this period, and be prepared for a reduction in the opening hours of shops and other facilities, with restaurants and cafes often working shorter hours, or closing during the day. Alcohol is not sold in public during the holy month, and bars will be closed. Hotels, however, will continue a regular service of serving food and drink, including alcohol to foreigners.

The law bans smoking, eating and drinking in public during the fasting hours and this is strictly upheld. Yet Jordan has a lively revival of Ramadan traditions including lavish banquets at the hour of breaking the fast and public gatherings during which traditional Ramadan sweets and drinks are offered.

Unlike other times in the year when the social life dies down at midnight, Jordanians stay up very late in Ramadan playing cards, listening to music, smoking hubbly-bubbly and chatting.

PART FIVE: FACTS AT YOUR FINGERTIPS

Visa and Immigration Requirements

Any non-Arab visitor to Jordan, whether entering on business or as a tourist, needs a visa. This is easily obtained, in most cases on entry into the country, or at diplomatic missions abroad. The fee for the visa, as well as the length of stay which is granted, depends on the visitor's nationality and passport.

Tourist visas generally take a day to obtain from a diplomatic mission. They are usually valid for a one month period.

Health requirements

Inoculations are not required unless you are travelling from an infected location. This applies if you have come from any country where yellow fever occurs. You may be asked to show your inoculation certificates at the point of entry into Jordan.

Departure tax

As of 1998, visitors and tourists to Jordan are required to pay a Departure Tax equivalent to 10 Jordanian Dinars when leaving the country by air. For those departing by land or sea (including crossings to the West Bank and Israel) the Departure Tax is 8 Jordanian Dinars.

For Jordanians residing in Jordan, the Departure Tax is 25 Jordanian Dinars, and 15 Jordanian Dinars for Jordanians resident outside Jordan.

These figures may be subject to change as time goes by.

Overseas Jordanian Missions

The Hashemite Kingdom of Jordan has embassies or consulates in the following cities: Abu Dhabi, Algiers, Ankara, Athens, Bahrain, Beijing, Belgrade, Berne, Baghdad, Bonn, Brasilia, Brussels, Bucharest, Cairo, Canberra, Damascus, Doha, Dubai, Geneva, Islamabad, Khartoum, Kuwait City, London, Madrid, Moscow, Muscat, New Delhi, New York, Ottawa, Paris, Rome, Rabat, Riyadh, Sana'a, Santiago, Tokyo, Tunis, Vienna and Washington DC. Honorary Consuls representing the kingdom's interests will also be found in most of the major cities of Europe.

International flights

Jordan is served by various airlines, with flights from all over the world. Royal Jordanian, the national airline, serves over forty international destinations.

Other airlines serving Amman's international airport include British Airways (in conjunction with Royal Jordanian), Air France, Alitalia, Egypt Air, Emirates Airways, Gulf Air, Iraqi Airways, KLM, Libyan Arab Airlines, Lufthansa, Olympic, Pakistan International Airways, Saudia, Singapore Airlines, Swissair, Turkish Airlines, and Yemenia. A number of chartered airlines fly tourists direct to Aqaba's international airport from Europe.

Royal Jordanian flies to the following cities from Amman: Abu Dhabi, Amsterdam, Ankara, Aqaba, Athens, Bahrain, Bangkok, Beirut, Belgrade, Berlin, Brussels, Cairo, Calcutta, Casablanca, Colombo, Damascus, Delhi, Dhahran, Doha, Dubai, Frankfurt, Geneva, Hanoi, Istanbul, Jakarta, Jeddah, Karachi, Larnaca, London, Madrid, Montreal, Moscow, Muscat, New York, Paris, Riyadh, Rome, Sana'a, Singapore, Toronto, Tripoli, Tunis and Vienna.

Arrival by ferry

The ferry terminal at Aqaba is complete with immigration facilities to receive passengers travelling on the Nweibeh to Aqaba ferry. The boat leaves Nweibeh in Egypt twice daily; at the same time another ferry leaves Aqaba bound for Nweibeh.

Arrival by road

From Syria the only border post is the Ramatha/Deraa border. JETT buses cross this border on routes between Amman, Damascus and Cairo. The road from Amman to Baghdad is good, but getting a tourist visa for Iraq is another story. There are two roads crossing from Jordan into Saudi Arabia but, again, getting a visa for Saudi Arabia is no easy matter. With the new climate of peace in the Middle East two new border crossings with Israel have been established. One links Eilat (in Israel) to the Jordanian resort of Aqaba, in the south. In north there is a new crossing via the Sharif Hussein Bridge, near Irbid. Visas — single entry only — to Jordan can be issued at both border posts. There are no problems in bringing your own vehicle into Jordan as long as you are not intending to sell it.

Crossing to the West Bank and Israel

For the West Bank, the King Hussein (Allenby) Bridge over the Jordan River is a 30-minute drive from Amman. Used by Palestinians living on the West Bank, foreigners and tourists can use it as well. Private vehicles and pedestrians are not permitted to cross the bridge. The only form of public transport across is by the JETT buses.

Before making the crossing you will need a permit from the Ministry of the Interior in Amman which takes about three days. You are not required to leave your passport at the Ministry and so can travel around the country in the meantime.

To get the permit you must submit one photograph, a revenue stamp of 50 fils (issued at the post office outside the Ministry) and complete a form. It may take an hour or so to apply for the permit, and another hour to collect it. This permit will entitle you to a one-month stay on the West Bank.

When crossing from the East Bank to the West Bank make sure that the Israeli officials give you their stamp of entry on a loose sheet of paper. If they stamp your passport you may not be permitted to re-enter Jordan. If you are making a trip to the West Bank ensure that you leave Amman as early as possible, as the last bus leaves the capital for the West Bank at 11.00.

For crossing into Israel there is the Sheikh Hussein border crossing in the north and the Aqaba/Eilat crossing in the south. These crossings can be used by anybody with visas to enter Israel except PNA residents and visitors with permits to enter PNA areas.

Customs

Most items carried by tourists are not subject to customs duty; these include radio, hair-dryer, camera, video equipment and so on. You may be requested to open your luggage for inspection. So far as duty allowances are concerned, you are permitted to take into Jordan 200 cigarettes or 25 grammes of tobacco and a one-litre bottle of spirits or two bottles of wine. Modest gifts brought into the country are exempt from customs duty.

Domestic air services

Jordan is such a small country, with such good roads, that the only domestic air service runs between Aqaba and Amman. The Royal Jordanian flight, which takes 45 minutes, leaves four mornings a week in either direction.

Road services

Jordan's road system, which spans more than 11,263 kilometres (7,000 miles) around the country, is generally good. You will find, however, that the more important roads are in the best shape. If you are venturing into the desert, to Qasr Tuba for instance, you will have to take a high clearance 4WD vehicle. For most other highways and B roads, a normal town car will suffice.

Three main roads bisect the country from north to south. They run roughly parallel to each other, and rise in importance from west to east. The first, running the length of the country down the Jordan River through Wadi Araba to Aqaba, is the Dead Sea Highway. General use is restricted at certain points. To its east is the extremely picturesque, but extraordinarily winding, Kings' Highway. It runs south from Amman, through Madaba, Kerak, Tafila, Shobak and Petra before twisting its way down to Aqaba. The last, and furthest to the east, is the well-used Desert Highway. Also known as Route 15, it is the only blue motorway road marked on maps of Jordan and it slices down the backbone of the country. Stretching from Damascus, it crosses into Jordan at Jabir before continuing through Mafraq, Zarqa, Amman and Ma'an, ending at Ras an Naqab, where it joins the Kings' Highway. The Desert Highway is well constructed and although busy with freight, does allow a swift passage for private vehicles.

North of Jordan, the sector between Amman and the Syrian border has a jumble of smaller interconnecting roads, linking the towns of Jerash, Ajlun, Irbid, Mafraq and others. A delightful way to pass a few hours is to drive around on these largely uncluttered roads, venturing through the small towns and villages in search of remnants of the past. Four roads lead to the eastern oasis of Azraq. One leads indirectly, from Mafraq, and heads to the Iraqi border. Another passes Qasr Hallabat en route from Amman. A third connects Amman's southern suburbs with Azraq. The last is little more than a fabled and ancient desert track which ventures south from Azraq into the desert.

Transportation from Amman's airport

Taxis are available from Queen Alia International Airport to take you into Amman (32 kms, 20 miles), a journey of about 30 to 45 minutes. At peak times allow considerably longer. You are required to buy a taxi ticket from the dispatch desk in the terminal before boarding the vehicle. This is presented to the driver. A fast and efficient bus service also connects the airport with Amman, leaving Abdali bus station every twenty minutes. A bus to the airport can also be boarded at Amra Hotel, situated at the beginning of the airport highway.

Passengers using Queen Alia Airport for international flights are requested to check in two hours before departure.

Taxi services

Taxis are readily available in Amman, Aqaba and other cities. They are not too expensive, and are generally yellow in colour with a green square on the door. Taxis have green number plates and a meter which ought to work. They are licensed to take four passengers. Take care, especially at night, that the driver knows his destination and is not taking you round in circles. Also make sure he is using the meter. A small tip is usual. The driver may ask for the full address of your destination.

Another type of taxi plies the major cities. Known simply as *servees*, they are communal taxis, usually white, and are often Peugeot 504s or Mercedes. Passengers are bunched tightly against each other. Similar to the buses, the cars take preordained routes — stopping at registered points around the city. The *servees* have the number of their route written on the front doors in Arabic. The fee is standard according to the route.

Car hire

All the main international car-hire companies operate in Amman, and some have offices in other cities. There are many Jordanian hire companies, but do check the contract and obtain good insurance. But, when hiring a car, bear in mind that in Jordan it is not possible to waive all damage liability. This means that, in the event of a crash, the driver is liable to pay at least the first JD 100 of the claim. The car hire agency usually requires a credit card slip to be signed by the driver and left at the hire office until the car is returned. Major car hire companies have offices at Queen Alia International Airport.

In addition, taxis plus driver can usually be hired from most companies for touring. Car hire can also be arranged through travel agents and hotels. Hire-vehicles have green number plates, while private cars generally have white licence plates.

Driving

Jordan is a small country that can be crossed by car in approximately four hours. Most of the sites a visitor would want to see are within a few hours' drive from Amman. Jordanians drive on the right-hand side of the road. Road signs are in Arabic and English, and should pose no problem. Take great care driving around towns, especially Amman, as roundabouts are common and potentially hazardous. Local driving habits are erratic, particularly around Amman and major highways.

An international driving licence is preferred, but generally a national driving licence, particularly if it has a photograph of the holder, is sufficient. For foreigners planning to live in Jordan it is necessary to obtain a Jordanian driving licence from the Driving Licence Bureau, which is situated in Marqa. To obtain the licence you must present your passport, three photographs, and driving licence from your own country. A driving theory test, a practical test, and an eye test might be necessary. A nominal fee is made for issuing the Jordanian driving licence. It is wise to get to the Driving Licence Bureau as early as possible.

Climate

The climate depends on which part of the country you are in, as altitude ranges from 400 metres (1,312 feet) below mean sea level at the Dead Sea, to high above sea level. The climate tends to be exceptionally dry during most of the year. Winter and spring are cooler and, during these seasons, most of the country's rainfall occurs.

The hottest months of the year are June to September, when temperatures rise to about 32°C in the more arid regions of Jordan. The period between December and February is the coolest, when temperatures stay around 15°C during the day. Prevailing winds sweep in from the north and, during winter, winds blow up from the south.

Jordan can be divided into three physiographic regions: the average temperature in Amman ranges from 8.1°C in January to 25.1°C in July. In Aqaba average temperatures range from 15.6°C in January to 32.5°C in July. There is an extreme variation in the climate of the desert between day and night, and between summer and winter. Summer temperatures can exceed 40°C. Winter nights can be bitterly cold, dry and windy.

	AMMAN	
	Celsius	Fahrenheit
January	8	46
February	9	48
March	12	53
April	16	60
May	21	69
June	23	74
July	25	77
August	26	78
September	23	73
October	21	69
November	15	59
December	10	50

	AQABA	
January	16	60
February	17	62
March	20	68
April	24	75
May	28	82
June	32	89
July	32	89
August	33	91
September	30	86
October	27	80
November	22	71
December	17	62

Currency

Jordan currency is the Jordanian Dinar, or JD. It is subdivided into 1000 fils. Jordanians between themselves use the subdivision of the piaster or qirsh. One JD consists of 100 piasters. Coins and paper denominations are both used.

The denominations are:

Silver Coins: 5 fils (0.5 qirsh); 10 fils (1 qirsh); 25 fils (2.5 qirsh); 50 fils (5 qirsh); 100 fils (10 qirsh); 250 fils; 500 fils.

Golden Coins, seven sided; Quarter Dinar; Half Dinar and One Dinar.

Paper Currency: Jordanian Dinars (JD) 0.5; 1; 5; 10 and 20.

The daily exchange rate is published in the local newspapers. Money can be exchanged not only at banks, but also at hotels in major towns.

Banks

Major international banks have offices in Amman, along with Jordan's own banks, some of which can be found in other cities around the world. Foreigners are permitted to open accounts at Jordanian banks in either Jordanian Dinars or in foreign currencies. Currency exchange offices operate under the guidelines and regulations of the Central Bank of Jordan. The Central Bank sets minimum and maximum interest rates for financial institutions to follow. Banks are open to the public between 09.30 and 13.30. Some banks have recently introduced afternoon hours for regular transactions, but if you want to change foreign currency in the afternoon you may have to do this at an hotel.

Credit cards

Although credit and charge cards are not as widely used as in the USA or Europe, they are accepted at most large hotels, car hire companies, tourist shops and restaurants. Remember that a credit card outside of these premises often has no meaning. Major cards accepted are: Access, MasterCard, Visa, Eurocard, American Express and Diners Club. Most have representatives in Amman should your card be lost or stolen.

The Kingdom

Jordan achieved full independence from Great Britain in 1946, before which it was the Emirate of Transjordan established in 1921. Since independence it has been known as the Hashemite Kingdom of Jordan.

The country has been ruled by three monarchs to date: H M King Abdullah bin Al Hussein (1921-1951); H M King Talal bin Abdullah (1951-1952); and H M King Hussein bin Talal (1952-present).

Government and Constitution

Jordan's legislative authority resides with the King and the parliament which is comprised of an Upper House (The Senate) and the Lower House (Chamber of Deputies). The King designates members to the Upper House, while the deputies of the Lower House are elected through national suffrage. Men and women over the age of nineteen are eligible to vote and the minimum age for a candidate to the House is thirty.

Jordan's ruling monarchy is that of the Hashemite line, the ancestors of the Prophet Mohammed. The lineage is continued with the next most acceptable male heir. At present, King Hussein has bestowed the responsibility of Crown Prince to his younger brother Prince Hassan bin Talal.

The monarch is Head of State, and has the capacity to approve laws, direct the government, order parliamentary elections and dissolve the Lower House. He appoints the Prime Minister and cabinet ministers upon the Prime Minister's recommendation. The cabinet is approved by parliament through a vote of confidence.

The Council of Ministers should submit its policies and plan of action for the approval of the Lower House of Parliament within a month of assuming office. A vote of no confidence by the House results in the resignation of the cabinet or the minister(s) in question.

The King is also the Supreme Commander of the Armed Forces and has the authority to declare war, conclude peace, as well as sign treaties with other states and nations.

The legislative authority

Jordan's present parliamentary system dates back to 1923 and consists of an 80-member elected Lower House and a 40-member Upper House. The Upper House must not exceed half the size of the Lower House. The Lower House initiates, debates and votes on legislation in conjunction with the government.

When a bill has been approved by the Lower House it is passed to the Senate for debate and a vote. If it is approved, it is passed forward to the King, who either grants consent by Royal Decree or returns it unapproved with justification for his refusal.

A bill becomes an Act of Parliament on being passed in both houses with a majority of two-thirds or more.

Constitution

The constitution of Jordan was written in 1949, before being promulgated in 1952, and later amended on several occasions. It maintains that Jordan is an hereditary monarchy with a parliamentary system. Various provisions define the rights and duties of the citizens of Jordan, and guarantee freedom to all in matters of religion and freedom of speech. The constitution defines the authority of the head of state.

Local government
Jordan is divided into twelve governorates — each headed by a governor and subdivided into smaller administrative regions. These governorates, which are essentially an extension of the central government, are supervised by the Ministry of the Interior. Governors enjoy wide administrative authority and in specific cases they exercise the powers of ministers.

National Charter
In November 1989 King Hussein announced plans to draw up a National Charter which would underline political pluralism and the democratic freedom of all Jordanians. Thus, in 1990, he appointed a 60-member commission to debate and formulate the National Charter. The draft was presented to the King in January 1991 and, in June 1991, it was approved. This National Charter stresses Jordan's national and pan-Arab identity and commitments.

There are currently 21 registered parties in Jordan representing almost the entire gamut of the ideological spectrum. In general, the parties can be grouped into leftists, centrists and Islamists. The leftists include Ba'athists, Socialists and Communists. The Islamic Action Front party, an offshoot of the Muslim Brotherhood movement, is considered the most influential and enjoys considerable popular support.

Democracy and human rights
Despite setbacks, Jordan has taken courageous steps towards democratisation, most of which are reflected in the emergence of human rights organisations and freedom institutions. Six human rights bodies are active in the Jordanian political arena and are slowly gaining influence over the development of the society and by raising awareness of public freedoms. They are: the Arab Organisation for Human Rights (Jordan Branch) established in October 1991; Amnesty International, established in February 1992; Centre for the Study of Freedoms, Democracy and Human Rights in the Arab World, established in February 1993; the National Society for enhancing Democracy and Freedoms, established in March 1993; the Freedoms Committee at the Lower House of Parliament, and the Freedoms Committee of the Union of Professional Associations.

Language
Arabic is the national language of Jordan, although English is widely spoken, particularly in the major cities. French is also spoken but to a lesser extent. Language courses are widely offered in Amman, teaching Arabic, French, German, Spanish, Russian, Turkish, Hebrew and Italian.

Religion
The state religion is Islam, as indicated in the Constitution. The majority of the population (95%) are Sunni Muslim. Those include other non-Arab minorities such as the Circassians and the Chechen who, towards the end of the last century, fled their homeland in Caucasia. The rest of Jordan's population are Arab Christians and Armenians of different denominations whose freedom of worship, opinion and association are guaranteed by the Constitution.

You are likely to hear the call to prayer (known as *Athan*) echoing out. Muslims are required to pray five times a day. The prayers are as follows: *Fajr* — the morning prayer; *Thuhur* — the noon prayer; *'Asr* — the late afternoon prayer; *Maghrib* — the sunset prayer; and *'Isha* — the night prayer. It is not compulsory to go to the mosque to pray although Muslims try to go at least on Fridays. You will see the devout unrolling small prayer rugs wherever they are, facing in the direction of Mecca.

The basis of the Muslim faith stems from the early years of the 7th century AD when the Prophet Mohammed received the *Word* from Allah and called upon those living around him to leave their pagan rituals and beliefs to follow Islam. Muslims consider their God to be the same as the God worshipped by Christians but disagree with the Christian divination associated with Jesus. In Islam, Mohammed is the Prophet of God, not His son. In the year AD 622 Mohammed was forced to leave Mecca with his followers. He went to Medina where support for his teachings escalated. It was this migration, known as the *Hijra*, which marks the beginning of the Islamic calendar.

By 630 AD, Mohammed had a massive following and headed back to Mecca to spread the Word of Islam once again. In the years that followed many people throughout the Middle East and North Africa converted to Islam.

Islam, which means *submission* in Arabic, implies that it is the duty of the people to submit themselves to worship and obey Allah — the one God. The Qur'an (also spelt Koran) is the Word of God spoken to Mohammed while he was in Mecca and Medina during the 7th century. It is the holy book of all Muslims.

There are five essential pillars central to the lives and conduct of all Muslims. These pillars, or *Arkan*, are as follows:

(1) *Shahada*: Muslims are required to turn towards Mecca and recite this prayer five times a day. Its words are the foundation of Islam, and profess a Muslim's absolute devotion to Islam: "There is no God but Allah, and Mohammed is

His Prophet". These words are the first that greet a newborn infant, and the last uttered at the grave.

(2) *Salah*: the recitation of a series of prayers, made five times during the day. These recitations of prayer are repeated three times and are accompanied by motions of devotion and homage to God. Before offering Salah one must cleanse oneself in a specific fashion (a process known as *Taharah*). At all mosques there are washing facilities, and you will see Muslims cleaning themselves thoroughly before starting to pray. There are two types of cleansing before offering prayer: the first is *Al-Wudu* (a partial wash or ablution); the other is known as *Al-Ightisal*, (which is a cleansing of the whole body). An ablution, known as *Tayammum* can be used. Being a dry ablution, this is adopted when there is no water available.

(3) *Zakat*: the act of bestowing alms and charity on those less fortunate than oneself. Today there is an obligatory property tax which is used to benefit the poor and needy. You will find that in Islamic countries beggars are treated with respect and generosity.

(4) *Ramadan*: this, the ninth month of the Islamic calendar, is reserved for special religious observances. It is a month of fasting during the hours of daylight. Ramadan commemorates the first month in which the Qur'an was revealed to the Prophet Mohammed. The actual timing of Ramadan changes each year depending on the phases of the moon.

The end of Ramadan is celebrated with the holy festival of *Eid al-Kabir* (also known as *Al-Adha*). These celebrations, occurring throughout the Islamic World, are the Muslim calendar's most celebrated time. People greeting each other in the streets call out '*Eidkum Mubarek*' (*May your Eid be blessed*). Large feasts generally mark the occasion.

(5) *Hajj*: the holy pilgrimage to Mecca — Islam's most sacred city. It is the duty of all Muslims to make the pilgrimage at least once in their lifetime. The journey is made in simple clothing — a white seamless robe and sandals. The pilgrim walks seven times around the *Kaabah* at the centre of Mecca's Holy Mosque.

Time

Jordan is two hours ahead of Greenwich Mean Time. Daylight saving time occurs between 1 April and 1 October.

Business hours

Government-run and most other offices are open from 08.00 to 14.00 hours every day except Friday when nearly all of them are closed all day. During the month of Ramadan working hours are usually reduced to between 09.00 and 14.00 hours. Shop opening hours depend on the location and the type of shop. Most of the shops open their doors between 09.00 and 10.00 and close before 20.30. Muslims close early or do not open at all on Fridays, and Christians follow similar rules on Sundays.

Tipping

Although many hotels and restaurants at the top end of the scale add a gratuity of about ten per cent, smaller service businesses, such as cafés, do not include a tip. In such cases it is polite to leave a gratuity of some kind in line with the quality of service you have received.

Communications

Jordan has a modern communications system. Direct dial international telephone and facsimile services are available throughout Jordan and to almost all countries. A rapidly increasing number of private citizens and corporations are making use of the Internet. Sending email is a fraction of the cost of international telephone calls — which tend to be high in Jordan. (See following 'Internet' for more information.

To make an international call, dial first 00 followed by the required country's international code, and then the local number. At present 110 nations worldwide can be reached by direct dialling from Jordan. Both Arabic and English telephone directories are available. Car telephones are quite common and the country is now studying tenders to introduce mobile telephones.

Facsimile services have become increasingly popular, and can be found at most businesses, hotels, offices, agencies and even at home. Telex services have also expanded through the provision of a central telex exchange which can handle 4,000 circuits.

Postal services are handled by the Post and Postal Savings Public Corporation (PPSPC) which organises and operates all related services. These include the issuing of new stamps and postal savings programmes, as well as public telephone services. Air and surface postal services are available for international mail. Telegram services are available through most of the nation's post offices. Most international express delivery companies also have representative offices in Amman and other large cities.

Internet

Jordan has quickly and efficiently staked a claim in the world of cyberspace.

The kingdom has numerous informative web sites, and a growing number of businesses and individuals are making use of email. Before you journey to Jordan have a look on the Internet. You will be able to find latest information, from currency exchange to business matters. Some of the best sources for information on Jordan are, somewhat ironically, outside the country. The CIA's site has good up-to-date data on Jordan (www.odci.gov/cia). While the 'Hashemite Kingdom of Jordan Home Page' provides a range of practical information detailing everything from the kingdom's National Charter and its record of Human Rights to cultural briefings and even the kingdom's radio schedule (www.mit.edu8001/activities/jordanians/jordan). The site, which contains a mass of information, is actually managed at the Massachusetts Institute of Technology (MIT) in the USA. An important source for American visitors is the US State Department's travel advisory to Jordan. (www.stolaf.edu/network/travel-advisories).

A key organisation in the Internet Industry in Jordan is NETS (National Equipment & Technical Services)

Telephone: Amman 619870;

Email: (infor@nets.com.jo)

Other useful Internet sites for news and information on Jordan, include:

• Jordanian Tourist Board: a useful place for starting research into the kingdom's tourist facilities and main attractions. (www.esinet.es/globanet/jordan)
The major sites on any tour of Jordan — Petra, Jerash, Amman and so forth — are well presented, each linked to the main page. The site includes photographs, currency details and travel tips. You can email the Tourist Board at: JTM@nets.com.jo.

• Arab Net: provides an extremely useful databank of reference information on the Kingdom of Jordan, as well as on all other Arab countries. The site is one of the core reference points when it comes to the Arab World. (www.arab.net)

• Directory of Middle East Resources on the Net: a practical, and well-maintained site, presenting a wide variety of cultural, economic and political material relating to all Arab nations. (www.yahala.com)

• Jordan Newsgroup: one of the primary newsgroups offering some of the more elusive information one might want to know about Jordan and the Middle East. (news.soc.culture.jordan).

Media

Jordan has a variety of privately owned mainstream and opposition newspapers and weeklies. Television and radio are state owned. The press itself is politically influenced, although sufficient space and time is allocated for literature, travel, the arts and business. The mainstream newspapers, although largely owned by shareholding companies, both private and public, tend to reflect the government's political message and its role and place in the Arab World at large. They are not, however, the voice of the government.

These newspapers include three Arabic dailies, *Al Ra'i*, *Al Dustour* and *Al Sha'ab* as well as one English daily, *The Jordan Times*.

Two new dailies appeared in October 1993: *Akher Khaber* (the latest news) is the only evening paper and is mainly distributed at traffic lights; and *Al Aswaq* (the markets) which is a business-oriented daily that also tackles major political news.

A political parties law, enacted in May 1992, paved the road for a number of political party papers which have emerged and folded according to the financial situation of the mother party. The political weight and distribution of these weekly publications have so far remained marginal to the more established mainstream newspapers.

The Islamists publish two weeklies, *Al Liwa*, which concentrates on regional Islamic issues with a moderate editorial line on Jordanian issues; and the newly established *Al Sabeel* weekly which has emerged as the voice of the powerful Islamic Action Front (IAF) party, the political arm of the Muslim Brotherhood Movement. The Communist Party publishes *Al Jamaheer* while other leftist parties publish *Al Ahali* and *Al Baath*. Centrist Parties' weeklies include *Al Ahd*, *Al Mustaqbal*, *Al Rasif* and a host of smaller newsletters. There are two tabloid weeklies: *Shihan*, considered as the second largest distributing publication in the country, and *Al Bilad*, which proposes itself as an opposition paper.

The Jordan News Agency, known as PETRA, is the country's official news agency. It supplies home news to local newspapers, radio and television, as well as to government departments and international subscribers. It offers a teleprinter network and a photographic service, and distributes news and features about Jordan in both Arabic and English. Jordan has one national television station. This started transmitting in April 1968 and now has two channels. Today Jordan Television (JTV) transmits not only to Jordan, but also to other countries in the Middle East such as Syria, the south of Lebanon, the West Bank and northern Saudi Arabia. Channel One is the main channel and broadcasts in Arabic. Channel Two offers a selection of programmes, most of which are in English, but it also provides some French and Hebrew programmes.

During the past year or so a wealth of new stations has become available to those who have a satellite dish. Jordanians can also subscribe to a cable television service which broadcasts, among other channels, the BBC and CNN.

Medical services

There are 47 private hospitals in Jordan with a total of 2,600 beds. Others are under construction. Pharmacists number approximately 4,300 and dentists 2,000.

The health care system has drastically

improved over the last two decades, placing it among the top ten countries of the world in reducing infant mortality. Life expectancy is 67 for males and 71 for females. The main provider of health services in Jordan is the public sector, complemented by the private sector in addition to international and charitable organisations. The highly professional standards of medical treatment in Jordan have attracted patients from neighbouring Arab countries such as Iraq, Syria and Yemen. The Ministry of Health operates 506 primary and secondary health clinics, as well as 161 maternal and child health care centres, 106 dental health clinics, and 15 centres for chest disorders.

In previous decades, physicians with overseas training often failed to return to the kingdom after their studies. But now, with increased incentives and state-of-the-art facilities, Jordan boasts some of the world's leading surgeons and medical practitioners. Patients travel from around the Middle East to Amman for diagnosis and operations of all kinds. Prices for operations, which must be approved by the Ministry of Health, are extremely competitive. Amman has become a showcase of medical science, and now offers the crème de la crème when it comes to sanatoria.

The Amman Surgical Hospital (3rd Circle, Amman) is well-known for its work in introducing new trends in medicine to the people of Jordan. The hospital has a telemedic link with the Mayo Clinic in Rochester, USA, permitting surgeons in the USA to co-operate with surgeons in Amman. The system, which relies on state-of-the-art satellite communication and video-imaging, has already saved hundreds of lives in Jordan.

Arab Centre for Heart & Special Surgery (5th Circle, Amman), which opened in 1994, is fully equipped to provide advanced diagnostic, surgical and rehabilitation services. The Centre, known for its pioneering treatment of cardiac cases, also treats those with kidney, bone marrow and diabetic disorders, as well as performing major organ transplants.

Jordan's Speciality Hospital (Shmeisani, Amman) provides a comprehensive range of treatments — ranging from simple out-patient operations to complex open heart and other surgeries. The hospital's facilities include the cutting edge of technology for corneal transplants and excismer laser surgery for treatment to correct short-sightedness.

The Child Welfare Hospital (between 7th and 8th Circles, Amman) is the capital's newest medical achievement. Catering to the kingdom's enormous child population, the hospital offers a wide range of medical treatments, and is dedicated to promoting child health. As with most of Jordan's major clinics and hospitals, most of the staff speak English.

Libraries

There are 40 public libraries in Jordan, 102 libraries in governmental institutions and departments, 7 libraries in the different cultural centres, 44 libraries at the universities and community colleges and 16 libraries for children.

Museums

Although Jordan is a country that is rich in history and archaeology, museums in Jordan also cover a variety of themes which include: children's heritage and science, folklore, jewellery, fine arts, military memorabilia, popular traditions, post and communications, coins, marine science, school books, and Islamic culture. Amman has the greatest number of museums, but there are several other museums in other tourist-attractive centres such as the Red Sea port of Aqaba, and the old city of Salt.

Clubs

Almost all of the recreational centres in Jordan are private ones and are confined to members. Although membership is somewhat hard to obtain, one may be allowed in as a guest of one of the centre's members. Such clubs include: The Royal Automobile Club, the Orthodox Club, Al Hussein Youth City, the American Women of Amman Club, YWMA and the YWCA and others.

Health and recreational clubs can also be found in 5- and 4-star hotels but membership is not essential, and non-residents can benefit from the hotel's services. The fee differs from one hotel to another and mostly depends upon the facilities provided.

There are also specialised clubs which offer facilities for one kind of sport or recreational activity and are often open to the public. These include: the Chess Club, the Riding Club, the Bowling Club and the Royal Jordanian Shooting Club.

Cultural clubs are dramatically increasing in the country. They offer a wide variety of activities including lectures, seminars and exhibitions. Their programmes are usually issued on a monthly or a weekly basis and their activities are regularly published in the daily Arabic and English newspapers. These clubs include: the Democratic Thought Forum, the Phoenix Gallery, the Arab Thought Forum, the Royal Cultural Centre, the Jordanian Writers Association, the Women's Union in Jordan, the Abdul Hamid Shoman Foundation, the French Cultural Centre, the British Council, the Goethe Institute, and the American Centre.

Energy

Jordan's national power grid runs on 220 volts/ 50 cycles AC, so most electrical appliances from Britain will function. Wall sockets in large hotels often take the 13 amp square three-pinned plug — as used in Britain — while a selection of other sockets and plugs are also in use. These include the Italian thin two-pinned plug, the three-pinned plug with round pins, and various others. If in doubt take a multi-purpose adaptor. American equipment requires both an adaptor and a transformer.

Weights and measures

Jordan operates almost entirely on the metric system. You may come across the measurement for land: the *dunum*. One dunum is approximately equal to 1,000 square metres (10,760 square feet).

Public holidays

Friday is the day of rest although Christians tend to take Sunday off. The following days are observed as national holidays:

1 May	Labour Day
25 May	Independence Day
10 June	Arab Revolt and Armed Forces Day
11 August	King Hussein's Accession to the throne
14 November	King Hussein's Birthday

Other religious holidays are determined by the Islamic lunar calendar and can vary in date by about two weeks from year to year. They are:

Lailat al Isra wal mi'raj (the Prophet's Night Journey)
Eid al-Fitr (the Feast of Ramadan)
Eid al-Adha (the Feast of Sacrifice)
Al-Hijra (Muslim New Year)
Mawlid Al Nabi (the Prophet's Birthday)

Christians are permitted as holidays:
Christmas Day
Boxing Day
Palm Sunday
Easter Sunday

Narcotics

The Jordanian authorities take an extremely serious view of drugs and drug trafficking. Penalties for possession and for any kind of trafficking are met with long jail sentences and fines. Whenever one is travelling in the Middle East take care to ensure that one's luggage is firmly fastened — preventing any would-be smuggler from using your bags.

Useful Arabic

Just a few words in Arabic will make your trip more enjoyable and, at the same time, bring gleaming smiles to the faces of all Jordanians with whom you speak.

Vocabulary and phrases:

Hello	Mar-haba
Good morning	Sabah el-khair
(In reply)	Sabah el noor
Welcome	Ahlan wa sahlan
(In reply)	Ahlan bekum
Greetings	Assalam 'alaikoom
(In reply)	'Alaikoom salalm
Good-bye	Ma'assalama
(when departing)	Fi aman allah
How are you?	Kaifa halak?
Do you speak English?	Hal tatakalum Al Engleaziah?
I do not speak Arabic	Ana la atakallum Al Arabiah
Please	Min fadlak
	(to a man)
	Min fadlik
	(to a woman)
Excuse me	Aatherni, Affwone
If God wills	Insha-allah
Thank you	Shuk-ran
No, thank you	Laa, shuk-ran
Yes	Nam
No	La
Take me to...	Khothni Ela...
Wait here	Intadhir Hona
I'm sorry	Muta'assef
Who is it?	Meen?
What is it?	Shoo ha-da Esh hada?
What is your name?	Ma Ismika?
My name is...	Ismi...
Where?	Wein?
Why?	Laysh?
What?	Matha?
How much is it? (money)	Bekome?
How many?	Kam?
How much does it weigh?	Shoo wazno?
I don't know	Ma ba'arif
Slowly	Shway shway
Stop	Waqqif

To the right	'al-ya-meen
To the left	'ash-shmal
Straight ahead	Dug-ri
Once	Marra
Twice	Marratain
I want	Bid-dee
I don't want	Ma bid-dee
What do you want?	Shoo bid-dak?
	(to a man)
	Shoo bid-dik?
	(to a woman)
What is that?	Shou hathaak?
How many kilometres?	Kam kilometre?
Where is the road to...?	Wain et-tareeq 'al...?
Is there air-conditioning?	Fee tabreed?
I want to eat	Bid-dee akul
I want to drink	Bid-dee ash-rab
Water	Mai
Tea	Sh'ay
Coffee	Qah-wa
Milk	Haleeb
Sugar	Sukkar
Market	Souq

Numbers:

zero	sifr
one	wahad
two	tenayne
three	talateh
four	arba'a
five	khamseh
six	siteh
seven	saba'a
eight	tamanyeh
nine	tissa'
ten	asharah

Days of the week:

Sunday	al-ahad
Monday	at-t'nayne
Tuesday	at-t'lateh
Wednesday	al-arba'a
Thursday	al-khamees
Friday	aj-juma'a
Saturday	as-sebt

In Brief

Archaeological & Ancient Sites — Jordan

Ain Mousa
Thought to be the spring which started when Moses struck a rock twice. Next to the spring are various newly excavated Byzantine churches.

Ain Zara
Thirteen sites from the Hellenistic era to the late Byzantine have so far been recorded and are now preserved as a natural and archaeological park.

Azraq Castle
Probably dating back to Roman times, the castle was renovated in AD 1237 by the Ummayeds, before being used this century as a base for T E Lawrence (of Arabia) during the Arab Revolt.

Bayir
Seventy kilometres south of Qasr Tuba, Bayir is deep in the desert. It is thought that the Ummayed adapted what was originally a Nabatean fortress at Bayir.

Beidha, Petra
Just north of Petra, the Beidha ruins equal Jericho in their antiquity. The ruins date back some 9,000 years.

Cave of the Seven Sleepers
Next to Amman's Mosque of the People of the Cave, the site is believed to be that which is mentioned in *Sura 18* of the Qur'an. It is comprised of several underground chambers containing sarcophagi cut from the rock.

Citadel, Amman
Most ancient area of Amman, overlooking the city. Site of the ruined Temple of Hercules and the Archaeological Museum of Jordan. The latter contains some of the Dead Sea Scrolls.

Crusader Fortress, Aqaba
A modest Crusader stronghold beside the Gulf of Aqaba. The garrison was built during the 12th century, and is in very good condition.

Deir Alla
Said to be the site where Jacob wrestled with an angel, excavations at Deir Alla have unearthed remains of a civilisation dating back to about 1600 BC. Of particular interest in the find has been a temple with a shrine; in addition to various incense burners and figurines.

Deir el-Kahf
Forty-five kilometres from Azraq, the black basalt ruins seem unending. The actual fortress, whose name meant *The Monastery of the Caves,* enclosed an entire community, complete with stables, living quarters, watchtowers and so forth.

Dhiban
Ancient once-walled city, most famed as the site at which the Mesha Stele was discovered in 1865. The stone, recounting the deeds of King Mesha, was partly destroyed during an altercation in 1865.

El-Mukhayyet, Mount Nebo
The small site at el-Mukhayyet houses a fine Byzantine mosaic floor, which was built in dedication to St Lot and Procopius.

El Qasr
South of Dhiban, El Qasr is the site of a ruined Nabatean temple. South of El Qasr is Al Rabbath, which is mentioned in the Bible.

Humaima
Thirteen kilometres from the Via Nova Traiana the remains found at Humaima are believed to be those of Auara, the town founded by the Nabatean King Aretas III in the 1st century BC. In the same vicinity are a 2nd-century AD Roman fort and 5 churches.

Iraq el-Amir: Caves of the Prince
Near to the Tobiad's palace are these caves, eleven in all, carved into the cliff face.

Irbid
Eighty-eight kilometres north of Amman, Irbid was constructed on the site of a Bronze Age settlement. It was once surrounded by a formidable black basalt wall, and is thought to be *Beth Arbel* of the Bible.

Jerash
Located 48 kilometres north of Amman, Jerash is one of the finest surviving Roman provincial cities in the world. Like other sites in Jordan, Jerash was one of the ten cities of the Decapolis. The ruins have been well renovated and are the scene of the annual Jerash Festival.

Among the many constructions are: Hadrian's arch, built in honour of Hadrian's visit to Jerash; the Oval Plaza, exceptional in its very shape; the once colossal Temple of Zeus; North and South Theatres; Street of Columns; Temple of Artemis, phenomenal in its size; the West Baths; the

Nymphaeum; the Ummayed Mosque; and a large selection of Byzantine churches.

Kerak Fortress, Kerak
The elaborate Crusader fortress is relatively well preserved with its subterranean chambers and storage rooms. Once stronghold of the dastardly Reynaud de Chatillon, the castle has had a colourful history.

Khirbet et Tannur
Site of a Nabatean temple, dating to the 1st century AD, and constructed on a precipitous slope.

Lisan Peninsula
The ruins of a Byzantine monastery complex, chapel and partly-preserved 6th- and 7th-century mosaic floors are located on the peninsula 6 kilometres west of Mazra'a. At the Ghawr Haditha cemetery east of the village of Haditha there are a great number of unusually-shaped tombs.

Mafraq
Now a modern town, possibilities for excavations are unlikely. The town is known to have been constructed on the foundations of an earlier community. Ruins of an Arab fortress, in addition to Nabatean and other relics have been unearthed.

Mosaic Map of Holy Land, Madaba
Most celebrated of all Madaba's important sites. The map, originally containing over two million mosaic cubes, depicts the Holy Land during the Byzantine era. A number of other important mosaic friezes are situated in the town of Madaba.

Mukawir
Now open to visitors, the old village of Mukawir has been partly renovated, believed to be the site where John the Baptist was beheaded.

Pella
One of the cities of the Roman federation of the Decapolis, Pella is yet to be seriously excavated. It is thought that Pella was inhabited during much of the last 6,000 years. Various buildings have been identified, among them are: a Roman Odeon; a Byzantine church, and two further churches, in addition to Ummayed constructions. Some archaeologists believe that, if excavated, Pella could yield buildings as great as those at Jerash.

Petra
Jordan's most illustrious archaeological site, Petra's ruins, are extensive. Constructed by the Nabateans as their capital, Petra's list of phenomenal structures is daunting. Two of the greatest are El Khazneh (the Treasury) and El Deir (the Monastery). Others include the Street of Façades; the Roman Theatre; the Urn, Corinthian, Palace and Silk Tombs; the Colonnaded Street; the Nymphaeum; the Triumphal Arch; Qasr el Bint; and the Turkamaniya Tomb.

Qalaat-al-Rabad, Ajlun
Constructed on the site of an earlier Saracen fortress (built by Saladin's nephew), with a sweeping vantage over all surrounding areas. It is superbly preserved and quite different in design from Kerak, Shobak, or other Crusader strongholds.

Qasr Ain es Sil
This farming estate with bathing complex was probably constructed on the foundations of an earlier Roman estate.

Qasr al-Abed: Castle (Palace) of the Slave
Ruins of an enormous palace, thought to have been built by the powerful Tobiad family, during the 2nd century BC.

Qasr Amra
Now a World Heritage Site this bathing complex is often considered to be the finest of all Ummayed constructions in Jordan. The complex houses various dining and lounging areas, in addition to a selection of baths, and a well. The ceilings of the chambers are decorated with exquisite plasterwork scenes.

Qasr Aseikhin
Built by the Romans as a small fortress, the so-called Qasr (meaning 'palace', which is a misnomer), is of modest significance.

Qasr Hallabat
Hallabat was constructed in the 2nd century AD, on the site of an earlier (perhaps Nabatean) fortress. It was later remodelled by the Ummayeds, who destroyed much of the Roman and Byzantine workmanship.

Qasr Kharana
Located on a plain, 55 kilometres east of Amman, Kharana is the best preserved of the Ummayed palaces. Dated as being built in AD 771, the walls are 35 metres long. Although Kharana might look like a fortress, historians believe that it was constructed as a palace or meeting place.

Qasr Mushash
The site is that of 18 Ummayed stone buildings, which are thought to have been a palace. Mushash was also gigantic in size.

Qasr Mushatta

Situated within Amman International Airport's perimeter, Mushatta is one of the most lavish Ummayed palaces ever built. The colossal yellow brick walls stretch 144 metres in each direction. Understandably, the palace was never completed.

Qasr Muwaqqar

Little remains today of the Ummayed palace which once stood in the town, although a huge water cistern can still be seen.

Qasr Shibib, near Zarqa

An Arab fortress, constructed on the site of a Roman stronghold, located above the Zarqa Spring.

Qasr Tuba

Rather like Mushatta, Tuba was planned on a gloriously grand scale, and was never completed. Unlike Mushatta, its location is anything but central. By land it can only be reached by driving at length over the desert. The remains of Qasr Jila are in the vicinity of Qasr Tuba.

Qasr Uweinid

Located 15 kilometres south-west of Azraq, the fortress was built from black basalt blocks. It has been dated to the 3rd century AD, and is known to have been a caravanserai en route from Amman to Arabia.

Qastal

Just west of Amman's International Airport, Qastal is one of the oldest Ummayed palaces. The remains include a mosque, central palace building, cemetery, baths, reservoir and dam.

Quweismeh

South-east of Amman, the village houses the site of a Roman crypt — first unearthed in 1881.

Roman Theatre, Amman

Constructed by the Romans to seat 6,000 spectators. The theatre was restored in 1970, and is still used for cultural events. In the west wing is the Museum of Popular Traditions; and in the east wing is the Folklore Museum of Amman.

Siq el Barid, Petra

Suburb of Petra, the ruins contain various interesting buildings and features. Most famous is the Painted House, site of several fine plasterwork scenes.

Shobak Fortress, Shobak

Constructed by Baldwin I, as a link in the chain of Crusader fortresses across the Middle East,

Shobak was gained by Saladin in 1189. The castle dominates surrounding areas, and was, at its height, home to 6,000 Christians. It was later renovated by the Mamluks during the 14th century.

Swafieh

Located between the 6th and 7th Circles of Amman, the Swafieh ruins of a Byzantine monastery house a superb Byzantine mosaic floor.

Syagha, Mount Nebo

The monastery of Syagha is in dedication to the last moment of Moses' life. It contains several superb Byzantine mosaic floors, and looks across the Jordan Valley to the Holy Land.

Teleilat Ghassul

Excavations continue at the large site of this ancient settlement where, in the Neolithic/Chalcolithic era of around 4500-3600 BC, Teleilat Ghassul was once the home of a prosperous farming community. Frescoes and wall paintings excavated in the 1930s are thought to be the second-oldest of their kind in the world, predated only by Neolithic-site frescoes at Catal Huyuk in Turkey.

The site has revealed limestone amulets, maceheads, cosmetic pallets, mortars, querns, hoe blades and animal bones dating from around 4400 BC.

Tel el Kheleifeh

Significant urban remains of a fortified city called Aila (Ayla) of the Nabatean-Roman-Byzantine era have been revealed by 1996 excavations and can be located 2 kilometres south of Tel el Kheleifeh and north-west of the small present-day town.

Tell Maquss, Aqaba

Ancient ruins, dating to about 3500 BC, at a community thought to have depended on smelting copper. Another important archaeological site in the area is that of Tel el Kheleifeh.

Thamudic Carvings, Wadi Rum

Deep in the Valley of Rum, the carvings, etched into the sheering rock faces, are of ancient origin.

The Cave of Lot at Deir Ain Abata

Recently discovered by the eminent Greek archaeologist, Constantinos Politis, the site has revealed the actual cave to which the biblical figure of Lot fled with his daughters during the destruction of Sodom and Gomorrah.

The site is perched precariously on a hillside overlooking the Dead Sea (near Safi). In addition to the Cave of Lot, a large and elaborate Byzantine Basilica has also been unearthed. Other finds include the monastery's refectory, reservoir, mosaic floors, numerous cairns, and other tombs, and Bronze Age pottery.

Umm el-Jemal
The black basalt remains of Umm el-Jemal cover a phenomenal area. It is thought that the community was constructed by the Nabateans, perhaps to cater for caravans trekking through the desert.

Umm el-Rassas
Site of a large and ancient encampment once surrounded by a formidable stone wall. On the northern extremity of the site are the remains of the Byzantine Church of St Stephen. The mosaic floor of the church is preserved. It is outstanding. A mysterious watchtower also remains at Umm el-Rassas (1,300 metres north of the settlement): strange in that there is one chamber at the top of the tower, with no apparent means to ascend to it. A chapel at the foot of the tower was unearthed in 1987.

Umm el Walid
Once a substantial fortified town the remains uncovered at Umm el Walid are believed to be those of a one-time caravan station with a number of rooms, a central courtyard and several ancient cisterns

Umm Qais
Known by the Romans as *Gadara* (and also one of the cities of the Decapolis), Umm Qais is located 518 metres above mean sea level. It looks over Lake Tiberias, the Yarmouk River and the Golan Heights. The ruins have revealed several important archaeological finds. These include: a North and West Theatre; the Basilica of Gadara; the Decumanus Maximus; a set of baths.

Archaeological & Ancient Sites — West Bank

Church of the Nativity, Bethlehem
Sacred to Christians, the church is said to be the site at which Jesus was born. A church, erected by Constantine during the 4th century, was destroyed by fire in the 6th century.

El Aqsa Mosque
Just to the south of the Dome of the Rock, on the mosque's steps, King Abdullah, the grandfather of King Hussein, was assassinated in 1951. The mosque, on whose site other mosques have also stood, dates back to the 11th century.

Haram esh-Sharif
The sacred enclosure, covering some 30 acres, on the apex of Mount Moriah, upon which is situated the fabulous Dome of the Rock, in addition to the El Aqsa Mosque.

Hisham Palace, Jericho
Located 5 kilometres north of Jericho, the Hisham Palace was constructed by the Ummayeds during the reign of the tenth Ummayed Caliph (AD 724-743) but was never completed. Much of the site has been devastated by earthquakes, although the fine *Tree of Life* mosaic remains in good condition.

Maram al-Khalil Mosque, Hebron
Sacred to Islam and Judaism, the mosque was built over the cave of Machpelah. A synagogue and a mosque adorn the site.

Qumran
Thirty kilometres south of Jericho, Qumran became famous in 1947 when a shepherd boy found in its caves the Dead Sea Scrolls. The scrolls are the manuscript of the ancient biblical text of Isaiah: the oldest known Hebrew texts in the world.

Tel-es-Sultan, Jericho
The site illustrates well the antiquity of Jericho, the city near it. Jericho is the oldest continuously inhabited city on earth. Tel-es-Sultan dates back to Neolithic times, and is dominated by a Neolithic watchtower.

The Church of the Holy Sepulchre
One of the most important sites in Christianity, the church is said to stand on the direct point where Jesus was not only crucified, but buried. The church, constructed on the site of a former church (built by Emperor Constantine) was erected in the 12th century.

The Dome of the Rock
Constructed by the Ummayeds in the 7th century, the Dome of the Rock is sacred to Islam. From there, it is said, the Prophet Mohammed ascended to heaven to receive the Qur'an from God. The rock itself is reputed to contain his footprint.

The Gates of Jerusalem
Eight in total, the gates of Jerusalem's old city are inextricably linked to the city's history. They are: Herod's Gate; Gate of St Stephen; the Golden Gate; the Dung Gate; the Zion Gate; the Jaffa Gate; the New Gate; and the Damascus Gate.

Wildlife Reserves

Azraq Wetland Reserve

A few years ago, Azraq's ancient oases seemed as if they were destined for total extinction. The waters, pumped as they were to feed the thirsty inhabitants of Amman, had all but disappeared. But then, mercifully, an international effort sought to preserve Azraq's great birthright as the region's prime wetland. Water was pumped back into the area and life was nurtured there once again. Now, as the fragile ecosystem claws its way back from the brink of extermination, there are plans to reintroduce into the reserve's 12 square kilometres (5 square miles) wild horses, buffalo and other creatures which did not survive the droughts of the early 1990s.

Shaumari Wildlife Reserve

Shaumari Reserve is Jordan's most important wildlife sanctuary, located 12 kilometres (7 miles) south of Azraq. It covers an area of some 22 square kilometres (8 square miles) and is encircled by a mesh fence.

The park, which was conceived in 1975, is under the authority of the Royal Society for the Conservation of Nature. It has concentrated on various specific projects, and has succeeded immeasurably with projects such as Operation Oryx, as well as which, the Syrian wild ass (onager) and ostriches are bred there, their numbers having been decimated in recent years through hunting and drought.

Unfortunately Shaumari's projects, and popularity as a tourist site, have been drastically hindered in the last decade by lack of water in the area. The abundant springs at Azraq are being tapped, largely to supply Amman with water.

D'ana Nature Reserve

To preserve the rugged landscape's flora and protect its fauna and avifauna from hunting and poaching, the D'ana Nature Reserve, reached from the King's Highway between Tafila and Shobak, was founded in 1990. Of its plant life, nearly 600 species have already been identified.

Included among its 200 recorded mammals and reptiles are the ibex, mountain gazelle, badger, wolf, hyena, jackal and the hitherto unknown tiny Blandford's fox.

The reserve is important for its birdlife, having a wide variety of tree cover. Of the 150 bird species identified, some have never before been recorded in Jordan and some 45 species are considered to be in global decline or threatened with extinction. D'ana is thought to have more than 90% of the known breeding population of the rare Syrian serrin.

This is a wildlife reserve with a difference, inasmuch as evidence shows that man had resided there for around 6,000 years; Palaeolithic, Egyptian, Edomite, Nabatean and Roman.

Wadi Mujib Wildlife Reserve

South of Dhiban and north of Kerak and reached by the King's Highway, the reserve's location is in the dramatic scenery of Jordan's 'Grand Canyon' — the Wadi Mujib. Covering 212 square kilometres (82 square miles) where the altitudes range from below Dead Sea Level to 800 metres (2,625 feet) the reserve extends from the Dead Sea to the eastern highlands and is famous for its scenery and flora, not least its many species of wild orchid. Nubian ibex are the most likely animals to be seen there. Roman milestones on the south edge of the *wadi* still line the course of an ancient Roman road.

Dibbin National Park

North of Amman, the Dibbin park is located just off the old road which winds its way to Jerash. Its rivers are fed by Mount Gilead's melted snows and the lush prairies provide shelter for the park's flora and birdlife. Resident animal species most likely to be sighted, though no longer as frequently as they once were, include red squirrel, wild cat, Egyptian mongoose, red fox, Asiatic jackal and striped hyena.

Future protected areas

Seven locations have been designated as future reserves to protect the flora, fauna and birdlife which already live there and where it is hoped that other creatures which once made them their home can be reintroduced. These include: **Burqu'** on the Syrian border; **Wadi Bayir** in the eastern desert 440 square kilometres (170 square miles); **Rajil** in the Wadi Rajil east of Azraq; **Abu Rukbah**, near Kerak; **Wadi Jarba** in the south; and at **Jebel Masada** where a 460-square-kilometre (286-square-mile) reserve is intended in the Wadi Araba and a road to reach it is to be constructed. At **Wadi Rum,** 510 square kilometres (197 square miles) of rocky hill country is being set aside to preserve the ibex, gazelles and smaller creatures of this lonely and wild terrain.

Demographic Profile

Location

Situated near the south-eastern coast of the Mediterranean Sea, Jordan shares borders with Syria to the north, Iraq to the east, Palestine and the West Bank to the west and Saudi Arabia to the east and south.

The land of Jordan and its people have been moulded by centuries of passing civilisations. Jordan has always been the crossroads between east and west, and its centrality has given it strategic and economic importance, making it a vital trading and communication link between countries, peoples and continents.

Area

Excluding the Dead Sea Jordan is a country of 92,300 square kilometres (57,345 square miles) which can be crossed by car in approximately four hours. However, its diverse terrain and landscape impart a feeling of its being larger than it is.

Population

Jordan's population was estimated at 4.44 million in 1997, not including those living in the West Bank. Jordan's high fertility rate of 6.6 and declining mortality rate have caused a considerable increase in the population, which averages 3.5% annually.

Jordan's stability in a turbulent region has attracted large numbers of refugees and temporary residents from neighbouring regions such as the West Bank, the Gaza Strip and Lebanon. In recent years it has also seen tens of thousands of Jordanian expatriates returning from abroad.

Jordan's strong rurally-based lifestyle, grounded in the nation's villages and deserts, has taken a slight shift in recent years. The trend has been to urbanise. About 73% now resides in towns. However, the Jordanian cultural identity is firmly rooted in rural and desert communities. Approximately 38% of the population lives in Amman.

Language

Arabic is Jordan's official language, although English is spoken widely. French and German are also spoken by a few people, especially those who have commercial or cultural interest in France or Germany. Jordan's Circassian community have managed to retain their Circassian language, as well as speaking Arabic.

Television and radio media both offer English and French programmes. There are two English publications: *The Jordan Times*, published daily, and *The Star*, published weekly.

Religion

The majority of the population (95%) is Sunni Muslim. They include a small minority of Chechens and Circassians, who originally came from the Caucas region in the Soviet Union. Christians constitute 4% of the population and the remaining one per cent are Druze or Armenians or are from the very small contingent of Baha'is. The Druze sect is derived from the Ismaili branch of Shi'ite Islam. Baha'is are also originally Muslims who migrated from Iran in 1910.

Literacy

Basic education (from grades 1 to 10) is compulsory and free in Jordan. About a third of the population was recorded as being students for the scholastic year 1997. Females constituted about half of the student body throughout the academic system. The number of school teachers was 55,216 and the number of schools was 3,917 for the same year. There are 681 kindergartens, only two of them are governmental and the rest are run by the private sector. The kingdom has 11 private and 6 public unversities.

By 1997 the educational infrastructure had increased Jordan's literacy rate to 85%.

Health services

Health care has been at the forefront of Jordan's national agenda. The country achieved a comprehensive child immunisation programme in 1988. The country offers both private and public health care.

The Ministry of Health operates some 560 primary and secondary health clinics; 161 maternity and child health care centres; 110 dental clinics.

Preventive medicine and immunisation are given priority; with school health care services and health education taken very seriously.

Public health is maintained by testing water and food (both imported and locally produced); environmental cleanliness is monitored.

Eighty-five per cent of all Jordanian babies are delivered in hospitals (a figure which stands at around 46% in other Arab countries).

After several failures, the kingdom witnessed the birth of the first test-tube baby in April 1987 at the hands of the Arab World's pioneer of test-tube babies, Dr Zeid al Kilani. Operating at his al Farah Hospital, Dr al Kilani now successfully treats infertility by microinsemination and receives patients from different parts of the region. Figures released by the Eighth World Congress on IHV in Japan, reveal that twenty-five of 452 women who conceived by microinsemination worldwide were treated at Dr al Kilani's centre.

Population growth:	3.5%	Infant Mortality Rate:	32.3 deaths/1000 population
Birth Rate:	37.32 births/1000 population	Life Expectancy:	Male 70.43 years
Death Rate:	4.02 deaths/1000 population		Female 74.21 years

Gazetteer

(Distances are in kilometres)

Ajlun
Amman 73, Aqaba 409, Jerusalem 151

Amman
Aqaba 335, Jerusalem 88

Aqaba
Amman 335, Jerusalem 400

Azraq
Amman 115, Aqaba 445, Jerusalem 198

Bethlehem
Amman 101, Aqaba 413, Jerusalem 17

Irbid
Amman 88, Aqaba 424, Jerusalem 160

Jerash
Amman 48, Aqaba 383, Jerusalem 127

Jerusalem
Amman 88, Aqaba 400

Kerak
Amman 129, Aqaba 285, Jerusalem 190

Ma'an
Amman 216, Aqaba 121, Jerusalem 265

Madaba
Amman 30, Aqaba 332, Jerusalem 81

Mafraq
Amman 72, Aqaba 407, Jerusalem 40

Salt
Amman 29, Aqaba 364, Jerusalem 51

Petra
Amman 262, Aqaba 133, Jerusalem 328

Zarqa
Amman 23, Aqaba 358, Jerusalem 111

Listings

Airlines

Amman

Adria Airways
Petra Travel &
Tourism Co
Shmeisani
Tel: 670267/698004

Aeroflot
Intercontinental
Hotel
PO Box 7303
Tel: 641510

Air Algeria
Al-Karmel Travel
and Tourism
PO Box 926497
Tel: 688301/695876

Air Bosna
Abu Annab
Tourism
Tel: 856488/863208

Air Canada
Nahas Travel &
Tourism
PO Box 182346
Tel: 630879

Air France
Shmeisani
PO Box 35252
Tel: 666055/698317

Air India
Al-Karmel Travel
& Tourism
PO Box 926497
Tel: 695876/688301

Air Lanka
Grand Travel
PO Box 2152
Tel: 682140/628596

Air Ukraine
Hadeel Travel
Tel: 5535610/646155

Alitalia
First Circle
Jabal Al-Hussein
PO Box 2136
Tel: 625203

American Airlines
Space Travel &
Tourism
PO Box 925072
Tel: 669068/668069

American West
Airlines
Abdali Commercial
Centre
Tel: 694802

Austrian Airlines
Shmeisani
PO Box 1803
Tel: 693845/694604

AZAL
Azerbaijan
Airlines Pan
Mediterranean
Tours
Tel: 646155

Balkan Airlines
Grand Travel
PO Box 2152
Tel: 611740/682146

Belgian Airlines
(Sabena)
Sevilla Travel
Tel: 675888/683674

British Airways
Hashweh Corp.
Shmeisani
Tel: 828801/862288

British Midland
Abdali Commercial
Centre
Tel: 694801/2

Cathay Pacific
Shmeisani
Tel: 653691/2

Czechoslovakian
Airlines
Grand Travel
PO Box 2152
Tel: 630956/682140

China Airlines
Petra Travel &
Tourism Co
Tel: 670449/613680

Continental
Airlines
Grand Travel
PO Box 2152
Tel: 682140/628598

Cyprus Airlines
Petra Travel &
Tourism Co
Shmeisani
Tel: 670267/670493

Delta Airlines
Ambassador
Services
PO Box 811855
Tel: 643661

Ethiopian Airlines
Al-Karmel Travel
& Tourism
PO Box 926497
Tel: 688301/695876

Egypt Air
Zaatarah Co
King Hussein St
Tel: 630011

El Al
Tel: 702526

Emirates Airlines
Abdali Al Sayegh
Centre
Tel: 643341/643353

Eva Air
Ammon Shipping
Transport
Tel: 684775

Garuda Indonesia
Tel: 680801/680944

Gulf Air
Abdali
PO Box 9829
Tel: 653613/653621

Iberia
Zaid Travel & Tours
King Hussein St
Tel: 637827/644036

Iran Air
Nahas Travel &
Tourism

PO Box 182346
Tel: 630879

Iraqi Airways
Abdali
Tel: 638600

Japan Airlines
Nahas Travel &
Tourism
PO Box 182346
Tel: 630879

Jet Airways
Abdali
Tel: 646190/653613

KLM
King Hussein St
PO Box 1304
Tel: 655267

Kenya Airways
Al-Karmel Travel
& Tourism
PO Box 926497
Tel: 688301/2

Korean Airlines
United Travel &
Tourism
Tel: 662236/676624

Kuwait Airline
Shmeisani
Tel: 690144/5

Libyan Arab
Airlines
King Hussein St
Tel: 643831/2

Lufthansa
Shmeisani
Tel: 601744

Malaysia Airlines
King Hussein St
Tel: 639575/653446

Malev Hungarian
Grand Travel
PO Box 2152
Tel: 640200/1

MEA
King Hussein St
Tel: 636104

Olympic Airways
Grand Travel
PO Box 2152
Tel: 682140/630125

Oman Air
Abdali
Tel: 646190/653621

Pakistan
International
Airlines, Jordan
International
King Hussein St
Tel: 625981

Palestinian
Airlines
Al-Karmel Travel
Tel: 688301/695876

Philippine
Airlines
Asean Travel
King Hussein St
Tel: 640200/1

Polish Airlines
Jordan
International
PO Box 7086
Tel: 625981

Qantas
Hashweh Corp
PO Box 7056
Tel: 862288/828801

Qatar Airways
Petra Tours
Shmeisani
Tel: 684526/684576

Royal Jordanian
Tel: 607300
663525 (Sales)
678321 (Reser.)

Royal Wings
Tel: 875201/5

Saudia
King Hussein St
Tel: 639333/6

Scandinavian
Airlines, Amin
Kawar & Sons

PO Box 7806
Tel: 699701/2/3

Singapore Airlines
Avia Tourism &
Transport
PO Box 1061
Tel: 676177/86

Sudan Airways
Diana Travel &
Tourism
Tel: 694501/3

Swissair
Jordan
Intercontinental
Hotel
Tel: 659791

Syria Airways
Seikalys
Tel: 622147/8

Taram (Romania
Airtransport)
Petra Tours
Tel: 630380/613670

Thai Airways
Amin Kawar &
Sons, Shmeisani
PO Box 7806
Tel: 699701/2/3

Transacro Airlines
Salam Travel
Tel: 665269/665688

Trans
Mediterranean
Airways
Amin Kawar &
Sons, Shmeisani
PO Box 7806
Tel: 699701/2/3

Turkish Airlines
3rd Circle
Riyadh Centre
Tel: 659102/112

TWA
Khoury Travel
Agency
PO Box 7704
King Hussein St
Tel: 623430/622684

United Airlines
United Travel
Agency
Tel: 641959

US Air
Abdali Commercial
Centre
Tel: 694801

Uzbekistan
Airways
Expo Travel &
Tours
Tel: 691768

Varig Brazilian
Airline
Zaatarah & Co
Tel: 630011

Yemen Airways
PO Box 2152
Tel: 5514165

Yougoslav Airlines
Avia Tourism &
Travel
PO Box 1061
Tel: 604911

Archaeological Foundations

American Centre
of Oriental
Research (ACOR)
Tel: 846117
Fax: 844181

British Institute at
Amman for
Archaeology &
History
Tel: 841317
Fax: 837197

Department of
Antiquities
Restoration Centre
Tel: 644482
Fax: 615848

Department of
Antiquities
Tel: 644336
Fax: 615848

Franciscan Institute
Mount Nebo
Tel: (09) 801186

Friends of
Archaeology
Tel: 695682
Fax: 696682

German Protestant
Institute for
Archaeology
Tel: 842924
Fax: 836924

Insitute Francais
d'Archaéologie du
Proche Oriente
Tel: 611872
Fax: 643840

Italian-Jordanian
Institute of
Archaeological
Sciences
Tel: 757246
Fax: 757247

Petra National
Trust
Tel: 686338

University of
Jordan
Archaeology
Dept
Tel: 843555 Ext 3412

Art Galleries & Museums

Amman
Alia Art Gallery
Abu Bakr
As-Siddiq St
1st Circle
Jabal Amman
Tel: 639350

Almushraq
Showroom
Shmeisani
Near Chinese
Embassy
Tel: 690964

Art Centre
Showroom
Baladna Gardens St
Tel: 687598

Baladna
Showroom
Wasfi Al-Tal St
Tel: 657132

Darat Al-Funun
Jebel Weibedeh
Tel: 643252

Fakhir Al-Nisaa
Showroom
Ministry of Culture
Gallery Abaad
Mecca St
Tel: 814257

Gallery Al Aein
Wadi-Saqra St
Tel: 644451

Gallery Alia
Jabal Amman
1st Circle
Tel: 639303

Gallery Aseelah
Wasfi Al-Tal St
Tel: 698512

Gallery
Ashbeelieh
Amra Hotel
Tel: 723696

Gallery of
Contemporary
Jordanian Artists
Al-Muthana
Al-Takhasusi St
Tel: 699914

Gallery of Plastic
Artists Union
Jebel Weibedeh
Tel: 623297

Gallery Orfali
Um Uthaiyna
Tel: 826932

Housing Bank
Gallery
Shmeisani near
Plaza Hotel

Jordan
Archaeological
Museum
Citadel Hill
Tel: 638795

Jordan Folklore
Museum
The Roman
Amphitheatre
Tel: 651742

Jordan Museum
of Popular
Traditions
The Roman
Amphitheatre
Tel: 651760

Jordan National
Gallery, Muntazah
Jabal Luwiebdeh
Tel: 630128

Martyr's Memorial
Sports City
Tel: 664240

Nabateans Gallery
Dabouq
Tel: 841363

Phoenix Gallery
Wasfi Al-Tal St
Tel: 664240

Rawak Al-Balqua'a
Fuheis
Tel: 720677

Rowak Hamourabi
Wasfi Al-Tal St

Royal Cultural
Centre
Queen Alia St
Smeisani
Tel: 661026

The Gallery
Jordan
Intercontinental
Hotel
Tel: 641361 ext 2183

Jerash
Jerash Arts Gallery
Main Road

Jerusalem
Gallery Anadiel
27 Salah Eddin St
Tel: 288750

Yarmouk
Yarmouk
University
Museum of
Jordanian
Heritage
Irbid
Tel: (02) 271100
Ext: 2341

Banks

Amman Bank for
Investment
Jabal Amman
Tel: 642701
Fax: 645270

ANZ Grindlays
Bank, Shmeisani
Tel: 660201
Fax: 656552

Arab Bank Plc
Shmeisani
Tel: 607231
Fax: 606793

Arab Banking
Corporation —
Jordan, Shmeisani
Tel: 664183
Fax: 686291

Arab-Jordan
Investment Bank
Shmeisani
Tel: 607126
Fax: 681482

Arab Land Bank
Jabal Amman
3rd Circle
Tel: 644065

Bank Al-Mashrek
Shmeisani
Tel: 624161

Bank of Jordan
Jabal Amman
Tel: 644327
Fax: 656642 '

Banque Nationale
de Paris
Jabal Amman
Tel: 641932

Beit Al-Mal
Saving &
Investment for
Housing
Jabal Al Hussein
Tel: 641644
Fax: 644089

British Bank of
the Middle East
Jabal Al Hussein
Tel: 636175
Fax: 692904

The Business Bank
Shmeisani
Tel: 672543
Fax: 672459

Cairo-Amman
Bank, Downtown
Amman
Tel: 639321
Fax: 639328

Central Bank
of Jordan
Amman
Tel: 630301
Fax: 638889

Citibank
3rd Circle
Jabal Amman
Tel: 644065
Fax: 658693

Darco for
Investment
& Housing
Shmeisani
Tel: 661197

Housing Bank
Abdali
Tel: 667126
Fax: 678121

Industrial
Development Bank
Jabal Amman
Tel: 642216
Fax: 647821

Jordan Finance
House for
Development &
Investment
Shmeisani
Tel: 663141
Fax: 683247

Jordan-Gulf Bank
Shmeisani
Tel: 624171/2
Fax: 664110

Jordan Industrial
Estates
Corporation
Tel: 295152
Fax: 295248

Jordan
Investment
& Finance Bank
Shmeisani
Tel: 665145
Fax: 681410

Jordan Islamic
Bank for Finance
& Investment
Shmeisani
Tel: 661220
Fax: 666326

Jordan-Kuwait
Bank

Near Parliament
House
Abdali, Amman
Tel: 662126
Fax: 687452
Telex: 21994

Jordan National
Bank
Jabal Amman
Tel: 642391
Fax: 628809
Telex: 21206

National Portfolio
Securities
Shmeisani, Amman
Tel: 673101
Fax: 688793

Rafidein Bank
Jabal Amman
Tel: 624365
Fax: 649305
Telex: 21334

The Real Estate
Financial
Corporation
(REFCO)
Shmeisani
Tel: 663160
Fax: 668573

Real Estate
Investment
(AKARCO)
Abdali
Tel: 670744
Fax: 699513

Societe Generale
Shmeisani
Tel: 660016
Telex: 23191

Union Bank for
Savings &
Investment
Shmeisani
Tel: 607011
Fax: 666149
Telex: 21875

Car Hire

Amman
Al Andalusiah
Rent A Car
Gardens St
Tel: 606821
Fax: 606961

Al-Arz Rent
A Car
Tyche Hotel
Tel: 671470
Fax: 695544

Al Jawad Rent
A Car
Tel: 606125

Almasq Rent
A Car
Wasfi Al-Tal St.
Tel: 5535644
Fax: 5531655

Al Safeer Rent
A Car
Safeer Motel
Tel: 691505/602312

Al Samer Rent
A Car
Tel: 689645
Fax: 863219

Al-Waha Rent
A Car, Sports City
PO Box 960462
Tel: 674105
Fax: 682161

Amani Rent
A Car
Dahat Alrabiah
Tel: 5510150

Assaraya Rent
A Car, King
Abdallah Gdns
Tel: 684771
Fax: 684973

Atlantic Rent
A Car, Al-Jbeha
Yajouz St.
Tel: 845934

Atlas Rent A Car
Shmeisani
Tel: 697469
Fax: 692567

AVIS Rent A Car
King Abdallah
Gdns
PO Box 961003
Tel: 699420
Fax: 699430

Budget Rent A Car
Shmeisani
Tel: 698131
Fax: 673312

Cruise Rent A Car
Wadi Saqra St
Tel: 5530176
Fax: 5530176

Dalia Rent A Car
5th Circle
Tel: 5528258

Europcar
Forte Grand Hotel
Tel: 674267

Europcar
Marriott Hotel
Tel: 601350

Europcar
Regency Hotel
Tel: 601360

Fadi Rent A Car
Wadi Saqra
Commercial
Centre
Tel: 5535568
Fax: 5535568

Firas Rent A Car
Shmeisani
Tel: 602082
Fax: 616874

Heart Car Rental
Commodore
Hotel
Tel: 682582

Hertz
Middle East Hotel
Tel: 668958
Fax: 688406

International Rent
A Car
3rd Circle
Jabal Amman
Tel: 641073
Fax: 641079

Shahin Rent A Car
University Road
Tel: 848095

Star Rent A Car
Sport City Square
Tel: 604904
Fax: 604904

U-Drive
Tel: 669376
Fax: 669398

Cinemas & Theatres

Amman
Al Hussein Cinema
Tel: 622117

Al Khayam Cinema
Tel: 622950

Ammoun Theatre
Abdali
Tel: 618274

Basman Cinema
Tel: 630126

Cavalier
(Above Olivier Restaurant)
Abdoun
Tel: 819564

Coconut Grove
Abdoun
Tel:

Concord Cinema
Shmeisani
Tel: 677420

Irish Pub
Dove Hotel
Shmeisani
Tel: 697601/2

Jugglers
Forte Grand Hotel
Shmeisani
Tel: 696511

Marriott Sports Bar
Marriott Hotel
Shmeisani
Tel: 607607

Nabil Al Mashini's Theatre
Abdali
Tel: 675571

Nabil & Hisham Theatres
1st Circle
Tel: 625155

Philadelphia Cinema
Tel: 634149

Philistine Cinema
Tel: 622119

Plaza Cinema
Shmeisani
Tel: 699238

Raghdan Cinema
Tel: 622198

Saluté
(at d'Angelo)
Jebel Amman
Tel: 628212

Scandals
San Rock Hotel
Um Utheina
Tel: 813800

Shepherd Hotel Disco
Shepherd Hotel
Jabal Amman
Tel: 639197

Talk of the Town
Middle East Hotel
Shmeisani
Tel: 685211

The Cellar
Al-Qasr Hotel
Shmeisani
Tel: 666140/698671

Versaille Cinema
Tel: 635304

Vis-a-Vis
Turino, Sweifiyeh
Tel: 816690

Courier Services

DHL Worldwide Express
PO Box 92711
Tel: 818351

Aramex International
Shmeisani
PO Box 3371
Tel: 664510/590

TNT Skypack International
PO Box 35202
Tel: 651414/9423

ZWA Aviation & International Trading
PO Box 12
Tel: 819560/690

Cultural Centres

Amman
American Centre
Abdoun
PO Box 676
Tel: 820101

Abdel Hamid Shoman Foundation
1st Circle
Jabal Amman

British Council
Jabal Amman
PO Box 634
Tel: 636147/8
Fax: 656413
Telex: 21823

French Cultural Centre
Jabal Luweibdeh
PO Box 9257
Tel: 637009/636445

Goethe Institute
3rd Circle
Jabal Amman
PO Box 1676
Tel: 641993
Fax: 612383

Haya Arts Centre
Shmeisani
PO Box 35022
Tel: 665195

Royal Cultural Centre
Shmeisani
PO Box 19193
Tel: 661026

Spanish Cultural Centre
3rd Circle
Jabal Amman
PO Box 815467
Tel: 624049/610858

Turkish Cultural Centre
Jabal Amman
Rainbow St
PO Box 2357
Tel: 639777

Emergency Numbers

Amman
Ambulance & First Aid
Tel: 193

Blood Bank
Tel: 749121

Complaints:
Amman Municipality:
Tel: 839970/1

Electricity:
Tel: 750981/2/3

Hotel:
Tel: 642304

Price:
Tel: 661176

Directory Assistance
Tel: 121

Emergencies (Civil Defence)
Tel: 199/829701

Fire Brigade
Tel: 622090/3

Operator-assisted overseas calls
Tel: 010230

Police
Tel: 192/621111

Highway Police
Tel: 843402

Traffic and Accident
Tel: 896390

Public Security Dept.
Tel: 630321

Queen Alia International Airport
Tel: 0853200

Royal Jordanian Flight Information
Tel: 0853200

Water Authority
Tel: 897468

Foreign Diplomatic Missions

Algeria
3rd Circle
Jabal Amman
Tel: 641271/2

Australia
4th Circle
Jabal Amman
Tel: 673246/7
Fax: 673260

Austria
3rd/4th Circle
Jabal Amman
Tel: 644635
Fax: 612725

Bahrain
Shmeisani
Tel: 664148
Fax: 664190

Bangladesh
Tel: 689988
Fax: 659923

Belgium
5th Circle
Jabal Amman
Tel: 675683
Fax: 697487

Brazil
3rd Circle
Jabal Amman
Tel: 642169
Fax: 612964

Bulgaria
Al Mousel St
Tel: 5529391
Fax: 559393

Canada
Shmeisani
Tel: 666124
Fax: 689227

Chad
Tel: 672736

Chile
Abdoun
Tel: 680673
Fax: 702500

China
Jakarta St
Tel: 5519136
Fax: 5518713

Colombia
Tel: 652688
Fax: 645669

Cyprus
Tel: 677619/677559
Fax: 743308

Czech Republic
Al-Ameen St
Tel: 665105
Fax: 692239

Commission of
the European
Communities
Tel: 668192
Fax: 686746

Denmark
Tel: 603703
Fax: 672170

Djibouti
Tel: 656273
Fax: 647814

Egypt
3rd Circle
Jabal Amman
Tel: 605202
Fax: 640772

Equador
Tel: 625495
Fax: 750339

Finland
Tel: 824676/
824654
Fax: 824726

France
Jabal Amman
Tel: 641273/4
Fax: 659606

Germany
Jabal Amman
Tel: 689351
Fax: 685887

Greece
4th Circle
Jabal Amman
Tel: 672331/2
Fax: 696591

Guatemala
Tel: 665948
Fax: 661450

Honduras
Tel: 622550
Fax: 658321

Hungary
Rashid
Tel: 815614
Fax: 815836

Iceland
Shmeisani
Tel: 687396/698851
Fax: 698852

India
1st Circle
Jabal Amman
Tel: 622098
Fax: 659540

Indonesia
Abdoun
Amman
Tel: 5538911
Fax: 5538380

Iran
3rd/4th Circle
Jabal Amman
Tel: 641281
Fax: 641383

Iraq
1st Circle
Jabal Amman
Tel: 623175
Fax: 637328

Ireland
Hay Al Jamali
District
Tel: 614268
Fax: 630878

Italy
Jabal Luweibdeh
Tel: 638185
Fax: 659730

Jamaica
Tel: 864361
Fax: 701121

Japan
4th/5th Circle
Jabal Amman
Tel: 672486/671428
Fax: 672006

Kuwait
4th Circle
Jabal Amman
Tel: 675135
Fax: 681971

Lebanon
2nd Circle
Jabal Amman
Tel: 859111

Libya
Shmeisani
Tel: 693101
Fax: 693404

Luxembourg
Tel: 688093
Fax: 688094

Malaysia
Shmeisani
Tel: 676076
Fax: 672088

Malta
Tel: 667112
Fax: 665680

Mauritania
Tel: 5535133
Fax: 5535135

Mexico
Tel: 641157

Morocco
4th Circle
Jabal Amman
Tel: 641451
Fax: 641634

Netherlands
Tel: 691525
Fax: 692214

New Zealand
Tel: 636720
Fax: 634349

North Korea
Shmeisani
Tel: 666349
Fax: 812821

Norway
3rd Circle
Jabal Amman
Tel: 644932
Fax: 644894

Oman
4th/5th Circle
Jabal Amman
Tel: 686155
Fax: 689404

Pakistan
Jabal Luweibdeh
Tel: 622787
Fax: 611633

Palestine
Jabal Hussein
Tel: 677517
Fax: 661727

Panama
Tel: 642899
Fax: 616699

Peru
Tel: 691715
Fax: 690882

Philippines
2nd Circle
Jabal Amman
Tel: 827001
Fax: 827003

Poland
3rd Circle
Jabal Amman
Tel: 637153
Fax: 618744

Portugal
Tel: 5531203
Fax: 5531204

Qatar
4th/5th Circle
Jabal Amman
Tel: 648346
Fax: 648374

Romania
Jabal Luweibdeh
Shmeisani
Tel: 667738
Fax: 684018

Russia
Shmeisani
Tel: 641158
Fax: 647448

Saudi Arabia
5th Circle
Jabal Amman
Tel: 814154/5
Fax: 826154

Senegal
Tel: 680329/689461
Fax: 689463

Seychelles
Tel & Fax: 823262

Slovenia
Tel: 861542
Fax: 818819

South Africa
Tel: 812288
Fax: 811194

South Korea
Jabal Amman
Tel: 660745/6
Fax: 660280

Spain
Zahran St
Jabal Amman
Tel: 614166
Fax: 614173

Sri Lanka
Tel: 671549
Fax: 683905

Sudan
3rd Circle
Jabal Amman
Tel: 644251
Fax: 644187

Sweden
4th Circle
Jabal Amman
Tel: 669177
Fax: 669179

Switzerland
4th Circle
Jabal Amman
Tel: 686416
Fax: 698685

Syria
3rd Circle
Jabal Amman
Tel: 641076
Fax: 669179

Thailand
Tel: 622344
Fax: 653217

Tunisia
4th Circle
Jabal Amman
Tel: 674307
Fax: 605790

Turkey
2nd Circle
Jabal Amman
Tel: 641251
Fax: 612353

United Arab
Emirates
3rd Circle
Jabal Amman
Tel: 704781
Fax: 704781

United Kingdom
Abdoun
Tel: 823100/88
Fax: 813759

Uruguay
Tel: 635577
Fax: 625565

USA
2nd Circle
Jabal Amman
Tel: 5920101
Fax:820123

Vatican
Tel: 627711
Fax: 692502

Yemen
3rd/4th Circle
Jabal Amman
Tel: 642381
Fax: 654717

ICRC
Tel: 688645
Fax: 688649

UNDP
Shmeisani
Tel: 668171
Fax: 676582

UNESCWA
Tel: 694351
Fax: 694981

UNHCR
Tel: 629571
Fax: 640049

UNICEF
Wadi Saqra
Tel: 629571
Fax: 640049

UNRWA
Shmeisani
Tel: 669194
Fax: 685476

UNTSO
Shmeisani
Tel: 696240

WHO
Um Utheina
Tel: 684651
Fax: 667533

Health Clubs & Gyms

Amman
Al Hussein
Sports City
University Road
Tel: 667181

Body Must
Amra Forum Hotel
6th Circle
Tel: 815071

Brunswick
Bowling Centre
1st Circle
Tel: 891401

Marriott Centre
Marriott Hotel
Shmeisani
Tel: 660100

Orthodox Club
Abdoun
Tel: 810491

Plaza Fitness
Centre
Plaza Hotel
Tel: 686956

Power Hut Gym
Shmeisani
Tel: 686349

RoyalAutomobile
Club
8th Circle
Tel: 815410

Outside Amman
Ashtar Ma'in
Tel: (08) 545500
Fax: (08) 545550

Dead Sea Hotel
Tel: (09) 802028
Fax: (09) 184194

Hospitals

Amman
Al-Basheer
Hospital
Al-Ashrafieh
Tel: 775111/28

Al-Ahli Hospital
Abdali
Tel: 664164

Al Amal Hospital
Tel: 607155

Al-Khalidi
Maternity
Hospital
Jabal Amman
Tel: 644281/4
Fax: 616801

Al-Muasher
Hospital
Jebal Hussein
Tel: 667227/8

Amman Surgical
Hospital
3rd Circle
Tel: 641261/210
Fax: 641260

Aqileh Hospital
Jabal Amman
Tel: 642441

Arab Centre for
Heart & Special
Surgery
5th Circle
Tel: 865199
Fax: 865282

Farrah Maternity
Hospital
Zahran District
Tel: 644440

Hussein Medical
Centre, Sweileh
Amman
Tel: 856856

Ibn Al Haitham
Hospital
Tel: 695564
Fax: 606644

Italian Hospital
Al-Muhajreen
Tel: 777101/2

Islamic Hospital
Abdali
Tel: 680127/130

Jabal Amman
Maternity Hospital
Jabal Amman
Tel: 842362

Malhas Hospital
First Circle
Tel: 636140

Palestine Hospital
Shmeisani
Tel: 607071

Queen Alia
Hospital
Tel: 686100

Shmeisani Hospital
Shmeisani
Tel: 607431

The Child Care
Hospital
Airport Road
Tel: 864180/3

The Speciality
Hospital Shmeisani
Tel: 693693

University Hospital
University of
Jordan
Tel: 845845

Aqaba
Princess Haya
Hospital
Tel: (033) 14111

Zarqa
Government
Hospital
Tel: (099) 83323

Zarqa National
Hospital
Tel: (099) 00560

Hotels

Ajloun
(2-Star)
Ajloun
PO Box 97
Tel: (04) 462524

Al-Rabadh Castle
PO Box 73
Tel: (04) 462202

(5-Star)
Amman
Amman Marriott
Shmeisani
PO Box 926333
Tel: 607607
Fax: 670100
Telex: 21145

Forte Grand
Shmeisani
PO Box 950629
Tel: 696511
Fax: 674261
Telex: 23266

Jordan
Inter Continental
3rd Circle
Jabal Amman
PO Box 35014
Tel: 641361
Fax: 645217
Telex: 21207/21267

Philadelphia
Al-Hussein Bin
Ali St.
PO Box 6399
Tel: 607100
Fax: 665160
Telex: 21859

Regency Palace
Queen Alia St
PO Box 927000
Tel: 607000
Fax: 660013
Telex: 22244/54

(4-Star)
Amman
Alia Gateway
Near Queen Alia
International
Airport
PO Box 39158
Tel: (08) 51000
Fax: (08) 51029
Telex: 23361

Amman
International
University Road
PO Box 2500
Tel: 841712
Fax: 841714
Telex: 21873

Amra Forum
6th Circle
PO Box 950555
Amman 11195
Tel: 815071/858071
Fax: 814072/858106
Telex: 22012

Jerusalem
International
University Road
PO Box 926265
Tel: 607121/696541
Fax: 696882
Telex: 22330

(3-Star)
Amman
Al-Qasr
Shmeisani
PO Box 926192
Tel: 695480/1
Fax: 689673
Telex: 23937

Ambassador
Shmeisani
PO Box 925390
Tel: 605161
Fax: 681101
Telex: 21628

Amman Crown
Radio & TV
Station Rd
PO Box 1318
Tel: 758182
Fax: 758180
Telex: 22269

Carlton
3rd Circle
Jabal Amman
PO Box 811666
Tel: 654200
Fax: 655833

Commodore
Shmeisani
PO Box 927292
Tel: 607185/225
Fax: 668187
Telex: 21760

Darotel
Shmeisani
PO Box 9403
Tel: 607193
Fax: 602434
Telex: 23888

Firas Palace
Jabal Al Weibdeh
Tel: 650404
Fax: 650122

Geneva
7th Circle
Jabal Amman
Tel: 858100
Fax: 858111

Grand Palace
Queen Alia St
PO Box 922444
Tel: 691131
Fax: 695143
Telex: 21292

Hillside
Jordan
University St
Tel: 839481/4
Fax: 839485

Hisham
4th Circle
Jabal Amman
PO Box 5398
Tel: 644028
Fax: 647540
Telex: 21887

Liwan
Sweifiyeh
PO Box 851851
Tel: 858125
Fax: 858620

Lotus
Shmeisani
Tel: 683368
Fax: 604136

Middle East
Shmeisani
PO Box 19224
Tel: 5517150
Fax: 5517160
Telex: 21159

Olympia
5th Circle
Jabal Amman
PO Box 1569
Tel: 810150
Fax: 827113
Telex: 21808

Qasr Firas
Jabal Al Weibdeh
Tel: 650404
Fax: 650122

Ramada
7th Circle
Abdallah
Ghousheh St
PO Box 334
Tel: 816722/816817
Fax: 825941

San Rock
International
Jabal Amman
PO Box 9032
Tel: 813800
Fax: 813600
Telex: 22211

Shepherd
Jabal Amman
PO Box 2020
Tel: 639197
Fax: 642401
Telex: 21410

Turino
Swifeh
PO Box 5011
Tel: 863944
Fax: 863051

Tyche
PO Box 3190
Tel: 607114
Fax: 664013
Telex: 21729/23207

Region
Po Box 2490
Tel: 689071/81
Fax: 689091

(2-Star)
Al Safeer
PO Box 20188
Shmeisani
Tel: 602316
Telex: 24186

Al-Arz
Sport City
PO Box 19287
Tel: 676092
Fax: 676091

Al-Concord
PO Box 183494
Tel: 613133/44

Al-Jabal
Al Rasheed
PO Box 929167
Tel: 662327
Fax: 681411

Al-Mamoura
Middle East Circle
PO Box 510367
Tel: 778174
Fax: 744667

Al-Manar
Shmeisani
PO Box 20730
Tel: 662186
Fax: 684329
Telex: 21624

Al-Sabeel
Jabal Amman
PO Box 2206
Tel: 630571/613572
Fax: 630572

Amman Orchid
PO Box 940537
Tel: 604114
Fax: 606961

Ammoun School
Jabal Amman
PO Box 950271
Tel: 671133/4
Fax: 671132
Telex: 22011

Babelon Tower
Shmeisani
PO Box 851569
Tel: 700489/481
Fax: 700498

Balqa Palace
Sweileh
Tel: 843459
Fax: 842262

Blue Marine
Shmeisani
PO Box 926038
Tel: 667165/6

Cameo
Jabal Amman
PO Box 5058
Tel: 644515
Fax: 644579
Telex: 21720

Canary
Jabal Luweibdeh
PO Box 9062
Tel: 638353
Fax: 645353

Caravan
Jabal Luweibdeh
PO Box 9062
Tel: 661195/6
Fax: 661196

Dove
Jabal Amman
PO Box 950701
Tel: 697601/2
Fax: 674676

Firas Wings
Jabal Al-Weibdeh
PO Box 9119
Tel: 622103/4
Fax: 621999

Granada
Jabal Amman
PO Box 2321
Tel: 622617
Fax: 638031

Hala Inn
Jabal Amman
PO Box 182423
Tel: 644642/906
Fax: 612311
Telex: 21188

Holy Land
University Road
PO Box 921194
Tel: 841309

Merryland
Abdali
PO Box 9122
Tel: 654052
Fax: 657392

New Park
PO Box 1790
Tel: 612144/648144
Fax: 648145

Qasr Al-Balka
PO Box 395
El Jubaihah
Tel: 843291
Fax: 842262

Ramallah
PO Box 182157
Tel: 636122
Fax: 639551

Region
Dahiet Al-
Rasheed
PO Box 2490
Tel: 689071
Fax: 689091

Royal
PO Box 19112
Tel: 843335/6

Rum Continental
PO Box 109
Tel: 623162/611962
Fax: 611961
Telex: 21245

Salah Eldeen
PO Box 6820
Tel: 623518/4508
Fax: 634118

Select
Jabal Luweibdeh
PO Box 9906
Tel: 637101
Fax: 637102

Seveen
Jabal El-Hussein
PO Box 921888
Tel: 603578

Sultan
PO Box 151325
Tel: 639710

(1-Star)
Amman
Abu-Nawas
El-Wehdat
PO Box 443
Tel: 754547

Al-Anwar
PO Box 23221
Tel: 647166/7

Al-Munzer
Abdali
PO Box 926595
Tel: 639469

Al-Qasr Al Abasi
PO Box 150958
Tel: 638505

Al-Remal
Abdali
PO Box 910477
Tel: 630670
Fax: 615585

Alsinan
El-Wehdat
PO Box 620367
Tel: 753707

Ameer Al-Shark
PO Box 183437
Tel: 656590

Amman Al-Jadid
El-Wehdat
PO Box 621000
Tel: 778673/4

Asia
PO Box 187546
Tel: 648851
Fax: 648852

Bethlehem
Razi St
Jabal Al-Hussein
Tel: 611305

City
Jabal Amman
PO Box 2734
Tel: 642251

Cleopatra
Abdali
PO Box 19158
Tel: 636959

Diamond Star
PO Box 150691
Tel: 775129/34

Green Paradise
PO Box 962052
Tel: 834955

Gulf
El-Wehdat
PO Box 620765
Tel: 771016

Halton
Jabal Amman
PO Box 7550
Tel: 622381

Hammoudeh
PO Box 8766
Tel: 630568

Happy Land
Tel: 639862

Jerusalem Jewel
Tel: 613970
Fax: 615565

Jowhert Al-Quds
Abdali
PO Box 7334
Tel: 649482

Karnak
Al-Weibdeh
PO Box 6095
Tel: 638125

Lipton
Al-Weibdeh
PO Box 7351
Tel: 637580

Lords
Al-Weibdeh
PO Box 6293
Tel: 622167

Lu'lu't Hala
Al-Weibdeh
PO Box 16107
Tel: 778554

Manzel El-Zahra
PO Box 910449
Tel: 835230

Nefertiti
Shmeisani
PO Box 926258
Tel: 603865

Nehal
Tel: 654130/1

Nobel
PO Box 6420
Tel: 638703

Palace
Manko Market
PO Box 6916
Tel: 624327

Sun Rise
Abdali
Tel: 621841

Wadi Al-Neel
PO Box 23488
Tel: 636973

Aqaba
(4-Star)
Aqaba Gulf
PO Box 1312
Tel: (03) 316636
Fax: (03) 318246

(3-Star)
Aquamarina I
(Beach Hotel)
PO Box 96
Tel: (03) 316250/4
Fax: (03) 314271
Telex: 62249

Aquamarina II
(City Hotel)
PO Box 96
Tel: (03) 315165/8
Fax: (03) 315169
Telex: 62308

Aquamarina III
(Royal Hotel)
PO Box 96
Tel: (03) 319425/9
Fax: (03) 313569
Telex: 62249

Coral Beach
PO Box 71
Tel: (03) 313521
Fax: (03) 313614
Telex: 62227

Crystal
Tel: (03) 322001
Fax: (03) 322006

Holiday
International
PO Box 215
Tel: (03) 312426
Fax: (03) 313426
Telex: 62263

Miramar
PO Box 60
Tel: (03) 314340/1
Fax: (03) 314339
Telex: 62275

Petra
International
PO Box 1088
Tel: (03) 316255/8
Fax: (03) 314270
Telex: 62347

(2-Star)
Alcazar
PO Box 392
Tel: (03) 314131/2
Fax: (03) 314133
Telex: 62242

Aqaba Hotel
PO Box 43
Tel: (03) 312056
Fax: (03) 314089
Telex: 62275

Al-Shuala
PO Box 211
Tel: (03) 315156
Fax: (03) 315160

Nairoukh II
PO Box 1138
Tel: (03) 312980
Fax: (03) 312981

(1-Star)
Al-Abasi
PO Box 158
Tel: (03) 313403

Al Ameira
PO Box 383
Tel: (03) 312559

Al Jameel
PO Box 1077
Tel: (03) 314118

Al Khouli
PO Box 579
Tel: (03) 312207

Al Manara
PO Box 477
Tel: (03) 313711

Al Nahr Khaled
PO Box 387
Tel: (03) 312456

Al Nouman
PO Box 1009
Tel: (03) 315142

Al Yamamah
PO Box 283
Tel: (03) 314621

Nabrokh
PO Box 908
Tel: (03) 312984

Nairoukh I
PO Box 1138
Tel: (03) 319284

Nigmet Al-Aqaba
PO Box 1407
Tel: (03) 316480

Palm Beach
PO Box 4
Tel: (03) 313551

Red Sea
PO Box 65
Tel: (03) 312156

Zahrat Al Urdon
PO Box 113
Tel: (03) 314377

Azraq
(2-Star)
Al-Sayad
PO Box 830633
Amman 11183
Tel: 647610/1
Fax: 644988

Azraq Resthouse
Tel: 64711/6
Telex: 21607

Dead Sea
(4-Star)
Dead Sea
Saltland Village
PO Box 184194
Amman
Tel: (08) 546101
Fax: (08) 688100
Telex: 23238

Dead Sea
Resthouse
Tel: (05) 572900

Dibbin
(2-Star)
Dibbin Resthouse
PO Box 2863
Tel: (04) 452413
Telex: 21607

Irbid
(3-Star)
Al-Razi
PO Box 2131
Tel: (02) 275515/6
Fax: (02) 275517

Hijazi Palace
PO Box 1115
Tel: (02) 247267
Fax: (02) 279520
Telex: 51540 Hijaz

(2-Star)
Hemmeh
PO Box 52
Tel: (02) 242606/
241758

(1-Star)
Al Nasim
PO Box 1397
Tel: (02) 274310

Omayyah
PO Box 287
Tel: (02) 245955

Sah Al Noum
PO Box 184
Mukheiba
Tel: (02) 217203

Kerak
(2-Star)
Mu'ta Palace

Kerak Resthouse
PO Box 95
Tel: (03) 351148

Ma'in
Ashtar Ma'in
(4-Star)
Ma'in Spa Village
PO Box 801
Tel: (08) 545500
Fax: (08) 545550

Petra and Wadi
Mousa
(5-Star)
Grand View
PO Box 11
Wadi Mousa
Tel: (03) 336871
Fax: (03) 336984

King's Way Inn
PO Box 71
Wadi Mousa
Tel: (03) 336797/8
Fax: (03)336796/7

Petra Movenpick
PO Box 214
Tel: (03) 337111
Fax: (03) 337112

Petra Plaza
Tel: (03) 336407
Fax: (03) 337096

Taybet Zaman
Resort
PO Box 2
Wadi Mousa
Tel: (03) 339107/8
Fax: (03) 339101

(4-Star)
Petra Forum
PO Box 30
Wadi Mousa
Tel: (03) 336266
Fax: (03) 336977
Telex: 64001

Petra Resthouse
PO Box 5
Tel: (03) 336014

(1-Star)
Al Nabatian
Castle
Tel: (03) 339399
Fax: (03) 339350

Qasr Al-Petra
PO Box 3390
Petra-Wadi Mousa
Tel: (03) 336723

Rose City
PO Box 61
Petra-Wadi Mousa
Tel: (03) 336440

Tafila
Jordan Palace
Hotel

Zarqa
(1-Star)
Andaleeb
PO Box 748
Tel: (09) 981351
Fax: (09) 987702

Serviced Apartments

Amman
(5-Star)
El Yassmin Suites
PO Box 3335
Tel: 643214/8
Fax: 643219

(3-Star)
Gondola House
PO Box 17196
Tel: 815556
Fax: 828847

Olympia
5th Circle
PO Box 1569
Tel: 810150
Fax: 827113

Turino Flat-O-Tel
Sweifiyeh
Tel: 863944

(2-Star)
Al-Maqsura
PO Box 811666
Tel: 698222
Fax: 690671

Al-Safeer Motel
PO Box 20188
Tel: 602312
Fax: 602329

Comfort Suites
Sweifiyeh
Tel: 865987
Fax: 865997

Darotel
Shmeisani
Tel: 607193
Fax: 602434

Media

Akher Khabar
Shmeisani
Tel: 682066

Al Aswaq Arabic
Daily (business)
University Road
Tel: 687691

Al Dustour
Arabic Daily
University Road
Tel: 664153
Fax: 667170

Al Rai Arabic Daily
University Road
Tel: 667171
Fax: 661242

Al Sabeel
Abdali
Tel: 692852

Al Ufuq Magazine
Shmeisani
Tel: 606261

Jordan Times
University Road
Tel: 667171
Fax: 696183

The Star English
Weekly
Jabal Luweibdeh
Tel: 648298

Foreign Media
Agence France
Press
Randa Habib
Tel: 644978

Al Hayat/BBC
Salameh Ne'mat
Tel: 602186

ARD German
Radio
Ghadeer Taher
Tel: 659772

Associated Press
Jamal Halaby
Tel: 614660

CNN
Stephen Cotsonis
Tel: 650412

Italian News
Agency (Ansa)
Nermeen Murad
Tel: 697520

Reuters News
Agency
Jack Redden
Tel: 623776

United Press
International
Sana Atiyeh
Tel: 687956

Wall St Journal
Peter Waldman
Tel: 617945

Washington Post
Nora Boustani
Tel: 666549

Mobile Phones & Pagers

Amman
Al-Andalus
Jordanian Co
Tel: 682932
Fax: 826861

Jordan Mobile
Telephone Services
Tel: 863750
Fax: 863770

Jordan Radio
Paging
Tel: 865999

Restaurants

Middle Eastern
Restaurants
Abu Ahmad
Tel: 641879

Al Bustan
Jordan University
Street, Amman
Tel: 661555

Al Diwan Al
Arabi, Shmeisani
Tel: 607150

Al Kalha
Sweifeh
Tel: 864242

Al Mansaf
Marriott Hotel
Tel: 607607

Al Waha
Tla' Al-Ali
Al Waha Circle
Tel: 831734

Cameo
Tel: 644515

Darotel
Tel: 607193

Nouroz
Tel: 642830

Specialised
Restaurants

Chen's (Chinese)
Tla'a Al Ali
Tel: 5518214

Bonita (Spanish)
3rd Circle
Tel: 615060/1

China House
Tel: 693004

Indian
Tel: 819829

Kashmir (Indian)
Jabal Amman
Tel: 659520

Maison Verte
(French)
Shmeisani
Tel: 685746

Mamamia
(Fast food Italian)
Tel: 682122

Napoli (Italian)
Dahiat Al-Rabiah
Tel: 5538504

Olivier (French)
Abdoun
Tel: 819564

Peking (Chinese)
Shmeisani
Tel: 660250

Romero (Italian)
3rd Circle
Jabal Amman
Tel: 644227

Royal Jordanian Airlines

Offices Worldwide

Australia
Sydney
Concorde Int.
Travel
403, George St
NSW 2000
Tel: (02) 93219222
Fax: (02) 92903641

Austria
Vienna
Parking10/1/4/5
1010 Wien
Tel: 5135333
Fax: 5135465

Bahrain
Manama
Chamber of
Commerce Bldg
King Faisal
Highway
PO Box 1044
Tel: 253315
Fax: 210175

Belgium
Brussels
Mont des Arts 9/15
1000 Brussels
Tel: 5127070/6710
Fax: 5142167
Telex: 26121

Canada
Montreal
1801 McGill
College
Tel: (514) 2881655
Fax: (514) 2881647

Toronto
45 St Clair, Ave West
Ontario M4V 1K9
Tel: (416) 9623955
Fax: (416) 9609162

Cyprus
Larnaca
Airport Office 34
Larnaca
International Airport
Tel: (04) 643286
Fax: (04) 643021

Nicosia
66 Makarios Ave
Cronos Court
Tel: (02) 375124
Fax: (02) 369196

Egypt
Alexandria
Moh'd Ibrahim
Selim St.
Tel: 4839926
Fax: 4840345

Cairo
Zamalek Sporting
Club, 26 July St
Mohandeseen
Tel:3443114/3467540
Fax: 3462446

France
Paris
12 Rue De La Paix
75002 Paris
Tel: (42) 444580
Fax: (42) 604819

Germany
Berlin
Budapest Strasse
14a, 10787 Berlin
Tel: (030) 2115661
Fax: (030) 2115607
Telex: 304842

Frankfurt
Muenchener St 12
6000 Frankfurt
Tel: (069) 231853/
54/55
Fax: (069) 234802
Telex: 412686

Greece
Athens
80-88 Syngrou Ave
Athens 11741
Tel: 9242600-603
Fax: 9242604

Iraq
Baghdad
Sa'adoun St
Palestine Int.
Hotel Building
PO Box 3306
Tel: 8866088/77

Ireland
Dublin
3, Clyde Road
Ballsbridge
Dublin 4
Tel: 1 8423144

Fax: 1 8423637
Telex: 31415

Rome
Via Barberini 50
Tel: (06) 4787055
Fax: (06) 4884600

Jordan
Amman
Housing Bank
Commercial Centre
Queen Noor St
PO Box 302
Tel: 607300
Fax: 672527
Telex: 21501

Aqaba Holiday
International
Hotel
PO Box 376
Tel: 314477
Fax: 316555
Telex: 62221

Irbid
Baghdad St
PO Box 245
Tel: 243201/2
Fax: (02) 243382

Libya
Benghazi
Jamil Abdelnaser
Street
PO Box 2783
Tel: 9093017/6155

Tripoli
Imhemed Al
Moghareyef St
PO Box 1273
Tel: 4441565/4442453
Fax: 4446695

Morocco
Casablanca
Tour Atlas Place
Zellaqa
Casablanca 2000
Tel: 442525
Fax: 305975

The Netherlands
Amsterdam
Parnassusweg 209
1077 DG
Tel: (020) 6733386
Fax: (020) 6753326

Pakistan
Karachi
Hotel Metropole
Mereweather Rd

Karachi 75520
Tel: 5660458-60
Fax: 5682026

Qatar
Doha, 2nd Floor
Volkswagon
Roundabout
Tel: 351422
Fax: 329438

Saudi Arabia
Dahran
King Abdul Aziz St
PO Box 108
Tel: 8949532
Fax: 8949604

Riyadh
Mashael Al-Riyadh
Building
Altameen St
Olaya
PO Box 7373
Tel: 4625697/6405
Fax: 4659940

Switzerland
Geneva
6 Rue Adhemar
Fabri,1201 Geneva
Tel: (022) 7328051/2
Fax: (022) 7322424
Telex: 412358

Spain
Plaza de Espana
No 18, Torre de
Madrid Bldg
Ground Floor
28008 Madrid
Tel: 5422443
Fax: 5415827

Syria
Damascus
29 Ayyar St
PO Box 2887
Tel: 2211267/8681

Tunisia
Tunis
14 Avenue de
Carthage
Tel: 255194
Fax:340281

Turkey
Ankara
Tunali Hilmi Cad
No. 110/2
Kavaklidere
Tel: 312-4278872
Tel/Fax: 312-
4278694

Istanbul
Merkez Apt no 163
2nd Floor, Elmadag
Tel: (212) 2304074
Fax: (212) 2345410

UAE
Abu Dhabi
Sh Khalifa St
PO Box 4163
Tel: 226832
Fax:318209

Dubai
Dubai Pearl Bldg
Deira Side
PO Box 4534
Tel: 232855
Fax: 236997

United Kingdom
London
32 Brook St.
WIY IAG
Tel: (0171)8786300
Fax: (0171) 6294069

Manchester
Suite 3
Lancaster Bldg
77 Deansgate
Tel: (0161) 832 4847
Fax: (0161) 833 4457
Telex: 669380

USA
Chicago
6 North Michigan
Ave, Suite 803
IL 60602
Tel: (312) 2361702
Fax: (312) 2362526

Detroit
6 Parklane Blvd
Suite 122, Dearborn
Michigan 48126
Tel: 800 2230470
Fax: 313 2716667

Houston
3336 Richmond Ave
Suite 216
Texas 77098
Tel: 713 524 3700
Fax: 713 524 4071

Los Angeles
6033 West
Century Blvd
Suite 760
Los Angeles
California 90045
Tel: 310 215 9627
Fax: 310 215 0142

Miami
7200 Corporate
Centre Drive NW
19th St, Suite 401
Miami
Florida 33126
Tel: 305 599 0800
Fax: 305 599 0222

New York
535 Fifth Avenue
18th Floor
NY 10017
Tel: 212 949 0060
Fax: 212 949 0488

Washington
1660L St NW
Suite 305
Wash DC 20036
Tel: 202 857 0401
Fax: 202 857 0446

Yugoslavia
Belgrade
Prizrenska 7
Tel: 030 2115661
Fax: 031 2115607

Taxis

Amman
Abu Shusa Taxi
Office
Wadi Al Remam St
Tel: 782892

Ahmad Taxi
Jabal Luwebdeh
Tel: 622038

Al A'meer Taxi
University St
Tel: 272005

Al Alamain Taxi
Office, Shamil St
Tel: 982936

Al Ali Taxi
Main St
Tel: 842474

Al Amir Taxi Office
Al Ashrafieh Abu
Dhabi St
Tel: 771051

Al Balqa Taxi
Office
Wasfi Al-Tal St
Tel: 552141

Al Bashir Taxi
Office

Al-Dastour St
Tel: 790551

Al Borj Cars Office
Shmeisani
Tel: 661028

Al Hamrah Taxi
Office
The Turkish
Embassy
2nd Circle
Tel: 641833

Al Jamiah Taxi
Al Ahram St
Tel: 274899

Al Marij Taxi
Office
Abu Nussair
Tel: 832200

Al Masude Taxi
Wadi Al Remam St
Tel: 780344

Al Maydan Taxi
Office
Tel: 998438

Al Medan Taxi
Al Farouq St
Tel: 998438

Al Nahdah Taxi
Office
Al Aqbat St
Tel: 663002

Al Nuzha Taxi
Office
Abdel Rahman
Al-Qurashiy St
Tel: 610558

Al Qudds Taxi
The Commercial
Market
Tel: 552719

Al Rasheed Taxi
Al Maidan St
Tel: 552136

Al Saaid Taxi
Zemelly St
Tlaa Ali
Tel: 604422

Al Salam Taxi
Al Maidan St
Tel: 552455

Al Saraya Taxi
Association
Complex
Tel: 556521

Al-Shab Taxi
Wasfi Al Tal St
Tel: 243636

Al Shaheed Taxi
Office
Shaffeq Rshaidat St
Tel: 272592

Al Yarmouk Taxi
Office
Al Dastour St
Tel: 790924

Al Zemzawi Taxi
Office
Tabr Bour Abu
Alia St
Tel: 886789

Alia Taxi
Al Maidan St
Tel: 552550

Amer Taxi Office
The Commercial
Market
Abu Nussair
Tel: 835500

Amman Taxi Office
Al Mahatta
Officers's Quarter
Tel: 651424

Arifa Taxi Office
Nazzal
Tel: 793106

Bashaar Taxi Office
Al Tafaylah
Quarter
Abu Haneefah St
Tel: 781511

Da'san Taxi Office
Madaba St
Tel: 740388

Feras Taxi Office
Princess Haya St
Tel: 841058

Firas Taxi
Omar Bin Al
Khattab St
Tel: 243007

Hatem Taxi Ofiice
Wadi Al Remam St
Tel: 781615

Jaffa Taxi Office
Al Fhaiss
Shaker Circle
Tel: 729355

Jaffa Taxi Office
Al Ashrafieh
Barot St
Tel: 776133

Jordan Taxis Office
Petra Centre
Saqf Al Sail St
Tel: 637581

Khalid Taxi Office
Khaled Bin
Al-Wahlid St
Tel: 623715

Marj Al-Hammam
Al-Dalah Circle
Tel: 711164

Moawga Taxi
Office
Tabr Bour St
Tel: 897250

Nayed Taxi Office
Abu Alanda
Shukh Quarter
Tel: 731662

Nazeh Taxi
Abu Al-Alaa
Al-Muari St
Tel: 610845

Omayya Taxi
Al-Shaheed St
Tel: 775780

Port Said Taxi
King Abdallah St
Tel: 272194

Raja'ai Taxi Office
Tabr Bour Tariq St
Tel: 692333

Rami Taxi
Al Maidan St
Tel: 552452

Samir Taxi Office
Al-Shafee St
Tel: 777144

Sultan Taxi
Al-Furousiyah St
South Marka
Tel: 757988

Swaiss Taxi Office
Al Fhaiss Horse
Circle
Tel: 729111

Tabr Bour Taxi
Office
Tabr Bour Jora'an

Street
Tel: 679829

Tame Taxi Office
Al Sweifieh
Tel: 813581

Taxi Al Tajj
Al Tajj St
Tel: 774692

Taxi Jabi
Main St
Tel: 811406

Taxi Philistine
King Abdallah St
Tel: 985510

Taxi Yafa
Al Shafieh St
Tel: 776133

Yazan Taxi Office
Tabr Bour Tariq St
Tel: 698333

Travel Agents

Amman
Alawali Tours
Shmeisani
Tel: 696467/8
Fax: 694422

Al-Barakah
2nd Floor
Kaheel Bldg #4
Tla'a Ali
PO Box 910782
Tel: 699025/3348

Al Buraq Travel
& Tourism
Madaba St
PO Box 7094
Tel: 778015
Fax: 787928

Alfadi Travel
PO Box 926961
Tel: 668452/696452
Fax: 622594

Alhani Travel &
Tourism
PO Box 1092
Tel: 695701/2
Fax: 695705
Telex: 23051

Al-Jawwal Travel
& Tourism

King Abdallah
Gardens
PO Box 5506
Tel: 681422
Fax: 681422

Al Jazy Travel &
Tourism Bureau
90 Queen Noor St
PO Box 921409
Tel: 666499
Fax: 662112
Telex: 21600

Al-Karmel Travel
King Hussein St
PO Box 926497
Tel: 688301/695876
Fax: 688302
Telex: 24038

Al-Maha Tours
6th Circle
Jabal Amman
PO Box 140900
Tel: 819805
Telex: 22232

Al Rahhal
Abdali
PO Box 911094
Tel: 683773

Al Shurafa Travel
King Hussein St
PO Box 6471
Tel: 623388/636293

Al Tawfiq Travel
Al Abdali
PO Box 9331
Tel: 655661/638379
Fax: 655662

Amin Kawar &
Sons Travel
Shmeisani
PO Box 7806
Tel: 637195/624596
Fax: 604649
Telex: 21634

Amman Tourism
Ahli Bank Bldg
PO Box 815457
Tel: 644321/614321
Fax: 658018
Telex: 22227

Apollo Travel &
Tourism
Al-Hussein Ben
Ali St
PO Box 811519
Tel: 641083/698886

Fax: 657999
Telex: 22330

Arab Express Tours
Amman Marriott
Hotel
Tel: 677344/687344
Fax: 687344

Arab Falcon
Suite 102
Shmeisani-Al
Hamra Building
PO Box 830172
Tel: 685520/5
Fax: 683410
Telex: 23603

Areen Travel
Tourism
Abdali Trade
Centre Bldg
PO Box 926557
Tel: 684980/1
Fax: 684981

Asean Travel &
Tourism
King Hussein St
PO Box 6024
Tel: 640200/1
Fax: 618202
Telex: 21194

Ashtar Tours
PO Box 425114
Tel: 616419/3
Fax: 616428
Telex 23238

Atlas Travel &
Tourist Agency
King Hussein St
PO Box 7131
Tel: 637586/624262
Fax: 610198
Telex: 21750

Aviatourist Tourism
& Transport Service
PO Box 1061
Tel: 676186/177
Telex: 22346

Aya
A Ghosheh St
PO Box 140808
Tel: 826086/4
Fax: 826086
Telex: 23510

Azure Travel &
Tourism
King Hussein St
PO Box 7067

Tel: 655377/1799
Telex: 21453

Banna Travel
Tourism Co
PO Box 5237
Tel: 644763/651663
Fax: 651663

Bayader Travel &
Tourism, 8th Circle
Wadi Seer
PO Box 338
Tel: 824055/863755
Fax: 824055

Bayan
Shamia Bldg
Wasfi Al-Tal St
PO Box 211704
Fax: 683465

Beit El Makdes
Tourism & Travel
Kuhail Trading
Centre, Gardens St
PO Box 961820
Tel: 695528/9

Best Tours
99 Abdalhamid
Sharaf St
PO Box 1807
Tel: 669532/8608
Fax: 682560
Telex: 22056

Cedars Tours
Al Saeigh
Commercial Centre
PO Box 5031
Tel: 614659/727

Da'd Tourism
Main St
PO Box 5529
Tel: 772558/754406
Fax: 754407

Darna Travel &
Tourism Co
Shamroukh
Center Bldg
PO Box 8049
Tel: 655514/647084
Fax: 613638
Telex: 24320

Deema Tours
Agency, Sa'ad
Commercial Bldg
Gardens St
PO Box 35154
Tel: 692823
Fax: 692824

Delta Travel &
Tourism, Prince
Mohammad St
PO Box 496
Tel: 625562/639188

Derbi Tours
King Hussein St
PO Box 811634
Tel: 610933/1860
Fax: 611860
Telex: 21409

Diana Travel
Abdali Commercial
Centre
PO Box 910545
Tel: 694501/2
Fax: 668041
Telex: 24567

Eastern Services
Peace Bldg
PO Box 815408
Tel: 621775
Fax: 656270
Telex: 23023

Elwan Travel
Agency, Abdali
PO Box 9829
Tel & Fax: 646190

Expo Travel &
Tours
PO Box 960329
Sports City
Tel: 691768
Fax: 685274

Farah Travel
& Tourism
Queen Noor St
Shmeisani
PO Box 930240
Tel: 689515
Fax: 689516

Friends Tours
Al-Sayegh
Commercial Centre
PO Box 840
Tel: 617506/7
Fax: 617507

General Tours
King Hussein St
PO Box 184561
Tel: 624307/90
Fax: 610460
Telex: 23958

Gerizim Travel &
Tourism
King Hussein St

PO Box 20820
Tel: 656350/1
Fax: 656351

Global
PO Box 1092
Tel: 695701/2
Fax: 695705
Telex: 23051

Global Tours &
Travel
PO Box 815339
Tel: 667160/125
Fax: 683801
Telex: 21158

Golden Holiday
PO Box 925356
Tel: 654650
Fax: 690882
Telex: 21153

Golden Jubilee
King Hussein St
PO Box 183065
Tel: 618824/5

Golden Star
Tourism
Ras El-Ein
PO Box 151259
Tel: 770565/750861
Fax: 750861

Granada Travel
King Hussein St
PO Box 9773
Tel: 638126/419
Fax: 638419

Grand Travel
PO Box 2152
Tel: 699037/0401
Fax: 690402
Telex: 2119

Green Wings
Shmeisani Issam
El-Ajloni St
PO Box 5610
Tel: 699097/83

Habi Tours
PO Box 17
Wadi Seer
Tel: 818813
Fax: 811627

Hala Travel &
Tourism
Al-Wehdat
Madaba St
PO Box 20611
Tel: 777283/8567
Fax: 778588

Hisham
International Tours
Zahran Building
47 Al-Hussein Bin
Ali Main St
Tel: 698180/1
Fax: 689307
Telex: 21628

International
Holiday Planner
Jordan Insurance
Bldg, 3rd Circle
Jabal Amman
PO Box 921506
Tel: 642869/689307
Fax: 648174
Telex: 21379

International
Tourist Travel
Services
Jawhart Amman
Building
PO Box 9673
Tel: 669130/938
Telex: 23121

International
Traders
Shmeisani
PO Box 408
Tel: 607014
Fax: 669905
Telex: 21441

International
Wings Tours
Agency
King Hussein St
PO Box 20833
Tel: 618182/3
Fax: 618183
Telex: 21142

Jerash Tours
Abdalhamid
Sharaf St
Shmeisani
PO Box 7086
Tel: 683003/4
Fax: 683004

Jerusalem Express
Travel
King Hussein St
PO Box 6622
Tel: 685196
Fax: 688126
Telex: 22151

Jordan
International
King Hussein St

PO Box 7086
Tel: 625981/655156
Fax: 615721

Jordan Travel
Bureau
King Hussein St
PO Box 1078
Tel: 625585/1220
Fax: 628585
Telex: 21480

Jordan Visitor
Services
Alouzi Centre
PO Box 685
Tel: 604464/74
Fax: 604474

Karim Tours &
Travel, Madaba St
PO Box 520225
Tel: 772337

Khoury Travel
Agency
King Hussein St
PO Box 1704
Tel: 623430/2684
Fax: 622684

Lawrence Tours
Grand Palace Hotel
PO Box 92587
Tel: 664916/1121
Fax: 683439
Telex: 23550

Lords Travel &
Tourism
1st Floor, Akarco
Centre, Abdali
PO Box 815361
Tel: 692710/1
Fax: 692711

Makkah
Shmeisani
PO Box 910564
Tel: 697217/6217
Fax: 697217

Middle East Tours
Shamieh Trading
Centre
Wasfi Al-Tal St
PO Box 811915
Tel: 683494/652310
Fax: 681903

Muhana Tours
PO Box 960847
Tel: 834885/5885
Fax: 834885

Nahas
King Hussein St
PO Box 182346
Tel: 622826/5535
Fax: 629333

National Tours
Rafiq Al Athem St
PO Box 3103
Tel: 682053/4
Fax: 680424
Telex: 23501

Nawas Tourist Co
PO Box 968
Tel: 622184/654184
Telex: 21331

Near East Tourist
Centre, Jordan
Intercontinental
Hotel
PO Box 2518
Tel: 642943/1906
Fax: 659792

Near East Tourist
Agency, Azzahra St
PO Box 19105
Tel: 282194/6351
Telex: 262200

Palmyra Tours &
Travel
Abdul Hameed
Sharaf St
PO Box 922502
Tel: 686195
Fax: 686194
Telex: 23340

Pan Arabian Travel
King Hussein St
PO Box 3265
Tel: 623806/645640
Telex: 23042

Pan East Tours
55 Islam Al-Ajlouni
Street, Shmeisani
PO Box 182478
Tel: 606420/1
Fax: 685421
Telex: 23873

Pan Mediterranean
Tours & Travel
Tel: 657255/646155
Fax: 657255
Telex: 22307

Pan Pacific Travel
& Tourism
King Hussein St
PO Box 959

Tel: 621688/638387
Telex: 21191

Paradise Travel &
Tourism, Al-Swafiya
Fahad Centre
PO Box 850278
Tel: 861831
Fax: 861830

Petra Travel &
Tourism
King Hussein St
Tel: 667028/670267
Telex: 21715

Petridis Tours &
Travel
King Hussein St
PO Box 336
Tel: 636123/53
Telex: 21886

Plaza Tours
Wadi Saqra Centre
PO Box 950531
Tel: 690946/7
Fax: 690947
Telex: 22071

Ramada Tours
King Hussein St
PO Box 921092
Tel: 639059/659205
Fax: 659205

Razan Travel &
Tourism Agency
King Hussein St
PO Box 182440
Tel: 647614/615614
Fax: 615614

Round The World
Travel & Tourism
Middle East Circle
Wehdat
PO Box 621241
Tel: 787334/750655

Safe Travel
Abdul Hameed
Sharaf St
Shmeisani
PO Box 962135
Tel: 605535
Fax: 605554

Salam Tours
Abdali
PO Box 20750
Tel: 665688/269

Sara Tours
Jabal Al-Weibdeh
PO Box 910152

Tel: 645654
Fax: 635262

Seikalys Tours
Prince
Mohammad St
PO Box 479
Tel: 622147/8
Fax: 603550

Shepherds Tours
Tyche Hotel
Shmeisani
PO Box 3190
Tel: 661114/5
Fax: 664103
Telex: 21729

Sindbad Travel
Madaba St
Al Wehdat
PO Box 620661
Tel: 752750/7750
Fax: 757750

Skyways Travel
King Hussein St
PO Box 1747
Tel: 637205/616592
Telex: 22151

Space
Shmeisani
PO Box 925072
Tel: 669068/8069
Fax: 688919
Telex: 22388

Stars Tourism
8th Circle
Bayader Wadi
Al Seer
PO Box 140886
Tel: 827140/1
Fax: 827141

Sun Tours
King Hussein St
PO Box 182008
Tel: 627212
Fax: 621108
Telex: 22288

Tajco
Prince Moh'd St
PO Box 1652
Tel: 622902/25
Fax: 622925
Telex: 21987

Tania Tours
Shmeisani
PO Box 2586
Tel: 699260/1
Fax: 699261
Telex: 21513

Tawfiq Zaatarh &
Company
Prince Moh'd St
PO Box 926436
Tel: 642332
Fax: 611186
Telex: 21889

Terra Sancta
Tourist Co
Karim Centre
Firas Circle
PO Box 2136
Tel:625203/636038
Fax: 646116
Telex: 21782

Top Tours
PO Box 911191
Tel: 5539509
Fax: 5519446

Travel Services
Office
Peace Building
Jabal Al-Webdeh
PO Box 926400
Tel: 624355/136
Telex: 22262

Travel & Tourism
3rd Circle
Jabal Amman
PO Box 3278
Tel: 652150/3150
Fax: 614150
Telex: 24570

Trust Tours
Agency, Shmeisani
Tel: 683200/1
Fax: 672282

Tyche Travel &
Tourism
Shmeisani
PO Box 960376
Tel:663150/671150
Fax: 690150

United Travel
Agency
PO Box 35241
Tel: 641959
Fax: 610095
Telex: 23293

Universal Travel
& Tourism Agency
King Hussein St
PO Box 20499
Tel: 656130
Fax: 655011
Telex: 22276

Wazzan Travel
King Hussein St
PO Box 2484
Tel:623180/637339

World Class Travel
Rawhi Centre
Khalidi St
PO Box 926422
Tel: 642899
Telefax: 616699

Yasmin Travel
Al-Wahlid St
Jabal Hussein
PO Box 922702
Tel: 643570/1
Fax: 643572
Telex: 23119

Zaatarah & Co
King Hussein St
Tel: 636011/0011
Fax: 655011
Telex: 21889

Aqaba
Sun Tours
Corniche St
PO Box 1796
Tel: 318700
Fax: 318701

Petra
Petra Moon
Tourism
Wadi Mousa
PO Box 59
Tel: (03) 2156665
Fax: (03) 2156666

Zarqa
Alaseel
Tel: (09)909027

Shammas Travel
& Tourism
PO Box 69
Tel: (09) 992744/5
Fax: (09) 984014
Telex: 41454

Ministries

Administrative
Development
Jabal Amman
Tel: 692434

Agriculture
University
Highway
PO Box 961043

Amman
Tel: 686151
Fax: 686310

Culture & Youth
University
Highway
PO Box 1794
Amman
Tel: 604701
Fax: 604717

Education
Abdali
PO Box 35262
Amman
Tel:847671/607181
Fax: 837616

Energy & Mineral
Resources
Jabal Amman
PO Box 140027
Amman
Tel: 817900
Fax: 818336

Finance
PO Box 85
Amman
Tel: 636321
Fax: 643121

Foreign Affairs
Jabal Amman
PO Box 35217
Tel: 644361/529
Fax: 648825

Health
Jabal Amman
PO Box 86
Amman
Tel: 665131
Fax: 688373

Information
Jabal Amman
PO Box 1854
Amman
Tel: 641467
Fax: 648895

Interior
Jabal Hussein
PO Box 100
Amman
Tel: 702811
Fax: 606908

Justice
Shmeisani
PO Box 640
Amman

Tel: 663101
Fax: 680238

Labour
Abdali
PO Box 8160
Amman
Tel:698186/607481
Fax: 667193

Municipal, Rural
& Environmental
Affairs
Jabal Amman
Tel: 641647/393
Fax: 648895

Planning
Jabal Amman
PO Box 555
Amman
Tel: 644466
Fax: 649341

Prime Minister
Jabal Amman
Tel: 641211

Public Works &
Housing
Abdali
Tel: 607481
Fax: 684759

Religious Affairs
PO Box 659
Amman
Tel: 666141
Fax: 602254

Social
Development
Jabal Amman
Tel: 603191
Fax: 603198

Tourism &
Antiquities
Jabal Amman
PO Box 224
Tel: 642311
Fax: 648465

Trade, Industry
& Supplies
Abdali
PO Box 2019
Tel: 663191
Fax: 603721

Transport &
Telecomms
Jabal Amman
Tel: 607111

Water & Irrigation
Shmeisani
PO Box 80
Tel:689400
Fax: 642520

Bus Companies

Amman
Abu-al-Ragib
Alasfahan St
Jabal Al-Jofeh
Tel: 613550
Al-Badeh Transit
Office
King Hussein St
Tel: 982030

Al-Wafa
Transport Co
Middle East Circle
Tel: 788618

South District Bus
Co Office
Middle East Circle
Tel: 784304

Tabbalat
Transport Office
Middle East
Circle
Tel: 770500

Credit Card Offices

American Express
International
Traders
Abdul Hameed St
Sharaf, Shmeisani
Amman
Tel: 661014

Visa
Jordan Payment
Services Co
7th Floor
Housing Building
PO Box 930026
Amman
Tel: 680574/5
Fax: 680570

Bibliography

A brief bibliography follows for those interested in further readings on Jordan, the Middle East and Islam.

Journey Through Jordan (1994), by Mohamed Amin, Duncan Willetts and Sam Kiley, published by Camerapix, Nairobi.

Seven Pillars of Wisdom (1976), by T E Lawrence, published by Penguin, New York.

Antiquities of Jordan (1967), by G Lankester Harding, published by Lullworth Press, Kent.

Jordan: Its People, Its Society, Its Culture (1958), by George Harris, published by New Haven; Human Relations Area Files.

Handbook of Palestine and Trans-Jordan (1934), by Sir H Luke & E Keith-Roach.

A History of Jordan and its Tribes (1958), by F W Peake Pasha, published by University of Miami Press, Miami.

Arab Command: A Biography of F W Peake Pasha (1942), by C S Jarvis.

Jordan (1978), published by the Ministry of Information, Amman.

The Kingdom of Jordan (1958), by R Patai.

Jordan: A Meed Practical Guide (1983), by Trevor Mostyn, published by Meed, London.

Hussein's Kingdom (1966), by Winifred Carr, published by Leslie Frewin, London.

The Hashemite Kingdom of Jordan (1958), by P G Phillips: Research Paper 34, published by University of Chicago.

A Short History of Trans-Jordan (1945), by B U Toukan.

Uneasy Lies The Head (1962), by His Majesty King Hussein of Jordan, published by Heinemann, London.

My War With Israel (1969), by His Majesty King Hussein of Jordan, published by Peter Owen, London.

A Study on Jerusalem (1979), by His Royal Highness Crown Prince Hassan of Jordan, published by Longman Group, London.

Palestinian Self-Determination: A Study on the West Bank and Gaza Strip (1981), by His Royal Highness Crown Prince Hassan of Jordan, published by Quartet Books, London.

Search for Peace (1984), by His Royal Highness Crown Prince Hassan of Jordan, published by Macmillan & Co, London.

Petra (1989), by Iain Browning, published by Chatto & Windus, London.

Jerash & the Decapolis (1982), by Iain Browning, published by Chatto & Windus, London.

The Dead Sea Scrolls (1986), by John Allegro, published by Penguin, Middlesex.

Azraq: A Desert Oasis (1973), by Bryan Nelson, published by Allen House, London.

Insights and Guide to Jordan (1981), by Christine Osborne, published by Longman Group, Essex.

The Art of Jordan (1991), by Piotr Bienkowski, published by Alan Sutton Publishing, Stroud.

Hussein: A Biography (1972), by Peter Snow, published by Barrie & Jenkins, London.

Hussein of Jordan (1960), by Gerald Sparrow, published by George Harrap, London.

Hussein of Jordan (1989), by James Lunt, published by Macmillan, London.

Travels in The Unknown East (1992), by John Grant, published by The Octagon Press, London.

Alone in Arabian Nights (1992), by Sirdar Iqbal Ali Shah, published by The Octagon Press, London.

History of the Arabs (1974), by Philip K Hitti, Macmillan & Co, London.

Cultural Research (1993) Edited by Tahir Shah, published by The Octagon Press, London.

A Literary History of the Arabs (1930), by R A Nicholson, published by Cambridge University Press, Cambridge.

A Soldier With the Arabs (1957), by Sir John Bagot Glubb Pasha, published by Hodder & Stoughton, London.

A Short History of the Arab People (1969), by Sir John Bagot Glubb Pasha, published by Hodder & Stoughton, London.

The Story of the Arab Legion (1969), by Sir John Bagot Glubb Pasha, published by Hodder & Stoughton, London.

The Arabs in History (1950), by Bernard Lewis, published by Oxford University Press, London.

The Middle East Bedside Book (1991), by Tahir Shah, published by The Octagon Press, London.

The Arabs (1978), by Thomas Kiernan, published by Sphere Books, London.

Inside the Middle East (1982), by Dilip Hiro, published by Routledge & Kegan Paul, London.

The Arab of the Desert (1959), by H R P Dickson, published by George Allen & Unwin, London.

Marvels of the East (1938), by Richard Halliburton, published by Geoffrey Bles, London.

Saladin: Prince of Chivalry (1930), by Charles J Rosebault, published by Cassell & Co, London.

Travels & Adventures in Arabia (undated), by William Perry Fogg, published by Ward, Lock & Co, London.

The Businessman's Guide to the Middle East (1977), by Lillian Africano, published by Harper & Row, London.

The Koran (1956), Translated by N J Dawood, published by Penguin, Middlesex.

The Oriental Caravan (1933), by Sirdar Iqbal Ali Shah, published by Denis Archer, London.

Dictionary of Islam (first published 1885), by Thomas Patrick Hughes, published by Rupa & Co, Bombay.

The Legacy of Islam (1979), by Joseph Schacht, published by Oxford University Press, London.

The Spirit of Islam (undated), by Ameer Ali, published by Christophers, London.

The World of Islamic Civilization (1974), by G Le Bon, published by Editions Minerva, Geneva.

Islamic Literature (1963), by Najib Ullah, published by Washington Press, New York.

Petra — A Traveller's Guide (1994 — revised 1996), by Rosalyn Maqsood.

Tracks and Climbs in Wadi Rum, Jordan (1987 — revised 1994), by Tony Howard, Cicerone Press.

Jordan Revealed (1996), by Anthony King, Boxer Press.

EVIL EYE
285